Peter Norton's Guide to

THE NORTON UTILITIES® 6.0

Peter Norton's Guide to

THE NORTON UTILITIES® 6.0

Peter Norton
Judi N. Fernandez
Ruth Ashley

BANTAM BOOKS
NEW YORK · TORONTO · LONDON · SYDNEY · AUCKLAND

Peter Norton's Guide to the Norton Utilities® 6.0
A Bantam Book / October 1991

All rights reserved.
Copyright © 1991 by Peter Norton
Cover design © 1991 by Bantam Books, Inc.
Interior design by Nancy Sugihara

Produced by Micro Text Productions, Inc.
Composed by Context Publishing Services, San Diego, CA

ISBN 0-553-35343-8

Published simultaneously in the United States and Canada

Bantam Books are published by Bantam Books, a division of Bantam Doubleday Dell Publishing Group, Inc. Its trademark, consisting of the words "Bantam Books" and the portrayal of a rooster, is Registered in U.S. Patent and Trademark Office and in other countries. Marca Registrada, Bantam Books, Inc., 666 Fifth Avenue, New York, New York 10103.

PRINTED IN THE UNITED STATES OF AMERICA

0   9   8   7   6   5   4   3   2   1

PREFACE

The Norton Utilities 6.0 includes all the familiar and famous utilities of previous versions, plus many new features to help you protect your data, recover lost data, and generally improve your interactions with DOS. This book shows you how to use all the utilities included in version 6.0.

> If you're already in trouble and in need of the recovery utilities, go directly to Appendix A. Do not pass Go; do not collect $200; and in particular, do not do *anything* to your disk until you have successfully rescued the lost data from it.

The main part of this book is designed for the reader who does not have immediate recovery needs, and wants to install the utilities and learn to use them in an orderly fashion. We'll look at the utilities in the order that you will probably begin to use them. We start with the Install and on-line Help programs, which you'll naturally want to use right away. From there we'll show you how to use the main Norton menu.

Chapter 2 discusses Disk Editor as a device for exploring your disks. Armed with this knowledge, you'll be able to try out the other utilities and see what your disk looks like before and after using one of the utilities.

The next few chapters introduce utilities that you might want to start using immediately: the ones that protect your data from accidents like unintentional erasures or reformattings, and the utilities that improve the performance of your system by speeding up your hard disk.

Next, you'll learn how to protect your data from outside influences: viruses, sabotage, and espionage. And since you can't prevent *all* problems, the next section will show you how to recover data when things do go wrong.

The final section of the book contains a variety of tools to make your life easier. These utilities round out and improve upon the facilities provided by DOS.

This book is intended for anyone who needs or wants to use the Norton Utilities. It is especially appropriate for those who are new to the utilities and are having difficulty figuring out how, when, and where to use them.

The Norton Utilities 6.0 is also an excellent guide for those who are upgrading their systems; version 6.0 looks completely different from earlier versions (the user interface has been redesigned) and contains several new, useful features. All the old features are still there, but some of them have changed not only their looks but their names. In addition, several new utilities make an appearance.

You do need to know a bit about DOS in order to use this book. You should know what a file and a directory are, how to boot and reboot, how to name a file and a directory, and the most elementary commands like DIR and COPY. If you feel that you don't know enough, start out with Appendix B: A Dab of DOS, and then turn to Chapter 1.

Conventions Used in This Book

We have used some typographical conventions in this book to help you identify certain types of elements:

- In regular text, ALL CAPS are used for filenames, directory name, drive names, and commands (for example, UNERASE D:\INFO.DAT).

- **Boldface** has been used for the names of menus, dialog boxes, and the options they contain.

- In statements that show the format for typing a command, ALL CAPS have been used for special words, which must be included as is (for example, UNFORMAT d:).

- *Italics* have been used in commands for items that must be replaced with a value of some kind (for example, UNFORMAT *d:*, where *d:* means that you must insert a drive name, as in UNFORMAT A: or UNFORMAT C:).

- We have used square brackets for optional items in commands (for example, UNERASE [*filename*], where the filename is optional. Any item not in square brackets is required.

- Finally, vertical lines {|} have been used for mutually exclusive alternatives (for example, ECHO [ON| OFF | *message*], where you can follow the required word ECHO with the word ON, the word OFF, or with a message).

ACKNOWLEDGMENTS

We're very grateful to several people who went way beyond the call of duty to help us during the writing of this book:

Larry Colker at Symantec
Scott Clark
Kevin Goldstein at Symantec
Henri Isenberg at Symantec
Stephen Guty and the staff at Bantam Electronic Publishing

Thanks to you all.

CONTENTS

3   SETTING UP YOUR SYSTEM   77

14 DISK EDITOR AS AN EDITOR   283

15 SYSTEM INFORMATION   299

1

INTRODUCTION

During the 1980s, the Disk Operating System (DOS) grew to be the universal operating system for IBM and compatible personal computers. (An *operating system* is a set of programs that control the basic resources of your computer: memory, the processor, the disk storage, the monitor, and the keyboard. All other programs have to go through the operating system to access these resources.) Unfortunately, DOS has a few shortcomings. For example, many people need to protect sensitive information from unauthorized users. Yet DOS has no facility to do so.

This is where the Norton Utilities enter the arena! These programs have been specifically designed to fill in DOS's lapses and to give you additional control over your computer. Like DOS, the Norton Utilities have grown and improved over the years. Now they have reached version 6.0, with dozens of useful programs, modern graphics-oriented screens, and the ability to "point and shoot" with the mouse with many of the utilities. In addition to rounding out DOS, they add on capabilities to diagnose and improve the performance of your computer, to protect your data from all the nasty things that go bump in the night, and, perhaps most importantly, to recover as much data as possible when something does go wrong.

Like the Norton Utilities, DOS has grown and improved over the years. In fact, the newest versions include some facilities that Norton has offered right from the start, such as the ability to recover a file that was accidentally deleted. But the DOS versions of such facilities are pretty elementary, whereas the Norton versions have been expanded and polished over a number of years so that they are as powerful and flexible as you could ever ask for, and yet are very easy to use.

The Norton Utilities do not replace DOS, they work hand in hand with it, enhancing and supplementing DOS's basic features. The Norton Utilities 6.0 can work with any version of DOS through DOS 5.0.

Getting Acquainted with the Utilities

What's a *utility?* In computerese, it's a program that helps you manage your computer and its disks. Compare this to an *application*, which lets you "apply" your computer to an external process—business, household, or personal. Your word processor, spreadsheet, and database manager are applications; the Norton Utilities are utilities. They won't balance your checkbook or send out a personalized mailer, but they will help you rescue data from a damaged disk, recover a file that you accidentally erased, and prevent unauthorized access to sensitive data.

The entire collection of Norton Utilities can be divided into four general categories: NDOS, command-line utilities, graphic utilities, and other utilities.

NDOS

DOS includes a *command processor* that gives you the ability to start up programs by entering commands. A number of essential programs are built into the command processor, such as COPY (to copy files), TYPE (to display files), and DIR (to display directories). Norton's NDOS replaces the DOS command processor with a new and improved one. The NDOS command processor includes all of the DOS features, frequently improving them, and adds many more commands of its own. Once you have installed the Norton Utilities and rebooted, NDOS takes over as your command processor (unless you suppressed it during installation). You'll soon start to notice differences from DOS, even in very basic things such as the messages displayed by COPY and DIR.

Command-Line Utilities

The Norton Utilities include a set of utilities that are executed from the command prompt. They fall in a different category from the graphic utilities because they simply display the information you've requested and then they stop. There's no opportunity for—nor is there any need for—interaction between the user and the utility. Briefly, the command-line utilities are:

- FA Displays and changes file attributes
- FD Changes date and time stamps for files
- FL Locates files
- FS Displays file sizes
- LP Prints files
- TS Searches for text in files

Graphic Utilities

The majority of Norton Utilities require interaction between you and the program to establish what is wanted. When you start up one of these utilities, it uses windows, menus, and dialog boxes to communicate with you. You can use the mouse as well as the keyboard to respond to it. Because this type of communication is called a *graphic interface*, we refer to these as the *graphic utilities*.

In most cases, a graphic utility remains active until you specifically terminate it and you can repeatedly use it on different files or drives. The graphic utilities fall into four categories: recovery, speed, security, and tools.

Recovery Utilities

Recovery utilities can help you rescue data in situations where you would ordinarily lose it, such as when you accidentally delete all the files on your hard disk or drop a valuable diskette in a puddle. There are eight recovery utilities:

- *Norton Disk Doctor (NDD)*: Diagnoses and corrects many kinds of disk problems that could cause you to lose data.
- *Disk Editor*: Lets you view and edit every part of the disk, including areas not normally available such as the system information at the beginning of each disk. Norton Disk Doctor fixes disk problems automatically, but Disk Editor lets you get in there and fix a problem manually—byte by byte—which might help you rescue something that NDD can't quite handle. Disk Editor is also a fun tool because it lets you go exploring on

your disk, peeking into areas you're not "supposed to" and discovering for yourself how things work.

- *Disk Tools*: Provides a set of six rescue tools that can help you restore a disk that has gone bad and prevent future problems.
- *Erase Protect*: Saves deleted files in a special TRASHCAN directory for a while to make recovery easier.
- *File Fix*: Finds and fixes problems in Lotus 1-2-3, Symphony, dBASE, and compatible files.
- *UnErase*: Recovers deleted files and directories.
- *UnFormat*: To prepare a disk for use by DOS, it must be *formatted*, which makes any previous data on the disk inaccessible. UnFormat lets you rescue data from a disk that was accidentally reformatted.

Speed Utilities

Two utilities help to speed up your system. Both utilities operate on your disks, which are always the main bottleneck.

- *Calibrate*: Takes a number of steps to improve the performance of your hard disk, not only speeding it up, but also making it more reliable.
- *Speed Disk*: Reorganizes the data on a disk so you can access it faster.

Security Utilities

The security utilities help protect your programs and data from prying eyes, espionage, viruses, some forms of sabotage, and other possible threats. These three utilities can be used to set up any level of protection, from just plain horse sense to the highest level of defense against sophisticated, malicious forces.

- *Disk Monitor*: Prevents anybody from writing on your disks without your direct approval.
- *Diskreet*: Disguises sensitive data so that no one can read it unless they can find (or figure out) your password. Diskreet protects your data by *encrypting* it; that is, by translating it into apparent nonsense. If you can provide the correct password, it will also *decrypt* the data again; decryption restores data to its original, readable form.
- *WipeInfo*: Removes sensitive deleted data from your disk by completely obliterating it so that it can't be recovered or examined with Disk Editor.

Tools

This "miscellaneous" category includes many useful tools for managing your computer, from a program that compares your computer to others, to the Norton Utilities version of the better mousetrap: a fast, safe, and flexible format utility.

- *Configure*: Lets you change the way the Norton Utilities are set up.
- *Norton Control Center*: Gives you simpler, more direct control than DOS does over hardware characteristics such as serial ports and keyboard speed.
- *FileFind*: Helps you find those pesky lost files.
- *Norton Change Directory* (NCD): Graphically displays a disk's directory tree so that you can change to a different directory, add or delete directories, and rename directories.
- *Safe Format*: Formats disks easily, quickly, and safely.
- *System Information*: Provides all kinds of interesting and useful facts about your system, such as memory usage, drive statistics, and system usage information. System Information will even compare your computer's performance to that of several popular ones. (Take it along when you go computer shopping.)

Other Utilities

The Norton Utilities includes several other programs you'll find useful.

- *Install*: Helps you install the utilities on the hard disk. Installation isn't necessary for the recovery programs, which can be run from the emergency diskettes (so that, if you bought the utilities to resolve an immediate crisis, you can do so without destroying any data on the hard disk). But you must install the utilities before you can use any of the other programs.
- *Norton*: Provides a main menu from which you can access the graphic utilities, as shown in Figure 1-1. The Norton menu helps you find the program you want to use, advises you on solutions to hardware problems, and lets you set up the monitor and the mouse for use with the graphic utilities. You can also install other programs on the menu, so you can use it as the main access to your whole system, if you wish.
- *Help*: Displays on-screen assistance for every utility. Figure 1-2 shows a sample help screen for a graphic utility.

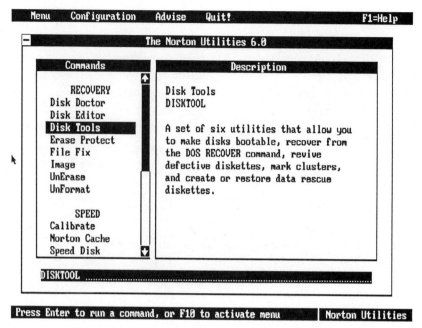

Figure 1-1   Norton Menu

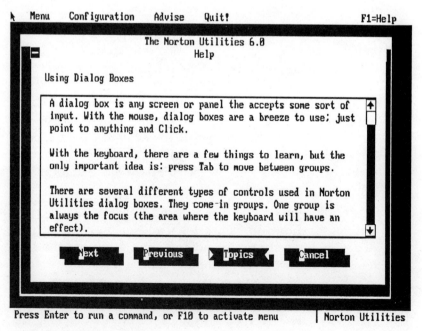

Figure 1-2   Sample Help Screen

- *Batch Enhancer*: The DOS batch facility lets you create your own programs by combining DOS commands, but it's very limited in what it can accomplish. Batch Enhancer gives you additional commands to make your batch jobs more effective and fun.
- *Norton Cache*: Bypasses a disk's sluggishness by storing data in memory, which is much faster.
- *Image*: Captures a snapshot of crucial system information to help you restore a disk later, if necessary.

Installing the Norton Utilities

> **Warning:** Do not install the utilities (or any other program) if you immediately need to recover data from the hard disk. You could destroy your chances of recovering the data. See Appendix A if you need to recover data before learning how to install or use the utilities.

Before you start installing the utilities, take the time to prepare for several decisions:

Color or black and white: The first question Install asks is whether you want to use color or black-and-white screens during installation. Some monitors might require black and white.

Which utilities to install: During installation, you can choose which utilities to install on the hard disk from a list of all the utilities. If you're not yet sure which utilities you'll use and have plenty of space on the hard disk, try installing them all. This way you can try them out and delete the ones you won't use. If disk space is limited, or if you know exactly which utilities you want to use, then unselect the ones you don't want. Install shows you how much room is on the hard disk and how much is taken up by the selected programs.

Drive and directory to use: You have to indicate which drive and directory you want Install to put the utilities in. It does not have to be an existing directory; Install will create the directory for you. Install will put the utilities in C:\NU if you don't specify otherwise.

Easy or advanced setup: Install includes a number of setup options, such as password protection and screen colors. You can choose an easy setup, in which case Install uses the default choices for all the setup options. But if you prefer more control, choose the advanced setup, which leads to a menu where you can handle each item individually. Even if you choose the easy setup, you can change setup options later on. The Configuration program and the Norton menu both give you access to all the setup options, which are described below:

Expand programs: To save disk space, many of the utilities are stored in compressed format. A compressed program has to be expanded when it's loaded into memory, which takes extra time every time you start it up. To save that extra startup time, you can expand the stored programs permanently. But keep in mind that you're trading time for disk space.

Renaming the utilities: If you would like, Install will rename the following utilities so that you can start them with shorter commands at the DOS prompt: Disk Editor (from DISKEDIT to DE); FileFind (from FILEFIND to FF); Speed Disk (from SPEEDISK to SD); and System Info (from SYSINFO to SI).

In addition, you can rename Safe Format from SFORMAT to either SF or just plain FORMAT. If you rename it as FORMAT, DOS's FORMAT program will be renamed as XXFORMAT so that it is still available on your disk if you need it.

Note: If you have DOS version 4.0 or later and plan to use the DOS BACKUP program, don't rename Safe Format as FORMAT. DOS BACKUP requires the use of DOS's FORMAT.

Password protection: If you are setting up the utilities for end users, you can establish passwords to block them from using powerhouse Norton Utilities programs such as Disk Editor and Disk Doctor. This can prevent others from trying to use facilities they don't completely understand.

Editing the Norton menu: You can also prevent end users from changing the Norton menu once you have it set up the way you like it. (Editing the Norton menu is explained later in this chapter.)

Hardware configuration: The graphic utilities have default settings for hardware features such as the screen colors and whether the mouse is left- or right-handed. Some of the default settings might not work well with your equipment. You can change any of these settings during installation, but you can also change them later on from the Configuration program or an option on the Norton menu, both of which are explained later in this chapter.

Tip: Use the default hardware settings until you try out the utilities. If you need to make a hardware change, you can do it easily from the Norton menu or the Configuration program.

Norton Cache: The configure menu provides an easy way to set up the Norton Cache program, which can be somewhat complex. Chapter 4 explains Norton Cache and what the setup options are all about.

Whenever DOS boots, it looks for two files named CONFIG.SYS and AUTOEXEC.BAT, which contain commands that set up your system during booting. If DOS finds them, it executes all the commands they contain. Install will make several changes to AUTOEXEC.BAT and CONFIG.SYS if you let it:

CONFIG.SYS: Install will add statements to CONFIG.SYS to install and Diskreet, NDOS, and Keystack during booting.

AUTOEXEC.BAT: AUTOEXEC.BAT usually contains a PATH command which sets up the search path—that is, the list of directories that DOS should search when looking for a program. Install will add the Norton Utilities directory to your PATH command so that you can start a utility from any drive or directory. In addition, it will add a command to set the NU environment variable, which Norton Utilities needs to find its files. It will also add statements to AUTOEXEC.BAT to start up Disk Monitor, Erase Protect, Image, and Norton Disk Doctor (to do a quick check of the hard disk) during booting.

How to Run Install

When you're ready to install the utilities, boot your system as you normally do. You should see a DOS prompt that looks something like this:

```
C:\>
```

This prompt tells you that DOS is ready to receive a command. (The first letter will be different if your boot drive is not drive C:.)

Insert the Norton Utilities **Install** diskette in drive A: and switch to that drive by entering this command (your entry is shown in boldface type):

```
C:\>A:        [press the Enter key]
A:\>
```

> **Note:** DOS commands can be typed in uppercase or lowercase. We show them in uppercase here to make them stand out from regular text.

Make sure the DOS prompt shows the letter A before continuing. Then enter the command INSTALL, like this:

    A:\>INSTALL   [press the Enter key]

The Install program will take over, and then all you have to do is follow the directions on the screen. If you're not sure how to move the cursor or select options, read the next section before installing your utilities.

The Norton Utilities Graphic Interface

One of the major enhancements in version 6.0 is a new and improved graphic interface. Most of the graphic utilities present a main screen, such as the one in Figure 1-1 (seen earlier). The screen has a menu bar across the top, a work area in the middle, and a message/status bar at the bottom.

Dialog boxes appear as needed in the work area. In Figure 1-1, the area enclosed by a box labeled "The Norton Utilities 6.0" is a dialog box. The help display in Figure 1-2 (seen earlier) is also a dialog box. Dialog boxes explain things and let you select options.

Menus

A *menu* is a list of commands to select from. Screens such as the one in Figure 1-1 include several menu names in the menu bar across the top. When you want to use a menu, you pull it down by pressing Alt plus the first letter of the menu name. Or you can press Alt or F10 to pull down the first menu, then press Right arrow and Left arrow to move from menu to menu. To pull down a menu using the mouse, click on its name. Figure 1-3 shows an example of a pulled-down menu.

To select a menu item from the keyboard, type the highlighted character, such as D for **Drive**, R for **diRectory**, or 1 for **1st copy of FAT**. (On monochrome screens, it's the first capital letter of the option name.) Or you can move the cursor to the option with Down arrow and press Enter. To select a menu item with the mouse, click on it. You can cancel a menu without selecting an item by pressing Esc or by clicking away from any option.

Items followed by three dots, such as **Drive** and **diRectory**, lead to dialog boxes that collect more information about the options you want. Items that appear in gray on a color screen are temporarily unavailable. On monochrome screens, unavailable items are enclosed in parentheses and have no capital letters, like **(clipboard)** in Figure 1-3.

Notice that many items are followed by key combinations such as Alt-D. These are *hotkeys* which select the option without pulling down the menu.

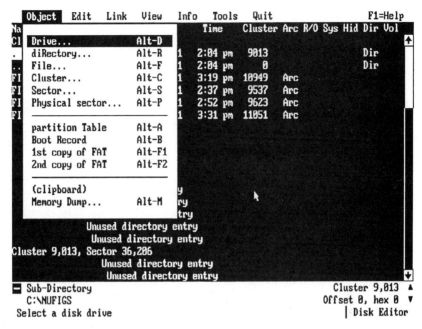

Figure 1-3   Sample Menu

This is the fastest and easiest way to select a menu option, as long as you can remember the hotkeys. They're as mnemonic as possible, so you will soon learn the ones you use most often.

> **Note:** Hotkeys work only when no menu or dialog box is present. If a menu is already pulled down, then you must select the desired option by normal means. If a dialog box is present, then you must deal with the dialog box and close it before you can use any menu item.

Dialog Boxes

Usually, a dialog box appears when you must choose options, enter a filename, and so on. The dialog box in Figure 1-1 includes two smaller boxes, labeled **Commands** and **Description**. The **Commands** box is known as a *list* box, because it presents a list of items from which to choose. The **Description** box is a message box; in this case, it describes the currently highlighted command from the list box. The dialog box in Figure 1-2 contains a message box and four *command buttons*, labeled **Next**, **Previous**, and so on. You select a command button to execute the command. For example, if you select **Next**, the next help topic is displayed in the message box.

Maneuvering in a Dialog Box

When you use a mouse, you don't have to worry about maneuvering in a dialog box. All you do is click on the options you want. But when you're working only with a keyboard, you have to move the cursor to the desired option in order to select it.

First you have to get the cursor to the right *control group*. Each input box, such as a list box, is a control group. A message box is not a control group; since it is output only, you can't move the cursor to it. The command buttons also comprise one control group. If a dialog box has more than one control group, the Tab key moves the cursor from control group to control group; you can use Backtab (Shift-Tab) to move to the previous control group. The effect of the Home, End, PageUp, and PageDown keys varies from dialog box to dialog box, and sometimes from control group to control group.

Once the cursor is in the right control group, you can move it from item to item with the arrow keys. For example, to move it to **File Fix** in Figure 1-1, you would press Down arrow twice. Some types of control groups have additional ways to highlight a specific item, as you will see in the following sections.

List Boxes

To select an item from a list box, click on it or move the cursor to it. You can move the cursor with the arrow keys. In addition, Home and End move the cursor to the first and last items.

If the list is too long for the box, you can scroll around in it. If you're using the keyboard, press PageUp, PageDown, Home, and End. The scroll bar at the right side of the box lets you scroll with the mouse. The solid rectangle, called the *thumb box*, shows the relationship of the current display to the entire list. In the example in Figure 1-1, approximately the top half of the list is showing in the box. Click on the Up arrow to move the cursor up one line; the Down arrow moves it down one line. Click on the gray bar above or below the thumb box to page up or page down. To move longer distances, drag the thumb box.

> **Note:** Some message boxes also require scrolling. Use the same techniques that you use for list boxes.

Command Buttons

Most dialog boxes have at least one command button—to get you out of the dialog box. (The dialog box in Figure 1-1 doesn't have one because the window includes a **Quit!** option in the menu bar.)

To move the cursor to a command button, tab to the desired button. Once the cursor is on the button, pressing Enter selects that button.

There is always one default command button; it contains the triangular pointers at the sides (see **Topics** in Figure 1-2). This is the button that will be selected whenever you simply press Enter. You don't have to move the cursor to it. Select any other button by clicking on it or by moving the cursor to it and pressing Enter.

Many dialog boxes contain an **OK** button, which puts the options you have chosen in the dialog box into effect; it also closes the dialog box. It's usually the default button, so all you have to do is select the options you want and press Enter.

Most dialog boxes also contain a **Cancel** button, which cancels the dialog box without putting new options into effect. In essence, it undoes any options you may have selected. You use **Cancel** to get out of a dialog box that you reached accidentally. You also use it if you change your mind after you have selected some options. You don't really have to select the **Cancel** button. Just press the Esc key or click both mouse buttons simultaneously.

Text Boxes

Figure 1-4 shows a dialog box with some other types of control groups. This particular dialog box appears when you select the FileFind utility so that you can tell it what file(s) you want to find.

At the top of the dialog box are two *text* boxes, which are used for entering file names, directory names, and any other data that must be entered from the keyboard instead of selected from a list. Often, a default value will be displayed in the text box when it first appears. In the **File Name** text box, *.* is the default value.

If you move the cursor to a text box by clicking on it with the mouse, *editing mode* is established. In this mode you edit the current value by inserting and deleting characters.

If you place the cursor in the text box by tabbing (instead of clicking), you will be in *replacement mode*. In this mode, the first thing you type replaces the *entire* current value.

But suppose you want to edit the current value, not replace it. You can switch to editing mode by pressing a cursor movement key such as Left arrow or End. Then go ahead and edit the item.

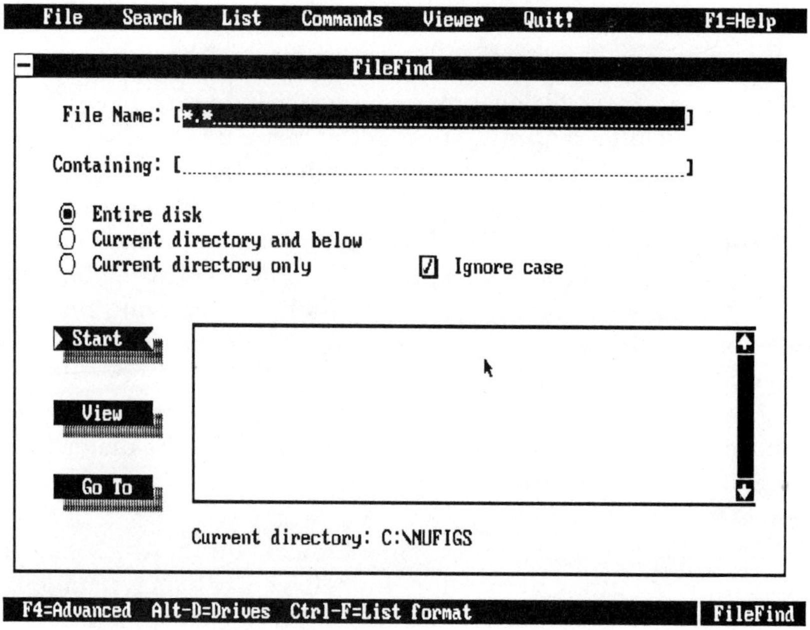

Figure 1-4   Sample Dialog Box

> **Tip:** The WordStar cursor movement keys work in text boxes.

Radio Buttons

In the section below the text boxes are three mutually exclusive options. These are called *radio buttons* because they behave somewhat like the buttons on your car radio; there must always be one and only one button selected. When you select a new radio button, the old button is automatically unselected.

To select a radio button with the mouse, click on it. To select one from the keyboard, move the cursor to it and press the Spacebar. (Most people want to press Enter instead of the Spacebar, but that selects the default command button rather than the radio button, so curb your natural instincts and learn to use the Spacebar.)

You can also select a radio button by pressing its hotkey—the first capitalized letter in its name. You must move the cursor into the control group first.

If more than one radio button has the same hotkey, as **Current directory and below** and **Current directory only** do in the example, the hotkey always selects the first one and you have to use some other means to select the other.

Check Boxes

The **Ignore case** option in Figure 1-4 is an example of a check box. It can be either on or off; an X or a check mark in the box means it's on. To toggle it on or off with the mouse, just click on it; you will see the mark appear or disappear. To toggle it with the keyboard, move the cursor to it and press the Spacebar.

> **Note:** The figure shows what radio buttons and check boxes look like with the EGA/VGA graphics options. If you don't use EGA/VGA graphics, then radio buttons appear as parentheses and check boxes appear as square brackets. You can control the graphics options from the Configure program or the Norton menu, discussed shortly.

Double-Clicking

Mouse users can select an option and complete the dialog in one fell swoop. Just double-click on the item you want to select: it could be an item in a list box, a radio button, or a check box. The dialog box closes and all new options (including the one you double-clicked on) are put into effect.

The Norton Menu Program

The Norton menu, shown in Figure 1-1, provides a gateway to all installed graphic utilities plus any other programs you add to it. This gives you several advantages. First, you don't have to remember commands; you can start a program by selecting it from the menu. Second, the menu helps you decide which program to use. Third, if you use any of the Norton Utilities general options to control the colors and graphics on your screen, you only have to specify the options once; they apply to all utilities that you start from the menu.

In addition to the menu function, the Norton menu includes an advisory function, which helps you diagnose and solve common hardware problems, and a configuration function, which lets you change your hardware settings easily.

Starting the Norton Menu

You must install the Norton utilities before you can use the menu program. When they're installed and ready to go, enter the following command at the DOS prompt:

```
NORTON [switches]
```

Table 1-1 lists several switches that are available for you to tailor the Norton menu, and all the utilities, to your preferences and environment. If you installed the utilities properly, the correct hardware settings are stored in a file named NU.INI and you shouldn't have to override them with these switches. But if NU.INI is missing or you weren't sure which settings to select during installation, you might need to specify one or more switches when you start up the menu, as in:

```
C:>NORTON /G1
```

Table 1-1   NORTON Command Reference

Format:

NORTON [switches]

Switches:

/G0	Disables graphic mouse display, graphic radio buttons, and graphic check boxes (necessary with some EGA/VGA monitors)
/G1	Disables graphic mouse display (necessary with some EGA/VGA monitors)
/G2	Disables graphics (icons) in dialog boxes
/BW	Disables the use of color
/HERC	For Hercules graphics displays
/LCD	Uses the LCD color set (necessry with some laptop displays)
/MULTITASK	Disables check for multitasking
/NOZOOM	Disables zooming of dialog boxes
?	Displays command reference on screen

When you specify a switch on the NORTON command, it applies to all utilities started from the menu. You can also specify switches on any command that starts a graphic utility from the DOS prompt, as in:

```
DISKEDIT /G0
FILESAVE /G1
SPEEDISK /BW /G1
```

/G0 and /G1 are used to suppress graphic features in case they are not compatible with your display. For example, if characters on your screen "fall apart" when you move the mouse, you need to suppress at least the graphical mouse feature. If radio buttons and check boxes don't look right, you need to use /G0 to get rid of the circles and boxes.

Use the /BW switch if the normal colors don't seem to work or if you prefer a black-and-white display for other reasons. Use the /LCD switch if you have an LCD display.

By default, dialog boxes zoom as they appear on the screen; that is, they start small and grow to full size. If your system is slow, you might not care to wait for this visual effect. Use the /NOZOOM switch to get rid of it.

The question mark (?) switch is a special case. When you use it, the program isn't started up. Instead, the command's format is displayed and the command prompt returns. Figure 1-5 shows an example of what this looks like.

Many utilities have additional switches unique to their function. You'll see those switches when you read about the individual utilities.

If you start your graphic programs from the Norton menu instead of the command prompt, you won't need the question mark switch. As you highlight a command in the **Commands** box, the information in the **Description** box includes a list of commonly used switches for that command.

```
Disk Editor, Norton Utilities 6.0, Copyright 1991 by Symantec Corporation

View and edit files and disk system areas.

DISKEDIT [drive:] [path] [filename] [/M] [/X:drives] [/W] [/SKIPHIGH]

    drive       Drive letter of disk to view/edit.
    path        Path of directory to view/edit.
    filename    File to view/edit.
    /M          Maintenance mode -- bypass DOS and look at disk directly.
    /X          Exclude drives from Absolute sector processing.
    drives      List of drives to exclude.
    /W          Enable write mode (turn off read only mode).
    /SKIPHIGH   Skip using high memory.
```

Figure 1-5   Sample Output from Question Mark Switch

Using the Menu

The Norton menu lists all available graphic utilities in a list box, grouped by topic. The **Description** box describes the highlighted command; it changes as you move the highlight in the **Commands** box. The text box at the bottom of the window shows the command that DOS will execute when you press Enter. The text box also changes as you move the highlight.

You can edit the command displayed in the text box before pressing Enter. For example, you might want to add a special switch or the name of a drive to work on. But it's rarely necessary to include specific details in the command. Most of the utilities include menus and dialog boxes to let you specify the options you want.

Suppose you want to start Disk Editor. If you're not sure what switches you want to use, you could highlight the **Disk Editor** command. The default command in the text box looks like this:

```
DISKEDIT
```

After reading the information in the **Description** box, you might want to add a drive name and the /M switch to the text box. You edit the text box to look like this:

```
DISKEDIT D: /M
```

When you press Enter, that is the command that is executed.

Suppose instead you know that you want to use just the default command. You could double-click on the **Disk Editor** option or highlight it and press Enter.

Setting Up the Norton Menu

Figure 1-6 shows the **Menu** menu, which is used to tailor the Norton menu to your needs. Through this menu, you can add commands and groups, change their descriptions, and delete them. You can also reconfigure your hardware settings.

Reminder: To pull down the **Menu** menu, press Alt-M or click on the word **Menu** in the menu bar.

Figure 1-6   Menu Menu

Sorting the Commands Box

The top portion of the **Menu** menu contains two mutually exclusive options: **Sort by Name** and **Sort by Topic**. By default, **Sort by Topic** is in effect. This means that the list in the **Commands** box is divided into topics (Recovery, Speed, Security, Tools, and any topics you have added to the list). Within each topic, commands are displayed in alphabetical order. The order of the topics themselves is not necessarily alphabetical; you set that order in a dialog box (which you'll see shortly).

If you would prefer to ignore topics and want to see all the commands in one, long, alphabetical list, choose **Sort by Name**.

Adding a Topic and Command to the Norton Menu

This section shows you step-by-step how to add new commands and topics to the Norton menu. You might not be ready for this now. If not, feel free to skip to the next topic ("Configuring the Utilities"). You can come back here when you're ready to adapt your Norton menu.

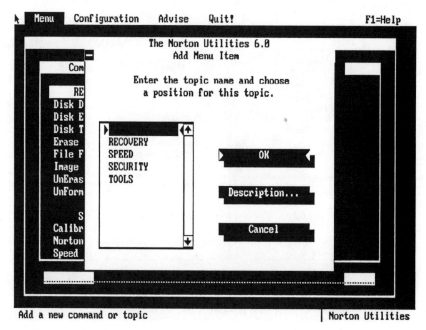

Figure 1-7   Add Topic Dialog Box

Tip: You can have up to ten topics in the **Commands** box.

Suppose you want to add a DOS topic and put a DISKCOPY command under it. You would start by selecting **Add menu item** from the **Menu** menu. A dialog box asks whether you want to add a topic or a command. In this case, we'll add the DOS topic first so we can put the DISKCOPY command under it. Figure 1-7 shows the dialog box that appears when you want to add a topic.

The list box shows all the current topics. At the top of the list is a blank space, indicated by pointers (➤), where you can type the name of a new topic.

After you type the topic name, you'll need to move it to its desired position in the list of topics (unless you want it to be first). To move it, press Down arrow until it reaches the desired position, or else click on the desired position. Then select **Description** so you can add a description for the topic. Figure 1-8 shows the resulting dialog box.

Type whatever description you want in the dialog box. This is the text that will appear in the **Description** box on the Norton menu when the topic is highlighted. For the DOS topic, it might be as simple as "DOS commands."

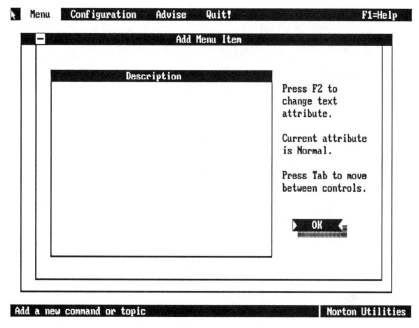

Figure 1-8 Description Dialog Box

When you select **OK**, the dialog box closes and the **Add Menu Item** dialog box returns. Select **OK** again to close the dialog box and see the new topic in the **Commands** box.

Now you're ready to add the DISKCOPY command to the list. Select **Add menu item** again. This time, when asked whether you want to add a topic or a command, select **Command**. Figure 1-9 shows the dialog box that appears next.

Tip: You can have up to 256 commands in the **Commands** box.

Next to **Name in menu**, type the name to appear in the **Commands** box on the main menu; in our example, you would probably type DISKCOPY, but the menu name doesn't necessarily have to be the same as the command itself. You could use Disk Copy, Copy Disk, or Copy a Diskette, for example.

New users tend to press Enter when they finish typing text in a text box, but you shouldn't press Enter too soon in a dialog box; it will complete the dialog and close the box before you're ready. When you finish the **Name in menu** text box, press Tab, not Enter, to get to the **DOS command** box. Then press Tab to get to the **Topic** box, and so on. If you do press Enter too soon,

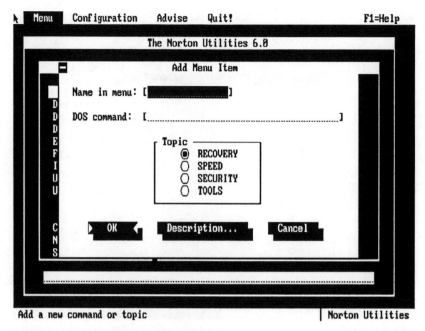

Figure 1-9   Add Command Dialog Box

you'll need to finish the definition using the **Edit menu item** option, discussed shortly.

> **TIP:** You can set up the utilities so that the Enter key acts like the Tab key. See page 25.

Next you type the default command in the **DOS command** box. In our example, you would probably want the default DISKCOPY command to duplicate a diskette in drive A:, so you would type DISKCOPY A: A:.

When entering a command in the **DOS command** box, you have no way of knowing what drive or directory will be active when the command is selected. If the program you are using is not on the program search path, then include the complete path name with the command, as in:

```
C:\DOS\DISKCOPY A: A:
```

Select a topic for the new command in the **Topic** box. Then select the **Description** button and type a description for the new command. The description is for your own use as well as end users for whom you are setting up the Norton menu. If you understand the command very well, you might not need to write much of a description. If end users will be using the command, then you might need to be more explanatory.

When you finish the description, you need to select **OK** twice: once to close the **Description** box and once to close the **Add Menu Item** box. When you return to the Norton menu, the new command will appear in the **Commands** box. Try it out to make sure it works properly.

If it doesn't, you can fix it up using the **Edit menu item** option on the **Menu** menu. The resulting dialog boxes show you the definition you created for the selected command or topic. All you have to do is correct or change the current definition and select **OK**.

If you select **Delete menu item,** a dialog box asks if you really want to remove the selected item. If you select **Yes,** the currently highlighted item is deleted from the menu. Be careful; if you accidentally delete the wrong item, you will have to define it again.

Configuring the Utilities

The **Configuration** menu, shown in Figure 1-10, lets you change the setup for all the utilities, not just the Norton menu.

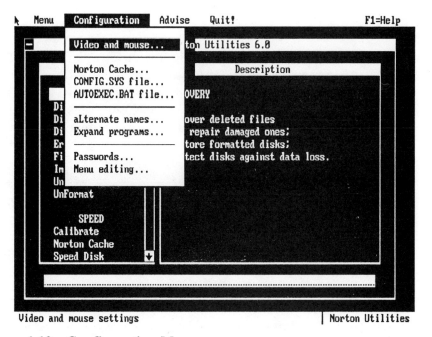

Figure 1-10   Configuration Menu

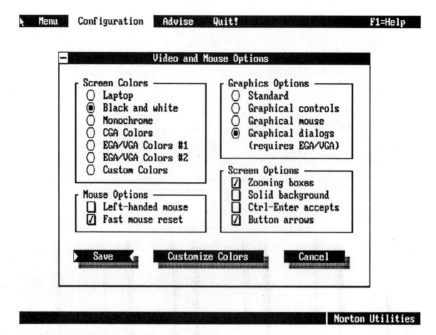

Figure 1-11   Video and Mouse Options

Video and Mouse Configuration

The **Video and mouse** choice brings up the dialog box shown in Figure 1-11. Here you can change your system setup permanently so that you don't have to use switches when starting up a utility. When you select **Save**, the current settings are saved in NU.INI and affect all future uses of the utilities until you change them again. You will also see the effect of any changes immediately on your screen.

> **Tip:** If you're not sure which settings are best for your hardware, you can experiment with them here and see immediately which produce the best results. That's one reason that we recommend that you make the changes here rather than during installation (which uses the same dialog box, by the way).

The **Graphics Options** are equivalent to the /G0 switch (**Standard**), the /G1 switch (**Graphical controls**), and the /G2 switch (**Graphical mouse**).

The **Graphical dialogs** option gives you full graphics on the screen. You must have an EGA or VGA monitor to use the graphic options.

The **Screen Colors** control group in the upper left corner gives you control over the basic color scheme. The various screen color options are available in case the default colors aren't clear on your monitor. You might also like to change colors just as a matter of personal preference. If none of the pre-selected color schemes works for you, choose the **Custom colors** radio button, then select the **Customize colors** command button to open a dialog box where you can select from a palette of colors for each element in the graphic interface. For example, you could set the color of the default command button to bright red on black and the non-default command button to blue on black.

The mouse options are not just a matter of personal preference, on the other hand (pun intended). If you use the mouse with your left hand, turn on **Left-handed mouse**. The function of the mouse buttons will be reversed so that you can click with the right button, and therefore still use your index finger. If you're having trouble with your mouse, try turning off **Fast mouse reset**; some mice work better without it.

The **Screen Options** section of the **Video and Mouse Options** dialog box includes several check boxes. **Zooming boxes** controls whether dialog boxes zoom or pop onto the screen. **Solid background** controls whether the background of each graphics screen is a solid color or stippled. **Ctrl-Enter accepts** causes the Enter key to move the cursor from item to item just as the Tab key does, and you have to press Ctrl-Enter to select the default command button. Some people prefer the Enter key to work this way. If you decide to choose this option, you'll have to remember to use Ctrl-Enter in places where the directions say "press Enter." **Button arrows** controls whether or not the default button is highlighted by arrow pointers. If the arrow pointers don't work on your monitor, use this option to turn them off.

Other Configuration Options

The rest of the **Configuration** menu gives you access to the setup options described previously in this chapter.

The Configuration Program

Figure 1-12 shows the dialog box that opens when you select the **Configuration** command from the **Tools** section of the **Commands** box. You can start up the same program by entering the command NUCONFIG at the command prompt. As you can see, this dialog box offers the same eight options as the **Configuration** menu; in fact, they lead to the same dialog boxes.

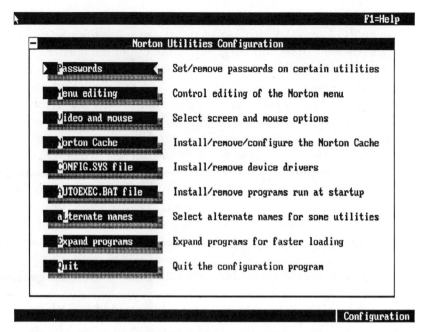

Figure 1-12   Norton Utilities Configuration Dialog Box

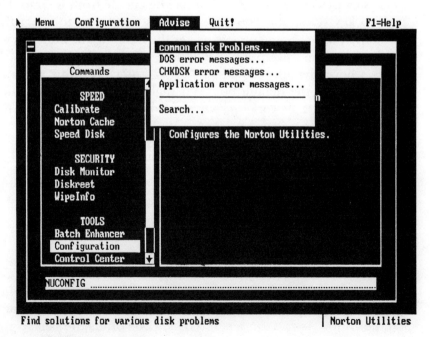

Figure 1-13   Advise Menu

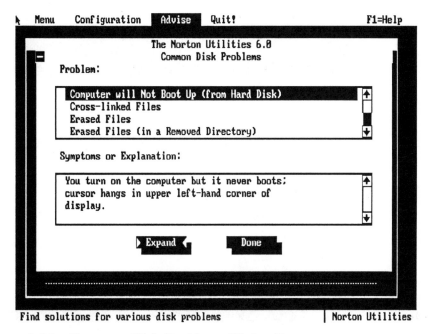

Figure 1-14   Common Disk Problems Dialog Box

On-Screen Advice

Figure 1-13 shows the **Advise** menu, which lets you look up solutions to hardware problems.

If you're having problems with your disk, select **common disk Problems**, which brings up the dialog box shown in Figure 1-14. The top section lists several common problems; you can scroll through it to see them all. The bottom section briefly explains each highlighted problem; it changes as you move the highlight.

When you find the closest description to the problem you are experiencing, select **Expand** to find out even more. Figure 1-15 shows the dialog box that opens if you expand "Missing files." It suggests possible actions you can take to solve the problem. You can scroll down and up to read the entire text. Buttons are included to let you start up a solution right away. Selecting **Done** returns you to the Common Disk Problems dialog box.

The **DOS error messages, CHKDSK error messages,** and **Application error messages** options work just like **Common disk problems** does. **Application error messages** includes error messages from commonly used applications such as WordPerfect and Lotus 1-2-3.

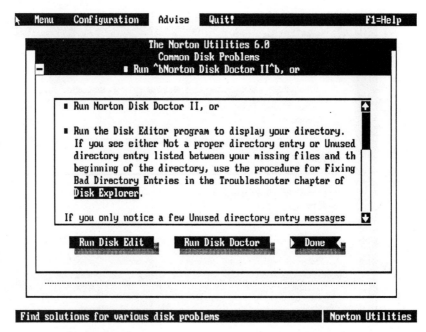

Figure 1-15   Expanded Advice

If you're not sure where to look for a message, you can use the **Search** option to find it. The resulting dialog box lets you enter up to 40 characters of text to search for. You can also select to include application error messages in the search, which makes the search take longer, or to just search the DOS and CHKDSK messages. All messages containing the search text are displayed so that you can choose the ones you want to expand.

Getting On-Screen Help

Any time you need immediate help with a utility, try the on-screen help system, which takes several forms. From the NDOS command prompt, you can enter the command HELP to open up an interactive Help window for all the NDOS and DOS commands. The initial windows displays an index of help topics to select from. Figure 1-16 shows what the Help window looks like when you select the DIR command from the index. (By the way, if you're familiar with DOS's DIR, notice how many more switches the NDOS command has; those are all additional features.) You can also reach this window by entering HELP DIR from the NDOS command prompt.

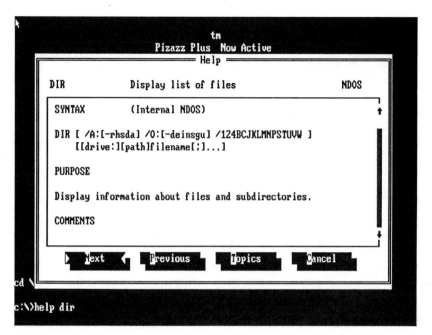

Figure 1-16   NDOS Help Window

You can scroll through the text to read the entire topic. The **Next** and **Previous** buttons take you to other topics in the index. The **Topics** button displays the index. And the **Cancel** button returns you to the NDOS command prompt.

Another way to see help information about a particular command is to enter the command name with the /? switch. Figure 1-17 shows the result of entering the command DIR /?. This information is often briefer than the NDOS Help system, but it's quick and it might be enough to tell you what you need to know.

A more extensive help system is available for graphic utilities. It pops up a dialog box that explains whatever you are currently working on. Figure 1-18 shows the dialog box that appears when you select help while the **Video and Mouse Options** dialog box is on the screen.

```
Display the disk volume label(s).

VOL [drive:]...
```

Figure 1-17   Command-Line Help Information

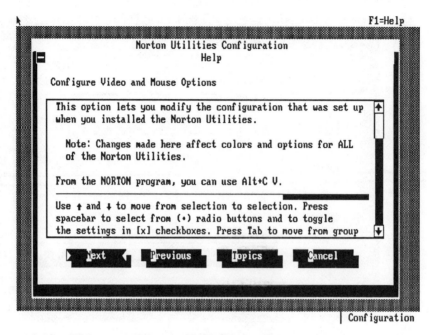

Figure 1-18   Video and Mouse Help Dialog Box

To select help, press F1 or click on "F1=Help" at the right end of the menu bar. Once in the help system, you can get to any topic for the current utility. The **Next** and **Previous** buttons let you scan topics in order. The order of topics usually starts with very general information—an introduction to the utility, how to use the help system, how to use menus and dialog boxes, and so on—then goes from the first option on the first menu to the last option on the last menu.

If you don't want to scan all the information, the **Topics** button takes you to an index where you can select the topic you want. Figure 1-19 shows a sample list of topics; this one is for the Norton menu.

Once you find the right topic, you can read all the text by paging down and up in it much like any other list box.

> **Tip:** Paging down and up moves within the description of a topic, while the **Next** and **Previous** buttons move from topic to topic.

When you're done with the help system, just press Esc or select **Cancel** to return to the utility with which you were working.

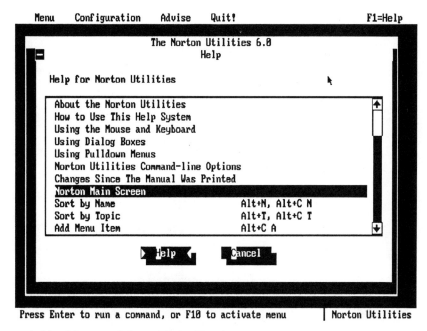

Figure 1-19   Norton Menu Help Topics

Looking Ahead

With the basics you have learned in this chapter, you can easily learn to use whatever utility you're most interested in. We'll start in the next chapter, which shows you how to use Disk Editor as an exploration tool. You can use Disk Editor to examine the before-and-after effects of the other utilities, which will help you understand exactly how they work. For example, you could examine the system areas of a diskette with Disk Editor, then reformat the diskette with Safe Format, and then examine the system areas again to see what changes were made. So, unless you're in a hurry to jump into one of the other utilities, we recommend that you continue on to Chapter 2 for a look at Disk Editor.

2

DISK EDITOR AS A DISK EXPLORER

Don't you wish you could just sit down and read a disk? Wouldn't you like to take a peek at the system areas at the beginning of the disk? Or find out what, if anything, is in the "unused" space? That's just what Disk Editor lets you do. You can examine any part of a diskette, hard disk, or RAM drive, even areas that don't belong to DOS. You can also examine the contents of any area of memory.

Disk Editor is fascinating for exploring your disks (especially hard disks), but it's also a very useful problem-solving tool. You can find data that "slipped between the cracks," examine deleted files before undeleting them, compare two files to see exactly where they're different, and more.

In this chapter, you'll see how to use Disk Editor to explore disks and memory, giving you a way to examine the effect of other utilities such as Disk Doctor and Diskreet as you read subsequent chapters. Chapter 14 shows you how to use Disk Editor for editing.

Starting Disk Editor

You can start Disk Editor from the DOS prompt or the Norton menu. To start it from the DOS prompt, you must enter the appropriate command, which might be DISKEDIT or DE, depending on whether you renamed DISKEDIT to DE during installation. (If you're not sure which one is correct for your system, try them both.) Include whatever switches you need with the

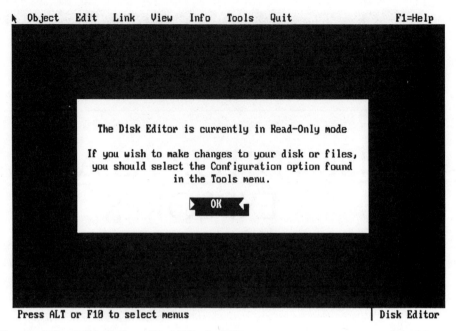

Figure 2-1   Disk Editor Read-Only Message

NORTON command, such as /G1 to disable the graphic mouse display or /LCD for laptop displays.

To start it from the Norton menu (refer back to Figure 1-1), select the **Disk Editor** option in the **Recovery** section.

The first time you start the Disk Editor, you should see the message shown in Figure 2-1. This message tells you that Disk Editor is set for exploration only; you can't edit with it. You can't accidentally change any crucial data in this mode.

To clear the read-only message and continue with Disk Editor, select the **OK** button. (All you really have to do is press Enter since that button is selected by default.)

Note: If you don't see the read-only message, someone has changed your Disk Editor configuration. Don't take chances: you really should change it back to read-only while learning how to use Disk Editor. Pull down the **Tools** menu; select the **Configuration** option; check the **Read Only** box; and select the **Save** command button.

After you see and acknowledge the read-only message, Disk Editor scans your disk. Then a screen similar to the one shown in Figure 2-2 appears. It shows

```
    Object   Edit   Link   View   Info   Tools   Quit              F1=Help
 Name     .Ext    Size     Date       Time    Cluster Arc R/O Sys Hid Dir Vol
 Cluster 6,184, Sector 24,889                                              ▲
 █████████          0    5-28-91    2:01 pm    6184                   Dir
 ..                 0    5-28-91    2:01 pm       0                   Dir
 NUBOOK   PZD     190   11-08-90    7:41 pm    6187   Arc
 PZP      COM   24576    7-28-90   12:49 pm    6188       R/O
 PZP      PZD     256    7-28-90   12:49 pm    7749
 PZP      PZO   89088    7-28-90   12:49 pm    7750
 PZP      PZX  110592    5-28-91    7:53 pm   13086
 ♂DLBOMB  TXT   50369    5-08-91    7:29 am   13161
 ♂OODPICS CFG    9349   12-13-90    4:09 am   13186   Arc
               Unused directory entry
               Unused directory entry
               Unused directory entry
               Unused directory entry
               Unused directory entry
               Unused directory entry
               Unused directory entry
 Cluster 6,184, Sector 24,890                                   ▶
               Unused directory entry
               Unused directory entry                                      ▼
 ─ Sub-Directory                                  Cluster 6,184   ▲
   C:\PZP                                         Offset 0, hex 0  ▼
   Press ALT or F10 to select menus              │ Disk Editor
```

Figure 2-2   Initial Disk Editor Screen

the current directory on the default drive. You can explore that directory or select something else to look at. You'll see how to interpret the directory later in this chapter.

Disk Editor Overview

In Disk Editor, you work on an *object*: a file, a directory, or whatever. Normally, the whole process of examining an object using Disk Editor looks something like this:

- Select the drive containing the object.
- Select the object you want to look at.
- Select the mode you want to view the object in.
- Examine the object.
- Link to related objects, if desired.
- Quit.

You'll see how these steps work as we explore each type of object in the following sections.

About Sectors and Clusters (and Bytes)

When you examine your disk with Disk Editor, you will see many references to *sectors* and *clusters*. Because the disk is spinning quite rapidly, the recording head can't read or write just one byte, or even 10 or 100 bytes. (A *byte* is an individual storage location where one indivisible piece of data, such as the letter "A," is stored.) The disk drive accesses data one sector at a time.

On personal computer disks, a sector is 512 bytes. The disk drive accesses data one sector at a time. Depending on the type of drive, the concentric circles called *tracks* where data is stored might be divided into 9 sectors (double-density diskettes), 15 sectors (high-density diskettes), or 17 or more sectors (hard disks).

Sectors are identified by a physical numbering scheme that specifies the side of the disk (starting with 0), the track number (starting with 0), and the sector number within the track (starting with 1). So the first sector on any disk is 0,0,1. The last sector on a double-density 5 1/4" diskette is 1,40,9. On a hard disk, it might be something like 5,818,17.

Because the physical numbers are awkward to work with (imagine trying to figure out how many sectors are between 2,12,5 and 4,625,2), DOS translates them into a straight sequential numbering scheme where the first sector on the disk is number 0. On a double-density 5 1/4" diskette, the last sector is 719. On a hard drive, it might be something like 41,801. Most of the time you will see and use the DOS sector numbers, but there are some cases where you will have to use the physical sector numbers.

On a larger capacity disk, there are too many sectors to reasonably keep track of individually, so DOS groups them together into *clusters*. A cluster is the basic file storage space for a disk. DOS gives a new file one or more whole clusters on the disk. Even if a file contains only one byte, it will occupy a complete cluster. DOS maintains a table at the beginning of every disk, called the File Allocation Table (FAT), where it keeps track of what's in each cluster on the disk.

A double-density diskette has only one sector per cluster, but a typical hard disk has four sectors per cluster. The first sectors on the disk, where the system information such as the FAT is stored, are not grouped into clusters. Only the data area, where files are stored, has clusters. Just to keep you on your toes, cluster numbers start with 2.

Exploring a Directory

A directory is an index of the files on a disk, much like the office directory in the lobby of a building. Each line in a directory is an entry that describes one file's name, size in bytes, starting cluster on the disk, and the date and time it was created or last modified. You can see all these fields in the directory view in Figure 2-2.

The directory entry also shows the file's *attributes*, which determine how the file is handled by DOS and other programs. The *hidden* attribute hides the file from the casual user: DOS doesn't display or process hidden files unless specifically told to. The *read only* attribute protects a file from being changed or deleted, but does not prevent it from being accessed. The *system* attribute is a combination of hidden and read only. The *archive* attribute indicates that the file has been modified since the last time it was backed up by a facility such as Norton Backup; basically, it indicates that the file needs to be backed up (or "archived").

Subdirectory Entries

Every disk has a main directory—called the *root* directory—which is placed at the beginning of the disk during formatting. For high-capacity disks, which can hold hundreds of files, you might want to establish *subdirectories* to group related files together. A subdirectory is a directory much like the root directory; it can hold any number of file entries and can have subdirectories of its own. Every subdirectory has a *parent* directory (the directory it branches off from) and may have one or more *child* directories (subdirectories that branch off from it), so that all the directories on the disk form a hierarchical structure, called a *directory tree*, with the root directory at the top.

The root directory is always named \ (a single backslash). Subdirectories have names just like filenames, such as NU, DOS, and DATABASE; you can include an extension, as in WORK.DBS, but most people don't bother.

When you list a directory with DOS's DIR command or examine it with Disk Editor, you will see entries for its child subdirectories. Every subdirectory takes up an entry just as a file does, with a name, time, date, starting location, and attributes (the size is always 0). In addition to other attributes, it always has the *directory* attribute. Every directory except the root directory always starts with two directory entries named . (a single period) and .. (a double period). The . entry describes the subdirectory itself while the .. entry describes its parent.

Volume Label Entries

DOS lets you assign each disk an 11-character name, called a *volume label*, which can keep you from mixing up your disks. For example, you might label your hard disk MAINDISK; you might label diskettes SCRATCH, BACK-UPDISK, and SAVEPICS. You will see the volume label, if present, when you examine a root directory under Disk Editor. It takes up one directory entry and has the *volume* attribute.

Viewing the Directory

When you list a directory with the DOS DIR command, you see only part of its information. For example, DOS doesn't show you the starting cluster or the attributes. It also doesn't list deleted files, nor does it show hidden or system files unless requested. When you explore a directory using Disk Editor, you see *all* the data in the directory. If you use the directory view, as in Figure 2-2, the information is even interpreted for you. The hexadecimal view (which you'll see a little later) shows you the raw data—byte by byte.

Note: The Norton Utilities includes a utility called Norton Change Directory that makes it simple to create and manipulate directories and volume labels.

The following sections show you how to view a directory with Disk Editor.

Selecting the Drive and Directory

Disk Editor starts by showing you the current drive and directory. But you can select any other drive and directory as an object. You start with the **Object** menu, shown in Figure 2-3.

Selecting the Drive

If the directory you want is on a different drive, you'll need to select the **Drive** option. Figure 2-4 shows the **Drive** dialog box. All your drives should be listed in the box on the left. Just select the one you want. When the dialog box closes, you'll see the current directory for that drive.

Reminder: To select the **Drive** option, either pull down the **Object** menu and select **Drive** or press Alt-D. To select a drive in the dialog box, move the highlight to it and press Enter, type its letter, or double-click on it.

Selecting the Directory

The **diRectory** option in the **Object** menu opens the dialog box shown in Figure 2-5. The box on the left shows the entire directory tree for the current drive. If the desired directory is showing, all you have to do is select it by clicking on it or by moving the highlight to it and pressing Enter.

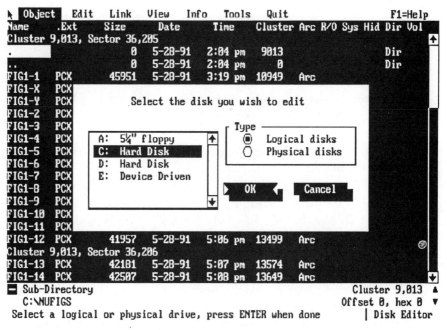

```
 ▶ Object   Edit   Link   View   Info   Tools   Quit                    F1=Help
Na │                                              Time   Cluster Arc R/O Sys Hid Dir Vol
Cl │ Drive...              Alt-D                                                          ↑
 . │ diRectory...          Alt-R        1  2:04 pm   9013                     Dir
   │ File...               Alt-F        1  2:04 pm      0                     Dir
FI │ Cluster...            Alt-C        1  3:19 pm  10949  Arc
FI │ Sector...             Alt-S        1  2:37 pm   9537  Arc
FI │ Physical sector...    Alt-P        1  2:52 pm   9623  Arc
FI │ ──────────────────────────────    1  3:31 pm  11051  Arc
FI │ partition Table       Alt-A        1  3:34 pm  11133  Arc
FI │ Boot Record           Alt-B        1  3:38 pm  11721  Arc
FI │ 1st copy of FAT       Alt-F1       1  3:48 pm  12981  Arc
FI │ 2nd copy of FAT       Alt-F2       1  3:49 pm  13051  Arc
FI │ ──────────────────────────────    1  4:56 pm  13127  Arc
FI │ (clipboard)                        1  5:00 pm  13203  Arc
FI │ Memory Dump...        Alt-M        1  5:01 pm  13274  Arc
FI └──────────────────────────────┘    1  5:03 pm  13346  Arc
FIG1-11  PCX       45323    5-28-91     5:04 pm  13422  Arc
FIG1-12  PCX       41957    5-28-91     5:06 pm  13499  Arc
Cluster 9,013, Sector 36,206
FIG1-13  PCX       42181    5-28-91     5:07 pm  13574  Arc
FIG1-14  PCX       42507    5-28-91     5:08 pm  13649  Arc                           ↓
━ Sub-Directory                                             Cluster 9,013  ▲
  C:\NUFIGS                                                 Offset 0, hex 0  ▼
Select a disk drive                                       │ Disk Editor
```

Figure 2-3   Object Menu

```
 ▶ Object   Edit   Link   View   Info   Tools   Quit                    F1=Help
Name    .Ext   Size     Date     Time    Cluster Arc R/O Sys Hid Dir Vol
Cluster 9,013, Sector 36,205                                                        ↑
 .                   0   5-28-91   2:04 pm   9013                     Dir
 ..                  0   5-28-91   2:04 pm      0                     Dir
FIG1-1   PCX     45951   5-28-91   3:19 pm  10949  Arc
FIG1-X   PCX┌────────────────────────────────────────────────────┐
FIG1-Y   PCX│  Select the disk you wish to edit                   │
FIG1-2   PCX│                                                     │
FIG1-3   PCX│                                  ┌─ Type ─────────┐ │
FIG1-4   PCX│ ┌──────────────────────┐ ┌───┐  │ ◉ Logical disks│ │
FIG1-5   PCX│ │ A:  5¼" floppy      ↑│ │   │  │ ○ Physical disks│ │
FIG1-6   PCX│ │ C:  Hard Disk       │ │   │  └─────────────────┘ │
FIG1-7   PCX│ │ D:  Hard Disk       │ │   │                      │
FIG1-8   PCX│ │ E:  Device Driven   │ │   │  ▶ OK ◀   Cancel     │
FIG1-9   PCX│ │                    ↓│ │   │                      │
FIG1-10  PCX│ └──────────────────────┘ └───┘                      │
FIG1-11  PCX└────────────────────────────────────────────────────┘
FIG1-12  PCX     41957   5-28-91   5:06 pm  13499  Arc
Cluster 9,013, Sector 36,206
FIG1-13  PCX     42181   5-28-91   5:07 pm  13574  Arc
FIG1-14  PCX     42507   5-28-91   5:08 pm  13649  Arc                           ↓
━ Sub-Directory                                             Cluster 9,013  ▲
  C:\NUFIGS                                                 Offset 0, hex 0  ▼
Select a logical or physical drive, press ENTER when done │ Disk Editor
```

Figure 2-4   Drive Dialog Box

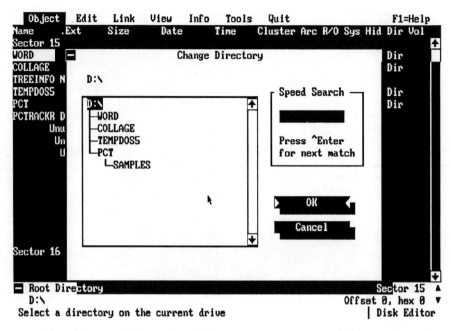

Figure 2-5   Change Directory Dialog Box

If the tree is so big that the desired directory isn't showing, you can scroll around in it or use Speed Search. To use Speed Search, type the first letters of the desired directory name. Each letter you type appears in the Speed Search box; at the same time, the cursor jumps to the next directory in the tree starting with that combination of letters. For example, suppose you want to find your NOVEL subdirectory. When you type an N, the highlight jumps to the NU directory. Then you type an O, and the highlight goes to NORTON. When you type a V, the highlight finally goes to NOVEL and you can press Enter to select it.

If the letter you type doesn't appear in the Speed Search box, there is no directory in the tree starting with that combination of letters. For example, suppose you type N-O-W instead of N-O-V. The N and O work, but the W produces no result and doesn't show up in the Speed Search box. There is no directory starting with NOW in the current tree. You can now type a V or some other letter as the third letter.

Pressing Ctrl-Enter jumps the highlight to the next directory starting with the same letter combination. For example, suppose you type NO; the NORTON directory is highlighted. Press Ctrl-Enter and the cursor jumps to NOVEL. Another press highlights NOVEMBER. When the highlight reaches the bottom of the tree, it cycles back to the top and keeps going.

When you select a directory and close the dialog box, the selected directory appears on the screen. Then you can choose the way you view the directory information.

Selecting the View

You can use any viewer on the directory, but the directory and hex viewers make the most sense. Figure 2-6 shows the **View** menu. You can see that the easiest way to select a view is to press a hotkey: F2 for hex, F4 for directory, and so on. The check mark identifies the current viewer.

The Directory Viewer

The directory viewer (see Figure 2-2) interprets the information stored in the directory. The top line (just under the menu bar) labels the directory fields:

Name and **.Ext**   The full name of the volume, directory, or file.

Size   The file's size, in bytes. (This field always contains 0 for directory and volume entries.)

Date and **Time**   For files, these fields show when the file was last modified. For directories and volume labels, they show when it was created.

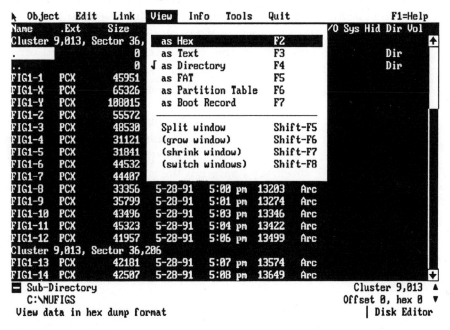

Figure 2-6   View Menu

Cluster	The first cluster of the directory or file. This is always 0 for a volume label and for the root directory.
Arc	This field shows "Arc" if the archive attribute is on and is blank if it's off.
R/O	This field shows "R/O" if the read-only attribute is on and is blank if it's off.
Sys	This field shows "Sys" if the system attribute is on and is blank if it's off.
Hid	This field shows "Hid" if the hidden attribute is on and is blank if it's off.
Dir	This field shows "Dir" when the entry identifies a subdirectory, not a file or a volume label.
Vol	This field shows "Vol" when the entry identifies the volume label. This can appear only in the root directory for a drive.

A directory is stored in sectors just like any other data on the disk. In the example in Figure 2-2, you can see two sector boundaries—one directly under the field headings and the other near the bottom of the display. This particular directory starts in cluster 6184, sector 24889, and continues into sector 24890. (You could page down to see more sectors.)

The first entry in any nonroot directory is the directory itself. Its name is always a single period (.). You can see in the status bar at the bottom of the screen that this directory's real name is PZP. It appears as PZP in the parent directory. But in the directory itself, it is always referred to by a single period. In the example, you can see that the directory was created on 5-28-91 at 2:01 pm. It starts in cluster 6184. And its only attribute is the directory attribute.

Similarly, the second entry in every nonroot directory is a double period, which identifies the parent directory. In this case, the parent directory was also created on 5-28-91 at 2:01 pm. It starts in cluster 0, a pretty good indication that it is the root directory. The path in the status line—C:\PZP—confirms that this directory's parent is the root directory.

Note: That cluster number isn't really a contradiction. Cluster 0 simply means that the root directory is located in the system area that comes before the first cluster, which is actually cluster 2.

The directory in the example contains 5 current files. The file named PZP.COM contains 24,576 bytes, was last modified on 7-28-90 at 7:41 pm, and starts in cluster 6188. It has the read-only attribute set.

The sample directory also has two deleted files, which you can identify by a sigma (σ) as the first character of the name. DOS places this character in the filename when you delete a file. The next time you add data to the disk, DOS will use these directory entries before it goes to the ones marked "Unused directory entry."

Because DOS fills in the directory from the top and always reuses deleted entries before unused ones, all the unused entries should come at the end of the directory. If you see real directory entries mixed in with unused directory entries, the directory is damaged (or it's not actually a directory).

A faulty directory might also contain invalid entries. On color monitors, Disk Editor displays invalid entries in a contrasting color. Disk Editor identifies such entries by invalid data in fields such as the date and time, which have limited values. For example, if the date field interprets as 15-45-07, Disk Editor will mark the entry as invalid.

Near the bottom of the screen is a two-line status bar. On the left, it shows the type of object ("Sub-Directory") and the path ("C:\PZP"). On the right, it shows the current position of the cursor within the object. Right now, the cursor is on the first byte of cluster 6184. If it said "Cluster 91, Offset 28, hex 1C," the cursor would be 29 bytes into cluster 91. Some programs report locations using the hexadecimal number system (which is based on 16 instead of 10), so the "hex" version is shown along with the decimal version, in case you need it. If you're uncomfortable with hexadecimal numbers, just ignore them.

The bottom line on the screen shows messages, which change as you pull down various menus and highlight various options.

Maneuvering in the Directory View

You can move about in the directory view using the mouse or the cursor keys. They work just like you would expect them to: the Up arrow moves up one line, the Home key jumps to the beginning of the object, and so on. Ctrl-PageUp and Ctrl-PageDown move backward and forward by sectors (so do the – and + keys on the numeric keypad when NumLock is off). With the mouse, click right on the gray part of the scroll bar to move by sectors. Ctrl-Home and Ctrl-End jump to the first and last entry in the current sector; click right on the up arrow and down arrow to accomplish the same effect.

Linking to Other Objects

When you're examining a directory, you might need to see one of the files or its FAT entries. You can switch to either of these objects without going through the **Object** menu by *linking* to it.

Figure 2-7 shows the **Link** menu. The available options depend on the object. For a directory, the **File** and **Cluster chain (FAT)** options are available. The same options are available if you use the hotkeys instead of the menu.

Suppose you are examining a directory and want to see a particular file, subdirectory, or the parent directory. You could highlight the desired entry and press Ctrl-F. Suppose you want to see the FAT entry for a file or directory; highlight it and press Ctrl-T. To get back to the original directory after linking, you would link back to it using Ctrl-D. If you highlight a volume, deleted, or unused entry, you won't be able to link with Ctrl-F. You'll either get a beep or no response at all.

The advantages of linking over changing objects via the **Object** menu are speed and convenience. You don't have to go through a dialog box to identify the object you want: the current cursor position identifies it. The disadvantage is that you're limited to certain related objects. You can't link from a directory to a cluster object or to a directory on another drive, for example.

```
  Object   Edit   Link   View   Info   Tools   Quit                F1=Help
Name       .Ext                                    Arc R/O Sys Hid Dir Vol
Cluster 9,013, Sec  File...                Ctrl-F                         ▲
 .                   (directory...)         Ctrl-D              Dir
 ..                  Cluster chain (FAT)... Ctrl-T              Dir
FIG1-1    PCX        (partition...)                 Arc
FIG1-X    PCX                                       Arc
FIG1-Y    PCX        (window...)                    Arc
FIG1-2    PCX                                       Arc
FIG1-3    PCX     48530   5-28-91   3:34 pm  11133  Arc
FIG1-4    PCX     31121   5-28-91   3:38 pm  11721  Arc
FIG1-5    PCX     31841   5-28-91   3:48 pm  12981  Arc
FIG1-6    PCX     44532   5-28-91   3:49 pm  13051  Arc
FIG1-7    PCX     44407   5-28-91   4:56 pm  13127  Arc
FIG1-8    PCX     33356   5-28-91   5:00 pm  13203  Arc
FIG1-9    PCX     35799   5-28-91   5:01 pm  13274  Arc
FIG1-10   PCX     43496   5-28-91   5:03 pm  13346  Arc
FIG1-11   PCX     45323   5-28-91   5:04 pm  13422  Arc
FIG1-12   PCX     41957   5-28-91   5:06 pm  13499  Arc
Cluster 9,013, Sector 36,206
FIG1-13   PCX     42181   5-28-91   5:07 pm  13574  Arc
FIG1-14   PCX     42507   5-28-91   5:08 pm  13649  Arc             ▼
■ Sub-Directory                               Cluster 9,013  ▲
  C:\NUFIGS                                   Offset 0, hex 0 ▼
View file's contents                         | Disk Editor
```

Figure 2-7   Link Menu

Quick Links

Disk Editor also has a Quick Links feature that makes certain links even easier. All you have to do is press Enter or double-click, and an automatic link takes place. For example, if you press Enter or double-click on a file entry, that file instantly becomes the object. Press Enter or double-click anywhere in a file, and you quick-link to its directory entry. A directory entry quick-links to that directory.

> **Note:** Quick Links is an optional feature. It's automatically on when you first install Norton Utilities. But if it doesn't work for you, someone has turned it off in your copy of Disk Editor. You'll see later in this chapter how to turn it on again.

Directory Information

In addition to examining the directory itself, you might want some overall information about it, such as its size and fragmentation. The **Info** menu, shown in Figure 2-8, provides access to information about the object and the drive it's on.

```
  Object   Edit    Link    View   Info  Tools   Quit                    F1=Help
Name    .Ext     Size      Date          r Arc R/O Sys Hid Dir Vol           ▲
Cluster 9,013, Sector 36,205   Object info...
.                     0   5-28-   Drive info...                        Dir
..                    0   5-28-   Map of object...                     Dir
FIG1-1   PCX      45951   5-28-                   Arc
FIG1-X   PCX      65326   5-28-91   2:37 pm  9537  Arc
FIG1-Y   PCX     100015   5-28-91   2:52 pm  9623  Arc
FIG1-2   PCX      55572   5-28-91   3:31 pm 11051  Arc
FIG1-3   PCX      48530   5-28-91   3:34 pm 11133  Arc
FIG1-4   PCX      31121   5-28-91   3:38 pm 11721  Arc
FIG1-5   PCX      31841   5-28-91   3:48 pm 12981  Arc
FIG1-6   PCX      44532   5-28-91   3:49 pm 13051  Arc
FIG1-7   PCX      44407   5-28-91   4:56 pm 13127  Arc
FIG1-8   PCX      33356   5-28-91   5:00 pm 13203  Arc
FIG1-9   PCX      35799   5-28-91   5:01 pm 13274  Arc
FIG1-10  PCX      43496   5-28-91   5:03 pm 13346  Arc
FIG1-11  PCX      45323   5-28-91   5:04 pm 13422  Arc
FIG1-12  PCX      41957   5-28-91   5:06 pm 13499  Arc
Cluster 9,013, Sector 36,206
FIG1-13  PCX      42181   5-28-91   5:07 pm 13574  Arc
FIG1-14  PCX      42507   5-28-91   5:08 pm 13649  Arc                         ↓
 ■ Sub-Directory                              Cluster 9,013    ▲
   C:\NUFIGS                                  Offset 0, hex 0  ▼
 Get more information on the selected object         | Disk Editor
```

Figure 2-8   Info Menu

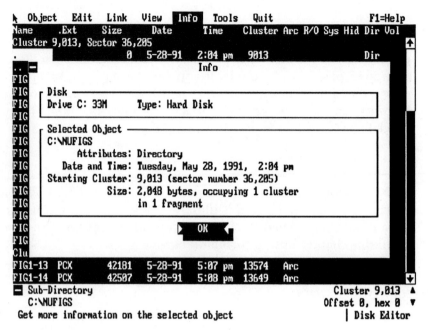

Figure 2-9(a)   Information for Directories

Figure 2-9 shows the dialog boxes that result from each option when a directory is the object. (Different objects produce different results from **Object info.**) The **Object info** and **Drive info** options provide general information, while **Map of object** shows you where the directory is located on the drive. (**Map of object** is not available for root directories since they're always in the same place.)

No matter what size the disk is, the map always fits on one screen, as shown in the example. The number of clusters represented by one block is adjusted to make the map fit. A message next to the **OK** button tells you how many clusters each block represents. In the example in Figure 2-9, each block represents 29 clusters because this is a 33M drive. For a 360K diskette, each block represents only one cluster. When the number of clusters per block is small, you can get a visual image of the object's layout from the map. But when each block represents 20 or more clusters, a directory could be broken into several pieces and still take only one block in the map.

Exploring a File

If you create a file with an application such as a word processor or spreadsheet, you can always look at it again and edit it using that same application. But what you see on your screen isn't necessarily the raw data

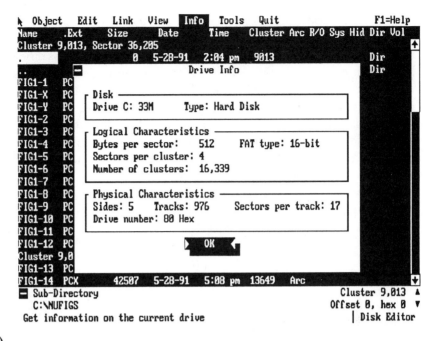

(b)

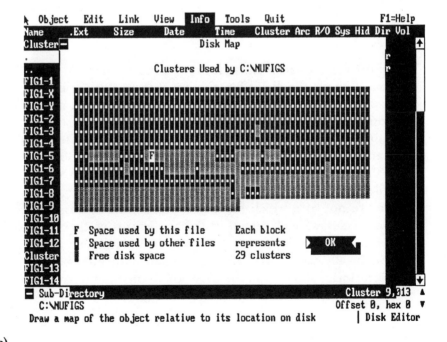

(c)

Figure 2-9   Information for Directories

in the file; the application interprets it for you much as Disk Editor's directory viewer interprets a directory. When you explore a file with Disk Editor, you can see the actual data in the file. You might find that it has a header, which is an area of administrative information at the beginning of the file. You might see the codes that start new lines, cause boldface type to appear, or center a heading.

Exploring files can tell you a lot about how your applications work. It might also help you figure out how to fix a file that has been damaged somehow and is being rejected by the application that created it. You could use Disk Editor to compare a "healthy" file to a damaged one, for example, and identify what the discrepancies are. After you learn how to use Disk Editor in edit mode (which is explained in Chapter 14), you could even try to repair the damaged file with Disk Editor.

> **Note:** You can explore program files with Disk Editor, but unless you're an experienced programmer, you won't be able to interpret what you see. Data files are much more satisfactory targets for the average user's exploration.

How to Explore a File

To explore a file, you can link to it or you can select it from the **Object** menu. Figure 2-10 shows the dialog box that results when you select the **File** option or press Alt-F. Since you can specify the drive and path in this dialog box, you don't need to use the **Drive** or **Directory** options first.

If you know the name of the file, you can type it in the text box at the top. You can include a drive and/or path with the name. So you could enter CHAP02 for a file in the current drive and directory, D:\NOVEL\CHAP02 for a file on another drive and directory, and so on.

If you're not sure which file you want, or where it is, you can use the selection boxes, which list items in alphabetical order. Start on the right with the **Drives** box. When you select a drive, the default directory for that drive is automatically chosen. Its path is listed above the **Files** box. Its parent and child directories show up in the **Dirs** box in the middle, and its files appear in the **Files** box.

> **Reminder:** Tab to move from box to box. Use the arrow keys to move within each box. Or double-click on the desired item.

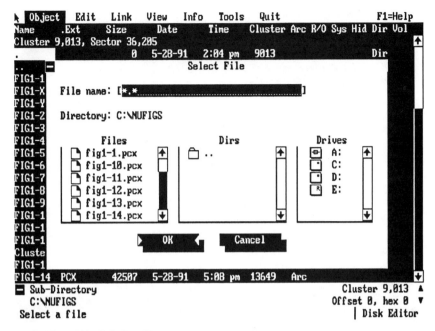

Figure 2-10   File Dialog Box

Once the drive is correct, you might need to find the correct directory. If it isn't showing in the **Dirs** box, select a subdirectory, if appropriate, or the parent directory, which always shows up as two periods (..). When you're looking at the root directory, there won't be any parent directory, but it will show up in all subdirectory listings. Each time you change the directory, the list in the **Files** box changes.

You can speed search by pressing the first letter (only) of the desired drive, directory, or file (depending on which box the cursor is in). The cursor jumps to the next item in the list starting with that letter. Press it again to jump to the next item starting with the same letter.

You can also limit the file list by entering a generic filename in the text box. Use ? to indicate one ambiguous character and * to indicate that the rest of the name or extension is ambiguous. For example, if you enter CH*.NOV in the text box, the file list would include CHAP01.NOV and CHANGES.NOV but not CHALLENG.PP3 or DELETES.NOV. (The default generic file name is *.*, which selects every possible filename.)

When you select the desired file, the dialog box closes and the file appears on the screen. What you see depends on the type of data the file contains. If it's ASCII data, Disk Editor automatically invokes the text viewer. If it's any other type of data, the hex viewer appears.

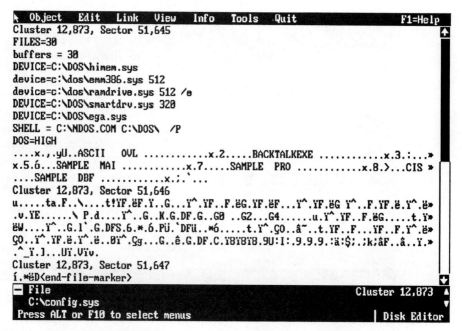

Figure 2-11   Text View

Text View

Figure 2-11 shows a file in text view, which interprets every byte in the file as an ASCII character. True ASCII text files should be very readable in this view. If you see a lot of extended characters, such as ï and â, the file is probably not really an ASCII file and you might do better in hex view.

This particular file is on a hard disk with four sectors per cluster. This short file occupies the minimum space—one cluster. All four sectors are included in the object, even though the file's data completely resides in the first sector; the rest is called *slack* and often contains old data left over from deleted files. You can pretty much tell where the file ends and the slack starts by the appearance of extended characters and periods (resulting from hex 00). That won't be the case when the slack space also contains ASCII text. Many ASCII files have an **<end-file-marker>** that shows up on the screen.

The status bar shows that the object is a file named C\CONFIG.SYS, which occupies cluster 12,873.

For lines wider than the screen, Disk Editor displays pointers (« and ») indicating that you can scroll in that direction. You can see pointers at the end of the slack lines in the figure.

Maneuvering in Text View

There is no cursor in the text view. You can't edit using this viewer, so there's no reason to have a cursor. The text view is for display only. (To edit text files, use a text editor or a word processor.)

You can scroll down and up in the object by the normal means. You can scroll right and left by clicking on the pointers at the beginnings and ends of long lines. Right arrow and Left arrow scroll sideways one character at a time, while Ctrl-Right and Ctrl-Left scroll sideways 39 characters at a time.

Selecting Text View

Text view appears automatically when you select an ASCII file as an object. You can switch to it from any other view by selecting **as Text** from the **View** menu or by pressing F3.

Hex View

Figure 2-12 shows the same file in hex view. With this view, you can see the actual value stored in every byte of the object. Hex view gives you the most raw information about an object, but makes little attempt to interpret it.

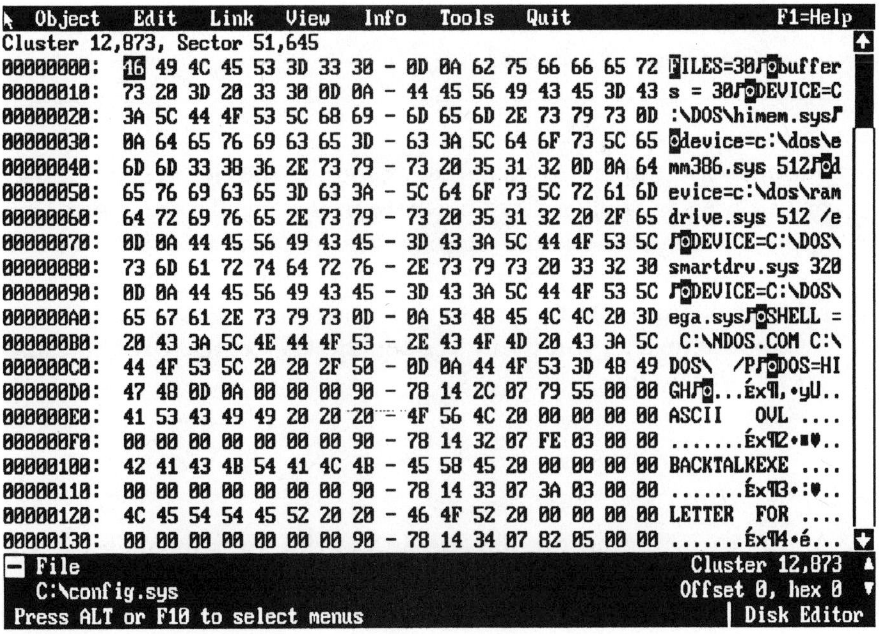

```
  Object   Edit   Link   View   Info   Tools   Quit              F1=Help
Cluster 12,873, Sector 51,645
00000000: 16 49 4C 45 53 3D 33 30 - 0D 0A 62 75 66 66 65 72  ILES=30  buffer
00000010: 73 20 3D 20 33 30 0D 0A - 44 45 56 49 43 45 3D 43  s = 30  DEVICE=C
00000020: 3A 5C 44 4F 53 5C 68 69 - 6D 65 6D 2E 73 79 73 0D  :\DOS\himem.sys
00000030: 0A 64 65 76 69 63 65 3D - 63 3A 5C 64 6F 73 5C 65   device=c:\dos\e
00000040: 6D 6D 33 38 36 2E 73 79 - 73 20 35 31 32 0D 0A 64  mm386.sys 512  d
00000050: 65 76 69 63 65 3D 63 3A - 5C 64 6F 73 5C 72 61 6D  evice=c:\dos\ram
00000060: 64 72 69 76 65 2E 73 79 - 73 20 35 31 32 20 2F 65  drive.sys 512 /e
00000070: 0D 0A 44 45 56 49 43 45 - 3D 43 3A 5C 44 4F 53 5C   DEVICE=C:\DOS\
00000080: 73 6D 61 72 74 64 72 76 - 2E 73 79 73 20 33 32 30  smartdrv.sys 320
00000090: 0D 0A 44 45 56 49 43 45 - 3D 43 3A 5C 44 4F 53 5C   DEVICE=C:\DOS\
000000A0: 65 67 61 2E 73 79 73 0D - 0A 53 48 45 4C 4C 20 3D  ega.sys SHELL =
000000B0: 20 43 3A 5C 4E 44 4F 53 - 2E 43 4F 4D 20 43 3A 5C   C:\NDOS.COM C:\
000000C0: 44 4F 53 5C 20 20 2F 50 - 0D 0A 44 4F 53 3D 48 49  DOS\  /P  DOS=HI
000000D0: 47 48 0D 0A 00 00 00 90 - 78 14 2C 07 79 55 00 00  GH    Ex ..yU..
000000E0: 41 53 43 49 49 20 20 20 - 4F 56 4C 20 00 00 00 00  ASCII   OVL ....
000000F0: 00 00 00 00 00 00 00 90 - 78 14 32 07 FE 03 00 00  .......Ex2 .....
00000100: 42 41 43 4B 54 41 4C 4B - 45 58 45 20 00 00 00 00  BACKTALKEXE ....
00000110: 00 00 00 00 00 00 00 90 - 78 14 33 07 3A 03 00 00  .......Ex3 .:.....
00000120: 4C 45 54 54 45 52 20 20 - 46 4F 52 20 00 00 00 00  LETTER   FOR ....
00000130: 00 00 00 00 00 00 00 90 - 78 14 34 07 82 05 00 00  .......Ex4 .é....
 File                                                Cluster 12,873
   C:\config.sys                                     Offset 0, hex 0
 Press ALT or F10 to select menus                  | Disk Editor
```

Figure 2-12   Hex View

Non-ASCII files appear automatically in hex view, as do clusters and sectors. You can use hex view with any object by selecting **as Hex** from the **View** menu or by pressing F2.

Each line displays 16 bytes. The left column shows the hex address of the first byte on the line. The middle area displays each byte in hex code—eight bytes before the dash and eight bytes after. On the right, each byte is interpreted in ASCII.

The status bar shows the type of object ("File" in this case), the name of the file or directory that the cursor is in, the cluster/sector, and the cursor position. For some objects, the cursor position shows the offset from the beginning of the current sector. For others, including files, the cursor position shows the offset from the beginning of the object. The cursor highlight appears on the same byte in both the hex and ASCII displays.

Maneuvering in hex view is identical to maneuvering in the directory view.

Linking from File Objects

When the object is a file, you can link directly to its directory entry or its FAT entries. Quick-link always goes to the directory entry.

> **Reminder:** Quick-link is activated by pressing Enter or double-clicking anywhere on the screen.

Suppose you wanted to take a quick look at the file size and attributes; just press Enter or double-click anywhere in the file. The appropriate directory appears with the file's entry highlighted. When you're done and want to get back to the file, press Enter or double-click on the file's entry again; Disk Editor will quick-link to the file.

Suppose instead you wanted to see the FAT entry. Use the **Link** menu or press Ctrl-T to link to the FAT.

File Information

Another way to find the file size and attributes is through the **Info** menu. Figure 2-13 shows the results of the **Object info** and **Map of object** options for a somewhat fragmented file; that is, its clusters are not all adjacent to each other. (The drive information stays the same no matter what object is selected, as long as it's on the same drive.)

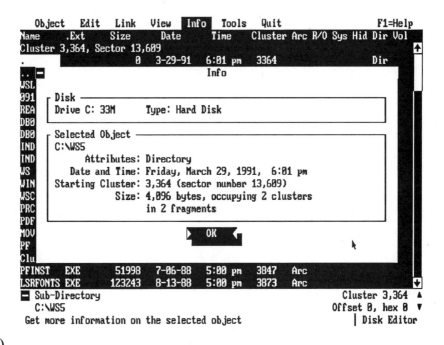

(a)

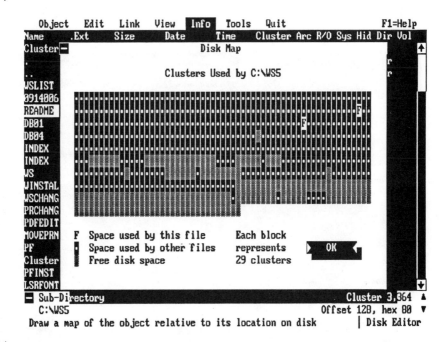

(b)

Figure 2-13   File Information Dialog Boxes

Exploring the FAT

You've probably seen directories and files before, but have you ever looked at a File Allocation Table? Figure 2-14 shows one, as seen in the FAT viewer.

Each entry represents one cluster on the disk, with the first entry representing cluster 2, the next cluster 3, and so on. Each entry contains the number of the next cluster in the chain of clusters that make up a file. In the example in Figure 2-14, cluster 4 contains the number 5, meaning that the next part of the file is in cluster 5. Likewise, cluster 5 points to cluster 10, cluster 10 points to cluster 11, and so on up to cluster 14, where the **<EOF>** (end-of-file) mark means that this is the last cluster in the file.

Selecting the FAT Object and View

Every disk actually has two complete FATs, which should be exact duplicates. Every time data is added to or deleted from the disk, DOS updates both copies of the FAT. DOS always uses the first FAT when accessing files; the second FAT is used only to identify problems. When you want to view the FAT, you probably want to view the first one. However, you might want to compare it to the second one. Later on in this chapter, you'll see how to do that.

```
 Object   Edit   Link   View   Info   Tools   Quit              F1=Help
Sector 1                                                                 ↑
                   <EOF>        <EOF>  »  5       ↳ »     18    <EOF>   <EOF>
 <EOF>    <EOF>  »   11    »    12   »   13    »     14    » <EOF>     16
   17       18       19        20       21       22       23       24
   25       26       27        28       29       30       31       32
   33     <EOF>      35        36       37       38       39       40
   41       42       43        44       45     <EOF>      47       48
   49       50       51        52       53       54       55       56
   57       58       59        60     <EOF>    <EOF>    <EOF>      64
 <EOF>       0        0         0        0        0        0        0
    0     <EOF>      75        76       77       78       79       80
   81       82       83        84       85       86       87       88
 <EOF>       0        0         0        0        0        0        0
    0        0        0         0        0        0        0        0
    0        0        0         0        0        0        0        0
    0        0        0         0        0      118      119      120
  121      122      123       124      125      126      127      128
  129      130      131     <EOF>     133     <EOF>    <EOF>       0
    0        0        0         0        0        0        0        0
    0        0        0         0        0        0        0        0
    0        0        0         0        0        0        0        0 ↓
 FAT (1st Copy)                                        Sector 1  ▲
 D:\COLLAGE\SHOW.EXE                               Cluster 4, hex 4 ▼
 Press ALT or F10 to select menus                 |  Disk Editor
```

Figure 2-14   File Allocation Table

To view the FAT, select the drive first. Then select either **1st copy of FAT** or **2nd copy of FAT** from the **Object** menu, or press Alt-F1 or Alt-F2. The FAT viewer appears automatically. To switch to the FAT viewer from another viewer, press F5.

The FAT View

The cursor rests on cluster 4, as you can see from the highlight. In the status line, the cursor position (bottom row on the right) also shows the cluster number where the cursor is. The first status line on the right shows the location of the FAT on the disk; since it's in the system area, it has no cluster number, only a sector number. The status bar also shows that this file is named SHOW.EXE. As you move the cursor around in the FAT, the filename changes to show you what file or directory you're in.

On a color monitor, the entire current cluster chain is displayed in a contrasting color, while on a monochrome monitor, it's marked by pointers (»). When you move the cursor into another file's cluster chain, the highlighting moves to the new cluster chain. The highlighting helps you see the entire chain, which can otherwise be difficult to find with fragmented files.

Look at cluster 2, which contains an <EOF> mark with no preceding cluster chain. This short file is contained in one cluster. The same situation exists in clusters 3, 6, 7, and so on.

A 0 in a cluster means it is currently unused and available. <BAD> marks a cluster that has been blocked out by the formatting program because of one or more bad sectors (sectors with unreliable recording surfaces).

Linking from FAT Chains

When the cursor is on a cluster belonging to a file, you can link to its directory entry by pressing Ctrl-D or to the file itself by pressing Ctrl-F. If the cluster belongs to a subdirectory, both Ctrl-D and Ctrl-F link to the subdirectory. When you're looking at a file or a directory, Ctrl-T links to its FAT entry.

Quick-link goes to the directory entry. To return to the FAT from the directory, you have to use Ctrl-T because a directory entry always quick-links to the file itself.

FAT Information

Figure 2-15 shows an example of the dialog box that results when you select **Object info** from the **Info** menu when a FAT is the object. The object map will not be available (because the FAT is always in the same position on the drive and is never fragmented).

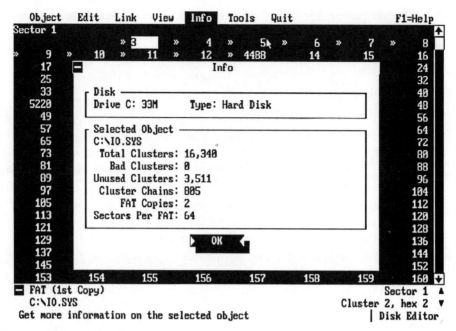

Figure 2-15   FAT Object Information

Exploring the Boot Record

The first sector on every disk contains a special record called the *Boot Record*, which identifies the type of disk, what program formatted it, its sector size, and other information that DOS needs. On bootable disks, the Boot Record also contains the small program that actually boots the system. On nonbootable disks, it contains a small program that displays an error message if you try to boot with the disk. The Boot Record is essential to accessing the disk; if it's missing or damaged, you will not be able to use the disk until you fix it (which can usually be done with Norton Disk Doctor).

To look at the Boot Record, select the drive first, if necessary, then select **Boot Record** from the **Object** menu or press Alt-B. To look at it in hex view, press F2; for the Boot Record view, press F7. Figure 2-16 shows a sample Boot Record in the Boot Record view.

The Boot Record view labels each field and shows you what the current object contains for that field. The **DOS Reports** column shows the values from the Boot Record for the same drive at the time that the system was booted. This can help you determine whether you're looking at a valid Boot Record.

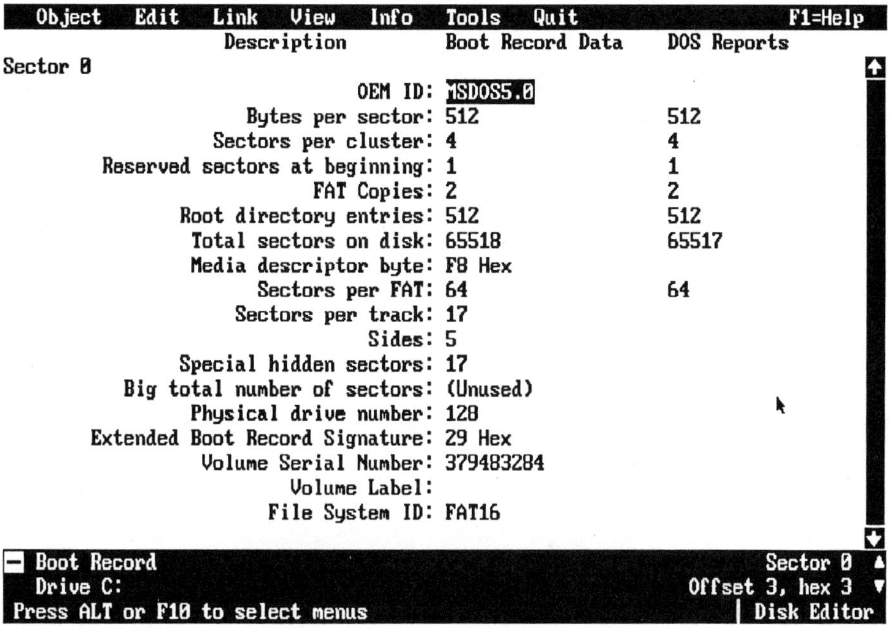

```
   Object   Edit   Link   View   Info   Tools   Quit                    F1=Help
                  Description            Boot Record Data    DOS Reports
Sector 0                                                                        ▲
                         OEM ID: MSDOS5.0
               Bytes per sector: 512                        512
             Sectors per cluster: 4                         4
     Reserved sectors at beginning: 1                       1
                    FAT Copies: 2                           2
         Root directory entries: 512                        512
           Total sectors on disk: 65518                     65517
          Media descriptor byte: F8 Hex
              Sectors per FAT: 64                           64
              Sectors per track: 17
                       Sides: 5
          Special hidden sectors: 17
     Big total number of sectors: (Unused)
          Physical drive number: 128                              ⬎
    Extended Boot Record Signature: 29 Hex
          Volume Serial Number: 379483284
                 Volume Label:
                File System ID: FAT16
                                                                               ▼
─ Boot Record                                                      Sector 0   ▲
  Drive C:                                                    Offset 3, hex 3  ▼
  Press ALT or F10 to select menus                              │ Disk Editor
```

Figure 2-16   Boot Record

> **Tip:** Sometimes the **Total sectors on disk** disagree by one. This is normal and does not indicate a problem.

There are no links available from the Boot Record. You'll have to go through the **Object** menu to get to other objects. Figure 2-17 shows the type of display you get when you select **Object info** from the **Info** menu.

Exploring the Partition Table

Another vital system area on hard disks is the Partition Table. Every hard disk must be partitioned before it can be used. Partitioning can divide the hard disk into separate drives, but even if you want only one drive on the disk, you still must partition it. The Partition Table is established by the DOS program FDISK (or a comparable program).

DOS can create two partitions, called the *primary* and *extended* partitions. The primary partition is usually the first partition on the disk and is called drive C:. This will be your bootable partition if you boot from the hard disk. The extended partition is simply another, nonbootable partition. Some

Figure 2-17   Boot Record Information

versions of DOS let you break the extended partition into several drives, so that partition might contain drives D:, E:, and so on.

Your hard disk might also have been partitioned by a non-DOS program such as Disk Manager. No matter what software creates or adapts the partitions, it must establish and maintain a correctly formatted Partition Table.

The Partition Table shows the beginning sector and the number of sectors in each partition on the disk. Without this information, DOS cannot find the partition on the hard disk and so will not be able to access the data on it. If your partition table gets damaged, Norton Disk Doctor can usually fix it.

Figure 2-18 shows a Partition Table object, which you can access from the **Object** menu or by pressing Alt-A. The Partition Table viewer is invoked with F6. The disk in this example has two partitions: the one labeled DOS-16 is a DOS partition; the other is a DOS extended partition.

> **Note:** The Partition Table is available as an object on hard disks only. Diskettes don't have Partition Tables.

Object	Edit	Link	View	Info	Tools	Quit			F1=Help

System	Boot	Starting Location			Ending Location			Relative	Number of	
		Side	Cylinder	Sector	Side	Cylinder	Sector	Sectors	Sectors	
DOS-16	Yes	1	0	1	4	770	17	17	65518	▲
EXTEND	No	0	771	1	4	975	17	65535	17425	
unused	No	0	0	0	0	0	0	0	0	
unused	No	0	0	0	0	0	0	0	0	▼

▬ Partition Table	Cyl 0, Side 0, Sector 1 ▲
Hard Disk 1	Offset 450, hex 1C2 ▼
Press ALT or F10 to select menus	Disk Editor

Figure 2-18   Partition Table

The **Starting** and **Ending Location** columns give physical sector addresses; the first partition starts on side 1, cylinder 0, sector 1 and ends on side 4, cylinder 770, sector 17. The **Relative Sectors** columns show the starting sector using DOS sector numbering: the first partition starts with sector 17.

> **Note:** The Partition Table is in side 0, track 0, and the rest of that track is skipped. That's why the partition starts on side 1 (sector 17).

The **Number of sectors** column shows the total number of sectors in the partition. You can multiply it by 512 to find out the number of bytes, or divide it by 2 for the number of kilobytes. The first partition in the example contains 33,545,216 bytes or 32,759K. (Disk Editor rounds this off to 33M in some displays.)

Linking from the Partition Table

The only available **Link** option is **Partition**, which acts the same as quick-link. Where it goes depends on your cursor position in the table. If it's on the current partition, it links to the Boot Record. If the cursor is on another partition, it links to that partition's Boot Record or Partition Table, which-ever is more appropriate.

Partition Table Information

When you select **Object info** for a Partition Table, the resulting dialog box shows you the Sector Signature, which is simply a value (hex 55AA) indicating that the Partition Table appears valid.

Exploring Clusters

You can select one or more clusters on the drive as an object. This is useful for exploring areas on the disk that don't belong to a file, directory, Boot Record, or Partition Table. For example, you could examine a deleted file or any "unused" space.

Select the drive first, if necessary. Then select the **Cluster** option (Alt-C) from the **Object** menu. Figure 2-19 shows the **Cluster** dialog box. If you enter numbers in both boxes, you delimit a set of clusters as an object. For example, to examine clusters 25 through 35, enter 25 in the first box and 35 in the second. To examine only cluster 25, enter 25 in both boxes.

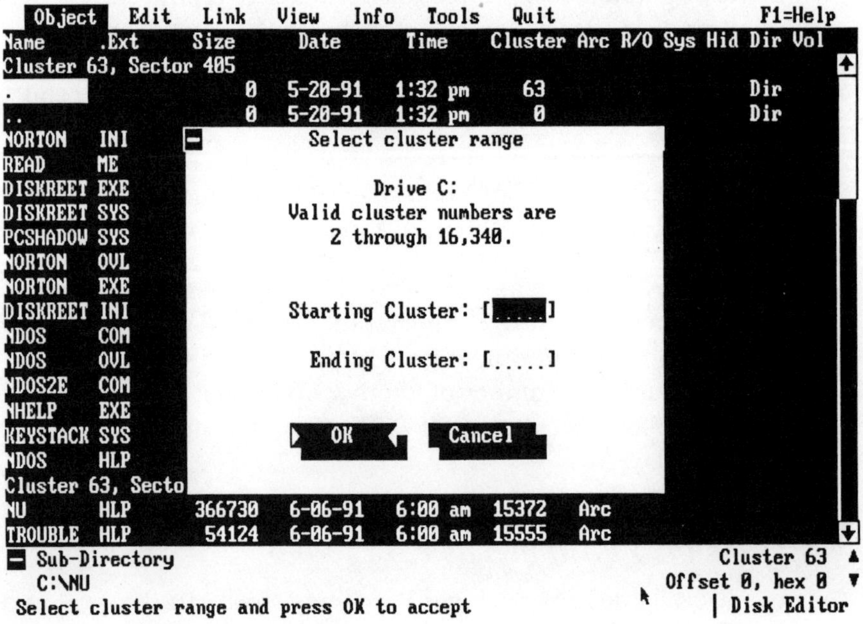

Figure 2-19   Cluster Dialog Box

If you enter 25 in the first box only, the entire drive is selected. Cluster 25 appears when you close the dialog box, but you can scroll from there to any other cluster on the drive.

The clusters appear in the most appropriate view for the starting cluster. As you move through the different clusters, the left part of the status bar tells you the names of files and directories you're in. When you're in unused clusters, the status bar says "Unused cluster (on drive x:)."

Linking from Clusters

The ability to link from a cluster depends on what it contains. If it's a file or a directory, the normal file or directory links are available. If it's an unused cluster, it will only link to the FAT entry. You can't link back to a cluster from other objects. You have to go through the **Object** menu to select a cluster as an object. (The cluster number on the status line helps you decide which cluster to select.)

Cluster Information

Object information differs depending on whether the object is a limited set of clusters or the entire range. Figure 2-20 shows the two dialog boxes. When a limited set of clusters is involved, then you just see the range of clusters. When the entire range is selected, Disk Editor tells you about the entity owning the current cluster, if any.

Exploring Sectors

Exploring sectors is similar to exploring clusters, but there are some differences. For example, you can explore the system area preceding the first cluster with this option. You can also get out of the current partition and examine any area on the disk. You start, as usual, by selecting the drive, if necessary. Then you can specify the desired sectors using either their logical (DOS) numbers or their physical coordinates.

Logical Sectors

To specify logical sector numbers, select the **Sector** option from the **Object** menu or press Alt-S. You'll get the dialog box shown in Figure 2-21. It shows you where the system and data areas are. You can enter both the starting and ending numbers to select a specific range, or just a starting number to select the entire drive.

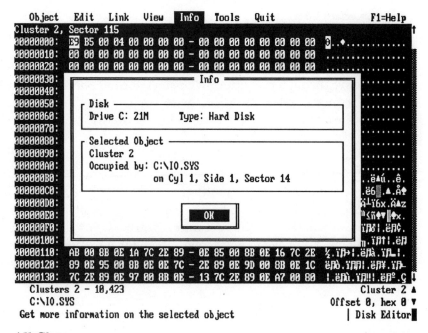

(a)   **All Clusters**

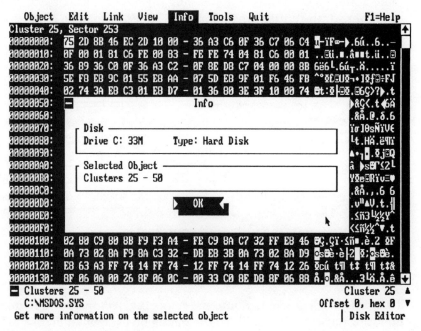

(b)   **Limited Set of Clusters**

Figure 2-20   Cluster Information

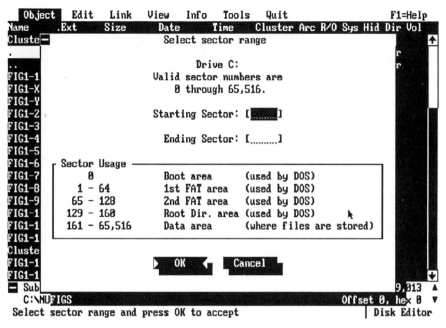

Figure 2-21   Sector Dialog Box

Physical Sectors

To use physical sector numbering, select **Physical sector** or press Alt-P. Figure 2-22 shows the resulting dialog box. You enter the starting sector coordinates and the number of sectors to be included in the object.

When you use logical sector numbers, only the sectors in the current drive are available. But when you use physical sector numbers, drives are ignored and the entire hard disk is available, which is why 83,538 sectors are available in this example.

The viewers, linking, and information are the same as for clusters, except that no object map is available for physical sectors.

Exploring Physical Disks

Sometimes you need to step outside DOS's logical formatting and explore the disk itself. With the **Physical Disk** option, you can access every sector on the disk, whether it's in a DOS partition or not. You could examine the data in a XENIX partition, you could examine an unformatted disk, or you could browse through those sectors following the Partition Table that DOS just "throws away."

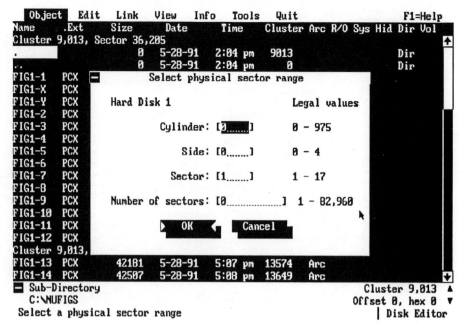

Figure 2-22   Physical Sector Dialog Box

Figure 2-23 shows the **Drive** dialog box with the **Physical Disks** radio button selected. Compare this to Figure 2-4, where the **Logical disks** button is selected. The drive names in the left-hand box have been replaced by descriptions of the disk hardware. All you have to do is select the unit you want to explore.

After selecting the physical disk, all physical sectors are automatically selected. You can select other objects if you wish, but physical sectors are the best way to access the unused portions of the disk.

Viewing Memory

To view any portion of the first megabyte of memory, select **Memory** as the object or press Alt-M. A dialog box prompts you for the starting and ending addresses in hexadecimal, with default values encompassing the entire range (0000 through FFFF). The low-order digit of the address is omitted because for each address you request, Disk Editor will display all 16 bytes from *xxxx*0 through *xxxx*F. That's one complete line in the hex view.

Viewing memory can come in handy when testing and debugging programs you're developing. But even if you never expect to develop or test a program in your life, you can still take advantage of this facility. You can

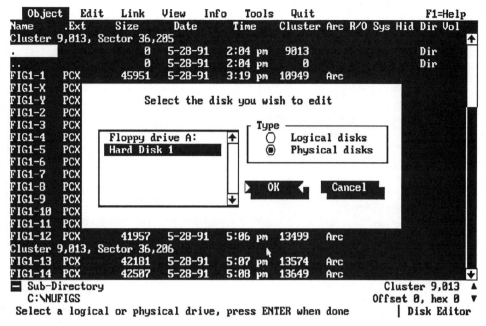

Figure 2-23   Physical Disk Options

rescue important data from memory if one of your applications crashes—but not if you had to reboot to recover from the crash. Suppose you spend a couple of hours developing a new database, but your database manager crashes before you save the database on disk. You can use Disk Editor to examine memory, find the database file, copy it to the clipboard, and write the contents of the clipboard on disk.

Tip: Viewing some memory addresses can cause your system to freeze up. If this happens to you, all you have to do is reboot and make a note about what addresses to avoid in the future.

Searching for Data

Disk Editor includes several tools to help you solve problems while exploring. They are included on the **Tools** menu shown in Figure 2-24. This chapter covers **Find, find aGain, Hex converter, ASCII Table,** and **cOnfiguration.** The other tools are covered in Chapter 14.

Suppose you have lost some data on your disk. In fact, you're not even sure whether it's in a current file or a deleted one. It might be in your primary

```
        Object   Edit   Link   View   Info  │ Tools │ Quit           F1=Help
       Name     .Ext    Size    Date      T┌────────────────────────────┐ol
       Cluster 9,013, Sector 36,205        │ Find...             Ctrl-S │  ▲
       .                      0   5-28-91  2│ (find again)        Ctrl-G │
       ..                     0   5-28-91  2│ Write to...          Alt-W │
       FIG1-1   PCX       45951   5-28-91  3│ Print as...         Ctrl-P │
       FIG1-X   PCX       65326   5-28-91  2│                            │
       FIG1-Y   PCX      100015   5-28-91  2│ (recalculate partition)    │
       FIG1-2   PCX       55572   5-28-91  3│ (compare windows...)       │
       FIG1-3   PCX       48530   5-28-91  3│ (set attributes...)        │
       FIG1-4   PCX       31121   5-28-91  3│ (set date/time...)         │
       FIG1-5   PCX       31841   5-28-91  3│                            │
       FIG1-6   PCX       44532   5-28-91  3│ Hex converter...           │
       FIG1-7   PCX       44407   5-28-91  4│ ASCII Table...             │
       FIG1-8   PCX       33356   5-28-91  5│                            │
       FIG1-9   PCX       35799   5-28-91  5│ cOnfiguration...           │
       FIG1-10  PCX       43496   5-28-91  5└────────────────────────────┘
       FIG1-11  PCX       45323   5-28-91  5:04 pm   13422   Arc
       FIG1-12  PCX       41957   5-28-91  5:06 pm   13499   Arc
       Cluster 9,013, Sector 36,206            ▶
       FIG1-13  PCX       42181   5-28-91  5:07 pm   13574   Arc
       FIG1-14  PCX       42507   5-28-91  5:08 pm   13649   Arc         ▼
        ■ Sub-Directory                            Cluster 9,013  ▲
          C:\NUFIGS                                Offset 0, hex 0  ▼
        Find a string or hex pattern in selected object          │ Disk Editor
```

Figure 2-24   Tools Menu

DOS partition or an extended partition. It might even be in an area that currently doesn't belong to a partition. You can use the **Find** feature to locate it if it still exists.

You'll need to know a key word or phrase that the lost data contains. It helps if that key doesn't appear in any other part of the disk so that **Find** doesn't locate the wrong data. But if you can't think of a completely unique key, then try to use one that appears infrequently on the disk.

The first thing you would do after starting Disk Editor is to select the object that you want to search. This might be all the clusters in one drive or even all the physical sectors on a hard disk.

Now you select the **Find** option (Ctrl-S) which results in the dialog box shown in Figure 2-25. As you type the key phrase in the ASCII box, its hex equivalent appears in the hex box. You can use the hex box if the key contains non-ASCII characters. Check **Ignore case** if you want to find any combination of uppercase and lowercase letters, or uncheck it if you want to search for phrases with exactly the same case as you typed.

Note: You can type up to 48 characters. To type non-ASCII data, tab to the Hex box and enter the desired hex values. The only acceptable values are the hex digits 0–F.

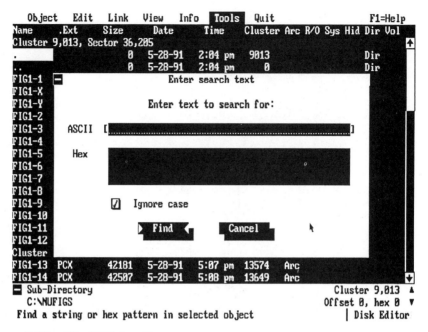

Figure 2-25   Find Dialog Box

When you close the dialog box, the search begins from the current cursor position and moves forward until the desired string is encountered or the end of the object is reached. For a long search, a dialog box advises you of progress; it contains a STOP button that lets you interrupt the search if necessary.

When the specified string is found, a display similar to the one in Figure 2-26 appears. The found string is highlighted. Since you're in hex view, the status bar shows the path, the filename, and the cluster or sector it's in. You can't link at this point, because more than one byte is selected. But if you move the cursor one character in either direction, then only one byte will be selected and you will be able to link to the directory, the FAT, the file, or whatever is most appropriate.

If this isn't the desired item, you could continue the search by selecting **find aGain**, Ctrl-G. It starts at the current cursor position and moves forward, looking for the same data string.

The Hex Converter

The **Hex converter** option from the **Tools** menu can be used to convert values between the hexadecimal and decimal number systems. Figure 2-27

```
  Object   Edit   Link   View   Info   Tools   Quit              F1=Help
00000090:  6E 6D 65 6E 74 0D 0A 20 - 20 20 20 20 20 20 20 20  nment♪◙        ▲
000000A0:  20 20 76 61 72 69 61 62 - 6C 65 3B 20 69 66 20 74  variable; if t
000000B0:  68 65 72 65 20 69 73 20 - 6E 6F 20 54 45 4D 50 20  here is no TEMP
000000C0:  76 61 72 69 61 62 6C 65 - 2C 20 74 68 65 6E 20 74  variable, then t
000000D0:  68 65 0D 0A 20 20 20 20 - 20 20 20 20 20 20 20 64  he♪◙            d
000000E0:  65 66 61 75 6C 74 20 69 - 73 20 74 68 65 20 57 69  efault is the Wi
000000F0:  6E 64 6F 77 73 20 64 69 - 72 65 63 74 6F 72 79 29  ndows directory)
00000100:  0D 0A 20 20 50 75 72 70 - 6F 73 65 3A 20 50 72 6F  ♪◙  Purpose: Pro
00000110:  76 69 64 65 73 20 74 68 - 65 20 6E 61 6D 65 20 6F  vides the name o
00000120:  66 20 74 68 65 20 64 69 - 73 6B 20 64 72 69 76 65  f the disk drive
00000130:  20 61 6E 64 20 64 69 72 - 65 63 74 6F 72 79 0D 0A   and directory♪◙
00000140:  20 20 20 20 20 20 20 20 - 20 20 20 74 6F 20 77 68             to wh
00000150:  69 63 68 20 57 69 6E 64 - 6F 77 73 20 72 75 6E 6E  ich Windows runn
00000160:  69 6E 67 20 69 6E 20 72 - 65 61 6C 20 6D 6F 64 65  ing in real mode
00000170:  20 6F 72 20 73 74 61 6E - 64 61 72 64 0D 0A 20 20   or standard♪◙
00000180:  20 20 20 20 20 20 20 20 - 20 6D 6F 64 65 20 73 77           mode sw
00000190:  61 70 73 20 6E 6F 6E 2D - 57 69 6E 64 6F 77 73 20  aps non-Windows
000001A0:  61 70 70 6C 69 63 61 74 - 69 6F 6E 73 2E 0D 0A 20  applications.♪◙
000001B0:  20 54 6F 20 63 68 61 6E - 67 65 3A 20 55 73 65 20   To change: Use
000001C0:  4E 6F 74 65 70 61 64 20 - 74 6F 20 65 64 69 74 20  Notepad to edit
000001D0:  74 68 65 20 53 59 53 54 - 45 4D 2E 49 4E 49 20 66  the SYSTEM.INI f ▼
━ Clusters 2 - 16,340                                Cluster 2,445  ▲
  C:\WINDOWS\SYSINI.TXT                            Offset 162, hex A2 ▼
  Press ALT or F10 to select menus                  │ Disk Editor
```

Figure 2-26   Result of a Search

shows the dialog box that results. As you type a value in any of the boxes, its equivalents appear in the other two boxes.

Caution: Don't try to use the hex converter to interpret values from the hex display. A personal computer does not always store numeric values in pure hexadecimal form. Sometimes it formats them with signs and exponents, stores them as complements, and/or reverses the bytes in a multibyte number. The hex converter does a pure conversion and would not interpret such values correctly. The hex converter is best used by power users who know exactly what they are doing.

The ASCII Table

The **ASCII Table** option on the **Tools** menu displays the character value for every possible value of a byte. One "page" from the table is shown in Figure 2-28.

ASCII, which stands for "American Standard Code for Information Interchange," standardizes the values for 0–127 only; values from 128–255 (the

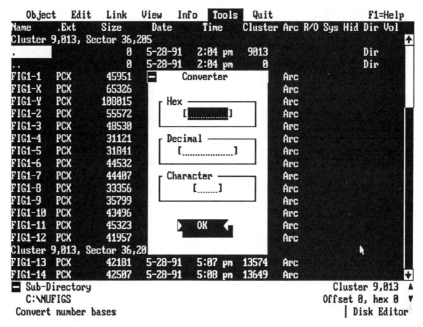

Figure 2-27   Hex Converter

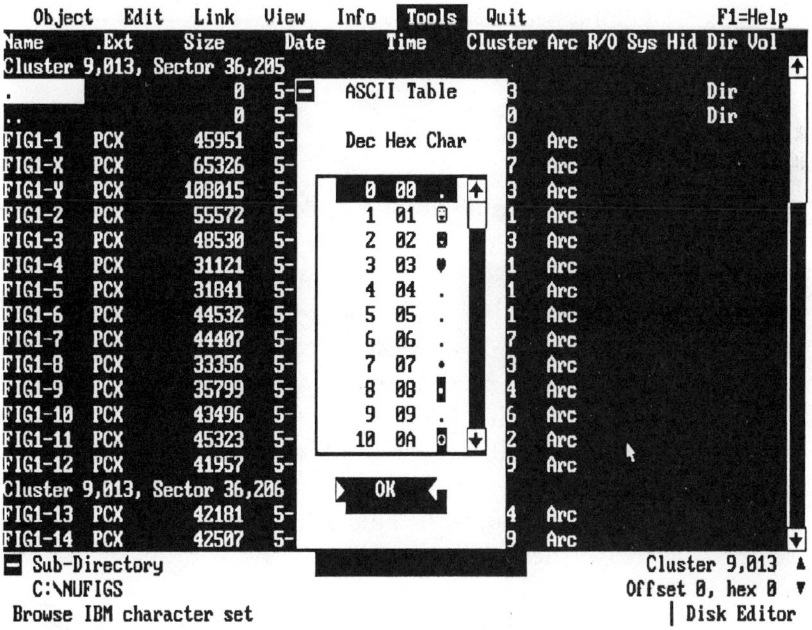

Figure 2-28   ASCII Table

maximum value of one byte) are generally used as graphics characters, but can change from program to program. For example, Microsoft Word interprets the value 212 as †, ™, ⌊, or → but Ventura Publisher interprets the same value as š, |, or ↖, depending on which font is used. The same program might produce a different character on your monitor and your printer.

You might also find some discrepancies in the values from 0–31. These were originally defined by ASCII as hardware control signals, not characters. Some software takes advantage of the values to provide 32 additional graphics characters, as you can see in the example.

The ASCII table shows the Norton Utilities' characters for all hex values. If you use a graphics mouse, some of the characters in the low 200s appear as dots; also, some characters change as you move the mouse.

Sometimes it comes in handy to print an object. You might want to retain printouts of your partition tables and boot records, for example. Or you might want to print a memory dump or a directory. The **Print As** option on the **Tools** menu lets you print the current object or save it as a disk file. A dialog box lets you select the printer or specify a path and filename if you want to store the printout in a disk file. You can also select the view for the printout if you don't want to use the current view.

Tip: Avoid writing any new files, such as a printout file, on a drive that is experiencing problems.

Using Two Windows

You can open up a second window under Disk Editor and view two objects at the same time. An example is shown in Figure 2-29. Each window has its own status bar. The active window contains the cursor; this is the window you are currently working on. It is the target of all keyboard and menu actions. You can tell which window is active by the position of the cursor. In the example in Figure 2-29, the second window is active, as you can see from the cursor in the OEM ID field.

Windowing is controlled from the **View** menu (refer back to Figure 2-6). The **Split window** option (Shift-F5) splits the screen into two windows. When the screen is split, this options changes to read **Unsplit window**, and you select it to close the active window. **Grow window** (Shift-F6) or **Shrink window** (Shift-F7) adds or subtracts one line from the active window, until the maximum or minimum size of the window is reached. The **sWitch windows** option (Shift-F8) activates the other window.

```
   Object  Edit   Link   View   Info   Tools   Quit              F1=Help
Name     .Ext   Size     Date       Time     Cluster Arc R/O Sys Hid Dir Vol
Cluster 9,013, Sector 36,205
 .                       0    5-28-91   2:04 pm    9013                   Dir
 ..                      0    5-28-91   2:04 pm       0                   Dir
FIG1-1   PCX    45951    5-28-91   3:19 pm   10949   Arc
FIG1-X   PCX    65326    5-28-91   2:37 pm    9537   Arc
FIG1-Y   PCX   100015    5-28-91   2:52 pm    9623   Arc
FIG1-2   PCX    55572    5-28-91   3:31 pm   11051   Arc
FIG1-3   PCX    48530    5-28-91   3:34 pm   11133   Arc
FIG1-4   PCX    31121    5-28-91   3:38 pm   11721   Arc
─ Sub-Directory                                        Cluster 9,013 ▲
  C:\NUFIGS                                             Offset 0, hex 0 ▼
                  Description        Boot Record Data    DOS Reports
Sector 0                                                                ▲
                      OEM ID: MSDOS5.0
              Bytes per sector: 512                 512
            Sectors per cluster: 4                  4
   Reserved sectors at beginning: 1                 1
                    FAT Copies: 2                   2
          Root directory entries: 512               512    ▶
          Total sectors on disk: 65518              65517           ▼
─ Boot Record                                          Sector 0
  Drive C:                                             Offset 3, hex 3
  Press ALT or F10 to select menus                    │ Disk Editor
```

Figure 2-29   Split Windows

You can also control windowing with the mouse. To split the windows, drag the status bar up. Change the sizes of the windows by dragging the top status bar to another position. Close either window by clicking on the close box at the left end of its status bar. Activate a window by clicking on it.

When the second window appears, it contains the same object and view as the first one. But you can switch to any object or view. For example, you could view a file in text view in one window and the same file in hex view in the other window. Unless you link them, which we'll explain in a moment, the two windows remain independent of each other.

Comparing Two Windows

Suppose Disk Doctor reports a discrepancy in the disk's two FATs and you want to see for yourself. Load the first FAT into Disk Editor's first window. Then split the windows and load the second FAT into the second window. Make sure the cursor is at the beginning of the FAT (it doesn't matter which window). Then select **Compare windows** from the **Tools** menu.

Disk Editor starts at the cursor position and works forward comparing byte 0 to byte 0, byte 1 to byte 1, and so on. A dialog box appears while the comparison is being made. When Disk Editor finds a discrepancy between the two objects, it stops the comparison and highlights the unmatching byte in the active window. You can switch to the same byte in the other window by pressing Shift-F8.

To continue the comparison, select **Compare windows** again. When the comparison reaches the end of the objects without finding any more discrepancies, it displays the message "No differences found."

Comparing the two copies of the FAT is just one application of the **Compare windows** feature. You might find many occasions to compare two similar objects. For example, you might want to compare a file on your hard disk with its backup copy on diskette to make sure they are identical. Or you might want to compare the header of a damaged file with the header of a healthy one to find the discrepancies.

Linking Windows

Suppose you want to examine a directory and several of its files. Open the directory in one window. Then split the windows and choose the **Window** option from the **Link** menu. The object in the second window becomes the file whose entry is highlighted in the first window.

As you move the cursor from entry to entry in the first window, the object in the second window changes to show you the highlighted file or directory. The most appropriate view is selected. When a deleted entry or unused entry is highlighted, the second window contains no object.

You can also put a FAT in the first window. As you move from cluster to cluster, the second window shows the contents of that cluster. Figure 2-30 shows an example of linked FAT windows.

Disk Editor Configuration

So far, we've shown you how Disk Editor works when you first install it. But there are several options you can set to change its behavior. Figure 2-31 shows the **Configuration** dialog box from the **Tools** menu, which controls the configuration settings.

The **Read Only** option controls whether or not you can make changes to the objects you're viewing. When it is checked, which is the default, you cannot make changes. Uncheck it if you want to actually edit an object. (Chapter 14 covers editing with Disk Editor.)

The **Quick Move** option controls the appearance of file and directory names in the status line. By default it is off, which means that file and directory names are constantly updated as you move the cursor through objects like the FAT or a set of clusters. But changing the status line display slows down your ability to move through the object, especially if you have a

```
 Object   Edit   Link   View   Info   Tools   Quit            F1=Help
 11953    11954  11955  11956  11957  11958   11959  11960
 11961    11962  11963  11964  11965  11966   11967  11968
 11969    11970  11971  11972  11973  11974   11975  11976
 11977    11978  11979  11980  11981  11982   11983  11984
 11985    11986  11987  11988  11989  11990   11991  11992
 11993    11994  11995  11996  11997  11998   11999  12000
 12001    12002  12003  12004  12005  12006   12007  12008
 12009    12010  12011  12012  12013  12014   12015  12016
 12017    12018  12019  12020  12021  12022   12023  12024
 12025    12026  12027  12028  12029  12030   12031  12032
```
```
 ▬ FAT (1st Copy)                                  Sector 47   ▲
   C:\NU\NU.HLP                             Cluster 11,959, hex 2EB7  ▼
```
```
d ^urename directories^u and change a.disk's ^uvolume label^u, and provides » ◆
our directories...But ^bthe real value of NCD^b is the time it saves at the.»
r ^C11...$ ^u(change drive)^u.  D:\>^rCD \wordproc\dan\ltrs\saved.89^r ^C11.»
89>_..you can simply type the first part of the endpoint name:..  C:\>^rNCD »
Cluster 11,959, Sector 47,990
tory)^u.  D:\WORDPROC\DAN\LTRS\SAVED.89>_..When an "endpoint name" in not un»
he same thing again to get to the.next match...Note: In order for NCD to do »
y structure occasionally to look... for any new directories. When NCD can't »
lso, if you... use ^bNCD MD ^b^udirname^u and ^bNCD RD^b ^udirname^u, you ca» ▼
```
```
 ▬ File                                           Cluster 11,959
   C:\NU\NU.HLP
 Press ALT or F10 to select menus                        | Disk Editor
```

Figure 2-30   Linked FAT Windows

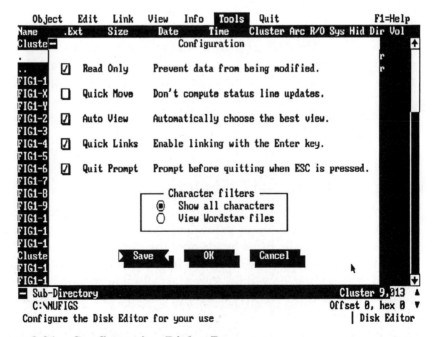

Figure 2-31   Configuration Dialog Box

slow computer. To speed it up, check this option, which removes the file/directory name display. In the FAT view, it also suppresses the highlighting of the cluster chain.

The **Auto View** option lets Disk Editor select the most appropriate initial view for the object. By default it is checked. If you uncheck it, Disk Editor will start up with Hex view. If you switch to another view, Disk Editor retains that view, no matter what object you switch to.

The **Quick Links** option enables quick links. By default, it is on. When it's off, pressing Enter or double-clicking on a view has no effect.

The **Quit Prompt** option controls whether or not Disk Editor displays a confirmation dialog box when you press Esc to exit. By default, this option is checked and you must confirm your decision to exit. If you find it annoying, you can uncheck this option. But you might occasionally exit Disk Editor when you press Esc inadvertently.

The **Character filters** determine how hex values are interpreted in character displays such as the text view or the character display in the hex view. By default, **Show all characters** is selected, which results in Disk Editor's normal character interpretation. But many WordStar files (and files that use WordStar format) produce erroneous results when their bytes are interpreted normally (they show up as graphic characters). To view a WordStar-compatible file, try the **View Wordstar files** option. Switch back to **Show all characters** to view non-WordStar files.

You can change the configuration temporarily or semipermanently. To make a change for a few minutes, select the options you want, then select the **OK** button. The dialog box will clear and Disk Editor will use the selected options. But when you terminate Disk Editor, the changes are forgotten; the next time you start it up, the default values will be in effect again.

To change the configuration more permanently, select **Save** instead of **OK**. The new settings become the defaults for future sessions—that is, until you change them again.

Accessing the Diagnostic Cylinder

Some hard disks include a *diagnostic cylinder*—a cylinder that's not available for partitions but can be used in low-level testing of the computer. Some park programs position the drive heads over the diagnostic cylinder if it exists.

Some programs store information in the diagnostic cylinder and expect to find it there the next time they start up. The problem is that no one controls access to the diagnostic cylinder. If you have several programs that use it, they might overwrite each other's data. After you run one program, another might stop working.

Norton Utilities 6.0 lets you access the diagnostic cylinder; you can view and edit the data there. Using Disk Editor's facilities, you could copy or print the contents of the diagnostic cylinder and restore them later on if need be.

To access the diagnostic cylinder, start up Disk Editor with the /M switch on the command line. This switch lets you examine any physical sectors on the disk, including the ones in the diagnostic cylinder.

To find out if you have a diagnostic cylinder, start up Disk Editor without the /M switch. When you choose the **Physical sector** option, the dialog box shows the total range of cylinder numbers. Now exit Disk Editor, start it up with /M switch, and select **Physical sector** again. If there is now one more cylinder number, that's your diagnostic cylinder.

Exiting Disk Editor

When you're done examining objects, you need to exit Disk Editor to get back to the DOS prompt or Norton menu. You might also want to exit Disk Editor temporarily. A temporary exit takes you to the DOS prompt so that you can run some commands. Then you can return to exactly where you were in Disk Editor when you exited. You could use this feature to compare how a directory looks under Disk Editor and DOS, for example.

To exit Disk Editor temporarily, pull down the **Quit** menu and select **Shell to DOS**. When you're ready to leave DOS and return to Disk Editor, enter the command EXIT at the DOS prompt.

> **Warning:** If you have exited Disk Editor only temporarily, do not start up any Terminate and Stay Resident (TSR) programs at the DOS prompt. They might contend with Disk Editor for memory space.

To terminate Disk Editor and return to either the command prompt or the Norton menu, whichever you came from, select **Quit Disk Editor** from the **Quit** menu or press Ctrl-Q.

Looking Ahead

Now you've learned enough about Disk Editor so it can be used to examine the results of the utilities as we discuss them in this book. If you haven't tried

Disk Editor yet, now would be a good time to take a few minutes and play around with it. Be sure you're in read-only mode!

When you're ready to go on, you'll probably want to turn your attention next to those utilities that can have the most immediate impact on your system—the ones that prevent data loss before it happens. Chapter 3 presents the three preventive utilities you should learn to use first (which you might already be using without knowing it): Safe Format, Image, and File Save.

3

SETTING UP YOUR SYSTEM

Many new computer owners suffer from the classic ICBM syndrome: It Can't Be Me. It goes something like this: "Other people delete files accidentally, but I'll never do that. And I would never inadvertently reformat a valuable diskette." If this sounds like you, listen up! These are the two most common causes of lost data, and *everyone does them*. So will you.

But you can set your system up right now to avoid losing files through accidental deletions and reformatting. The Norton Utilities include three preventive programs that preserve files in anticipation of these misfortunes. We are discussing them early so you can lock your particular barn *before* the horse is gone.

The Safe Format utility formats your hard disk (if that needs to be done) and all your diskettes without destroying previous files; you can get back to the old files if you have to. The Image utility captures a snapshot of your system area, which helps you find the old files. The Erase Protect utility preserves deleted files for a while so you can easily unerase them.

All three of these programs can be set up automatically during installation, so you might be using them already. In that case, you should understand what they are doing and how to control them.

Safe Format

Every disk must be formatted before you can use it. The process is somewhat different for hard disks and diskettes. We'll show you both processes.

Hard Disks

For a hard disk, formatting takes place in three stages, which must happen in order:

- *Physical* formatting divides the entire disk into *sectors* and tests each one for reliability by alternately writing and reading in it. Any unreliable sectors, which result from imperfections in the magnetic coating that covers the disk surface, are marked as "bad" and will not be used by the computer. (You can expect a small percentage of bad sectors on any new hard disk.)

  Physical formatting on hard disks is usually done at the factory. The Norton Utilities include a program to redo the physical formatting if you're having trouble with your hard disk. (This is the Calibrate program, which is explained in Chapter 5.)

- *Partitioning* creates one or more partitions on the hard disk. Each partition is a logically separate area that belongs to an operating system such as DOS, UNIX, or XENIX. Even if you use only DOS, you might have a *primary* DOS partition and a secondary partition, called an *extended* partition, so that you can set up two or more DOS "drives" on your hard disk. In other words, you can treat the hard disk as if it was two or more disks, partitioning it into drive C:, D:, E:, and so on.

  Partitioning is done by a DOS program called FDISK, which installs a Partition Table in the first sector to identify the size and location of each partition on the disk. It also identifies which partition to boot from when booting from the hard disk. Many dealers do the partitioning for you (sometimes without asking you what layout you want). If your hard disk has not been partitioned yet, you might have to use FDISK yourself or get an experienced friend to do it for you. You can use FDISK to change the partitioning later, but it will destroy your ability to access existing files. So you must be prepared to save all your files somewhere else (e.g. on diskettes) and restore them to the hard disk after repartitioning.

- *Logical* formatting sets up a drive specifically for DOS. It creates the system area containing the Boot Record, two copies of the FAT, and the root directory. Logical formatting is done by a format program such as DOS FORMAT or Norton Utilities Safe Format.

Diskettes

A diskette's format process involves only two steps, physical and logical; a diskette is not partitioned. Both steps are performed by the same format program; there is no separate physical format program for diskettes.

If you're using a version of DOS before 5.0, its FORMAT program automatically physically formats a diskette before logically formatting it. And because physical formatting involves creating the sectors, any previous data is erased from the diskette. People commonly reformat a diskette when they want to reuse it, eliminating the old directory entries and files. Unfortunately, people also frequently reformat the wrong diskette; for example, they put the right diskette in the wrong drive or vice versa. Once a diskette has been physically reformatted, you can't recover the previous data by any means normally available.

Safe Format Features

Norton Safe Format provides an alternative that is easier and safer than the DOS FORMAT program. It's easier because you can select options from a dialog box rather than having to compose a complicated command. It's safer because it includes several protection features that prevent data loss if you accidentally reformat the wrong disk:

- It checks for files before starting to format. If it finds any, it displays a warning message that lists the files. You must respond to the warning message to continue.

- It doesn't redo the physical format unless you specifically request a DOS-style format. Thus, you can usually recover the former data.

- Unless you request a DOS-style format, it saves the system area in a file called IMAGE.DAT on the disk. If you need to recover the previous data, the UnFormat and UnErase utilities can find IMAGE.DAT and use it to restore the old FAT and directories.

- By default, your hard disks are not included as options in the dialog box. This makes it harder for you to accidentally reformat them. When you do want to format a hard disk, you can add the hard disks to the dialog box, either temporarily or permanently.

Starting Safe Format

You can start Safe Format by selecting it from the **Tools** section of the Norton menu. Or you can start it from the DOS prompt. Its name might be SFORMAT or FORMAT or SF, depending on how your utilities are configured. If you're not sure, try each one.

No matter how you start it, the Safe Format screen shown in Figure 3-1 should appear.

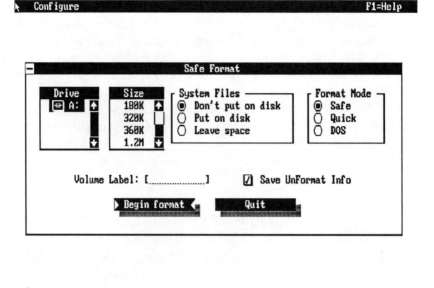

Figure 3-1   Safe Format Screen

Note: If you enter a FORMAT command and receive the message "Drive letter must be specified," you reached DOS's FORMAT instead of Norton's. Try the SF or SFORMAT command instead.

The Safe Format Screen

The Safe Format screen contains a dialog box and one menu. Figure 3-1 shows the default setting for each item in the dialog box. This is what it looks like after installation. You can use the **Configure** menu to set it up any way you like for the future.

Selecting the Drive and Size

Your floppy drives are listed in the left-hand box. Highlight or single-click on the drive you want to format. (Don't press Enter yet.) The drive's size should automatically be selected in the **Size** box. (If not, you need to redefine the drive using the **Configure** menu, discussed below.)

Sometimes you might need to format a lower density diskette in the selected drive (usually because it's the only disk you can find right now). For example, if you have a 5 1/4" 1.2M drive, you could format a 360K, 320K, or 180K diskette in it. In the **Size** box, select the size of the diskette you want to format. If a hard disk is selected, you cannot change the size.

Don't format a diskette for a higher density than the diskette itself is manufactured for. If you put a 720K diskette in a 1.4M drive, you should select the 720K size option. If you try to format it for 1.4M, you'll get a lot of bad sectors and the diskette will be unreliable.

Note: Formatting a double-density diskette in a high-density drive makes the diskette usable in that drive, but it might not work in a double-density drive or even in other high-density drives. A double-density drive has wider read/write heads and can pick up garbage on the edges of the tracks where the high-density drive doesn't write. So you really can't use your high-density drive to create a diskette for a friend in Oshkosh who has only double-density drives.

Select a System Files Option

The **System Files** box lets you choose whether or not you want to make the disk bootable. In order to boot from a disk, the Boot Record must contain a short program that loads DOS. The disk must also contain the files that DOS needs to load: two system files called *xxx*IO.*xxx* and *xxx*DOS.*xxx* (where *xxx* varies according to what version of DOS you're using), and the DOS command processor, which is called COMMAND.COM.

If you choose **Put on disk**, Safe Format installs the necessary Boot Record on the disk and copies the required files to it. You need to do this when you format your primary DOS partition for the first time, so that you can boot DOS from your hard disk. You should also prepare a couple of bootable diskettes so that you can boot your system if your hard disk fails. (If you can't boot, you can't use the Norton Utilities emergency disks to examine and fix your hard disk!)

If you choose **Leave space**, space at the beginning of the data area is set aside for the system files, but they are not actually copied to it. You would do this if the diskette is to be used by someone who has a different version of DOS. That person can make the diskette bootable later by installing the system files and COMMAND.COM on it. It's not always necessary to leave space for the system files in this situation. The Disk Tools utility can install DOS on any disk. But if someone doesn't have Disk Tools, the DOS SYS command must be used to accomplish the same function, and some versions of SYS cannot install the system files if adequate space has not been left at the beginning of the disk's data area. If you're sure that the later user will be able to install the system files, you can avoid wasting disk space by not choosing **Leave space**. But if you're not certain, then it's safer to leave the space.

Choose **Don't put on disk** if you don't care to make the disk bootable. This leaves the maximum amount of space for files. You'll probably want to format most of your diskettes this way; you really need only one or two bootable diskettes when your hard disk is bootable.

Choosing a Format Mode

Choose the type of format you want in the **Format Mode** box. Safe mode is the "standard" Norton Utilities format mode. It checks to see if the disk has already been formatted. If so, it doesn't do a physical format that would overwrite the data on the disk, which is a relatively slow and unnecessary process, anyway. All it does is check the sectors and replace the system area: the Boot Record, FATs, and root directory. This makes the disk look empty; the entire data area is available for new files. At the same time, the old data is still on the disk and can be rescued if need be. If the disk has never been formatted, Safe mode does both a physical and a logical format, and still takes less time than DOS.

Quick mode bypasses the step of checking the sectors. All it does is lay down new system areas. So it's slightly faster than Safe mode on old disks, but won't work on new, unformatted disks, which must be physically formatted.

DOS mode does a DOS-style format, but more quickly than DOS does. On a diskette, it does a physical format followed by a logical format. All former data is eliminated from the diskette and cannot be recovered. Even Image cannot save data from a DOS-style format on a diskette.

Use DOS mode if you actually want to eliminate the current data from the disk. But if you need to protect confidential data by completely obliterating it from a disk, a DOS-mode format might not be good enough. Some sophisticated electronic equipment can pick up traces of data from the edges of tracks. Use WipeInfo (explained in Chapter 7) to completely eliminate data from a disk.

> **Tip:** In most situations, use Safe mode. It will choose the format that is most appropriate for the disk.

Using the Image Facility

The Image facility saves a disk's system area in a file called IMAGE.DAT, which is placed in the last cluster of the disk. A logical format (Quick mode or Safe mode on an old disk) does not erase this file. The UnFormat program can find the IMAGE.DAT file even though it has no directory entry and use it to reestablish the former system area, effectively restoring the disk to its condition before formatting (as long as you didn't add any new files to the disk after reformatting it).

Although it's possible to rescue data after a logical format without the IMAGE.DAT file, it's a lot faster and easier if the file is present. Therefore, for your own protection, always select **Save UnFormat info** when reformatting an old disk.

You don't need to use Image with a new disk or a DOS-style reformatting. The physical formatting wipes out the Image data from the disk, so saving it would be a waste of time.

Assigning a Volume Label

Giving each volume a label is a good idea. The label shows up in directory listings and could prevent you from deleting or reformatting the wrong disk. You can enter up to 11 characters in the **Volume Label** box.

> **Note:** You can see the label of a disk at any time by entering VOL *d:* (where *d:* is the name of the drive), and you can change it through Norton Change Directory (explained in Chapter 17).

The Format Process

Once you have selected all the desired parameters, you start the format process by selecting **Begin Format**. Various messages keep you informed of what's happening. Many of the messages simply advise you of progress, but some are more important, such as this one:

The DOS Format mode DESTROYS all information on the diskette. The diskette cannot be unformatted, even if UnFormat information is saved. Are you sure you want to Format this diskette using the DOS Format mode?

This message appears when you've chosen DOS mode. If you didn't mean it, choose **No**. If you do want to do a DOS format, choose **Yes**.

Cannot save recovery info when formatting disk with different size. Do you wish to continue with the format?

You'll see this message when you're reformatting a disk to a different size from what it was before. For example, the disk is currently formatted as 1.2M and you're trying to format it as 360K. You can't use the Image feature in this case, since the old system areas won't be meaningful with the new format. This message is a warning that you're changing the size of the disk. Select **No** if you didn't mean to change the size of the disk. Select **Yes** if you want to forego Image and change the size.

Drive x: has the following files and subdirectories on it. [List box] Are you sure you want to Format it?

This message appears when the target disk contains data. Examine the list (it's scrollable) and make sure you're formatting the right disk. If not, select **No**. If you're sure you want to format the disk, select **Yes**.

Figure 3-2 shows the main message box that appears while the format takes place. The percentages and times dynamically track the format process. The space figures change if bad sectors are found. You can interrupt the format by pressing Enter or Esc, or by clicking the mouse button. For a quick format, you'll barely have time to see the box, but for a safe format or a DOS format, you'll be able to watch the numbers change. (If you're formatting a hard disk, you'll have time for a break.)

A message tells you when the format is successfully completed. When you select **OK**, the main dialog box reappears so you can format more disks, if necessary. When you're done, press Esc or select **Quit** to end Safe Format.

Formatting Problems

You might run into one of these problems while formatting:

- Bad sectors in the system area: If track 0 is unusable, the boot record cannot be installed and the disk is unusable. If this happens with a hard disk, contact your dealer.

- No room for IMAGE.DAT: If the disk is full, IMAGE.DAT cannot be saved. A dialog box asks if you want to continue or quit. You should probably quit, delete an unnecessary file, then restart Safe Format.

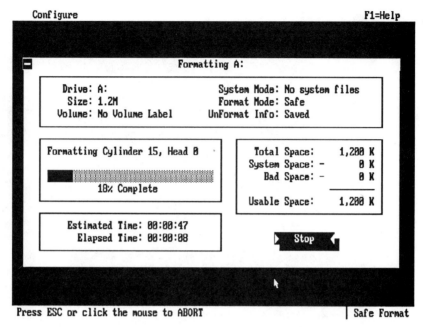

Figure 3-2   Format Progress Box

- Write-protected diskette: A write-protected diskette cannot be formatted. Safe Format terminates the format automatically in this situation. Remove the write protection and restart the format operation.

Configuration Options

So far, we've seen Safe Format in its default form. The **Configure** menu, shown in Figure 3-3, lets you add hard disks to the **Drive** box and lets you redefine your drives. You can also set up whatever default options (drive, size, format mode, and so on) you would like.

To format a hard-disk drive, select **Hard disks** (Alt-H). A dialog box explains the feature and lets you select **Allow hard-disk formatting.** When you close the dialog box, your hard disks are added to the main Safe Format screen. You should use the same process to remove them again after you have formatted the hard disk in question.

If Safe Format misreads your hardware and lists the wrong drive types, you can correct the situation via the **Floppy Types** option, which opens the dialog box shown in Figure 3-4. Select the drive in the left-hand box and its type in the right-hand box. When you close the dialog box, the specified drive information will appear on the main Safe Format screen.

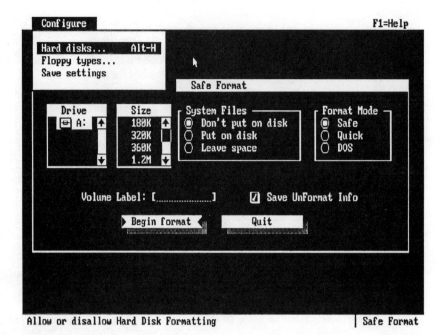

Figure 3-3 Configure Menu

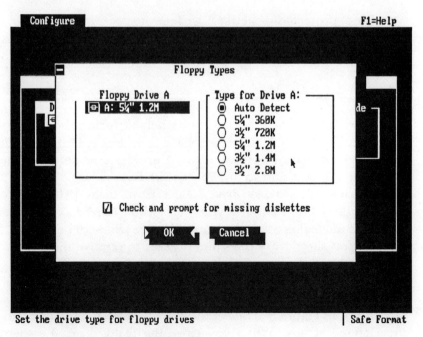

Figure 3-4 Floppy Types Dialog Box

By default, Safe Format checks to make sure a diskette drive contains a disk before starting the format operation. If the drive is empty, it gives you a chance to insert a diskette before continuing. If you would prefer not to spend the small amount of time it takes for Safe Format to check the drive, uncheck the **Check and prompt for missing diskettes** option. In that case, if a drive is empty, the format process will be terminated abruptly.

If you don't like the default settings for the main Safe Format screen, set it up the way you like it and choose **Save settings**. For example, suppose you want to include your hard drives in the **Drive** box, redefine drive B: as 360K capacity, and always save Image information. Set up the dialog box that way, pull down the **Configure** menu, and select **Save settings**. In the future, Safe Format will start up using those options. You can still change them for individual format situations, and you can save new settings whenever you want.

Command Format

Here is the complete format of the Safe Format command:

```
SFORMAT | FORMAT | SF [drivename] [switches]
```

Start the command with either SFORMAT, FORMAT, or SF, depending on your installation's setup. If you specify a drive, that drive will be selected in the dialog box. In addition to the standard Norton Utilities switches (shown in Table 1-1), you can use the switches shown in Table 3-1.

Notice in particular the /A (automatic) switch, which lets you run the format process completely from the command prompt; the Safe Format window does not appear. You can include whatever other switches you want to control the format options. Any option you don't specify uses its default setting. Once you have the default options set up the way you want, using /A will be much faster because the format takes place immediately after you enter the command.

Naming Safe Format

By default, the Safe Format program is named SFORMAT while the DOS format program is named FORMAT. You can rename Safe Format as either SF or FORMAT using the Configuration program. Many people like to rename it as FORMAT, which also renames DOS's format program to XXFORMAT, so that the standard FORMAT command will access Safe

Table 3-1   Safe Format Command Reference

Format:

SFORMAT | FORMAT | SF [*drivename:*] [*switches*]

Switches:

/1	Formats a diskette for single-sided use
/4	Formats a 360K diskette in a 1.2M drive
/8	Formats 8 sectors per track
/A	Automatic mode; does not display screens, menus, or dialog boxes
/B	Leaves space for system files on the disk
/D	Uses DOS mode
/F:*size*	Formats the diskette at the specified size
/N:*n*	Formats *n* sectors per track (*n* = 8, 9, 15, 18, or 36)
/Q	Uses Quick mode
/S	Copies system files
/T:*n*	Formats *n* tracks (*n* = 40 or 80)
/V:*label*	Installs label on disk

Format instead of DOS's format program. But don't do this if you use DOS's BACKUP program, which requires DOS's FORMAT program when you use the /F switch.

Image

If you capture image data every time you format a disk, you'll have little trouble unformatting it when that becomes necessary. Image data can also be valuable in recovering deleted files. The best setup for recovering files is Erase Protect, which is explained later in this chapter. But if you decide not to use Erase Protect, then you should capture image data frequently, not just when you format a disk. The Image utility can be used to capture image data whenever you want.

Note: Speed Disk also updates the IMAGE.DAT file. Chapter 5 explains Speed Disk.

Note: DOS 5.0 includes a Mirror facility that is similar to Image. Norton's UnErase and UnFormat programs can use either Mirror data or Image data.

How Image Works

Image captures the Boot Record, FAT, and root directory into a file in the root directory called IMAGE.DAT. It happens so fast, you might not even be aware that it worked.

Any former version of IMAGE.DAT is renamed as IMAGE.BAK. When it comes time to actually unformat a disk, IMAGE.BAK might contain the data you actually need. The UnFormat utility will find both IMAGE.DAT and IMAGE.BAK and ask you which one to use. UnErase, however, will find only IMAGE.DAT. You might have to erase IMAGE.DAT and rename IMAGE.BAK as IMAGE.DAT to get UnErase to use it.

A root directory has a limited number of entries available. If it's full, Image cannot function. It must be able to create the IMAGE.DAT file in the root directory. If Image displays a message saying that an error occurred while updating the image data, delete an unneeded file from the root directory or move something to another directory, then try again.

Image also cannot function if the drive is full. It will display a message advising you of the problem and terminate itself. You will need to delete at least one file to make room for IMAGE.DAT.

Don't delete or move IMAGE.DAT, or you'll defeat its purpose. Image creates it as a read-only file to prevent you from tampering with it. It's easy enough for you to undo the read-only protection, but don't do it. Just leave this file alone.

Running Image

You can run Image by selecting it from the **Recovery** section of the Norton menu or by entering the Image command, which has this format:

```
IMAGE [drivenames:] [/NOBACKUP] [/OUT]
```

The drive names specify the target drives. If you omit them, the current drive is used. The /NOBACKUP switch specifies that the current copy of IMAGE.DAT will be overlaid instead of renamed as IMAGE.BAK. The /OUT switch inhibits the progress messages that are normally displayed on your screen while Image is working; you might want to do this when running Image from a batch file such as AUTOEXEC.BAT, which is explained below.

Putting Image in AUTOEXEC.BAT

When DOS boots, it looks for a file called AUTOEXEC.BAT in the root directory of the boot drive. AUTOEXEC.BAT contains commands that you want to execute each time you boot. When you set up Norton Utilities during installation or with the Configure program, you have the option of including the Image command in your AUTOEXEC.BAT file. If you choose to do so, the following simple command is placed in your startup file:

```
IMAGE
```

Only the boot drive is protected by this command, and the /NOBACKUP switch is not included. You might want to adapt your AUTOEXEC.BAT file for more complete protection. For example, if you have three hard disk drives and prefer not to retain backups of IMAGE.DAT or to display Image messages, you might want to replace the simple Image command with this command:

```
IMAGE C: D: E: /NOBACKUP /OUT
```

Relationship to FRecover

Norton Utilities 4.5 had a similar program called FRecover that created a file named FRECOVER.DAT. If you are upgrading from version 4.5, the version 6.0 Image, Safe Format, UnErase, UnFormat, and Speed Disk programs will all treat FRECOVER.DAT just as if it was IMAGE.DAT.

Tip: Image is an important link in the chain of Norton Utilities' features that protect your data against loss due to accidental erasure, reformatting, and hardware or media failure. Always use the Image feature when reformatting a disk. If you don't use Erase Protect, use the Configure Utility to set up your AUTOEXEC.BAT file to automatically image all your hard drives during booting, and use Image whenever you make a major addition to a hard drive, such as a new directory, a new application, or a new file that might be fragmented.

Erase Protect

It's amazing how often you delete files without meaning to. You might enter a DEL command with a global filename that includes more files than you thought. For example, suppose you want to delete 20 files named DRAW1.GR, DRAW2.GR,...DRAW20.GR. You enter this command:

```
DEL DRAW*.GR
```

Later on, you discover that the command also deleted DRAWINGS.GR and DRAWMAX.GR. Now you need to recover those last two files.

Another easy way to delete the wrong files is to specify or imply the wrong drive and directory. Suppose you have just modified DRAW1.GR on drive C: and you want to delete an older version on drive A:. But you forget to include the drive name in the DEL command (and C: is the default drive):

```
DEL DRAW1.GR
```

You've just zapped the new version on drive C:. You have to use UnErase to get it back.

Recovering a file is easy if you discover your mistake immediately. But if it's some time later and you've added new data to the disk in the meantime, you might not be able to recover the whole file. Let's look at why this is.

When DOS deletes a file, it places a special delete code (hex E5) in the first character of the directory entry and zeros the FAT entries, but it doesn't actually erase the data in the clusters. At this point, Norton's UnErase has little trouble in recovering the file because the directory information is still available and it can guess at the FAT chain.

When you add a new file to the directory, DOS uses the first directory entry marked with the special delete code, overwriting and obliterating the former contents of that entry. Once the deleted file's entry has be reused, UnErase will have a much harder time recovering it—although it might still be possible. DOS also places the new file's data in the clusters with 0 FAT entries, obliterating any previous data in those clusters. It is impossible to recover the file that used those particular clusters.

Suppose you delete DRAW1.GR and copy FINISHED.MEM to the same directory. Could you now unerase DRAW1.GR? It all depends on whether FINISHED.MEM overlaid DRAW1.GR's directory entry and/or clusters. As you keep adding more files to the disk and expanding existing files, the probability of being able to unerase DRAW1.GR plummets.

How Erase Protect Works

Erase Protect counteracts DOS's normal behavior by preserving deleted files for a while, giving you more time to decide to unerase them. Erase Protect creates and maintains a special, hidden directory called TRASHCAN. Whenever you delete an eligible file, Erase Protect intervenes and prevents the FAT entries from being zeroed. It creates a new directory entry in TRASHCAN, pointing to the first cluster of the old file chain. It also maintains an index of all the files in TRASHCAN showing their original names, original directories, and when they were deleted.

The results of Erase Protect's actions are:

- The old directory entry is not preserved, so the file appears to be deleted from its original directory.

- The FAT entries are not zeroed, so DOS cannot reuse the file's clusters for new data.

- When you want to recover a file, UnErase knows how to use TRASHCAN to restore the file to its original directory.

Obviously, you don't want to preserve deleted files forever or you will quickly use up all your disk space with dead wood. Erase Protect includes several different methods of purging files from TRASHCAN. You can save them for a specified number of days or until TRASHCAN reaches a certain size. Also, Erase Protect will automatically purge files as necessary to make room for new data you add to the disk. Or you can view the files in TRASHCAN and select ones to purge.

You don't have to protect all deleted files with Erase Protect. You can specify which drives it should protect; you can even specify which types of files should be protected and which shouldn't.

Erase Protect is a terminate and stay resident (TSR) program, which means that, after it's loaded, it stays dormant in memory while you do other work. Every time a file is deleted, Erase Protect kicks itself on and saves the file, if appropriate. Then it goes dormant again. It also turns itself on to purge files when more disk space is needed for new data. It takes up only 8K bytes in memory when it is dormant.

How to Use Erase Protect

You can start Erase Protect by selecting it from the Norton menu or by entering the Erase Protect command, which has this format:

```
EP [switches]
```

Table 3-2 lists the possible switches. Use the /ON switch when you want to start Erase Protect automatically; it bypasses the Erase Protect dialog box and uses the default options.

Table 3-2   Erase Protect Command Switches

/ON	Turns Erase Protect on (current or default parameters are used)
/OFF	Unloads Erase Protect TSR from memory
/STATUS	Displays current Erase Protect status
/UNINSTALL	Unloads Erase Protect TSR from memory
/SKIPHIGH	Does not load Erase Protect into high memory

> **Note:** Your system might start up Erase Protect automatically from AUTOEXEC.BAT, depending on how the Norton Utilities are set up. An easy way to insert Erase Protect in AUTOEXEC.BAT is through the Configuration program, which inserts the command EP /ON.

When you start Erase Protect without the /ON or /OFF switch, the dialog box shown in Figure 3-5 appears. You use this dialog box to select the Erase Protect options and turn it on.

Choosing Drives

When you select the **Choose drives** option, the dialog box shown in Figure 3-6 appears. Check each drive that you want to protect, then select **ON**. To turn it off again, return to this dialog box and select **OFF**.

> **Tip:** Protect each of your hard drives but not your diskette drives. (Diskette protection takes too long and is usually unnecessary. Protect your diskette files by making backup copies.)

File Protection

By default, Erase Protect protects all files on the designated drives that have the archive attribute. Let's look a little more closely at the archive attribute to find out why this is.

Whenever a new file is added to a disk or an existing file is modified in any way, DOS turns its archive attribute on. The archive attribute says, in

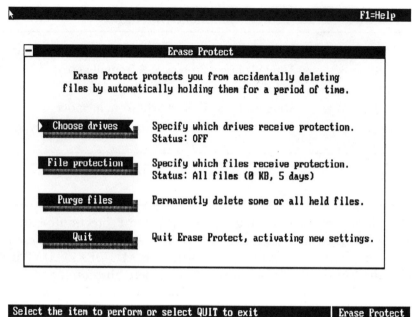

Figure 3-5   Erase Protect Dialog Box

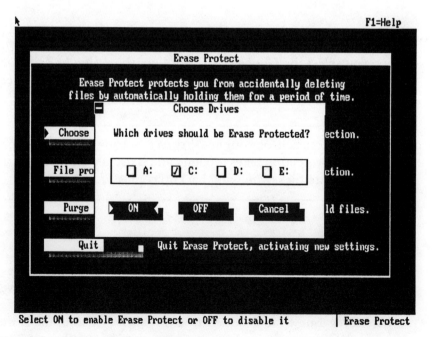

Figure 3-6   Choose Drives Dialog Box

essence, that the file needs to be archived (backed up). Whenever you make a backup copy of a file with a program such as Norton Backup, that program turns off the archive attribute, since the file no longer needs to be archived.

Therefore, when a file's archive attribute is on, it might be the only existing copy of the file in its current form, and it needs to be protected. So Erase Protect will protect it from deletion. When a file's archive attribute is off, a good backup copy of the current version (supposedly) exists and it does not need to be protected from deletion.

To limit the types of files that are protected by Erase Protect, or to save archived files as well as unarchived files, select the **File protection** button. Figure 3-7 shows the dialog box that appears.

You can control what types of files are protected by their extensions. To specify up to nine extensions for protection, type them in the **Files** box and select **Only the files listed**. Or you can protect all files except certain types by typing their extensions in the box and selecting **All files except those listed**. For example, suppose you don't need to protect any program files, since you have the original diskettes for all your programs. You could enter COM, EXE, BIN, and SYS in the **Files** box and select **All files except those listed**.

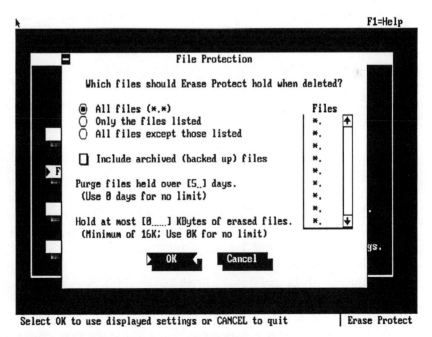

Figure 3-7   File Protection Dialog Box

> **Tip:** If you have diskette copies of all your program files, you can safely omit your program files from protection. But if your dealer installed programs on your hard disk without giving you diskette copies, then you should protect your program files, too.

To protect archived files as well as unarchived files, check the **Include archived (backed up) files** option. If you omit archived files, you can protect individual files later by using Disk Editor to turn on their archive attributes (Chapter 14 explains how).

Purging Deleted Files

You don't want to protect deleted files forever. Soon your entire disk would be filled up with deleted files. You must use some system to purge deleted files after a reasonable time. Three methods are available: automatic purging after a number of days; automatic purging when preserved files reach a certain size limit; and manual purging. The two methods of automatic purging are controlled from the **File Protection** dialog box.

To specify automatic purging after a number of days, enter a number in the appropriate text box. Each time Erase Protect starts up, it will examine every TRASHCAN directory for files that have been saved for longer than the specified number of days. It deletes those files from the directory; this time, they are really deleted.

> **Note:** The default time limit is five days.

To specify automatic purging when the deleted files reach a certain size, enter the number of kilobytes in the second text box. For example, you might not want the TRASHCAN directory to get larger than 2M. You would specify 2048K in the text box. Each time Erase Protect moves a deleted file into TRASHCAN, it checks the total number of bytes. When it exceeds the limit, the oldest files are deleted from the directory. ("Oldest" means those that were moved into TRASHCAN first; this has nothing to do with the original creation dates of the files.)

You can specify both a time limit and a size limit. Files will be purged when either limit is reached.

When you select **OK**, the **File Protection** dialog box closes and the main Erase Protect dialog box reappears. You will see the results of your choices next to the **File protection** button.

Selecting **Quit** in the main dialog box causes Erase Protect to start up using the options you have selected. They will stay in effect until you change them again. If you reboot, Erase Protect is turned off (unless it's started up in your AUTOEXEC.BAT file), but the current options are remembered for the next time you start it. Also, the preserved files continue to be preserved, even when Erase Protect is off.

> **Note:** When Erase Protect is turned off, it can't automatically purge files, which could cause space problems for new files unless you have specified a size limit for TRASHCAN.

Purging Files Manually

To purge files manually, start Erase Protect so that you get to the main dialog box. Then select the **Purge files** button. The dialog box shown in Figure 3-8 appears. All the files in TRASHCAN are listed. You can see the file's original directory and the date and time it was deleted by highlighting the file; the information appears below the list box.

Select files individually by clicking on them or by highlighting them and pressing Enter. Select a group of files by selecting the **Tag** button and

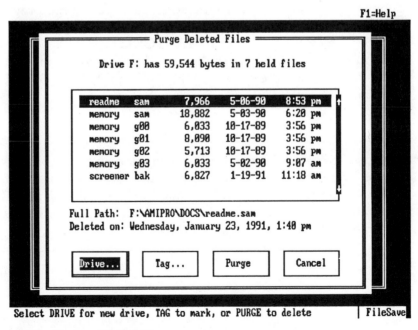

Figure 3-8   Purge Dialog Box

entering a global filename in the resulting dialog box. You can also tag a file by clicking the right mouse button on it or by highlighting it and pressing the Spacebar. When all the files you want to purge are tagged, select the **Purge** button. After the files are purged, you are returned to the main Erase Protect dialog box.

Network Considerations

You can use Erase Protect on network drives. All users' deleted files will be saved in TRASHCAN. Try to avoid purging manually, as no users' files will be saved while the Purge dialog box is on your screen. If you must purge manually, do it as quickly as possible.

Rescuing a File from TRASHCAN

Since TRASHCAN is hidden, you can't access it to save a file in the normal manner (i.e., by copying a file from it). But UnErase can access TRASHCAN easily. It will display a list of files available to be unerased, and you can select the ones you want. UnErase is explained fully in Chapter 9.

Removing Erase Protect from Memory

Suppose you need to free up memory space for a large program such as Ventura Publisher. You will probably need to remove all your TSRs from memory. Unless they're installed by AUTOEXEC.BAT, you can remove them by rebooting. Or you can back them out by uninstalling them. To uninstall Erase Protect, enter the command EP /OFF or EP /UNINSTALL; these two commands have the same effect.

Note: TSRs must be removed from memory in the reverse order that they were installed. If AUTOEXEC.BAT installs Erase Protect and Disk Monitor (in that order), and you later install a TSR called Grabber, you would have to uninstall the programs in this order: Grabber, Disk Monitor, Erase Protect.

Looking Ahead

If you haven't already done so, take the time now to decide how you want to use Safe Format, Image, and Erase Protect and use the Configuration program to set up. Be sure to check your AUTOEXEC.BAT to see if Image and Erase Protect are in there and adapt those commands as you wish. (You can edit AUTOEXEC.BAT with DOS 5.0's Edit program or your word processor, but be careful to use ASCII format.)

Once you have observed the elementary precautions to prevent data loss, it's time to turn your attention to improving your system's performance. Chapter 4 shows you how to set up and use Norton Disk Cache, which can dramatically speed up all your applications.

4

NORTON CACHE

Norton Cache sets up an area in memory to store disk data, cutting down on the number of necessary reads, and possibly writes, to the disk. The performance improvement for hard-disk data is noticeable. The overall effect is to make most of your applications run faster.

Essentially, you're trading memory for speed. The more memory space you can give to the cache, the faster your applications can perform. But even if memory is at a premium, you can still achieve good speed improvement with a minimum cache.

What types of programs benefit from disk caching? You'll notice a major improvement in any application that is disk intensive; that is, it reads from and writes to the disk a lot. This would include databases, spreadsheets, and word processors.

> **Tip:** If your system does not have extra memory (that is, more than 640K of RAM), don't use a disk cache on a regular basis; your memory space could be too crammed for your applications to function properly. But you might be able to start up a cache to speed up a particular disk-intensive operation, then shut it down again.

Background

It helps to understand a bit about disks and memory in order to use Norton Cache intelligently. This chapter explains some essential basics.

Disk Access

Disk drives are so much slower than the microprocessor and RAM that they could be compared to the tortoise and the hare. The processor and memory have no moving parts; everything is electronic, and data can move at nearly the speed of light. Disk drives involve electro-mechanical parts. A read-write arm, which holds the read-write heads over the tracks, must be moved to the correct track to access data; then it must wait until the desired sector rolls around. Hard-disk drives can do this about ten times faster than diskette drives, but the hard disk is still at least 50 times slower than RAM.

Disk-access speed is complicated by the fact that it always takes multiple reads to find the data you need. For example, suppose you want to read a short, unfragmented file named C:\STARPROJ\BUDGET91.DAT. Here are the steps the computer would take, assuming that nothing goes wrong:

1. Move the read-write head to the root directory location. Read one sector at a time from the root directory until you find the entry for the STARPROJ subdirectory.
2. Move the head to the FAT and read the sector containing the STARPROJ cluster chain.
3. Move the head to the first cluster of the STARPROJ subdirectory. Read one sector at a time until you find the entry for BUDGET91.DAT.
4. Move the head to the FAT and read the sector containing the BUD-GET91.DAT cluster chain.
5. Move the head to BUDGET91.DAT—finally! Copy all the sectors into memory (if possible).

It takes a minimum of five read-write head movements and five reads to access a simple file in a subdirectory. If the STARPROJ subdirectory and/or the BUDGET91.DAT file are fragmented, DOS might have to return to the FAT to find the next part of the subdirectory or file. And all this while, the processor might be idling, waiting for data so it can proceed.

Writing data on disk can take even more steps than reading. DOS must do multiple reads in the directories and FAT to find the correct sectors to write on. Then it might have to update the directory entry and possibly the FAT.

Memory Use

Ideally the computer would keep all data in RAM and not bother with disk drives; access would be virtually instantaneous. But unfortunately RAM is volatile: all its data is lost when you power down. So permanent files must be kept on some other device, such as a disk.

User memory is the portion of RAM where DOS stores the programs and data that it is currently working on, and this kind of memory is limited by DOS to 640K. (That's 640 *kilobytes*, where one kilobyte is 1024 bytes. For convenience, you can call a K one thousand bytes when you don't need to be more accurate.)

When DOS was designed, 640K of user memory seemed like more than anyone could possibly use. But as we progressed from text editors to word processors to desktop publishers and from line drawings to paintbrushes to scanners, that 640K got smaller and smaller. Today, it's not unusual for an application to demand 500K or more of RAM, leaving just enough room for DOS. There's frequently no room left over to create and use a disk cache while running a program like that.

Another range of memory lies above the 640K mark but below 1M (one *megabyte*, which is $1K^2$ or 1,048,576 bytes; you can call it one million bytes for short). This area is set aside by DOS for the memory in ROM-BIOS, your video card's memory, and so on. It is often called *high DOS memory* or *upper memory*. Some systems don't use all of high DOS memory for hardware. In some cases, 64K or even 128K could be made available as user memory, but you have to have a special memory driver for it. DOS alone has no facility to access upper memory as user memory. The special drivers usually come in conjunction with expanded or extended memory, discussed next.

To meet ever-expanding memory needs, we can now have extra memory installed over and above the 1M limit, which only some of your applications will be able to use. Depending on the type of computer you have, you could have many megabytes of extra memory. You must have a special memory driver to handle this memory, because DOS alone can't do it.

Two basic types of extra memory are available: expanded and extended. Some applications can use one type; some use the other. You might have one or both types. Extended memory is a more recent development and is generally faster than expanded memory, but more applications can work with expanded memory, simply because it's been around longer.

Many PCs don't use all the extra memory available to them because their applications don't use it or use only a small part of it. Sometimes an owner just doesn't understand the hardware and software well enough to set up the system to make maximum use of its extra memory. On the other hand, some systems are running out of space in the extra memory area, too. But chips are cheap (usually); it's easy and relatively inexpensive to add a few more megabytes of extra memory when you're running out. It's sometimes harder to get your applications to recognize and use it.

Needless to say, Norton Cache can build its disk cache in extended and/or expanded memory. It can make the cache a specific size, or simply take up all the available room. It can also store part of its own program management tables in upper and/or extra memory, leaving conventional memory for other software.

How Cache Works

Norton Cache sets up a special area called a *cache* somewhere in memory; you control its location and the size. You also control which disks are cached; you don't have to cache them all if you don't want.

Whenever the computer reads from a cached disk, Norton Cache looks first in the cache to see if the desired data is already present in memory. If it is, the data is read from the cache instead of from the disk. If it isn't, the data is read from the disk into the application's memory space *and* into the cache. The next time you read that same data again (which happens more frequently than you might think), it will be in the cache. When the cache is full, the data that has been used the least is overwritten with new data.

Imagine that you have just booted and the cache is empty. You enter the command to start your word processor. DOS reads the root directory from the disk so it can look up the location of the necessary subdirectory; the root directory gets stored in the cache. Then DOS reads the subdirectory, which goes into the cache. Then the word-processor program file is read; it also goes into the cache. As you continue through the day, the root directory will probably stay in the cache since it is accessed constantly. The subdirectory might stay in, depending on what else you do. The word-processing program will probably be overlaid by data files, other programs, and so on.

For even faster access, you can set up Norton Cache to predict what records you will want next and read them into the cache in advance. For example, suppose you read a sector from a database. Norton Cache can read the next 15 sectors into the cache (while the first sector is being processed), on the grounds that you will probably continue reading in sequence.

Norton Cache also includes a feature that will delay writes to the disk for a few seconds. This makes more sense than it sounds like. Usually, after you write a record, you start looking for the next one to process, which could involve several disk reads. Ordinarily, the system must wait for the write to be completed before it can start the next read. By delaying the write, you let the reads be performed first, thus giving the processor something new to work on before the previous record is written.

Another feature, called *IntelliWrites*, lets the system continue working on other things while the writes are being done. When IntelliWrites are used in conjunction with SmartReads, your applications can work on new records while the previous records are being written.

Norton Cache also provides a *status screen* that shows you the current configuration of the cache (which drives are cached, the size and location of the cache, and so on). It also shows you a *hit ratio*: the percentage of reads per drive that have come from the cache instead of the disk itself. The hit ratio can help you determine the best configuration for your cache.

Setting up the Disk Cache

The Install program might have already set up Norton Cache for you, depending on what options were chosen during installation. To find out, look in your CONFIG.SYS file for a statement something like this:

```
DEVICE=C:\NU\NCACHE.EXE [parameters]
```

Also, look in your AUTOEXEC.BAT file for a command like this:

```
NCACHE [parameters]
```

> **Note:** Even if Norton Cache is already installed on your system, read the following information. It will help you understand what is installed, and it could help you improve the cache's performance.

If you do need to install Norton Cache yourself, the easiest way is from the Configuration program, which you can start up from the Norton menu (refer back to Figures 1-10 and 1-12). Selecting the **Norton Cache** option opens the first dialog box shown in Figure 4-1. The dialog box opened by the **Advanced** button is also shown in Figure 4-1.

Preparing the System Configuration

Before you set up the disk cache, you need to pay attention to your current configuration, to eliminate any features that might interfere with Norton Cache. Primarily, you want to get rid of other disk-buffering devices. Even if you're a belt-and-suspenders type, avoid doubling up on data buffering; you'll waste time and memory. To check your current configuration, you'll need to examine, and possibly edit, your CONFIG.SYS and AUTOEXEC.BAT files. (We'll show you how in a minute.)

(a)   **Main Dialog Box**

(b)   **Advanced Dialog Box**

Figure 4-1   Norton Cache and Advanced Dialog Boxes

In CONFIG.SYS, remove any DEVICE statement that loads another cache driver, such as these:

```
DEVICE=SMARTDRV.SYS [parameters]
DEVICE=IBMCACHE.SYS [parameters]
```

This doesn't mean that you should eliminate every DEVICE statement; many of them install essential drivers. Just remove the ones that set up other caches.

There will probably also be a CONFIG.SYS statement that sets up several DOS buffers: areas in memory that let DOS read and store extra sectors to speed up future reads. The BUFFERS statement looks something like this:

```
BUFFERS=20
```

Buffers are neither necessary nor desirable when using a cache, so you should eliminate most of them. Don't eliminate them all, but cut down to a minimum of about 3. (You need a few buffers to speed up the boot process before the cache is installed.)

In CONFIG.SYS and AUTOEXEC.BAT, remove any command that installs DOS's FASTOPEN (which stores directory information in memory), which will look like this:

```
FASTOPEN [parameters]
```

You can examine CONFIG.SYS and AUTOEXEC.BAT through the System Info utility, but since you can't edit them there, you will probably want to use DOS 5.0's Edit program or your word processor. You need to exercise some caution, because if you edit them incorrectly, you might not be able to boot successfully. These guidelines should help you edit the necessary files safely:

1. Preserve your current versions of CONFIG.SYS and AUTO-EXEC.BAT by copying them as CONFIG.SAV and AUTOEXEC.SAV. You can do this by entering the following two commands:

   ```
   COPY C:\CONFIG.SYS C:\CONFIG.SAV
   COPY C:\AUTOEXEC.BAT C:\AUTOEXEC.SAV
   ```

   You should get the message "1 File(s) copied" after each command. If not, get someone to help you copy these files. Do not continue with these instructions until both files are safely copied.

2. Start up DOS 5.0's Edit program or your word processor and examine C:\CONFIG.SYS in ASCII format. Edit it if necessary and save it in

ASCII format. It's extremely important to work in ASCII format, as DOS cannot understand a file that has been stored in most word processors' standard formats. If you don't know how to use your word processor in ASCII format, take the time to find out before editing CONFIG.SYS. (DOS 5.0's Edit program automatically saves files in ASCII format.)

3. Repeat step 2 for C:\AUTOEXEC.BAT.

4. Reboot after editing the files. If you don't run into any trouble while rebooting, you can skip step 5.

5. If you run into trouble while booting (that is, if your system doesn't boot successfully or you get unexpected error messages), boot from a bootable diskette and enter these commands to restore the old CONFIG.SYS and AUTOEXEC.BAT:

```
COPY C:\CONFIG.SAV C:\CONFIG.SYS
COPY C:\AUTOEXEC.SAV C:\AUTOEXEC.BAT
```

If you get the message "1 File(s) copied" for both commands, you can safely enter the following two commands to delete the backup copies:

```
DEL C:\CONFIG.SAV
DEL C:\AUTOEXEC.SAV
```

You should now be able to reboot from your hard disk. (If not, get someone to help you.)

If you are unable to successfully edit CONFIG.SYS and AUTOEXEC.BAT, you'll probably need to get some outside help to install Norton Cache. If you can't find a knowledgeable friend to help you, you can call the technical-support staff at Symantec. Check your Norton Utilities documentation for the correct telephone number.

Decisions

You also need to make some decisions about exactly what you want to install: the size and location of the cache and which drives you're going to cache.

In terms of *location*, put the cache in extended or expanded memory if at all possible, since conventional memory is at a premium. If neither is available, you'll have to put it in conventional memory, which means you'll probably have to settle for a fairly small cache.

In terms of *size*, make it as large as possible unless it's in conventional memory. Memory allocated to Norton Cache is not available for other applications, so you need to know how much space to leave for the others.

Many applications, such as the latest versions of Lotus 1-2-3 and Ventura Publisher, are flexible in how much extra memory they can use; the more the better. In those cases, you might want to give half your extra memory to Norton Cache and leave half for other applications; you can adjust the allocations later based on what performance you observe. If you're using Windows 3.0, Norton Cache will lend it space from an extended or expanded memory cache on an as-needed basis. If you have to use conventional memory, then you should probably use the minimum configuration. If you find that some applications still can't get enough memory to run, you can remove Norton Cache temporarily, remove it permanently, or (preferably) install additional memory.

> **Tip:** The smallest effective cache is 64K.

In terms of which *drives* to cache, you certainly want to cache the hard-disk drive(s) that you use for the bulk of your work. Caching diskettes is not recommended because the cached data will be out of sync with the diskette if you change diskettes in the drive.

> **Tip:** Norton Cache works better with unfragmented files. We recommend using Speed Disk (explained in Chapter 5) regularly to keep files unfragmented.

Installing Norton Cache

You can use the Configuration program to install Norton Cache from either CONFIG.SYS or the command prompt. Most people install it from AUTOEXEC.BAT, but some systems require it to be installed as a device driver from CONFIG.SYS. If you install it from CONFIG.SYS, you can't remove it again without editing the appropriate DEVICE statement out of CONFIG.SYS and rebooting. If you install it from the command prompt (or AUTOEXEC.BAT), you can remove it with a simple NCACHE UNINSTALL command.

In the dialog box shown in Figure 4-1, choose the appropriate radio button in the **Loading** control group. Configuration will add an NCACHE command to CONFIG.SYS or AUTOEXEC.BAT depending on which button you choose. If you choose **Do not load the Norton Cache**, the NCACHE command is removed from whichever file it was in.

When you install the cache this way, all your hard drives are cached by default. You can also cache your diskette drives by checking **Cache floppy drives A: and B:** under the **Cache Options** control group. You'll see later in this chapter how to control caching on individual drives.

Loading into High Memory

If you have a 286 or higher, it might be capable of loading the cache software into high DOS memory (above 640K but below 1M) instead of conventional memory, which helps to save conventional memory for applications. In order to use high memory, a high memory manager such as DOS's EMM386.SYS must be installed.

If you know that your system is set up to use high memory, or if you're not sure, check the **Load in high memory** option. DOS will load Norton Cache into conventional memory if high memory is not available.

Working with IntelliWrites

Another way to speed up the system is with IntelliWrites. Without Intelli-Writes, each write to disk must be completed before processing can continue. IntelliWrites lets processing continue while a write is still taking place. To turn this feature on, check **Enable IntelliWrites** in the **Cache Options** control group. You should also take a look at the **IntelliWrites** control group in the Advanced dialog box.

Write-Back Buffers

The size of the Write-Back buffer determines how much data will be saved up and written to disk in one operation. The larger the buffer, the faster your system will run—up to the largest track size of the disks being cached. The Write-Back buffer size must be a value between 8K and 64K if IntelliWrites are enabled. When IntelliWrites are disabled, its value is 0. The default value depends on which **Optimize** option is selected in the lower-left corner of the Advanced dialog box; you'll learn about these options shortly.

You'll probably want to go with the default buffer size until you're sure that other parts of Norton Cache are operating as you want them. Then you might want to play with the Write-Back buffer size and see how it impacts performance.

Delay

IntelliWrites is usually used in conjunction with a Delay factor, which delays writes for a specified number of seconds. Not only does the delay give additional priority to reads, it actually cuts down on the number of writes because several writes in a row to the same sector (which is not uncommon, especially in directories) are stored up and written only once.

Waiting for the Command Prompt

When a program ends with IntelliWrites and Delay in force, all its remaining writes are written before the command prompt returns. You might notice the time lag. You can eliminate it with **Don't wait for write-back to display DOS prompt**. When you check this option, you can go on to your next operation while writes are finishing.

> **Warning:** If you choose this option, the command prompt is no longer a clue that write-backs are completed. Be very careful not to lose data by removing a diskette or powering down before all sectors are written.

Working with SmartReads

To enable SmartReads, check **Enable SmartReads** in the **Cache Options** control group. When SmartReads is enabled, you can control how far Norton Cache reads ahead using the **Size of the Read-Ahead buffer** option in the Advanced dialog box. The default size is 8K when SmartReads is enabled. You might want to make that value smaller to conserve memory or larger for more reading efficiency.

Cache Block Size

The block size of a cache is equivalent to the cluster size of a hard disk. When an element (a directory, a record, or a file) is read into the cache, it is allocated one or more blocks; the last block might have slack.

Your choice of a block size influences the speed and capacity of the cache. A small block size such as 512 bytes results in less slack, which increases the capacity of the cache; but it takes longer to access a larger element such as a 40K file, which would occupy 80 blocks. A large block size, such as 5K, speeds access of large elements but results in a lot more slack for small elements such as a 100-byte record, which would waste 5020 bytes.

In general, use a small block size if you'll be working with small elements such as database records or heavily fragmented files, and a large block size if you'll be dealing mostly with large, unfragmented files.

The block size influences the size of the management tables, and Norton Cache might need to adjust the block size to fit the management tables into the HMA or high DOS memory. So if you see that the cache is using a different block size than you specified, that's the reason.

Memory Usage

The **Memory Usage** control group is used to specify the size and location of the cache itself. The right-hand column shows the maximum amounts of memory available in three categories: Expanded, Extended, and Conventional. The first column shows the default amount Norton Cache will use from each type of memory if you don't change it. You can overtype these values to change the cache size.

> **Tip:** Be sure to leave enough room in extended or expanded memory for other applications that you might want to start up.

If you run Windows 3.0 in its enhanced mode, you need to pay attention to the middle column, which determines the minimum cache size when Windows needs to borrow memory from the cache. Windows often needs to borrow memory from a cache in order to provide enough space to its various programs. By default, Norton Cache makes the second column equal to the first column, which means that Windows can't borrow any memory from the cache. That makes the cache more effective but could lower the effectiveness of Windows. You can change the balance by overtyping the values in the middle column. For example, suppose you want to work with a 2000K cache but let Windows borrow 500K if needed. You would change the 2000K in the middle column to 1500K—your minimum cache size.

Using the Optimize Settings

At first, you might not be sure what cache factors to use. The **Optimize** control group in the Advanced dialog box gives you a simple way to set up the cache. If you select **Speed**, the Configuration program will select Read-Ahead, Write-Back, Delay, and Block factors for the fastest possible caching, usually at the expense of memory space. If you select **Memory**, the same factors will be chosen for low memory usage at the expense of speed. The **Memory** option disables SmartReads, IntelliWrites, and Delay. The **Efficiency** option finds a balance between the other two options.

Saving the Cache Configuration

When you have finished selecting options in the Norton Cache and Advanced dialog boxes, select **OK** to save them. Configuration will add the appropriate command to your AUTOEXEC.BAT or CONFIG.SYS file. The various parameters you have selected will be placed in a file called NCACHE.INI, which Norton Cache uses automatically during startup.

You can revise your cache setup by returning to the Norton Cache and Advanced dialog boxes and changing options. Don't forget to reboot to put your new changes into effect.

The NCACHE Command

Another way to install Norton Cache is to write your own command for CONFIG.SYS or AUTOEXEC.BAT (or even for the command prompt). When you do it yourself, you have even more options available to you than you do in the Configuration dialog boxes. Table 4-1 shows the complete format of the NCACHE command.

Table 4-1   NCACHE Installation Command Reference

Format:

NCACHE [*switches*] [*drive: switches* [...]]

or

DEVICE = *path*\NCACHE.EXE [*switches*] [drive:*switches*[...]]

Switches:

/INSTALL	Installs cache with default values; use when /EXT, /EXP, and /DOS are not specified
/OPTIMIZE=E|M|S	Sets up cache options for efficiency, memory, or speed
/DOS[=[-]*n*]	Sets up cache of *n* bytes in conventional memory; -*n* sets up cache of all but *n* bytes
/EXP[=[-]*n*[,*m*]	Sets up cache of *n* bytes in expanded memory and optionally specifies minimum cache size of *m* bytes when working with Windows 3.0 in enhanced mode; -*n* sets up cache of all but *n* bytes
/EXT[=[-]*n*[,*m*]	Sets up cache of *n* bytes in extended memory and optionally specifies minimum cache size of *m* bytes when working with Windows 3.0 in enhanced mode; -*n* sets up cache of all but *n* bytes
/BLOCK=*n*	Sets block size of *n*, which can be 512, 1024, 2048, 4096, or 8192; default is 8192

(continued)

Table 4-1   *(continued)*

/USEHIGH=ON|OFF	Enables or disables use of high DOS memory; default is ON unless a memory manager is used to load high
/USEHMA=ON|OFF	Enables or disables use of HMA; default is ON
/READ=n	Sets size of read-ahead buffer from 8K to 64K; default is 8K unless an /OPTIMIZE option is specified; 0 disables the read-ahead feature
/WRITE=n	Sets size of write-back buffer, from 8K to 64K; default depends on /OPTIMIZE option; 0 disables IntelliWrites
/DELAY=ss.hh	Specifies delay factor for IntelliWrites; default is 01:00 (one second) unless /OPTIMIZE is specified
/QUICK=ON|OFF	Enables or disables the return of the command prompt before delayed writes are completed
/INI=path	Specifies the location of the NCACHE initialization file
/REPORT[=ON|OFF]	Displays the full NCACHE report
/STATUS[=ON|OFF]	Displays partial NCACHE report
/[-]A	Activates or deactivates caching for a specific drive
/[-]I	Enables or disables IntelliWrites
/[-]W	Enables or disables write-through caching
/[-]P	Enables or disables write protection for a specific drive
/R[=[D]n]	Limits sector read-aheads to n bytes; D specifies dynamic read-aheads, in which NCACHE decides when to read ahead; default is /R=D8
/G=n	Does not cache reads larger than n sectors; default is 128

Differences from the Configuration Dialog Boxes

Many of the switches duplicate features found in the Configuration dialog boxes. But some switches provide additional features. For example, the /DOS, /EXT, and /EXP switches can specify the amount of space to leave for other programs instead of the amount to reserve for the cache. If you specify a parameter similar to this:

```
/EXT=-5-12
```

the cache will use *all but* 512K of extended memory. If you don't specify any cache size, you must include the /INSTALL switch, which creates a default cache.

Locating the INI File

Use the /INI parameter to specify the name and location of the file containing the cache's startup parameters, which is usually C:\NU\NCACHE.INI.

Controlling the Status Report

The /REPORT and /STATUS switches are used to indicate how much information you want displayed about the cache when it is started up. /REPORT displays a full report while /STATUS displays an abbreviated report.

Write-Through Caching

Suppose you read data such as a word-processor document from a disk (which causes it to be cached), update it, and write it back to the disk again. The cached copy will automatically be updated, too. That way, if you read the same data again, you will get the updated version from the cache. But if you create new data—such as a new document or a new record in a database— will it be cached when it is written? That depends on whether *write-through caching* is on or off.

When write-through caching is off, new data is not cached when it is written. You should use this setting when you know that you will not reread new data after writing it. For example, suppose you are setting out to add 50 records to your customer database. You probably won't want to reread them after writing them (at least not immediately), so you can safely turn write-through-caching off. That way, the new records won't push useful data out of the cache. You can turn write-through caching off with /–W.

To capture new data in the cache, leave write-through caching on (it's on by default) or turn it on with /W. Use this feature whenever you will be creating new elements that might be reread soon (such as when you create a new document with your word processor).

Drive-Specific Switches

Single-letter switches can also be applied to specific drives. Specify the drive name followed by the switches for that drive, as in:

```
NCACHE ... C: /P /R=D8 D: /G=5
```

This example turns on write protection and dynamic read-aheads for drive C: and limits reads for drive D:.

You can use Norton Cache to write protect a hard drive with the /P switch, which simply prevents all writes to that drive. To turn write protection off, enter another NCACHE command with the /-P switch, as in:

```
NCACHE D: /-P
```

Since the cache is already installed, you don't need any other parameters in the command.

The /R switch works in conjunction with the /READ switch to control read-aheads. /READ sets the size of the read-ahead buffer, but /R controls how much will be read ahead at once, up to the size of the buffer. You can use different /R switches for different drives, and you can change the factors as you work by entering NCACHE commands at the command prompt. Use lower /R values when working with small files and fragmented files. Use /R=0 to disable reading ahead when working with highly fragmented files or files that are accessed in random order instead of sequential order. If you're not sure when to use /R and when to disable it, use /R=Dn to let Norton Cache decide when to enable and disable it.

The /G (group sector) parameter controls the maximum size of a cached element and is intended to avoid overlaying cached data when a program is loaded. In this discussion, the word "element" refers to the amount of material that DOS tries to read in one chunk. In general, DOS will read data files a few sectors at a time but will load program files in larger chunks—up to 64K at a time. The /G parameter can take advantage of this fact to keep programs out of the cache. By specifying /G=8, for example, you prevent any element larger than eight sectors from being cached. The result is that most data files will be cached while most programs won't.

Why don't we want programs in the cache? When you load a program into memory, it stays there while it executes. There's no need to read it again or to write it, as you do with data files and directories. So caching a program gains nothing and pushes other data, which might be needed again, out of the cache. It is definitely to your benefit to use /G to keep programs out of the cache.

Tip: Try /G=8 to start with. You can experiment with higher and lower values and examine the results on your hit ratios later on. (We'll explain how soon.)

Dynamic Adjustments

The parameters we have discussed so far are usually included on the command that starts up Norton Cache. You might also want to enter

NCACHE commands at the DOS prompt to adjust the cache once it's running. Table 4-2 shows the NCACHE parameters that can be used for this purpose.

You can't change the cache's size or location, but you can enable/disable the various read and write features. For example, suppose you want to disable IntelliWrites while you run a particular application, then turn it back on again. You could enter this command to disable it:

```
NCACHE /-I
```

When you're ready to turn it back on again, you could enter this command:

```
NCACHE /I
```

Table 4-2   NCACHE Reconfigure Command Reference

Format:

NCACHE [*switches*] [*drive: switches* [...]]

Switches:

/RESET	Resets entire cache
/UNINSTALL	Removes cache and cache program
/SAVE	Saves current cache configuration in NCACHE initialization file
/DELAY=*ss.hh*	Specifies delay factor for IntelliWrites; default is 01:00 (one second) unless /OPTIMIZE is specified
/QUICK=ON|OFF	Enables or disables the return of the command prompt before delayed writes are completed
/REPORT [=ON|OFF]	Displays the full NCACHE report
/STATUS [=ON|OFF]	Displays partial NCACHE report
/[-]A	Activates or deactivates caching for a specific drive
/[-]C	Enables or disables caching
/[-]I	Enables or disables IntelliWrites
/[-]W	Enables or disables write-through caching
/[-]P	Enables or disables write protection for a specific drive
/R[=[D]*n*]	Limits sector read-aheads to *n* bytes; D specifies dynamic read-aheads, in which NCACHE decides when to read ahead; default is /R=D8
/G=*n*	Does not cache reads larger than *n* sectors
/F	Flushes cache for a specific drive

You can also deactivate the entire cache for a period of time, then reactivate it. To deactivate it, enter this command:

```
NCACHE /-A
```

When you're ready to reactivate it again, enter this command:

```
NCACHE /A
```

Deactivating the cache actually removes it from memory, letting another application have the memory space. If you just want to stop using the cache for a while, perhaps because an application is incompatible with it, use the /-C command:

```
NCACHE /-C
```

To start caching again, enter this command:

```
NCACHE /C
```

If you need to remove the cache program itself, along with the management tables and the cache, then you must completely uninstall it with the /UN-INSTALL parameter:

```
NCACHE /UNINSTALL
```

Like any other TSR, Norton Cache might not be in a proper position to be uninstalled. TSRs must be uninstalled in the reverse order that they were installed—last in, first out. So if you installed first a mouse driver, then Norton Cache, then Erase Protect, you must uninstall Erase Protect before you can uninstall Norton Cache, and you must uninstall Norton Cache before you could uninstall the mouse driver.

You also cannot uninstall Norton Cache if it was installed from CON-FIG.SYS. It must have been installed from the Command prompt or the AUTOEXEC.BAT file to be eligible for removal.

Once you have uninstalled Norton Cache, you can resume it again only by installing it from scratch. The former cache, and the former cache characteristics, will have been forgotten.

Controlling Individual Disks

Remember that you can cache different drives differently. For example, you could use IntelliWrites on your hard drive but not on your diskettes, you could disable caching on a particular drive without affecting the rest of the cache, and you can use different read-ahead factors for different drives. Any single-letter parameter name can be applied to an individual drive instead of the whole cache. Suppose you want to disable caching on drive A: for the next application. You would enter this command:

```
NCACHE A: /-A
```

Disabling IntelliWrites for Individual Drives

You might find that you don't like delaying writes to your diskette drives. You might not like taking the chance of removing a diskette before the writes are finished. Both /DELAY and /QUICK are general parameters, so you can't turn them on and off for specific drives. But IntelliWrites can be disabled for a specific drive, and by doing so, you also disable delays for that drive.

Suppose you want to start NCACHE using IntelliWrites and a two-second delay on drive C: but not on drive A: or B:. You would enter this command:

```
NCACHE /QUICK=ON /DELAY=2 A: /-I B: /-I
```

Flushing Data from the Cache

There can be situations where you want to flush all of one drive's data out of the cache, which you can do with the /F parameter. For example, suppose you want to write a file to drive A:, then examine the written version (not the cached version) to make sure nothing went wrong. You could flush the cached version with this command:

```
NCACHE A: /F
```

This flushes all of drive A:'s data out of the cache. If you enter /F without a drive name, it flushes the entire cache. You can also flush the entire cache with the /RESET parameter, which resets the cache to its initial state.

The Norton Cache Report

An example of Norton Cache's report is shown in Figure 4-2. The top part shows how the program, management tables, and cache are distributed in memory.

The **Total cache size** line tells you how much of the total cache is currently in use; it will be less than 100 percent when you haven't done a lot of work after installing the cache. The next section shows you what parameters are

Norton Cache, Norton Utilities 6.0, Copyright 1991 by Symantec Corporation

```
    Conventional memory:       128K cache    11K management    438K free
    High DOS memory:             0K cache    17K management      0K free
    Expanded (EMS) memory:       0K cache     0K management      0K free
    Extended (XMS) memory:       0K cache     0K management     11K free

       Total cache size is 128.0K - Currently using 44.0K  (34.3%)

DOS = 128K, 0K        BLOCK = 8192      USEHIGH  = ON        DELAY = 1.00
EXP = 0K, 0K          READ  = 8K        USEHMA   = ON        QUICK = ON
EXT = 0K, 0K          WRITE = 9K        OPTIMIZE = SPEED

        A   C   I   W   P      R      G      Cache Hits / Disk Reads
   A:   -   +   -   +   -      D8     128             0 / 0         (0.0%)
   B:   -   +   -   +   -      D8     128             0 / 0         (0.0%)
   C:   +   +   +   +   -      D8     128          3602 / 13371    (26.9%)
   D:   +   +   +   +   -      D8     128           106 / 1811      (5.8%)
```

Figure 4-2   Sample Norton Cache Report

in effect for the entire cache. The drive section at the lower left shows you
the options applied to each drive. The drive statistics on the lower right show
you how effective the cache has been so far, by drive. The cache hit ratio
shows the number of reads that have come from the cache and the total
number of reads. The percentage column interprets the hit ratio as a
percentage. Shortly after installing the cache, the hit ratio will be relatively
low, as the cache is not yet filled up. After a few minutes, the hit ratio for
your primary drive, at least, should be over 25 percent.

There's no way we can tell you what your hit ratios will reach; they're too
dependent on the characteristics of your cache and the applications you run.
But you can use the hit ratio statistics to find the best settings for your cache.
After performing normal work for a few hours, check your hit ratios. Then
reinstall your cache with a smaller or larger block size. A couple hours later,
check the hit ratios again. Keep adjusting the block size until you find your
maximum hit ratio. Then start to work on the read-ahead factors. When those
are maximized, start adjusting the time delay (if any). It might take several
days to discover the ideal settings for your system, but then you can relax
and use those settings every time, at least until you get new application
software that might require additional adjustments to the cache.

If you don't want to bother going through all that, you can rest assured
that you have significantly improved the performance of your system when
your hit ratios are over 25 percent.

The status screen, which is the top part of the full report, appears automatically every time you enter a command that changes the status of the cache. For example, when you install the cache, the status screen appears. It also appears when you disable/enable a drive, change the delay factor, and so on. You can display the status screen at any time by entering the following command:

```
NCACHE /STATUS
```

To display the full report, use this command:

```
NCACHE /REPORT
```

Looking Ahead

When you try out Norton Cache, you should notice a performance improvement with your applications. But that's not the only thing you can do to speed up your sluggish hard disk. The next chapter shows you two more programs that can make a dramatic difference in disk speed as well as reliability—Speed Disk and Calibrate. You should learn how to use both of these programs to set up your hard disk(s) for maximum performance.

5

SPEED DISK AND CALIBRATE

Speed Disk and Calibrate reorganize the data on your hard disk(s) for the fastest possible access. In addition, Calibrate can redo a hard disk's physical formatting to make it more reliable. To get your hard disk(s) in tip-top shape, you should probably run both programs right away (as soon as you finish reading this chapter). Then repeat them both periodically to keep your disks in good condition.

Speed Disk

Speed Disk reorganizes a hard disk to minimize read-write arm movements. This process is called *optimizing*, because it helps you achieve optimum disk speeds.

Background

Every time you access a different track on a hard disk, the read-write arm must move the recording heads to a new position—an agonizingly slow process (relative to computer speeds). The farther the distance to be moved, the longer it takes. Speed Disk's goal is to reduce the number of arm movements that are necessary as well as the distance of each arm movement. The four steps it takes to achieve that goal are explained in the following paragraphs.

123

Unfragmenting Files

Because DOS usually uses the first available clusters when it adds a new file to the disk or expands an existing one, a file might not get stored in adjacent clusters. For example, a new five-cluster file will be stored in clusters 105, 127, 210, 211, and 1014 if those are the first available clusters. Such a file is considered to be *fragmented* because its clusters do not form one consecutive chunk.

Fragmentation doesn't hurt a file, and DOS has no trouble retrieving all of it, but retrieval will be slower because of the extra arm movements involved in getting from fragment to fragment. Speed Disk speeds up file access by unfragmenting all the files on a hard disk. It actually moves the clusters around so that every file ends up in one piece.

Consolidating Free Space

New files get fragmented because deleted files leave individual available clusters (*free space*, in other words) scattered among the used clusters. Speed Disk will reorganize the clusters so that all available clusters come together at the end of the file area, inhibiting future fragmentation until more files are deleted.

Figure 5-1 shows what the file area looks like before and after consolidation. In the "before" half, unused clusters are spread all over the disk. In the "after" half, all the unused clusters have been moved to the end of the file area.

Optimizing Directories

The most heavily used objects on any disk are the root directory and the FAT. DOS must access each of them at least once in order to access every file. Next in line come the subdirectories, which are accessed much more frequently than any individual file. Since DOS might have to go back and forth among the root directory, the FAT, and a subdirectory several times to accomplish a single task, a lot of time will be saved if all subdirectories are located as close as possible to the root directory and the FAT. Speed Disk can reorganize a hard disk to position all subdirectories at the beginning of the file area, just after the FATs and the system files.

Optimizing Files

Again, to shorten arm movements, Speed Disk will move your most heavily used files so that they immediately follow the subdirectories.

(a)

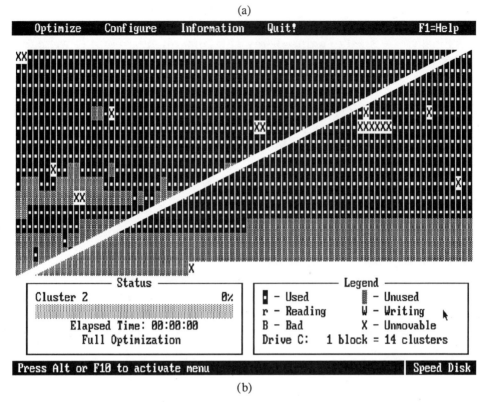

(b)

Figure 5-1   Effect of Consolidation

Other Speed Disk Functions

For your convenience, Speed Disk will also sort the entries in your directories in whatever order you specify: name, extension, date, or size. Additionally, you can obtain reports on disk usage, file fragmentation, and other factors that would influence your Speed Disk decisions.

Getting Ready for Speed Disk

Before you use Speed Disk the first time, you should back up each disk you plan to optimize. Some older disk controllers cannot handle Speed Disk's high-speed reading and writing and produce inaccurate results. If this happens to you, you will be able to restore your files from the backup copies.

If you suspect any problems with the disk's physical formatting–for example, if you have been getting intermittent read-write errors–you might want to run Calibrate before running Speed Disk. We'll talk about Calibrate later in this chapter.

Finally, you need to uninstall any TSRs that might attempt to write to the disk while it is being optimized. For example, if you have set an alarm that would copy something to the disk, be sure to disable it. Keep in mind that TSRs must be uninstalled in the reverse order that they were installed. So if you need to uninstall KEEPER, but MOUSE and GRABBER were installed after it, you would need to uninstall GRABBER, then MOUSE, and then KEEPER. (You have to look in each TSR's documentation to find out how to uninstall it.)

Running Speed Disk

Speed Disk must be installed before you can use it. To start Speed Disk from the Norton menu, select **Speed Disk** from the **Speed** section. Or you can enter either SPEEDISK or SD at the DOS prompt. Which command you enter depends on how your utilities were installed; if you're not sure, try them both. If you start Speed Disk from the DOS prompt, you can add whatever switches you would use to start the Norton menu (/G0, /G1, etc.).

Initial Screens

The first thing you'll see is a dialog box that says "Testing System Memory." Because Speed Disk must run most of the data on the hard disk through memory while reorganizing it, this test makes sure that memory appears reliable. If not, a message will warn you, and you should not use Speed Disk until you have had your memory repaired or replaced.

Next, you'll see the dialog box shown in Figure 5-2, in which you select the desired drive. Ignore the **Status** and **Legend** boxes for now; they become important later on.

Speed Disk analyzes the selected drive, producing a map and a recommendation somewhat like the screen shown in Figure 5-3. The map shows the layout of used clusters, unused clusters, bad clusters, and unmovable files. The **Legend** box helps you interpret the map.

The recommendation tells you what percentage of your files are not fragmented; the rest are fragmented. It also recommends the type of optimization you should do. In many cases, full optimization is recommended: that would include unfragmenting files, consolidating free space, optimizing directories, and optimizing files.

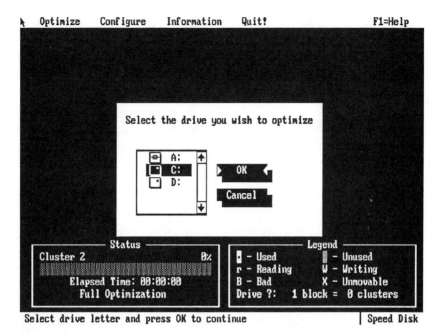

Figure 5-2   Drive Selection

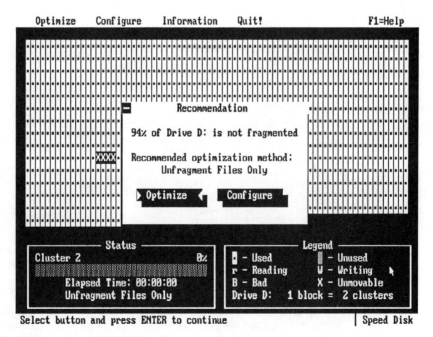

Figure 5-3   Speed Disk Recommendation

If you select **Optimize**, the recommended method of optimizing is invoked, using all the default options. If you choose **Configure** or press Esc, the **Configure** menu is pulled down so that you can set up the Speed Disk options you want to use.

> **Tip:** The first time you use Speed Disk, select **Configure** or press Esc so that you can set up Speed Disk for your own needs.

Getting Additional Information

Before you begin to configure Speed Disk, you should check out the reports available from the **Information** menu, which is shown in Figure 5-4. After you close the initial dialog box, the **Configure** menu is automatically pulled down. You can use the Right arrow key to move over to the **Information** menu.

The **Disk statistics** option opens a dialog box that shows the number of files, the number of directories, and so on. You can see an example of the Disk Statistics dialog box in Figure 5-5.

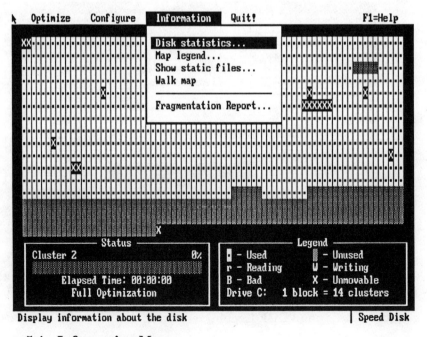

Figure 5-4   Information Menu

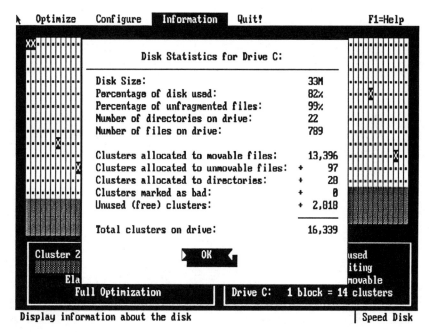

Figure 5-5   Disk Statistics

Most of the information will be self-explanatory, but notice the two fields dealing with movable and unmovable files. Any file or directory with the hidden or system attribute is considered unmovable; so is any file that belongs to an unmovable directory. This protects the DOS system files, which must be first on the disk (before subdirectories), the IMAGE.DAT file, which should be last on the disk, and other location-sensitive files. Unmovable files and directories will not be optimized; that is, they will not be repositioned or unfragmented.

> **Tip:** If you have hidden or system files or directories that you know are not location sensitive, and you would like them to be optimized, remove the inhibiting attribute with Disk Editor (Chapter 14 explains how). You can restore the removed attribute after optimization.

The **Map legend** option from the **Information** menu opens the dialog box shown in Figure 5-6, which gives a more complete legend for the drive map than can be shown on the main Speed Disk screen. You might need the

```
↖  Optimize    Configure   Information    Quit!                    F1=Help
╔═════════════════════════════════════════════════════════════════════╗
║XX                                                                     ║
║                                                                       ║
║            ┌─────────────────────────────────────────┐               ║
║            │              Disk Map Legend             │               ║
║            │  ───────────────────────────────────     │ X             ║
║            │  █  - Disk space used by files           │               ║
║            │  ▓  - Disk space optimized already       │               ║
║            │  ░  - Unused disk space                  │               ║
║          X │  X  - Disk space used by files that will not be moved    ║
║            │  B  - Bad disk space (untouched by Speed Disk)  X         ║
║            │  r  - Disk space that is being read      │               ║
║            │  W  - Disk space that is being written   │               ║
║            │  V  - Disk space that is being verified  │               ║
║            │  C  - Unused disk space that is being cleared│            ║
║            │                                          │               ║
║            │            ▶  OK  ◀                       │               ║
║            └─────────────────────────────────────────┘               ║
║  Cluster                                              ed              ║
║  ┌──────────────────────────┐  ┌──────────────────────────────────┐  ║
║  │    Elapsed Time: 00:00:00 │  │ r - Reading       W - Writing    │  ║
║  │    Full Optimization      │  │ B - Bad           X - Unmovable  │  ║
║  └──────────────────────────┘  │ Drive C:  1 block = 14 clusters  │  ║
╚═════════════════════════════════════════════════════════════════════╝
  Show the map symbols definitions                        │ Speed Disk
```

Figure 5-6   Map Legend

additional information during the optimization process itself, when many of the additional symbols will appear on your screen.

The **Show static files** option lists the unmovable files, somewhat like the list shown in Figure 5-7. This list is not editable in this dialog box, but you can build and edit an additional list of files you don't want moved by using the **Unmovable files** option from the **Configure** menu, which you'll see shortly. If **Show static files** is not available, there are no unmovable files on the currently selected disk.

The **Walk map** option makes the map available for you to examine individual blocks. (Actually, you can do this any time no menu is down and no dialog box is showing.) A map block is not necessarily the same as a cluster. Speed Disk always constructs the map to fit on the screen no matter how big the drive is; therefore, each map block might represent one cluster (for a 360K diskette) or many clusters (for a hard disk). The **Legend** box tells you how many clusters are represented by one block for the current map. In the example in Figure 5-7, each block represents 14 clusters.

When a map block represents more than one cluster, some of the clusters might be used, some unused, some bad, and some unmovable. A block is marked as unused if any cluster is unused, bad if any cluster is bad, and

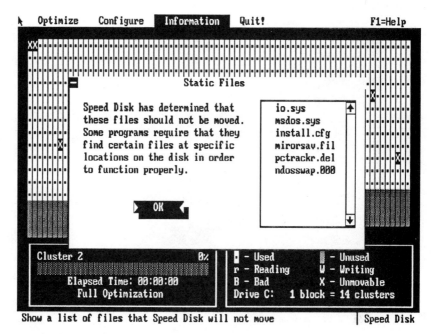

Figure 5-7   Static Files

unmovable if any cluster is unmovable. It is marked as used only if it contains no unused, unmovable, or bad clusters.

On the walk map, when you select a block (by highlighting it and pressing Enter or by clicking on it), a dialog box like the one in Figure 5-8 appears. You can see whether each cluster is used, unused, or bad. For clusters containing files, you can see the filename and whether it is fragmented, optimized (unfragmented), or unmovable.

The **Fragmentation Report** option produces a report like that shown in Figure 5-9. It shows a directory tree on the left so that you can select the desired directory. The box on the right shows fragmentation information for every file in the highlighted directory. The % column tells you how much of the file is contained in the main fragment.

If the subdirectory you want isn't showing in the directory tree box, you can scroll to it. Or you can use the Speed Search facility by starting to type its name. The highlight will jump to the next directory whose name starts with the letters you have typed so far. If that's not the one you want, you can type more letters of the name or press Ctrl-Enter to jump to the next directory name with the same beginning.

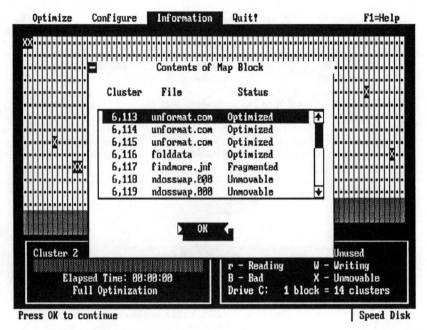

Figure 5-8   Map Block Contents

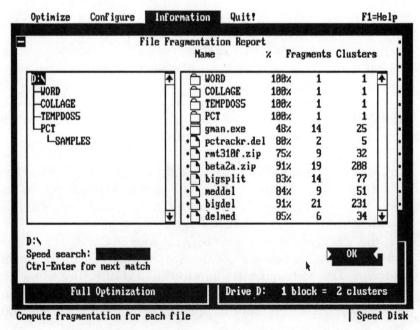

Figure 5-9   Fragmentation Report

Configuring Speed Disk

By the time you're finished checking information about the drive, you should have a pretty good idea what its problems are. Then you're ready to set up Speed Disk to solve them. You use the **Configure** menu, shown in Figure 5-10, to set up Speed Disk as you need it.

Directory Order

The **Directory order** option opens the dialog box shown in Figure 5-11, which you use to specify the order of the directories at the beginning of the data area. Once again, a directory tree appears on the left. On the right is the current directory order.

DOS uses a parameter called a *path*, which specifies directories to search when looking for programs. Whenever DOS can't find a program in the current directory, it searches every directory in the path, in the order listed, until it finds the desired program file. Therefore, the path directories are your most heavily used directories, with the first listed directory being the most heavily used, the second directory next, and so on. The path is established by a PATH command, which is usually included in your

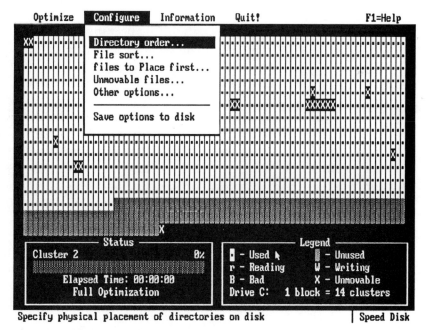

Figure 5-10   Configure Menu

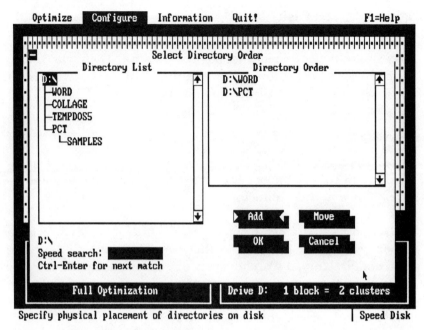

Figure 5-11   Directory Order Dialog Box

AUTOEXEC.BAT file to set the path during booting. You can see what your path is at any time by entering the following command at the DOS prompt:

```
PATH
```

By default, Speed Disk places the path directories in order at the beginning of the directory section. Since these are your most heavily accessed directories, you should leave them there. But if there are nonpath directories that you access often, you can add them to the **Directory Order** list. For example, if your work is primarily word processing, and you keep your current document files in the C:\DOCS directory, you should add it to the list.

> **Note:** If your path includes directories from more than one drive, only the directories on the drive being optimized are listed in the **Directory Order** box.

To add a directory to the list, highlight it in the **Directory List** box (you can use Speed Search to find it), then select the **Add** button. The directory will appear at the top of the list. Move it down to follow the path directories by highlighting it in the **Directory Order** box and selecting the **Move** button; alternatively, you can press the spacebar or click right on it. Pointers (➤) appear indicating that this is the directory to be moved. Then click on the desired position; the other directories move up and down as necessary. From the keyboard, use the Down arrow and Up arrow keys to move the directory to the desired new position. When the directory appears in the desired position, simply leave it there and go on to any other actions you need to do.

You can delete a directory from the list by highlighting its name in the **Directory Order** box, which causes the **Add** button to change into a **Delete** button. Select the **Delete** button to delete the directory.

When you're finished editing the **Directory Order** list, select **OK** to save it and close the dialog box. If you select **Cancel** instead, all your editing will be dropped and the original order will be reestablished.

Files to Place First

Use the **files to Place first** option to put heavily used files right after the directories, once again minimizing arm movements. Figure 5-12 shows the dialog box that opens when you select this option.

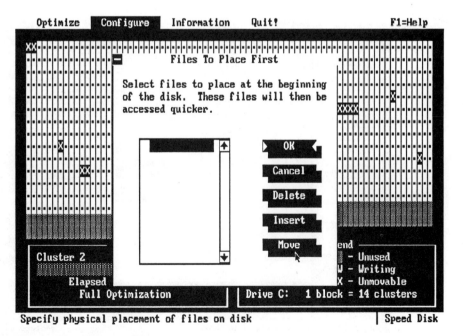

Figure 5-12   Files to Place First

You probably want to put program files (EXE and COM files) first because they are usually your most heavily used files. You might want to put their data files next. For example, if you use WordPerfect, you might want to put all WP*.* files next. Your most heavily used document files might come next: the database or spreadsheet that you work on every day, your appointment schedule file, and so on.

To add an item to the end of the list, position the cursor after the last item and type the new item. You can use a specific or global filename. To add an item in the middle of the list, position the cursor where you want the item to appear and select the **Insert** button; a blank space opens up so you can type the filename.

To delete an item, highlight it and press **Delete**. To move an item, tag it with the Move button, then move it just like you move a directory in the **Directory Order** list.

Unmovable Files

The **Unmovable files** option opens the dialog box shown in Figure 5-13. Any filenames that you enter in this box are included in the list of unmovable files. You would need to add files to the list only if they can't be moved for some reason.

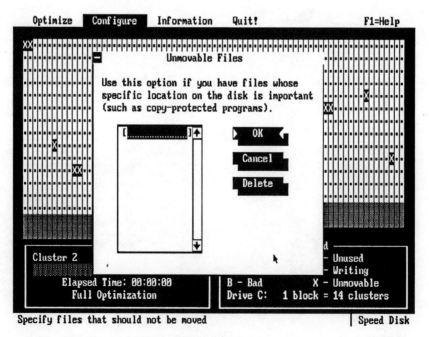

Figure 5-13   Unmovable Files Dialog Box

Other Options

The **Other options** item from the **Configure** menu opens the dialog box shown in Figure 5-14. The first option controls whether Speed Disk verifies data after it's moved. Verification takes longer, but the results are worth it.

> **Tip:** Don't try to optimize your disk in a hurry. Since Speed Disk will be moving most of your directories, programs, and essential data files, use the read-after-write option to make sure the result is 100 percent accurate.

The second option on this dialog box wipes data out of the unused area by overwriting it with nonsense data. If you have recently deleted confidential data, this will remove any traces of it from the disk. If you're genuinely concerned about removing all vestiges of former data from the disk, however, use WipeInfo instead. (WipeInfo is explained in Chapter 7.)

The third option simply beeps when the optimization is done. Optimization can take a long time and you'll probably go off and do something else while it's working. The beep lets you know that your computer is available again.

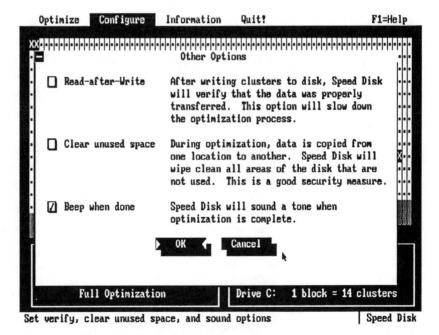

Figure 5-14   Other Options Dialog Box

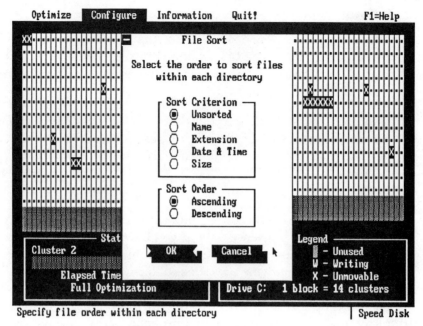

Figure 5-15   File Sort Dialog Box

Sorting Files

Files are listed in your directories in whatever order DOS adds them to the directory, with newer files replacing deleted files. When you list a directory with the default DOS DIR command or examine the directory with Disk Editor, the file entries seem to be in arbitrary order. If you would prefer the file entries to have some logical order, Speed Disk will do it for you. This will not make the access time any more efficient, but it might make your life a little easier.

To sort the file entries, select the **File sort** option from the **Configure** menu, which opens the dialog box shown in Figure 5-15. Select the sort criterion and order you would like. Then close the box again.

> **Note:** File sort does not sort the files themselves, just their directory entries.

Saving Your Configuration

Once you have set up Speed Disk with the best configuration for your disk, you can save it for future use by selecting **Save options to disk** from the

Configure menu. This saves your settings for all options on the **Configure** menu (plus the optimization method that you'll see soon) so that they will be the defaults the next time you optimize the same drive.

The settings are saved in a hidden file named SD.INI, which is placed in the root directory of the selected drive but is physically located at the end of the disk (along with IMAGE.DAT, if that file exists). SD.INI is specific to one drive. It will be used the next time you optimize the same drive. If you optimize another drive, Speed Disk will use that drive's SD.INI file or the default configuration if there is no SD.INI.

If you don't save your configuration, it will be used one time but will not be remembered after you terminate Speed Disk.

Doing the Optimization

After you have set up the configuration, you are nearly ready to start the optimization process, which is done from the **Optimize** menu shown in Figure 5-16. But you might still need to select an optimization method other than the recommended one. Figure 5-17 shows the dialog box that appears when you select **Optimization Method**.

You can select only one optimization method, but selecting any of the **Full** methods includes unfragmenting files and moving free space. **Full with**

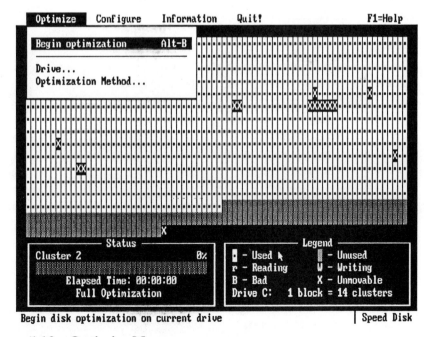

Figure 5-16   Optimize Menu

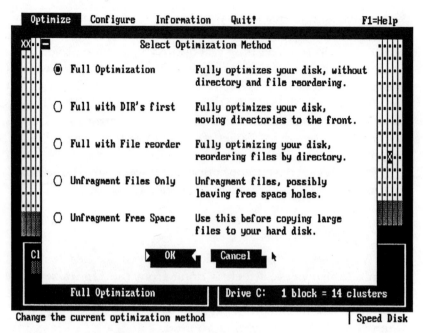

Figure 5-17   Optimization Method Dialog Box

DIR's first also moves directories, while **Full with File reorder** also moves files.

When you close the **Optimization Method** dialog box, return to the **Optimize** menu and select **Begin Optimization** (or press Alt-B). Speed Disk shows you what is happening as the optimization progresses. You will see the blocks on the map being read, written, verified, and completed. The **Status** box shows the percent completion and time elapsed, so if you don't care to watch, you know approximately when to come back. A dialog box tells you when it's finished and gives you the choice of selecting another drive to optimize, changing the configuration, or exiting Speed Disk.

If you chose to do another drive, that drive is analyzed just as the initial one was when you started Speed Disk, and a recommendation is displayed. Once again you will probably want to select **Configure** to set up the best configuration for the new drive, which can be saved in SD.INI.

The SPEEDISK Command

If you don't care to go through the Speed Disk screens, menus, and dialog boxes, you can use the SPEEDISK command, which has this format:

```
SPEEDISK or SD [drive:] [switches]
```

Table 5-1   Speed Disk Command Switches

/F	Full disk optimization
/FD	Full optimization with directories first
/FF	Full optimization with file reorder
/U	Unfragment files only
/Q	Quick compress: Combine free space only
/SN [-]	Sort files by Name (use – for descending order)
/SE [-]	Sort files by Extension (use – for descending order)
/SD [-]	Sort files by Date (use – for descending order)
/SS [-]	Sort files by Size (use – for descending order)
/V	Turn read-after-write Verify on
/B	Reboot computer after optimization

Table 5-1 shows the switches that are specific to this command. If you don't enter a drive name, the current drive is used. Any options that you don't specify with the switches are taken from SD.INI for the indicated drive. For example, if you want to do a full optimization plus optimize directories on drive D:, you would enter this command:

```
SPEEDISK D: /FD
```

or

```
SD D: /FD
```

The order of the directories will be taken from SD.INI on drive D:.

When you enter a command that includes a drive name and/or any switches, the initial Speed Disk screens and dialog boxes are bypassed. The specified optimization is begun immediately, with the progress screen displayed. When the optimization is finished, Speed Disk terminates itself and returns to the DOS prompt with no further dialog boxes or messages.

Calibrate

Calibrate performs two major functions that can improve not only the speed but also the reliability of your hard disk. The first function deals with your disk's *interleave factor*, which bears some explaining. DOS reads and writes data one sector at a time. To read two sectors in a row, it starts with the first sector, taking the time to store that data in memory. By the time it returns to read the second sector, the beginning of the sector has already spun past the read-write heads, and we must wait nearly a full revolution for it to return.

We can shorten the wait by rearranging the data to use every other sector, interleaving the sectors so that a 17-sector track looks like this: 1 10 2 11 3 12 4 13 5 14 6 15 7 16 8 17 9. Now by the time we return from reading sector 1, sector 2 is approaching the read-write heads and we can access it with a minimum wait. Since the track is circular, it wraps around at the end so that sector 10 is two positions after sector 9, just where it should be.

This example represents an interleave factor of 2:1, but some hardware might function most efficiently with a factor of 3:1 or even higher. A factor of 3:1 would look like this: 1 7 13 2 8 14 3 9 15 4 10 16 5 11 17 6 12. Calibrate is capable of determining your hard disk's best possible interleave factor and converting it to that factor.

Calibrate's second function is to redo the low-level (physical) formatting on the disk. A hard disk goes through three formatting stages: physical (low-level), partitioning, and high-level (logical). Each of these three is handled by a different program. The low-level formatting, which lays out the sectors on the disk, is usually done at the factory. It involves marking every sector and storing the checksums.

When a hard disk is in constant use, its physical formatting can begin to deteriorate, making some of the sectors impossible to access and perhaps causing DOS to refuse to access an entire file. Many factors can contribute to deteriorating physical formatting: degradation of the magnetic coating, slight realignment of the read-write arm, hardware malfunctions, power fluctuations, and user (that's you) interruptions are the most common. The last is caused when you power down or reboot while the sector is still being written and before the checksum can be brought up to date. You can avoid this by never powering down or rebooting when a disk access light is on.

Since low-level formatting involves a write-then-read test of every sector, most format programs cannot revive the physical format on the disk without destroying all existing data, but Calibrate can. It copies each sector into memory, tests the sector as much as you want, then restores it from the copy in memory. Therefore, you can use Calibrate to refresh the physical format on your hard disk with perfect reliability and safety.

You should use Calibrate as soon as possible to check and optimize your interleave factor as well as to refresh your low-level format. Then you should rerun it periodically (every 2 to 3 months) to keep your low-level format in good condition. And if you run into read-write errors on the disk, use Calibrate to identify and fix the problem.

> **Note:** If a sector does go bad—that is, the magnetic coating has become unreliable—Calibrate will find it, rescue as much data as possible from it, and block it out so it can't be used anymore.

Limitations

Calibrate can work only on unshared hard disks; it cannot handle diskettes, network drives, nor any kind of pseudo drive such as a RAM drive. (Disk Tools, which is explained in Chapter 12, can refresh the low-level formatting on a diskette.) It also can't change the interleave on hard disks with certain types of controllers. It will display a detailed explanation if it can't change your interleave.

Starting Calibrate

The Norton Utilities must be installed in order to use Calibrate. Also, it's a good idea to back up your hard disk before you use it the first time. Calibrate is incompatible with some types of disk controllers, such as translating controllers (some ESDI controllers) and those that do not permit interleave modifications (SCSI or IDE controllers). If you're not sure whether Calibrate is compatible with your controller, back up your drive(s) before you run Calibrate. (After the first time, you'll know whether it's compatible or not.)

To start Calibrate, select **Calibrate** from the **Speed** section of the Norton menu or enter CALIBRAT at the DOS prompt. The first dialog box briefly explains the utility and gives you a choice to **Continue** or **Quit**.

After you select **Continue**, the next dialog box lets you select the drive you want to calibrate.

System Tests

The next dialog box, which is shown in Figure 5-18, describes some general system tests that Calibrate performs before doing the actual calibration. When you select **Continue** on this dialog box, you will see a series of dialog boxes showing you the progress and results of these tests. The seek tests provide an animated display as they put your hard drive through its paces. Calibrate pauses after most of these tests so you can read the results and select **Continue**. You can safely interrupt the tests by selecting the **Stop** button if you decide not to continue; no harm will be done to your hard disk by interrupting a test.

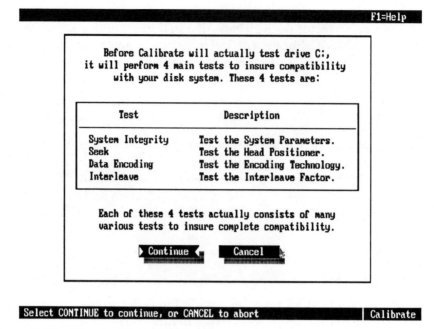

Figure 5-18   System Tests Dialog Box

The final test that is conducted in this series finds the ideal interleave. Figure 5-19 shows the display that is built on your screen as Calibrate tries out first a 1:1 interleave factor, then 2:1, and so on.

> **Note:** Calibrate will not test or display the interleave factor on hard disks where it can't change the interleave.

When Calibrate pauses after the interleave test, the graphic shows you several things. Each bar shows the number of revolutions that would be necessary to read an entire track using the indicated interleave factor. The word **Current** marks your current interleave while the word **Optimal** marks the best one. The bracket encloses the selected setting and the note box at the center top tells you how much performance improvement that represents. You can move the bracket to other interleave factors with the Left and Right arrow keys or by clicking on them. The message in the note box changes accordingly.

The position of the bracket identifies the interleave factor that will be set during the calibration, so if you move it away from the optimal setting, be

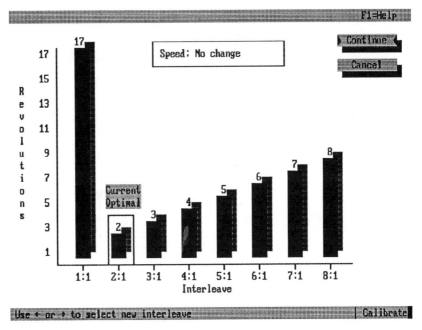

Figure 5-19   Interleave Test Display

sure to move it back again before selecting **Continue**. (If you don't want to change the interleave factor, move it to the current setting and select **Continue**.)

Pattern Tests

Figure 5-20 shows the dialog box that appears next. The pattern test is where the calibration actually takes place. You must indicate how thoroughly the disk surface should be tested during the pattern test.

If all you want to do is change your interleave factor, and you're not concerned about locating bad sectors, you can select **No Pattern Testing**.

If you select **Minimal Pattern Testing**, Calibrate tests each sector five times, using its five most difficult "patterns;" that is, five values that are especially difficult to write reliably on a disk surface. This is enough testing to find many errors, but it might not find them all.

For a more thorough test, select **Standard Pattern Testing**, which tests each sector with 40 different, difficult patterns. Standard testing will reveal most surface problems.

If you're experiencing an intermittent error and Calibrate doesn't find it with standard testing, you might have to resort to **Rigorous Pattern Testing**,

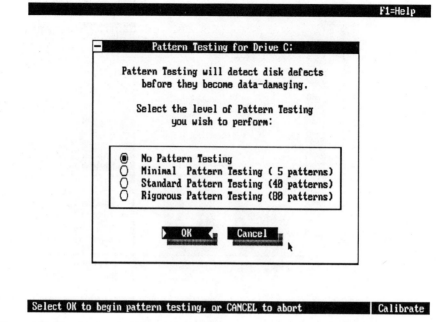

Figure 5-20   Pattern Test Dialog Box

which uses 80 different patterns on each sector. A rigorous test can take several hours on a large hard disk, but it should weed out sectors that are only marginally weak.

The Calibration Process

After you identify the level of pattern testing and select **OK,** the actual calibration begins. Figure 5-21 shows the progress screen that is displayed while the calibration takes place. The disk map is animated so you can see how things are going. The three progress boxes at the lower left help you determine how much longer the process will take. The **Finish** time will be adjusted frequently at first as Calibrate measures its own progress with your hard disk, but eventually it will settle down to an accurate prediction.

It is never wise to leave any one display on your monitor for long periods of time—it could "burn in" on some monitors (that is, it creates a permanent image on the screen). Since Calibrate might run for several hours, it includes a facility to replace the progress screen with a simple white-on-black message that moves every few seconds. All you have to do is press the Spacebar to

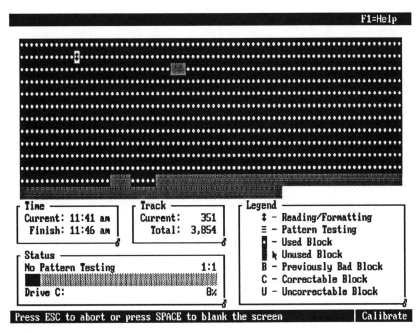

Figure 5-21   Calibrate Progress Screen

toggle back and forth between the full progress screen and the simple message. The message shows you the percentage of completion so you can estimate when the job will be done.

Calibrate Summary and Report

When the calibration is finished, a brief summary of the results appears on the screen. When you close that dialog box, the next box displays a detailed report, which you can view on the screen, print, and/or save in a disk file. The report shows disk characteristics, the results of all the various tests, and the results of the calibration.

Winding Up Calibrate

After you decide what to do with the report, Calibrate returns to the drive selection dialog box. You can select another drive and repeat the entire process, or you can select **Cancel** to terminate Calibrate.

Looking Ahead

Are you worried about viruses? Do you know what they are and how they get into your system? The next chapter explains a bit about viruses (and other problems) and how to use Disk Monitor to counteract them. Even if you think a virus will never happen to you, you should read at least the beginning of the chapter. You'd be surprised how vulnerable even the smallest computer system can be. (Disk Monitor also has a couple other functions you should know about.)

6

DISK MONITOR

If you're concerned about the security of your data—and everyone should be in this age of viruses—one of the programs that you should use on a regular basis is Disk Monitor, which has three major functions:

- The *Disk Protect* function prevents any unauthorized writes to your disks. You can protect your system areas, specific files, a combination of the system areas and specific files, or entire disks. Disk Protect slows down your applications a bit, of course, but it also lets you know when an unexpected program, such as a virus, is trying to write to your disk.

- The *Disk Light* function tells you when a drive is being accessed. The drive name appears in the upper-right corner of your screen whenever a disk is read or written. If you use a network drive or have your system unit hidden under your work stand where you can't see the drive lights, then Disk Light lets you know when it's safe to pop a diskette out of a drive or shut off the power.

- The *Disk Park* function parks your hard drive read-write heads when not in use. That is, it positions them over an unused area of the disk so that, if something or someone bumps your computer when the power is off, causing the read-write heads to crash into the disk surface, little harm is done. Many hard-drive units automatically park their own heads, but if yours doesn't, then you should park them whenever you power down, just in case.

A Brief Introduction to Viruses

A virus is a computer program that lies dormant in your computer for a while, then comes to life and begins wreaking havoc by indiscriminately erasing files from your hard disk, inserting invalid data in programs and/or files, and so on. A virus doesn't happen by accident; it's a very clever program created by someone who intends to do harm—out of malice, boredom, a twisted sense of humor, or just to prove that they can.

Viruses can be devilishly difficult to identify. They can be very short code buried in the middle of a seemingly innocent and useful program. Disk Monitor can prevent them from functioning by identifying and blocking any unauthorized writes to your disks.

How do viruses get into your system? The probability of a popular, name-brand program containing a virus is nearly null. But if you use freeware or shareware, or if you download software from a bulletin board (and that includes the major, nationwide on-line services), the chances can increase greatly. And, of course, if your system is set up so that other people can dial into it and upload programs onto your hard disk, your system is at great risk. The less you know about the source of a program, the more likely it is to contain a virus.

> **Note:** Symantec offers a separate program, called Norton AntiVirus, which gives you the most complete virus protection. It searches your disk for known virus strains, eliminating any that it finds, and monitors all work done on your system for virus-type activity.

Runaway Programs

Another form of software that can damage your system is a runaway program, which could be likened to an unintentional virus. A runaway program gets into a situation where it keeps writing to the disk after it should stop, going beyond the limits of its own files and into other areas of the disk. This can happen when a program has not been completely tested and perfected before you use it.

As with viruses, you are not in much danger of a runaway program when using name-brand software. But again, watch out for freeware, shareware, downloaded or uploaded software, and the like. Also, any software that is still in the development stages can be dangerous: prereleases of new applications, something a friend developed and wants you to try out, or something that you have developed yourself.

Starting Disk Monitor

You can start Disk Monitor from the Norton menu by selecting the **Disk Monitor** option from the **Security** section. To start it from the DOS prompt, enter the command DISKMON. (Disk Monitor command switches are explained later in this chapter.) Figure 6-1 shows the screen that appears when you first start Disk Monitor.

Using Disk Protect

The first option in the Disk Monitor dialog box, **Disk Protect**, is the one that protects your disk drives against unauthorized access. When you select it, the dialog box shown in Figure 6-2 appears. You use this dialog box to identify the level of protection desired and to specify which files should be protected, if that's appropriate.

If you protect the system areas, the Partition Table, Boot Record, system files, and COMMAND.COM are protected. This level of protection counteracts viruses and runaway programs that attack the system itself, but at the same time it lets you create, modify, and delete directories and files without interference (notice that the root directory and FAT are not protected).

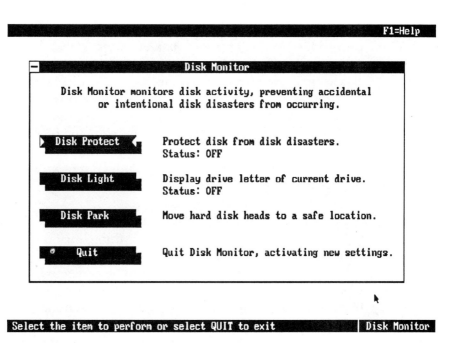

Figure 6-1   Disk Monitor Screen

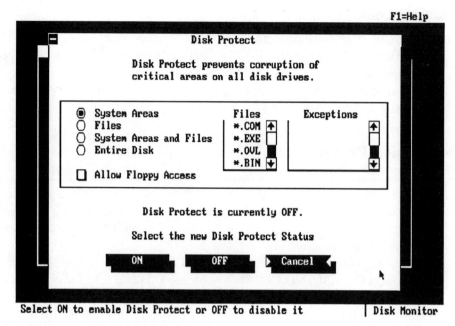

Figure 6-2   Disk Protect Dialog Box

If you protect files, then all the files that match the global filenames in the **Files** list box are protected, while any specific filenames listed in the **Exceptions** list box are excluded from protection. Any other files are not protected; nor are the system areas, the unused clusters, or directories.

By default, the **Files** box includes all program files; that is, all files with extension COM, EXE, OVL, BIN, and SYS. These are the files most likely to be attacked by viruses and least likely to be written to otherwise. However, you might find that some programs write to their own program files. If you find that you have a program like this, you might want to except its files from protection, just for convenience.

To protect both the system areas and the specified files, select the **System Areas and Files** radio button. To protect everything, including all files and unused clusters, select **Entire Disk**.

By the way, you can't select specific drives to be protected; by default, all drives are protected. However, to make life a little more convenient, **Allow Floppy Access** excludes your floppy drives from protection.

Once you have set up the protection features you want to work with, select the **On** button to install the Disk Monitor TSR, turn protection on, and return to the Disk Monitor main screen.

Once protection is on, you might find times when you want to turn it off again. To disable protection entirely, select **Disk Protect** to return to the Disk Protect dialog box and select **Off** or enter the following command at the DOS prompt:

```
DISKMON /PROTECT-
```

The current setup (level of protection, files included and excluded, and floppy protection) is retained for the next time you turn it on.

In some situations you might want to just lower the level of protection from **Entire Disk** to **System Areas and Files.** You can do this by returning to the Disk Protect dialog box, selecting the **System Areas** option, and selecting **On** again.

How Disk Protection Works

When you turn disk protection on, a TSR (Terminate and Stay Resident program—see page 92) is installed in memory to monitor all writes to disks; writes include not only new files and changes to files, but also deletions and updates to directories and the FAT. If you add a new file, several writes might be involved, both to the file area, the appropriate directory, and the FAT. If the entire disk is protected, you might have to respond to several disk-protect messages to complete the writing of just one sector.

Whenever Disk Monitor senses a write to a protected area, it interrupts your current work to ask for permission to write. If your monitor is currently in text mode—for example, if you're working at the DOS prompt or using a nongraphics word processor such as WordStar—then Disk Monitor pops up a dialog box like the one in Figure 6-3. If you select **Yes,** the write operation continues. (The dialog box might pop up several times in a row as DOS attempts to update the directory and the FAT.)

```
c:\>del autoexec.bat
Deleting c:\autoexec.bat
```

Figure 6-3   Write Attempt Dialog Box

If you select **No,** DOS tells the program attempting the write that a write-protection error occurred. The next thing you might see is a message from the program saying that the disk or file is write-protected.

If you select **Disable Protection,** then the write is permitted and protection is turned off. If you disable write protection so that you're not interrupted during an important task, don't forget to enable it again later.

If your monitor is currently in graphics mode, Disk Monitor can't pop up the dialog box. Instead, it simply beeps and rejects the write operation. You'll probably see an error message from your graphics-mode application that the disk is write-protected.

Tip: We suggest that you include a DISKMON command in your AUTOEXEC.BAT file to protect your system areas at all times; no programs should ever write to these areas without your knowing about it. If you are about to run a high-risk program such as an untested or a shareware program, then increase your level of protection to include the entire hard disk during the time that the program is in operation. For newly installed freeware or shareware, you might protect your system areas and your program files for several days, just to be on the safe side.

Using Disk Light

Has Norton Disk Doctor or DOS's CHKDSK ever found a bunch of orphaned and cross-linked clusters on one of your disks? How did they get there in an otherwise healthy system? Is DOS slightly flawed, so that it makes occasional, small mistakes when writing to the FAT? Are read-write heads just a touch unreliable, so that occasionally they write the wrong number in the FAT? Do microscopic magnetic particles fly through the air and land on your hard disk, changing a bit here and there? Or is this the work of disk devils?

The answer is: None of the above. In an undamaged system, FAT errors can occur when DOS is interrupted before it can complete updating the FAT for file and directory changes. The interruption is often the result of power failures or surges, but it can also be caused by a user who reboots, powers down, or ejects a diskette too early. The lights on your disk drives tell you when the disk unit is being accessed, and you should avoid rebooting, powering down, or ejecting the busy diskette when a light is on.

But what if you have a drive whose light you can't see? For example, what if you use a network drive, a RAM drive, or drive on a card? Or what if you have your system unit hidden somewhere so that you can't see the drive lights? Then you can use the Disk Light option to display the equivalent of a

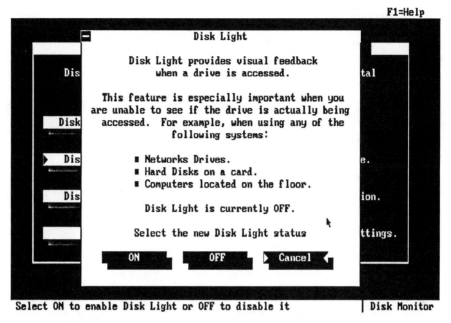

Figure 6-4   Disk Light Dialog Box

drive light right on your screen, so that you know when your drives are being accessed.

The second option in the Disk Monitor dialog box, **Disk Light**, calls up the dialog box shown in Figure 6-4. To turn Disk Light on, select the **On** button. To turn it off again, return to this dialog box and select **Off**.

When Disk Light is on and the screen is in text mode, a small box appears in the upper-right corner of your screen whenever a disk is accessed. The box contains the name of the drive and an arrow indicating whether the drive is being read (→) or written (←). The box tends to flash on and off as several short reads or writes occur in a row. If you have any hidden drives, always check the Disk Light before powering down or popping a diskette. This is doubly important when you are using Norton Cache with delayed writes.

When the screen is in graphics mode, such as when you are working with Windows or DOS Shell, the Disk Light cannot be displayed. You should always terminate such programs and return to the Norton menu or the DOS prompt before powering down.

Tip: If you have any drives whose lights you can't see, install Disk Light in AUTOEXEC.BAT so that drive lights will appear on your screen whenever you're in text mode.

Using Disk Park

Disk Park positions your hard-disk heads to protect your disk when the power is off. In their normal position, read-write heads are positioned only a fraction of an inch above the tracks. Any kind of blow to the disk drive—caused by someone bumping into the computer, an earthquake, or some other unexpected occurrence—can bounce the heads onto the tracks, destroying whatever data they touch and perhaps damaging the disk surface itself. To avoid such a calamity, you should always park the heads when you shut down your computer, which moves the heads to a safe zone away from the tracks. Many types of disk units park their own heads automatically. But if yours doesn't, use the **Disk Park** option or the following command to park your heads before powering down:

```
DISKMON /PARK
```

When you select the **Disk Park** option, the dialog box shown in Figure 6-5 appears. Do not select **Cancel,** simply shut off the power. If you do any other action, you might cause the heads to be moved out of the parked position again.

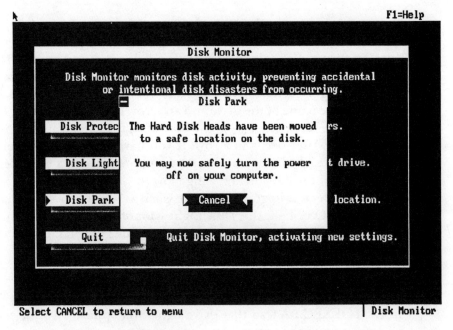

Figure 6-5   Disk Park Dialog Box

Parking the heads doesn't freeze them. If you subsequently give a command that accesses the disk, the heads will be unparked and used automatically.

Disk Park doesn't affect a network drive; it would make no sense to attempt to park the disk heads on a network drive when other people are still using the drive. In all likelihood, your network drive parks itself when it is powered down.

Tip: Find out if your hard drive parks its heads automatically. If not, then make it a practice to use Disk Park whenever you power down.

The DISKMON.INI File

The first time you use Disk Monitor, it creates a DISKMON.INI file, which records the options you select. If anything happens to your DISKMON.INI file, your Disk Monitor setup will be forgotten and the original, default setup (as shown in Figures 6-2 and 6-4) will be reestablished.

Disk Monitor Switches

Table 6-1 shows the switches you can use with the Disk Monitor command (in addition to the general switches that you can use with all Norton Utilities commands, as shown in Table 1-1). You can use these switches to control Disk Monitor without going through the dialog boxes. If you decide to install Disk Monitor from AUTOEXEC.BAT, use the switches to turn on the

---

Table 6-1   Disk Monitor Command Reference

Format:

```
DISKMON [switches]
```

Switches:

/LIGHT[+|-]	Turns the disk light feature on or off
/PARK	Parks the disk heads on all drives
/PROTECT[+|-]	Turns the disk-protect feature on or off (Parameters stored in DISKMON.INI determine what is protected)
/SKIPHIGH	Does not load Disk Monitor into high memory
/STATUS	Displays the current status of Disk Monitor features
/UNINSTALL	Uninstalls Disk Monitor from memory

---

features you want. For example, if you want to turn on Disk Protect and Disk Light during booting, you would enter this command in AUTOEXEC.BAT:

```
DISKMON /PROTECT+ /LIGHT+
```

You might need to uninstall Disk Monitor if you need its memory space for an application. Disk Monitor's TSR takes up about 8K in memory. Disabling it with /PROTECT- and /LIGHT- does not unload the TSR from memory. Only the /UNINSTALL switch will do that.

The /UNINSTALL switch works only if Disk Monitor was the last installed TSR. TSRs must always be uninstalled in the reverse order from their installation. If you install Norton Cache, Disk Monitor, and a mouse driver, in that order, then you must uninstall the mouse driver before you can uninstall Disk Monitor.

If you have some programs that require Disk Monitor to be disabled or turned off, create short batch files to turn off or uninstall Disk Monitor, run the program, then enable or install Disk Monitor again. For example:

```
DISKMON /UNINSTALL
CARDSORT
DISKMON /PROTECT+ /LIGHT+
```

This batch file uninstalls Disk Monitor, runs a program named CARDSORT (which probably demands all available memory), then starts up Disk Monitor again. If you just need to disable disk protection for a particular program, such as a program that works only in graphics mode, then your batch file might look like this:

```
DISKMON /PROTECT-
VP
DISKMON /PROTECT+
```

This file disables the Disk Protect feature and starts a program called VP. When VP terminates, it enables Disk Protect again. The level of protection remains the same as it was before (unless you used VP to alter or delete the DISKMON.INI file).

Tip: See Chapter 15 for brief information on how to create a batch file.

Looking Ahead

If you deal with sensitive data—by which we mean any kind of data that unauthorized people should not see—then you're probably aware that viruses are not the only type of artifice you have to watch out for. The next two chapters show you two utilities that prevent people from reading the sensitive data on your disk: WipeInfo and Diskreet. WipeInfo totally eradicates deleted data from your disk so that no one can find any traces of it. Diskreet encrypts (encodes) your active files so that no one can read them but you.

If you have sensitive data on your disk right now, you should take the time to read both chapters and learn to use these two utilities. If you used to have sensitive data, but you deleted it, it might still be on your disk and very readable by anyone who knows what they are doing. Chapter 7, on WipeInfo, explains why such deleted data stays on your disk and how to get rid of it once and for all.

If you don't deal with sensitive files, then you might want to skip to Chapter 9 and learn how to recover erased files.

7

WIPEINFO

The hard disk sitting on your desk right now could be full of information you don't want others to see—information you thought you had deleted. Someone could find it with UnErase, UnFormat, and/or Disk Editor.

Your personal computer has four features that combine to retain data on your disks that you thought was eliminated:

- DOS doesn't erase data when it deletes a file; it simply marks the directory entry and the clusters for reuse. Until they are reused, the former data is still there.

- Even when a cluster is reused, the new file might not completely fill it, leaving an area at the end called *slack*. The previous data remains in the slack area.

- Many disk format programs don't erase the old data when they reformat a disk. Earlier versions of DOS erase a diskette but not a hard disk. DOS 5.0 and Norton's Safe Format don't even erase a diskette unless you ask them to.

- Disk heads aren't accurate enough to write new data exactly over old data, so even when clusters have been erased or overwritten, traces of the old data might exist and can be picked up by some sophisticated hardware.

These characteristics come in handy when you need to UnErase files or UnFormat a disk, but they can be disastrous when you're trying to eliminate confidential data from your disks. Suppose, for example, that you use a diskette for backing up a group of sensitive files. Later on you reformat the diskette and use it to send some files to a client. The recipient might be able to lift all or part of the supposedly deleted data from the diskette.

Suppose you rent a computer for a project involving government secret information. At the end of the project, you delete all the files from the hard disk and reformat it. After you return the computer to the dealer, the next user could find and read the deleted data with Disk Editor! No sophisticated hardware is required for this task.

WipeInfo can be used to completely obliterate deleted data from your disks by overwriting it with generic data. Two levels of wiping are available:

- A fast method that overwrites the data once, which is sufficient to protect it from access with software such as UnErase and Disk Editor.
- A slower but very thorough "government" method that overwrites the data several times with different values and verifies the results. The government method, which meets U.S. Department of Defense standards, will eliminate all residual data so that, even with special hardware, detection is impossible.

WipeInfo will wipe an entire drive, all the unused clusters on the drive, selected files, or the slack area of selected files, according to your specifications. When it wipes files, it also marks the directory entry for reuse, zeros the rest of the directory entry so that its former contents can't be detected, and zeros the FAT entries. In other words, the files are both deleted and wiped.

> **Tip:** A government wipe of an entire hard drive can take several hours; a government wipe of an entire high-density diskette takes more than an hour.

As an additional benefit, WipeInfo can also be used to delete files without wiping them, with some strong advantages over the DEL command in earlier versions of DOS. It will seek files matching a global filename throughout an entire subtree, not just one directory. It will delete hidden and/or read-only files, if requested. And it will let you confirm each file selected for deletion, if requested.

Starting WipeInfo

You can start WipeInfo by selecting it from the Norton menu (**Security** section) or by entering the command WIPEINFO from the DOS prompt. Figure 7-1 shows the first dialog box that appears, where you select what you want to do next.

Configuring WipeInfo

The first time you use WipeInfo, you probably need to set up the configuration you want: the wipe method, the value to be used in wiping, and so on. After that, you need to go to the **Configure** dialog box only to use different settings from the defaults you have established. Figure 7-2 shows the dialog box that opens when you select the **Configure** button.

The **Fast Wipe** method, which is the default method, overwrites the area once with whatever value you specify (0 is the default).

The **Government Wipe** method writes first 1s then 0s, repeating those two patterns as many times as you specify (3 is the default). Then it writes a specified character (hex 246 is the default) and rereads the area to verify that

Figure 7-1   Initial WipeInfo Dialog Box

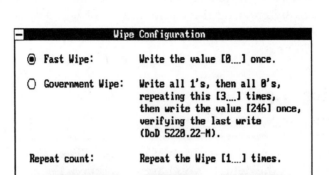

Figure 7-2   WipeInfo Configure Dialog Box

every byte contains the correct character. If it encounters any problems during verification, it displays a message that the wipe might not be valid. By the time the heads have revisited the same tracks seven or more times, they have probably totally eliminated all vestiges of the former data so that no equipment or software could pick it up.

Repeating the Wipe

To be extra sure, you can repeat the specified wipe method up to 999 times, providing more security than even the most cautious person with the most secret data could ever need. For example, if you repeat a default government wipe 10 times, you would write on the tracks 70 times and verify them 10 times.

Saving the Configuration

If you just select **OK**, WipeInfo remembers the current settings only until it terminates. Selecting **Save settings** stores them in a file so they become the defaults for all future wipes.

Wiping Drives

To wipe either a complete drive or the unused clusters from a drive, select the **Drives** button from the initial WipeInfo dialog box (see Figure 7-1). The dialog box shown in Figure 7-3 appears next.

All your drives are listed, including RAM drives but not network drives. You can select any or all of them.

If you wipe an entire drive, the system area is destroyed, too. Therefore, you will need to reformat the drive or diskette after the wipe is done. The Partition Table remains intact, so repartitioning is not necessary. If a hard disk contains several drives, only the specified drives are wiped.

The **Wipe unused areas only** option wipes only the unused clusters, which eliminates residual data from deleted files as well as any data left over when the disk was last reformatted. However, it does not wipe residual data residing in the slack of current files; you'll need to use the **Files** options (which are explained below) to eliminate that residual data.

After you have selected the drives and the method, select **Wipe** to begin the wipe process. The next dialog box gives you a chance to change your mind, then the wipe begins in earnest. Wiping progress is displayed in a progress box, which includes a button to interrupt the wipe.

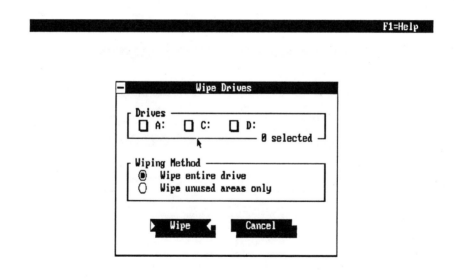

Figure 7-3   Wipe Drives Dialog Box

> **Tip:** When wiping entire drives, WipeInfo does the least crucial areas (unused clusters) first so you have some time to change your mind and stop the process.

Wiping or Deleting Files

Figure 7-4 shows the dialog box that appears when you select the **Files** button in the initial dialog box. You use this dialog box to delete and wipe files, delete files without wiping them, or wipe slack areas at the end of files.

You must enter a filename in the text box; it can be a global filename and it can include a path. For example, suppose C: is the current drive and you want to wipe all files that start with F90 from the root directory of drive D:. You would enter D:\F90*.* in the text box.

If you check **Include subdirs**, WipeInfo looks for files not only in the specified (or implied) directory but in all its children and all their children, down to the lowest level. For example, suppose you want to wipe all files on drive D: (every directory) that start with F90. You would enter D:\F90*.* in the text box and select **Include subdirs**.

The **Confirm each file** option comes in handy when a global filename is involved, since there's always the danger of accidentally selecting a file you

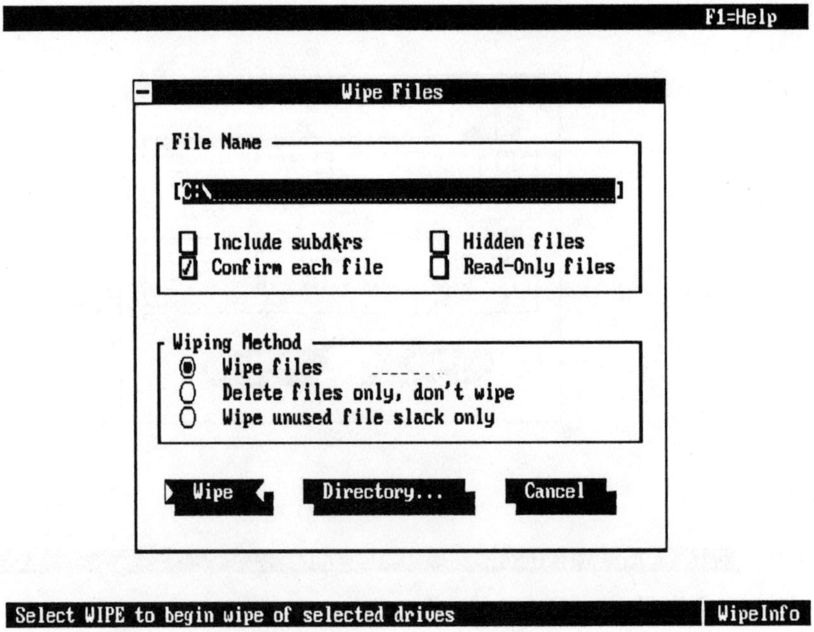

Figure 7-4   Wipe Files Dialog Box

didn't intend to. With **Confirm each file** checked, WipeInfo displays each selected filename, and you must choose **Skip**, **Wipe**, **Auto**, or **Stop**. **Skip** bypasses wiping or deleting the selected file. **Wipe** goes ahead with the operation; if the **Delete files only** option is selected, this button says **Delete** instead of **Wipe**. **Auto** turns off file confirmation, so that all remaining selected files will be wiped or deleted automatically. **Stop** terminates the wipe or delete operation entirely, returning you to the initial WipeInfo dialog box.

Warning: After selecting **Auto**, you can no longer interrupt the process with **Stop**.

Ordinarily, read-only files and hidden files are excluded from wipe or delete operations. But you can include them by checking **Hidden files** and/or **Read only files**.

The wiping method determines what is actually wiped, if anything. If you chose **Wipe files**, all files matching the filename are selected to be wiped. **Delete files only, don't wipe** causes matching files to be selected for deletion in the same manner that DOS deletes files. The **Wipe unused file slack only** option wipes residual data in the slack area at the end of each selected file's last cluster. Slack data has no effect on the current file, but it might contain confidential information left over from a file that you deleted or encrypted.

To start the wipe process, select **Wipe**. A warning box gives you a chance to change your mind, then WipeInfo begins selecting and wiping or deleting as instructed. A Stop button lets you interrupt the process.

Interaction with Erase Protect

Files wiped or deleted with WipeInfo are not preserved by Erase Protect. If you wipe them, they are gone forever. If you merely delete them, they are candidates for UnErase, but the Erase Protect information will not be available.

Some Sample Applications

Let's take a look at how you can use WipeInfo to protect your confidential data.

Wiping an Entire Hard Disk

Suppose you are returning a rented computer and want to make sure the hard disk is completely blank. Start WipeInfo and select the **Configuration** button. Select **Government Wipe** using all default values. A repeat count of 1 is probably fine unless you want to be extra careful. Select **OK** to get back to the initial dialog box, then select the **Drives** button. On the **Drives** dialog box, select all the drives on the hard disk, select **Wipe entire drive**, and select **Wipe**. On the warning dialog box, select **Wipe** again. The wipe will take several hours, depending on the size of the drive.

When the wipe is done, you won't be able to boot the computer from the hard disk. Someone will have to boot from a floppy and reformat the hard drives.

Eliminating Confidential Data

Suppose you have just deleted PATIENTS.DB, and you want to eliminate all residual patient data from your hard disk. This means you need to find and eliminate backup copies and earlier versions as well as residual data in unused clusters and slack areas. Start WipeInfo, select **Configuration**, and set up the wipe configuration as you want it; a standard **Fast Wipe** is probably sufficient to protect this type of data. Then go back to the initial dialog box and select **Files**. Enter the name \PATIENTS.* in the text box and check these boxes:

> Include subdirs
> Hidden files
> Read-Only files
> Confirm each file

Select the **Wipe Files** option and select the **Wipe** button. Examine each selected filename carefully; if it's a backup copy or an earlier version of PATIENTS.DB, select **Wipe**; otherwise select **Skip**.

Check your database documentation; does it make backup files under any other names? If so, wipe those, too. Then select **Files** again, enter the filename *.*, uncheck the **Confirm each file** box, and select **Wipe unused file slack only**. This will wipe the slack area in every file on the drive. Finally, select **Drives** and wipe all the unused clusters.

Deleting a Group of Files

Suppose you want to delete all the BAK files from your hard disk, but they don't need to be wiped. Start WipeInfo and select **Files**. Enter *.BAK in the text box and select these options:

Include subdirs

Hidden files

Read-Only files

Since these are backup files, it's probably not necessary to confirm each one. Finally, select **Delete files only, don't wipe** and select the **Wipe** button.

The WIPEINFO Command

If you prefer commands to dialog boxes, you can specify most of the wipe parameters in the WIPEINFO command, which is shown in Table 7-1.

You can specify either a drive name or a filename, but not both, and the switches must be appropriate for the one you specify.

If you specify a drive name and omit the /E switch, the entire drive is wiped. If you specify a filename (which can be global and include a path) and omit both /N and /K, all matching files are wiped. There are no switches for the confirm, hidden, and read-only options; your default settings are used for those parameters.

Table 7-1   WIPEINFO Command Reference

Format:

```
WIPEINFO [drive: | filename] [switches]
```

Switches:

DISK ONLY

/E	Wipes unused space ("Empty" space) only

FILES ONLY

/N	Delete oNly, don't wipe
/K	Wipe slacK only
/S	Include Subdirectories

EITHER DISKS OR FILES

/Gn	Government wipe; repeat 1s and 0s *n* times
/Rn	Repeat entire wipe *n* times
/Vn	Use wipe Value *n* (*n* can be 0 to 255)
/BATCH	Don't open WipeInfo window

The /G*n* switch specifies a government wipe, with the *n* indicating the number of times the 1s and 0s are written; any number less than 3 is ignored.

Reminder: /G0 through /G2 are standard Norton switches controlling the use of graphics (described in Table 1-1). If you use /G0 through /G2 here, they act just like they do with any other Norton Utilities command.

Looking Ahead

As you've seen, WipeInfo protects deleted data by completely removing it from your disk. But it can't help you protect data that you're still working on. The next chapter shows you how to use Diskreet, which disguises the data in files so that no one can access it without a password.

If you won't be working with sensitive data now, you might want to skip ahead to Chapter 9, which shows you how to recover erased files.

8

DISKREET

Do you have information on your computer that you don't want others to see? Whether it's your new, blockbuster screenplay, your secret recipe for Chicken Magnani, your company's five-year plan for total market saturation, or the latest design in strategic weapons systems, the best way to protect it is to encrypt it.

Encryption alters data so that it can't be understood by anyone who doesn't know how to decrypt it again. *Decryption* restores the data to its original, readable form. Figure 8-1 shows the same file before and after encryption. The encryption method used is secure enough that even an expert could not break the code. Any type of data can be encrypted: text, programs, databases, spreadsheets, and graphics, for example.

The Diskreet utility encrypts and decrypts files. It offers two methods of encryption: standard and DES. The standard method is fairly fast but might not be as secure as the DES method. It's an excellent choice for protecting data against non-professional snoopers; you'll probably want to use it for novels and screenplays, proprietary recipes, Friday's pop quiz, company confidential memos, as yet unpublished research findings, and the like.

The DES method, which meets the U.S. government's Data Encryption Standard, is slower but much more secure. It can protect your data against professional code crackers; use it for industry, government, and military confidential information.

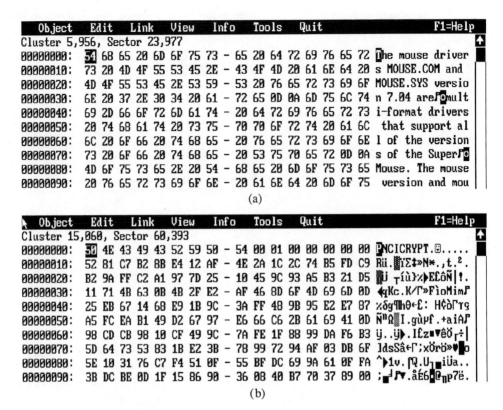

Figure 8-1   **Example of Encryption**

Note: Diskreet is not sold outside the United States. If you have the international version of the Norton Utilities, you won't have Diskreet available to you.

Diskreet can encrypt/decrypt individual files or it can create a pseudodrive called an NDisk and encrypt/decrypt all the files stored there. There are advantages to each method. If you have only a few, unrelated files to be encrypted, then you'll probably want to treat them individually. If you work daily with many encrypted files, you'll find an NDisk more convenient.

Diskreet has one other important security function: It can lock your keyboard and blank your screen so that no one else can use them when you're away from your computer. You can unlock them again by entering the correct password.

Diskreet Passwords

The entire encryption system is built around passwords. Every individually encrypted file has its own password; so does every NDisk. The password not only controls access to the files, it also acts as the key upon which the encryption is performed. That is, it becomes part of the algorithm used to encrypt and decrypt the file.

Warning! If you forget a password, you will never again be able to decrypt the files it protects. Choose your passwords carefully.

You also need a main password that you use for general Diskreet functions such as unlocking your keyboard.

A password can be from 6 to 40 characters long. Any characters can be used, including spaces and graphics characters.

There's no sense in encrypting files if your passwords aren't good enough. Imagine that you're trying to crack someone else's password. What are the first things you would try? The person's name, address, phone number, social security number, spouse's name, children's names, and so on. You would also look around the room for a note containing the password.

If all you're trying to crack is Professor Peabody's midterm exam, you'd probably soon give up. But what if someone will pay you several million dollars for the decrypted file? You'd probably pull the room apart inch by inch looking for the password. You'd find out the names of all Professor Peabody's relatives, friends, pets, and favorite performers; in fact, you'd probably compile a complete history of Professor Peabody, looking for significant words and phrases. You'd probably be willing to spend months at it.

Now put yourself on the other side of the fence. For the best protection, you need to come up with passwords that you can remember without writing them down, but that are not associated with you in any way. Rather than using phrases that have meaning to you, such as AUNT RUTH, SAINT LOUIS, and L. A. DODGERS, you should go for totally unrelated (but still rememberable) phrases like U. S. GRANT, WILLIAM TELL, ENTREZ VOUS, FAMILY FUN, and HIGHWAY #101.

If you need so many passwords that you have to develop a system or write them down, try this method. Find one 10-character, unmeaningful, rememberable phrase with no repeated characters: MONEYTALKS, JAMES POLK, REALITYNOW, and PIG BREATH would all be good. For this example, we'll use IDON'TCARE. Each time you need a password, make it up out of those ten characters, which can be repeated. For example, you could use

CARTER, RADIATION, and CAN'TDO. These passwords don't have to be remembered, so you can also use nonsense such as D'CREIO'T, ORA'EDI, and 'TNAICON. To write the password down, you encode it by writing the digits representing each character's position in the key phrase. For example, you would encode CAN'TDO as 7845623 because C is the seventh character in IDON'TCARE, A is the eighth character, and so on. An E would be coded as 0.

With this method, you have to remember only one phrase—the key phrase—which you never write down anywhere. If someone finds your list of encoded passwords, they'll see something like this:

Five-year plan   1052531
Ten-year plan   24665121
Fall line (first draft) 204561213
Winter '91 results   52378523

As long as they can't find or figure out your key phrase, they can't decode your passwords.

Starting Diskreet

To start Diskreet, select the **Diskreet** command from the Norton menu (**Security** section) or enter DISKREET at the DOS prompt. Figure 8-2 shows the dialog box that appears first, in which you indicate whether you want to work with individual files (the **Files** button) or NDisks (the **Disks** button).

Working with Files

There are several strong advantages to working with individual files instead of NDisks:

- Each file can have its own password; if someone cracks a password, they access only one file.
- Individually encrypted files are not automatically decrypted when you access them; you can back them up and telecommunicate them in encrypted format.
- Individual files take up less space than an NDisk since you must allocate all the NDisk space at once, even if you don't use it.

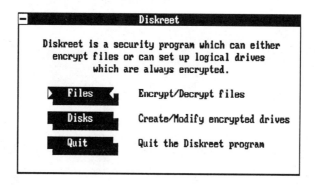

Figure 8-2   Initial Diskreet Dialog Box

> **Tip:** For maximum security, encrypt files individually, using a different password for each file. That way, if someone cracks a password, they gain access to only one file.

File Options

Figure 8-3 shows the screen that appears when you tell Diskreet that you want to work with files. This is a blank Diskreet screen with the **File** menu pulled down.

Before you actually encrypt any files, you should probably examine the file options to see if you want to make any changes. Figure 8-4 shows the dialog box that appears when you select **File options** from the menu. In addition to choosing between the proprietary and DES methods, several other options are available.

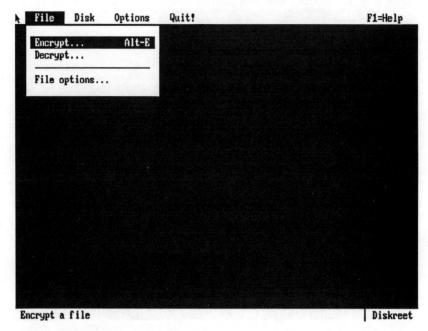

Figure 8-3   File Menu

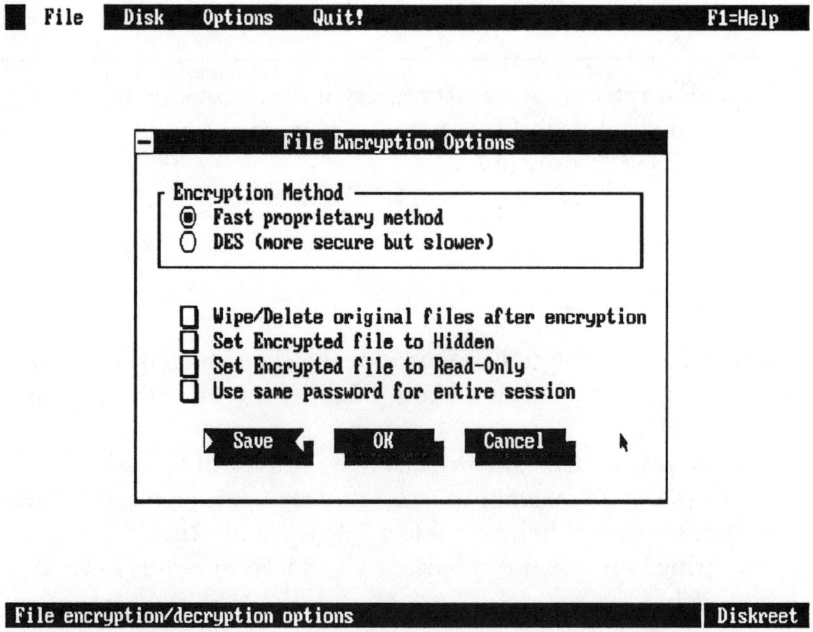

Figure 8-4   File Options

Wiping Original Files

Diskreet does not "encrypt in place"; that is, it does not replace the original file with an encrypted file. When the encryption process is finished, both the original and the encrypted versions exist on the disk unless you ask Diskreet to wipe the original file from the disk. Wiping is much more secure than simply deleting the original because the wipe process overwrites all the original data with zeros, preventing someone from examining the deleted file with Disk Editor.

> **Warning:** The wipe process used by Diskreet does not conform to U.S. government security standards. For the most secure wipe, use WipeInfo after encrypting instead of this option.

By the way, Diskreet automatically wipes the encrypted file when it is decrypted again.

Protecting Encrypted Files

To provide an additional measure of protection for valuable files, you can give them the hidden and/or read-only attribute. These attributes help to prevent you from accidentally erasing them, especially when using a global filename. They also prevent casual users from seeing them in a DOS directory and perhaps deleting them accidentally or on purpose. But keep in mind that any user sophisticated enough to use Disk Editor or FileFind can easily circumvent these attribute switches.

Using a Single Password

Some people prefer to use the same password all the time; it's not as secure, but maximum security isn't always necessary. Others like to use one password for a group of related files, much as an NDisk does. You can use the same password for all the files you encrypt and decrypt in one session by selecting **Use same password for entire session**. Diskreet will ask for the password once and apply it to all the files you encrypt and decrypt until you terminate Diskreet or turn off the option.

> **Tip:** If you find that you need to use a different password, you can return to this dialog box and turn the option off, after which you will be required to supply individual passwords for every file that you encrypt and decrypt. If you turn the option back on again in the same session, the password that will be applied to future encryptions and decryptions will be the last one that was entered while the option was turned off.

Saving Your File Options

If you close the **File Encryption Options** dialog box by selecting the **OK** button, the options you chose apply to the current session only. They are forgotten when you terminate Diskreet, and the default options are in effect again the next time you start it. To make your options more permanent, select the **Save** button. Your options become the default options when you do this. Whichever way you complete the dialog, you will be returned to the main Diskreet screen with the **File** menu pulled down.

Encrypting Files

Figure 8-5 shows the dialog box that appears when you select the **Encrypt** option from the **File** menu or press Alt-E. This dialog box works just like the one in Disk Editor (see Figure 2-10).

> **Tip:** If you enter a global filename, all matching files are combined into one encrypted file. Decryption separates them into individual files again.

When you select the desired file(s) and complete the dialog, the next dialog box asks you for the name of the encrypted file, suggesting *filename*.SEC (for SECured) as the default. You can enter another name if you wish. Then a dialog box asks for the password unless you are using the same password for the entire session and have already entered it. As you type the password, asterisks appear in the dialog box instead of the characters you type; this way, no one else in the room can see your password. To make sure that you don't make a typing error while typing "blind," Diskreet requires you to enter the

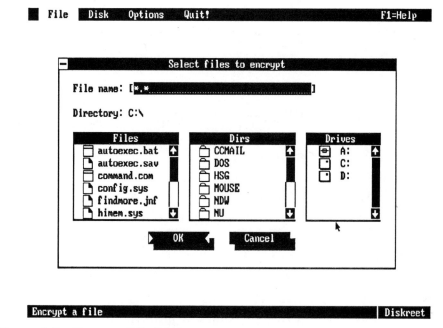

Figure 8-5   Encrypt File Dialog Box

password a second time. It warns you if the two entries don't match, and you have to start over again with the first one.

After you enter a password, you will see a series of progress boxes as the encryption takes place. The first box tells you that Diskreet is "combining" the original file(s) with the encryption file; Diskreet copies each original file's data into the encryption file and adds some administrative information. The next box follows the progress of the encryption itself. If the original file is to be wiped, the next box shows you its progress. Finally, you'll see a message that the encryption is complete.

Eliminating Unencrypted Versions

The application that creates the unencrypted version of a file might also create backup and working copies without your knowledge. Although most applications delete their working files when they terminate normally, they don't actually erase the data from the disk. Residual data from the file might exist in unused clusters and slack areas, where someone using Disk Editor could find it.

When you encrypt an individual file, you should be sure to get rid of all its backup copies and residual data using these techniques:

- Avoid, wipe, or encrypt all backup copies. (Read the application's documentation to find out how what backup files are made and how to avoid them.)

- Avoid, wipe, or encrypt automatic time-save copies. (Read the application's documentation to find out what time-save copies are made and how to avoid them.)

- Find and wipe or encrypt all copies in other drives and directories. (Use Norton FileFind to locate them.)

- If Erase Protect is enabled, purge copies of deleted files saved in TRASHCAN.

- After all of the above, wipe all unused clusters and file slack to eliminate residual data from deleted files. (Use the WipeInfo utility.)

Warning: Since it clears all unused clusters, the last step will make it impossible for you to unerase any files or subdirectories not preserved by Erase Protect.

Decrypting Files

The decryption process is almost the same as encryption:

- You select the file to be decrypted. You can enter a global filename in the text box to limit the files displayed in the list box, but you can't use a global filename to select multiple files to be decrypted. You have to decrypt one file at a time. Also, you don't provide a name for the decrypted file. Diskreet always decrypts to the original path and filename.

- You enter the password—just once when decrypting. A message tells you if it's the wrong password.

- A series of progress boxes show you that (a) the file is decrypted; (b) original files are "extracted" from the decrypted file; and (c) the encrypted file is wiped.

If a file with the original file's name is found on the disk, Diskreet displays the dialog box in Figure 8-6. Your best move at this point is to cancel the

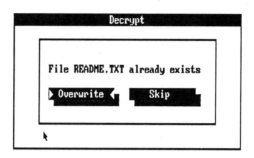

Figure 8-6   File Exists Dialog Box

decryption by selecting **Skip**; examine the indicated file and rename it or delete it, whichever is more appropriate; then start the decryption again. When you cancel the decryption, the data has already been decrypted within the encrypted file. A dialog box gives you the choice of reencrypting it or deleting it. It's safest to reencrypt it until you can decide what to do.

Working with NDisks

An NDisk is a portion of your hard drive set aside for encrypted files. It is actually a hidden file, which is managed by a special driver called DISKREET.SYS so that it behaves like a drive. Your applications see it as a separate drive where directories can be created and files can be stored and retrieved, just like any other drive.

Any file that you store in an NDisk is automatically encrypted using the NDisk's password. Any file that you access in the NDisk is automatically decrypted as long as you have previously opened the NDisk using the correct password.

There are several advantages to using NDisks in preference to individually encrypted files:

- You can encrypt and decrypt many files using only one password, which makes life much simpler.

- Once the NDisk is open, encryption and decryption are transparent; that is, you aren't even aware of them. You might notice that the NDisk "drive" is slower than your other hard drives.

- When you create a new file in the NDisk, most applications will also create backup copies and working copies using the same path. Therefore, all backup and working copies will also be encrypted. You don't have to worry about finding and wiping unencrypted copies and residual data.

- You can set up your NDisks to close automatically when you press a hotkey and/or when your keyboard has not been used for so many minutes.

- Your NDisk can give you an audit report of the number of successful and unsuccessful open attempts. The audit report can warn you that someone has been trying to crack your password.

- You can set up some of your NDisks to be opened automatically during booting (as long as you can enter the correct passwords).

Preparing Your System for an NDisk

You must create an NDisk before you can use it. But even before that, you have to get ready for it.

The DISKREET.SYS Statement in CONFIG.SYS

Before you can work with NDisks, you must load the NDisk driver by entering the necessary DEVICE statement in CONFIG.SYS and rebooting. Place this statement in your CONFIG.SYS file:

```
DEVICE=path\DISKREET.SYS
```

The *path* should reference the directory containing your Norton Utilities, which is probably C:\NU. (See page 107 for instructions on how to edit CONFIG.SYS.)

> **Tip:** The Configuration program will generate the correct statement
> for you if you wish. Start up Configuration and select **CONFIG.SYS
> file.** Check the option that says **Load the DISKREET.SYS driver (data
> encryption).**

DISKREET.SYS will load itself into extended memory if it can. If you load
an extended memory driver such as HIMEM.SYS, place the DISKREET.SYS
statement somewhere after the HIMEM.SYS statement. If you load Norton
Cache (or any other program that uses all available extended memory), put
the DISKREET.SYS statement before the NCACHE statement if you want
Diskreet to use extended memory. For example, if you load HIMEM.SYS,
DISKREET.SYS, and Norton Cache, and you want DISKREET.SYS to use
extended memory, you would put the statements in this order:

```
DEVICE=C:\HIMEM.SYS
DEVICE=C:\NU\DISKREET.SYS
DEVICE=C:\NU\NCACHE
```

After you have put the DISKREET.SYS statement into CONFIG.SYS, be sure
to reboot so that it takes effect. Figure 8-7 shows the message that appears
during the first boot after inserting the DISKREET.SYS statement in CON-
FIG.SYS. This message means that DISKREET.SYS could not find its startup
file, named DISKREET.INI, so it created one using the default settings for
all options. You will see this message only the first time because after that,
DISKREET.INI exists.

Organizing Your Hard Disk

If your hard drive has not been optimized lately, the new NDisk might be
fragmented and its access time will be slower. If you optimize the drive later,
the NDisk won't be unfragmented because it's hidden, and Speed Disk does
not move hidden files. Therefore, you should use Speed Disk to reorganize
your disk before you create the NDisk; when selecting Speed Disk options,
be sure to use the one that moves all the unused space to the end of the disk.
That's your best guarantee that your NDisk will not be fragmented.

If you do need to optimize the NDisk after it is created, you can unhide it
before starting Speed Disk. You'll see the command for unhiding NDisks
later in this chapter.

```
DISKREET(tm)      Norton Utilities 6.0
Copyright 1991 by Symantec Corporation

No DISKREET config file to read (DISKREET.INI).
DISKREET's Main Password has been cleared.
Instant close keys have been reset to LEFT + RIGHT shift keys.
AUTO-CLOSE TIME-OUT interval has been set to five minutes and DISABLED.
Keyboard lock & screen blank has been DISABLED.
NDISK drive count set to one.

***************    PRESS ANY KEY TO CONTINUE    ***************
```

Figure 8-7   First DISKREET.SYS Message

Creating the NDisk

To create an NDisk, start Diskreet and select the **Disks** option on the opening
dialog box. A dialog box tells you that there are no NDisks and asks if you
want to define one. When you select **Yes**, the next dialog box asks you to
select the host drive (which cannot be a network drive). Figure 8-8 shows the
dialog box that appears next, where you set up the characteristics of the
NDisk.

Filename and Description

Remember that an NDisk is actually a file as far as DOS is concerned. It needs
a filename just like any other file. You assign the main part of the filename.
Its extension will be @#!.

You can also give it a description of up to 30 characters. The name and
description appear in Diskreet's list of NDisks and in NDisk messages. If you
have more than one NDisk, the name and description can help you identify
the one you want. Many users like to put the encoded password in the NDisk
description. (You can see examples in Figures 8-9 and 8-10.)

Audit Information

The audit information displays a dialog box similar to the one shown in
Figure 8-9 every time you open the NDisk. You can see the last time it was
opened, the last time someone tried to open it (if it was a failed attempt, the

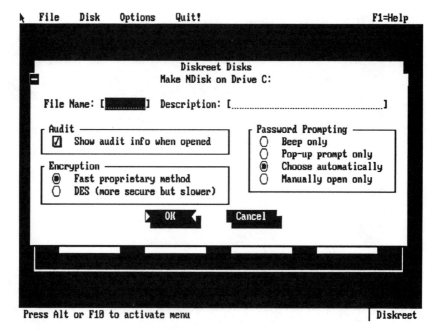

Figure 8-8   Make NDisk Dialog Box

word FAILED flashes next to this line), and the number of unsuccessful attempts to open it. This information should immediately warn you if someone has been trying to open your NDisk without your permission.

Encryption Method

The next control group in Figure 8-8 lets you select the encryption method. Whatever method you choose applies to every file in the NDisk. The encryption method can't be modified after the NDisk is created.

Password Prompting

If you wish, Diskreet will open the NDisk automatically when it is referenced for the first time after booting. For example, suppose the NDisk's drive name is F: and you enter this command after booting:

```
DIR F:
```

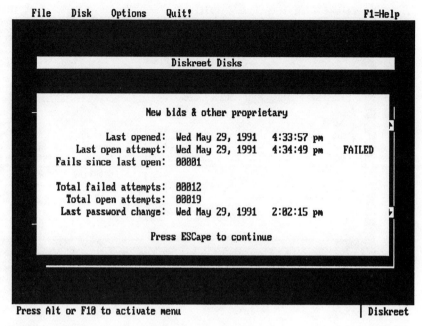

Figure 8-9 NDisk Audit Information

If automatic opening is in force, Diskreet will immediately ask you for the password and, if you can supply the correct one, open the NDisk. Then the DIR F: command will be completed. If you can't enter the correct password after three tries, DOS will report that the drive is not ready. This is the same error you get when you try to use an empty diskette drive.

You don't have to enable automatic opening. You can set up an NDisk so that it can be opened only manually. Then you must start Diskreet or enter the correct Diskreet command to open it.

If you don't want an NDisk opened automatically, choose **Manually Open only** when defining it. If you choose any other option in the **Password Prompting** control group, the NDisk will be opened automatically.

> **Note:** You'll learn shortly about a third opening option—opening automatically during booting.

When an NDisk must be opened manually, you might find it difficult or impossible to open from within an application. For example, suppose you have developed a new file using your word processor and now you're ready to save it to the NDisk, which is not currently open. DOS passes a not-ready error to the word processor. What happens next depends on the word processor. Most likely, you'll have to save the file on another (unencrypted) drive, quit the word processor, use Diskreet to manually open the NDisk, copy the file to the NDisk, then wipe the unencrypted version.

This problem doesn't arise when the NDisk is opened automatically. With the word processor still on the screen and waiting to save the file, Diskreet asks you for the password, opens the NDisk, and returns control to the word processor, which continues as normal. As you can see, the advantage lies with automatic opening.

When you use automatic opening, you can control the nature of the prompt Diskreet uses to ask for the password. If you use **Pop-up prompt only**, Diskreet always displays the dialog box shown in Figure 8-10, no matter what application is on the screen. Notice that the NDisk's name and description are included in the dialog box. If you have included your encoded password in the description, it's right there for you to use.

The dialog box works fine with text screen, but it can mess up a graphics screen so that, after the dialog box closes, you have to force the application to rewrite the screen.

The **Beep only** option suppresses the dialog box; no prompt appears on the screen. Instead a high alternating two-toned signal sounds. You have to realize what the signal means and type the password without being able to see what you type. The password is processed when you press Enter. If the password is incorrect, the signal sounds again. If you don't enter the correct password after three attempts, a low two-toned signal sounds and a not-ready error is issued.

```
c:\pzp>dir e:
```

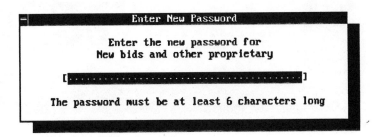

Figure 8-10   Password Prompt

There can be two problems with this method. First, if you have two or more NDisks, you might not know which one is being opened and therefore which password to enter. Second, if you're also running other TSRs that use beep prompts, such as Disk Monitor, you might not know which TSR is beeping, although they do use different types of beeps.

The **Choose automatically** option combines the other two, using the pop-up box when the screen is in text mode and the beep in graphics mode. It's not perfect, but it's the best choice unless you really need to see the dialog box every time.

NDisk Size

When you complete the dialog box shown in Figure 8-8, the dialog box shown in Figure 8-11 appears next. Unlike most files, an NDisk will not expand automatically into more clusters when needed. You must manually control its size, so be sure to allocate plenty of space to hold future files. But you're not stuck with the size you initially allocate. We'll show you later how to make it larger or smaller.

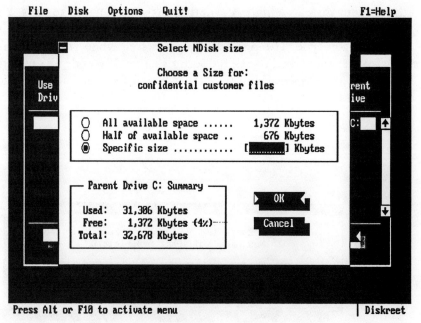

Figure 8-11   NDisk Size Dialog Box

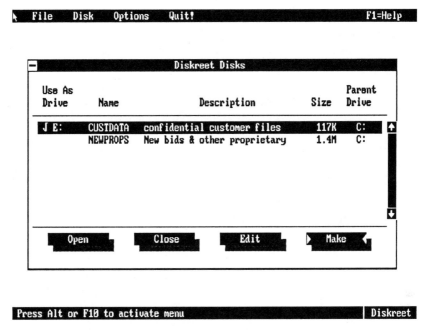

Figure 8-12   Diskreet Main Screen with NDisk List

Creating the NDisk

The next dialog box asks for the password—twice. Then Diskreet asks you what drive name to assign to the disk. Usually, only one drive name is available, and all you have to do is press Enter. Then Diskreet creates the NDisk while a progress box keeps you informed.

The new NDisk is opened automatically and the main screen reappears looking like Figure 8-12. Whenever you start Diskreet to work with disks, the screen includes a dialog box showing the status of your NDisks. A check mark next to the drive letter indicates that the NDisk is open.

> **Note:** The size shown for the NDisk will be larger than the size you specified; the additional space is for administrative information.

Setting Up the Main Password

You will often need the main password when working with NDisks. The first time you use Diskreet after DISKREET.INI is created, the main password will be null; all you do is press the Enter key when the main password is requested. You should set up your own main password as soon as possible for better protection. For maximum security, you should also change your main password every so often.

To set up or change the main password, select **Change main password** from the **Options** menu. You'll have to enter the current main password (to prove you know it) and then the new one (twice).

Tip: If you ever forget your main password, delete DISKREET.INI and reboot. Diskreet will recreate DISKREET.INI with a null password. (All your other options will also be reinitialized; see Figure 8-7 for the complete list.)

Using the NDisk

For the most part, you use an NDisk just like any other drive. There are only a few exceptions.

Encrypting Existing Files

To encrypt existing files, simply copy them to the NDisk, as in the following example, where drive F: is the NDisk:

```
C:\>COPY WORK*.DB F:
```

Don't forget to delete the original files and any other unencrypted copies as well as to wipe residual data from the unused clusters.

Creating New Encrypted Files

If you use an application to create a new file in the NDisk, make sure the application puts all its backup and working copies in the NDisk, too, so they don't go to an unencrypted area. You'll have to check the application's documentation to find out how to do this. It might involve making the NDisk the default drive or assigning a path and a name to the new file as soon as you open it. You might need to set the default path in the application's setup.

If you can't figure out how to force the application to put backup and working files on the NDisk, then you'll have to delete the backup files, purge the TRASHCAN copies, and wipe residual data, just as you do with files that were created outside the NDisk.

NDisk Directories and Files

You can use DOS commands, Norton Change Directory, or the utility of your choice to create and manipulate a tree-structured directory in an NDisk. You can view, print, copy, delete, and otherwise manipulate files. But you can't use low-level programs such as DOS FORMAT and CHKDSK on the drive. (You can use Norton's Safe Format and Disk Doctor to accomplish the same functions, however.)

If you want to use Erase Protect for deleted NDisk files, you must enable Erase Protect for the NDisk's drive name.

Closing NDisks

As long as the NDisk is open, anyone can access its files. No additional password is required, and the files are decrypted automatically. Therefore, it's best to keep your NDisks closed when they're not in use.

You can close an NDisk manually by starting Diskreet for disks (see Figure 8-12), highlighting the NDisk, and selecting the **Close** button. You can close all open NDisks at once by selecting the **Close all** option from the **Disk** menu or by entering the following command at the Command prompt:

```
DISKREET /CLOSE
```

NDisks are automatically closed when you power off or reboot. You can also set up Diskreet to close NDisks automatically under certain circumstances.

Closing by Timeout

If you wish, Diskreet will close all NDisks after the keyboard has not been used for a few minutes. To set this feature up, pull down the **Options** menu and select **Auto-close timeouts**, which opens the dialog box shown in Figure 8-13. (You might have to enter the main password.)

To turn the feature on, be sure to select the check box so that a check mark appears. You can also change the number of minutes if 5 doesn't suit you. Then select **OK**.

An automatic closure is only temporary. The next time you reference an NDisk, Diskreet asks for its password (even if it must normally be opened manually). When you enter the correct password, all temporarily closed NDisks are reopened, even though some of them have different passwords.

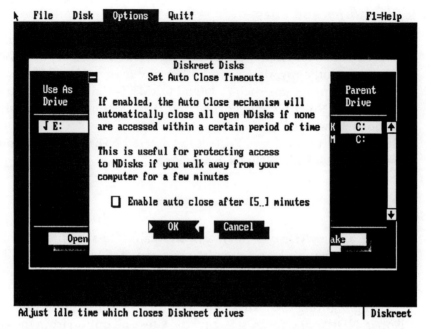

Figure 8-13   Auto-Close Timeouts Dialog Box

> **Tip:** Turn this feature on even if you plan to set up a hotkey. If you forget to use the hotkey when you walk away from the computer, the automatic timeout will still protect your files (unless someone gets to them before the keyboard times out).

Closing by Hotkey

For better security, you should intentionally close your NDisks when you walk away from the computer, not wait for them to time out. You can set up a quick-close hotkey to do a temporary closure of all open NDisks. Figure 8-14 shows the dialog box that appears when you select **Keyboard and screen lock** from the **Options** menu. This dialog box is used to set up the quick-close feature as well as keyboard and screen lock (discussed later).

Select **Enable Quick-Close** to turn on the quick-close feature. By default, the quick-close hotkey is both Shift keys pressed simultaneously, but you can select any one of the displayed choices.

Once the quick-close feature is enabled, develop the habit of hitting the hotkey whenever you leave the computer. Reopening the files is the same as for timeout closures.

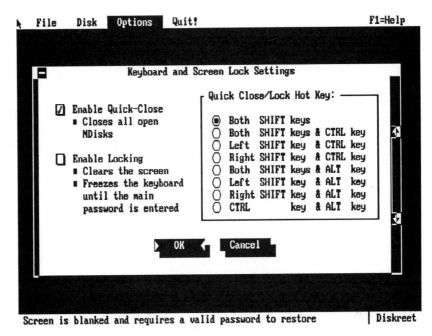

Figure 8-14   Keyboard and Screen Lock Dialog Box

Opening NDisks

You've already seen how NDisks can be opened automatically. To open an NDisk manually, highlight it on the Diskreet **Disks** screen (Figure 8-12) and select the **Open** button. You'll be asked for the disk's password.

> **Note:** There is no switch to open an NDisk from the command prompt.

Assigning Drive Names

As you know, an open NDisk has a drive name, which you use to access its files. But drive names are not permanently attached to NDisks. You assign a drive name when you open an NDisk; when you close it, the drive name is disassociated from it and could be used for another NDisk. Normally, Diskreet makes only one drive name available for NDisks. If you have only one NDisk, you would always assign the one drive name to the one NDisk.

If you have multiple NDisks but only one drive name, then you can have only one NDisk open at a time. Whenever you open an NDisk, a dialog box asks for the drive name. When you select the only available drive name and it's already assigned to another open NDisk, Diskreet automatically closes that NDisk in order to open the next one.

You can have two or more NDisks open at once by asking Diskreet for more drive names. Select **System settings** from the **Options** menu, which causes the dialog box in Figure 8-15 to open. (You might have to enter the main password.) The top part of this dialog box is explained later. You use the bottom control group to request more drive names.

After you select the desired number of drive names and select **OK**, a dialog box advises you that the new options won't take effect until you reboot. The two command buttons are **Reset** and **Don't reset**. Select **Reset** to reboot immediately (which will close your open NDisks, of course), which makes the new drive names available. Select **Don't reset** to return to the Diskreet screen.

Tip: Since an open NDisk can be vulnerable to abuse if you forget to close it when you leave your computer, it's good practice to open only one NDisk at a time. Having only one drive name forces you to do this. Avoid requesting more drive names unless you really need to have two or more NDisks open simultaneously.

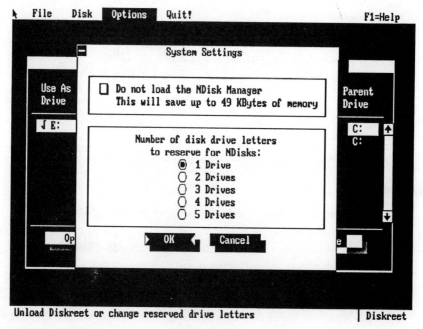

Figure 8-15   System Settings Dialog Box

Opening NDisks during Booting

You can set your NDisks up to be opened during booting, if desired. Select **startup Disks** from the **Options** menu, which produces the dialog box shown in Figure 8-16. (You might have to enter the main password.)

The dialog box shows how each drive name is set up for opening during booting. To specify that a drive should be opened, highlight it and select the **Edit** button. The next dialog box lists the names of the available NDisks; select the one that you want opened on the designated drive during booting. You must also choose whether you want to be prompted for a password **As soon as machine starts up** (the default) or **The first time the drive letter is used.**

Recall that when you create an NDisk, you select the type of password prompt to be used when the NDisk is automatically opened (refer back to Figure 8-8). If you choose to open an NDisk during booting, the selected prompt will occur as part of the boot process, and you must respond to it at that time (or the boot can't continue). However, if you choose **Manually open only** when you define an NDisk, then later select one of the automatic startup options for that NDisk, Diskreet will change **Manually open only** to **Choose automatically.**

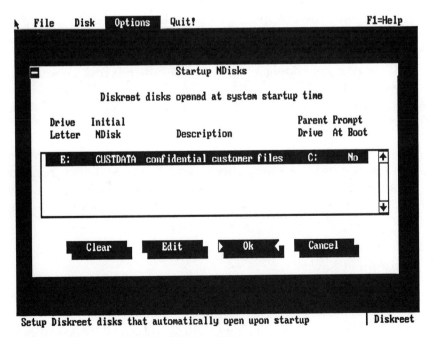

Figure 8-16   Startup NDisks Dialog Box

If you change your mind about opening an NDisk during booting, you can undo it by returning to the **Startup NDisks** dialog box, highlighting the drive you want to change, and selecting the **Clear** button.

Wiping NDisks

For an extra security precaution, you can ask Diskreet to automatically wipe NDisk clusters whenever any of the following events occur:

- When the NDisk is created, all its clusters are wiped of any previous data.

- When the NDisk is expanded, the added clusters are wiped of any previous data.

- When the NDisk is shrunk, the released clusters are wiped of any residual encrypted data.

- When the NDisk is deleted, all its clusters are wiped of any residual encrypted data.

To set up NDisk wiping, select **Security** from the **Options** menu. (You might have to enter the main password.) Figure 8-17 shows the dialog box that opens.

The **Quick Clear** option, which is the default, does not do any wiping. **Overwrite** wipes the clusters once, while **Security wipe** wipes them several times for maximum security, but takes longer, of course.

Changing the wiping option affects future NDisk actions but does not affect existing NDisks. If you have already shrunk an NDisk, for example, the released clusters would not be wiped in retrospect. You would need to use WipeInfo to wipe them.

> **Tip:** It's really not necessary to wipe encrypted data from your disk unless you think your passwords have been cracked. The encryption should be enough protection as long as your passwords are secure.

Searching for NDisks

When you start Diskreet and select the **Disks** option, Diskreet finds and lists all the NDisks on your hard drives, but it doesn't look on your floppy drives. To find and use NDisks on your floppy drives, you must ask Diskreet to search for them with the **Search floppies** option from the **Disk** menu (Alt-S).

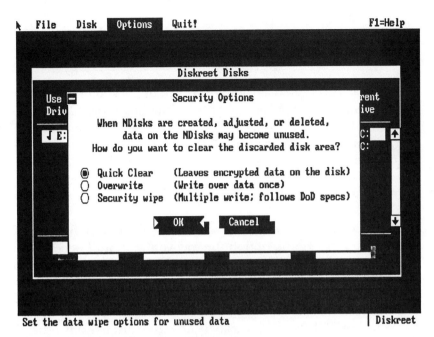

Figure 8-17   Security Options Dialog Box

Diskreet asks you which drive to search, finds the NDisks on that drive, and adds them to the list on the screen. Then you can open them if desired.

Copying, Backing Up, and Deleting NDisks

You can copy or back up a complete NDisk just like any other hidden file, using the name *filename.@#!*. You might have to unhide it first, depending on what copy or backup software you use. For example, DOS's COPY command can't work with a hidden file.

You can unhide all the NDisks on the current drive by entering the command DISKREET /SHOW. After you have processed them, you should hide them again by entering the command DISKREET /HIDE. To show or hide NDisks on another drive, use /SHOW:*d* and /HIDE:*d*, where *d* is the drive name of the host drive.

When you copy or back up a complete NDisk as a file, you copy its encrypted files and all the empty space, too. If you just want to copy or back up one or more files from the NDisk, open it and handle them like any other files, as in these commands (where E: is the NDisk's drive name):

```
C:\>COPY E:\*.DB3 A:
```
   (copies files from the NDisk to drive A:)

or

        C:\>BACKUP E:*.DB3 A: (backs up files from the NDisk to drive A:)

The files are decrypted as they are copied or backed up. If you copy them to
another NDisk, they will be decrypted from the source NDisk, then encrypted
again on the target NDisk.

You can delete an individual file using the normal means, as in this
command:

        C:\>DEL E:*.DB3

You can delete an entire NDisk with the **Delete** option from the **Disk** menu.
First, set up the wiping option the way you want it, if necessary. Then close
the NDisk if it's open. Finally, select the **Delete** option. You will be required
to enter the correct password.

> **Warning:** Deleted NDisks can be unerased just like any other files. But
> if you wipe the NDisk during deletion and if Erase Protect isn't enabled
> for the host drive, you won't be able to unerase the data.

Changing NDisk Definitions

As you work with an NDisk, you might find that you want to change some
of its characteristics: audit information, write protection, size, and so on.

You can get to a dialog box similar to the one shown in Figure 8-8 by
highlighting the NDisk and selecting **Edit**. Notice that the **Options** control
group includes a **Write protection** check box.

> **Note:** You can't change the encryption method in this dialog box.
> Once the NDisk has been created, the encryption method can't be
> changed.

NDisk Write Protection

After you have placed files in the NDisk, you might want to write-protect the
whole NDisk so that no files can be changed or deleted; you also won't be

able to add any more files to it. You can turn the write-protect feature on and off, so you can write-protect it now, then edit the definition again later to remove the write protection.

Changing the Size

To make the NDisk larger or smaller, you should take several steps:

- Make a backup copy of the entire NDisk for safety's sake. A power loss during a size change could result in serious data loss.
- Check the wiping options and select the one you want.
- Highlight the NDisk's name in the Disks screen and select the **Adjust size** option from the **Disk** menu. After entering the correct password, the next dialog box asks whether you want to expand or shrink the NDisk. Figure 8-18 shows the dialog box that opens when you select **Expand**; the **Shrink** dialog box is similar.

After you select the desired size and select **OK**, progress boxes keep you advised of what's happening.

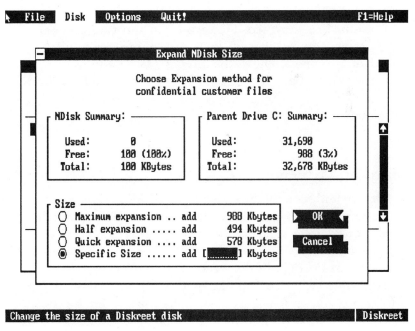

Figure 8-18   Expand Dialog Box

Changing the Password

You can change an NDisk's password, with the option of reencrypting all the existing files using the new password.

> **Tip:** For maximum protection, change your NDisk passwords regularly. If you think someone has cracked a password, reencrypt existing files using the new password.

Follow these steps to change a password:

- Make a backup copy if you plan to reencrypt. A power loss during reencryption could result in serious data loss.
- Highlight the NDisk and select **change disk Password** from the **Disk** menu. You will be asked for the current password.
- You are given the option of changing the description (because many people like to store the encoded password in the description).
- Next you must enter the new password (twice).
- Select **Quick** or **Full** change. If you select a **Quick** change, existing files are not reencrypted. However, you must access them using the new password, even though their encryption key is still the old password. But if someone knows the old password and the encryption algorithm, they might be able to manually decrypt those files. So if you think that someone has cracked the NDisk's password, choose **Full** change, which reencrypts everything.

Keyboard and Screen Lock

Keyboard and screen lock provides an additional measure of protection for your files. When triggered, it blanks the screen and renders the keyboard (and mouse) useless. The keyboard isn't really locked in the traditional sense, but all entries are ignored except one: your main password, which immediately restores both the screen and the keyboard.

To enable keyboard and screen lock and set up the hotkey, use the same dialog box shown in Figure 8-14. Turn on the **Enable locking** option and select the desired hotkey. If both quick-close and locking are enabled, the same hotkey triggers both of them.

Table 8-1   DISKREET Command Parameters

/ENCRYPT:*filename*	Encrypts the specified file(s)
/DECRYPT:*filename*	Decrypts the specified file
/PASSWORD:*password*	Specifies password for encryption or decryption
/SHOW [*d:*]	Removes hidden attribute from NDisks on *d:* drive
/HIDE [*d:*]	Restores hidden attribute to NDisks on *d:* drive
/CLOSE	Closes all open NDisks
/ON	Enables the Diskreet device driver
/OFF	Disables the Diskreet device driver

The DISKREET Command

Some Diskreet functions can be accomplished from the DOS command prompt, without going through the Diskreet screen, menus, and dialog boxes.

Table 8-1 shows the command format. Only one file can be processed per command. If you omit the /PASSWORD parameter, Diskreet prompts you for the password.

Suppose you want to individually encrypt a file. You could enter a command like this:

```
C:\>DISKREET /PASSWORD:TRX5L-23 /ENCRYPT:D:\YEREPORT\TRIALBAL.DAT
```

The first dialog box you would see asks for the name of the encrypted file, suggesting TRIALBAL.SEC. To decrypt the same file again, you would enter this command:

```
C:\>DISKREET /PASSWORD:TRX5L-23 /DECRYPT:D:\YEREPORT\TRIALBAL.SEC
```

Decrypting Files That Were Never Encrypted

You might accidentally attempt to decrypt a file that isn't encrypted. For example, in the above command, you might mistakenly use the filename TRIALBAL.DAT instead of TRIALBAL.SEC. One of the first things that Diskreet looks for is its own signature in the file header (you can see it in Figure 8-1). If not found, Diskreet does not attempt to decrypt the file, displaying an error message instead.

Unloading the DISKREET.SYS TSR

DISKREET.SYS takes up about 50K of memory. If it resides in extended memory, you probably won't have any problem with it. But if it resides in conventional memory, you might need to unload it sometimes to make room for a large application.

To unload the TSR, choose **System settings** from the **Options** menu. In the resulting dialog box, turn on the option called **Do not load the NDisk driver**. This adds a /U switch to the DISKREET.SYS statement in CONFIG.SYS, which has a similar effect to removing the statement, except that it's easier to reverse.

Like all changes to CONFIG.SYS, you must reboot to put it into effect. When you complete the **System settings** dialog, a dialog box asks if you want to reset (reboot) now; you can choose between **Reset** and **Don't reset**.

When you do reboot, you'll see the DISKREET.SYS startup message, but it will say that the device driver is not loaded. You can still encrypt and decrypt individual files, but none of the options on the **Disks** or **Options** menus are available, and you will not be able to access any NDisks.

> **Tip:** If boot messages go by too fast for you to read, you can press the Pause button to temporarily pause the boot process. Any key except Pause resumes it.

To reload DISKREET.SYS, start Diskreet and select **Disks**. The dialog box shown in Figure 8-19 opens. Select **Activate** to remove the /U from the DISKREET.SYS statement. In the next dialog box, select **Reset** to reboot immediately, which will now load DISKREET.SYS.

Enabling and Disabling Diskreet

There may be cases where you want to disable Diskreet for a while without actually unloading it from memory. The command DISKREET /OFF disables DISKREET.SYS so that you cannot access any NDisks. You can enable it again by starting up Diskreet (with no switches) or by entering the command DISKREET /ON.

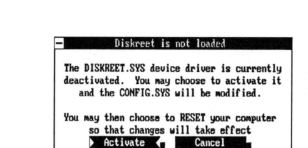

Figure 8-19   Diskreet Not Loaded Message

Looking Ahead

So far, we have shown you how to set up your system for maximum
performance and data protection. But problems can still occur, and the next
few chapters show you how to recover from them. In Chapter 9 you'll learn
how to use perhaps the most famous Norton Utility—UnErase, which recovers a file after you delete it.

9

UNERASE

The UnErase utility can be used to recover deleted files and subdirectories under a wide variety of circumstances. At the simplest level, you can recover a file that has been preserved by Erase Protect with 100 percent reliability. Without Erase Protect, you can still recover deleted files whose directory entries and clusters are intact, although you might have to manually adjust some clusters. Even if a file has been partially overwritten, you can recover whatever clusters are still available. And if all else fails, a manual UnErase facility lets you search the unused clusters for specific data and build a new file out of whatever clusters you find. These last two facilities might not always be wholly satisfactory, but you know what they say about half a loaf.

Background

DOS's way of handling files, directories, and the FAT make recovery possible on the one hand and difficult on the other. Figure 9-1 shows a directory and FAT that we will use to demonstrate how DOS works.

- When it deletes a file, DOS overwrites the first character of the file's directory entry with hex E5 (which appears on your screen as σ), which marks that directory entry as available. But it does not erase the rest of the directory entry. In particular, the deleted file's size and starting cluster number are still available until the directory entry actually gets

205

```
  Object   Edit   Link   View   Info   Tools   Quit                    F1=Help
Name      .Ext    Size      Date       Time    Cluster Arc R/O Sys Hid Dir Vol
Sector 15
⊡ESEG      DAT        9   2-18-91    6:54 pm      227   Arc
MIGRATE    EXE    53278  12-05-90   12:39 pm        5   Arc
RU         STY     1024  12-05-90   11:48 am       36   Arc
FIG4-1     PCX    47611  12-05-90   11:50 am       92   Arc
⌐OOD11     DOC    22528  12-05-90   12:52 pm        5   Arc
KOTC       IMG    12157  12-05-90   11:51 am      270   Arc
FIG4-3     PCX    46671  12-05-90   11:52 am      294   Arc
TAB4-1     DOC     3584  12-05-90   11:52 am      386   Arc
CHAP05     DOC    24064  12-05-90   11:53 am      393   Arc
FIG3-1     PCX    42656  12-05-90   11:54 am      440   Arc
FIG3-2     PCX    45785  12-05-90   11:55 am      524   Arc
FIG3-3     PCX    45009  12-05-90   11:55 am      614   Arc
FIG3-4     PCX    43653  12-05-90   11:58 am      702   Arc
FIG3-5     PCX    50592  12-05-90   11:59 am      788   Arc
FIG3-6     PCX    51301  12-05-90   12:00 pm      807   Arc
FIG3-7     PCX    61507  12-05-90   12:08 pm      988   Arc
Sector 16
FIG3-8     PCX    69795  12-05-90   12:09 pm     1109   Arc
FIGS03     VGR      276  12-05-90   12:09 pm     1246   Arc
  Root Directory                                        Sector 15 ▲
  A:\                                              Offset 0, hex 0 ▼
  Press ALT or F10 to select menus                    | Disk Editor
```

(a)   **Directory**

```
  Object   Edit   Link   View   Info   Tools   Quit                    F1=Help
Sector 1
                     ▣0           0          0          6          7          8
      9        10         11         12         13         14         15         16
     17        18         19         20         21         22         23         24
     25        26         27         28         29         30         31         32
     33        34         35         58         37      <EOF>         39      <EOF>
     41     <EOF>         43         44         45         46         47      <EOF>
     49     <EOF>         51      <EOF>         53         54         55         56
     57     <EOF>         61          0          0         62         63         64
     65        66         67         68         69         70         71         72
     73        74        227          0          0          0          0          0
      0         0          0        235          0          0         87         88
     89        90         91        185         93         94         95         96
     97        98         99        100        101        102        103        104
    105       106        107        108        109        110        111        112
    113       114        115        116       -117        118        119        120
    121       122        123        124        125        126        127        128
    129       130        131        132        133        134        135        136
    137       138        139        140        141        142        143        144
    145       146        147        148        149        150        151        152
    153       154        155        156        157        158        159        160
  FAT (1st Copy)                                          Sector 1 ▲
  Drive A:                                         Cluster 2, hex 2 ▼
  Press ALT or F10 to select menus                    | Disk Editor
```

(b)   **FAT**

Figure 9-1   Sample Directory and FAT

reused for a new file. In Figure 9-1, you can see that the first and fifth files have been deleted from the directory.

• When deleting a file, DOS zeros its FAT entries, making them available to other files. But it does not erase the clusters themselves; the deleted file's data are still available on the disk until its clusters are reused by other files (or wiped). You can see 15 available clusters in Figure 9-1.

• DOS 5.0 has introduced a new feature called *delete-tracking*, which keeps a temporary record of the former location of deleted files. Unlike Erase Protect, delete-tracking does not preserve the clusters themselves; all it does is record where they were. But even that can help UnErase recover a file that hasn't been preserved by Erase Protect. Delete-tracking is optional, so you have to turn it on for each drive you want to track, with a command like this:

```
MIRROR /Tdrive: [/Tdrive:] ...
```

If you don't use Erase Protect, you might want to place a MIRROR command in your AUTOEXEC.BAT file to track each of your hard drives. It's not as good protection as Erase Protect, but it's better than nothing.

• When adding a file to a directory, DOS uses the first available entry starting from the top of the directory. If you add a file to the directory shown in Figure 9-1, it will use the first entry, because it's the first available one.

• When adding a file to a disk, DOS usually uses the first available clusters, starting from the beginning of the disk or partition. If you add a five-cluster file to the disk in Figure 9-1, the file will probably go into clusters 2, 3, 4, 59, and 60.

• When expanding an existing file, DOS usually uses the next available cluster. In Figure 9-1, if you expand the file currently in cluster 5, it will probably expand into cluster 59.

Figure 9-2 shows the layout of a directory entry and its relationship to the file's cluster chain in the FAT. Essentially, the directory entry identifies the size of the file and points to the first cluster in the chain. Each FAT cluster entry contains the number of the next cluster in the file's chain. EOF (end-of-file) indicates the last cluster in the chain.

In the example, the file named SMARTSET.TBL is 7516 bytes long, requiring four clusters. It resides in clusters 101, 103, 104, and 106. Cluster 102 is bad, and cluster 105 is available (probably because its file was deleted after SMARTSET.TBL was created).

Suppose we deleted SMARTSET.TBL and now we want to recover it. Also assume for the time being that Erase Protect and delete-tracking are not

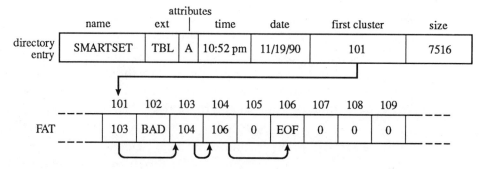

Figure 9-2   Directory and FAT Entries for a File

enabled. Immediately after deletion, the directory entry (except for the first character) is intact and the data still exists on the disk; the FAT information has been lost, however. At this point the prognosis for recovery is good, but not excellent. UnErase can find the first cluster number and the size of the file in the directory entry; from the size, it knows how many clusters to look for. Knowing the way that DOS assigns clusters, it can make a pretty good guess at what the cluster chain was. (In the case of SMARTSET.TBL, it would assume that the four clusters were 101, 103, 104, and 105, which would be incorrect. However, you could work with UnErase to find and recover the right clusters.)

Complications with Unerasing

Now suppose you add data to your disk before you recover SMARTSET.TBL. If you add new data to a file, it expands into the next available cluster, which might be the first cluster of SMARTSET.TBL. When that happens, the prognosis for recovery drops from good to poor. UnErase can still find the directory entry, but it can see from the FAT that the former first cluster is in use by another file.

Let's go a step further and add some new files to the directory before recovering SMARTSET.TBL so that its directory entry is overlaid. Now UnErase cannot find any trace of the file by name, even though some of its clusters might still be intact. However, it can help you find at least some of the clusters. You can examine unused clusters one by one or search unused clusters for particular types of data structures (such as Lotus 1-2-3 and Symphony) or for a particular string of characters (such as "John Smith").

As you locate clusters, you can build a file from the appropriate ones. It's unlikely that you can reconstruct a complete file this way, but you might be able to save several hours' worth of data.

Now let's look at another situation. Suppose that, in addition to deleting the file, you also deleted the directory it was in. You can recover a subdirectory just like any other file, as long as the data is still available; then you can try to recover the files in it. But if the subdirectory's entry in its parent directory has been reused, you might have trouble getting to the file you want, even though the subdirectory's data is still intact somewhere on the disk. In this case, UnErase will do a lost-name search: It searches the unused clusters for all abandoned directory entries. If the directory entry is located, UnErase can then try to recover the file.

   In the final analysis, if the data is somewhere on the disk, UnErase can help you find and recover it. It could take from a few seconds up to an hour or longer, depending on the condition of the file's directory entry, its first cluster, and its remaining clusters.

Using Erase Protect and Delete-Tracking

When Erase Protect is turned on, it intercepts DOS's normal behavior and preserves the clusters of a deleted file in its TRASHCAN directory. It also preserves control information about the original name and directory of the file. UnErase uses the Erase Protect information to recover the file. Since the clusters have been preserved, there are no problems in recovering it.

   If a file has already been purged from TRASHCAN when you try to recover it, its clusters might still be available for recovery, but you'll have to use manual recovery methods.

   UnErase uses delete-tracking information, if available, to recover a multiple-cluster file when Erase Protect has not preserved it or has purged it. In such cases, UnErase doesn't have to guess at where the clusters were, which can be inaccurate when the file was fragmented. Also, UnErase can compare delete-tracking information to the FAT and warn you when some of a file's clusters have been reused.

   However, there are cases where clusters recovered through delete-tracking aren't completely correct. Suppose the file named TIRELESS was in clusters 1280, 1281, 1285, and 1286. After TIRELESS was deleted, a file named TEMP0005.$#$ used clusters 1280 and 1281, but it was subsequently deleted and 1280 and 1281 are available again. If you try to recover TIRELESS now, UnErase compares the delete-tracking information to the FAT and sees that all the clusters are available. But when you examine the recovered file, you'll find that the first two clusters contain data from the other file. This type of situation happens quite a lot because of the way that applications such as word processors and database managers create and delete temporary files as they work. You'll see shortly how you can tell the difference in UnErase between a file that is preserved by Erase Protect, one that has only delete-tracking information available for it, and one that has neither.

   Another source of information about the former location of a file is the IMAGE.DAT file saved by the Image program and the MIRROR.FIL file saved by DOS's Mirror. Both of these files contain copies of earlier root directories and FATs, which UnErase will use to find the clusters belonging to a file if no better information is available. The problem with the information supplied by IMAGE.DAT and MIRROR.FIL is that it could be out of date. UnErase includes command switches to prevent the use of IMAGE.DAT and MIRROR.FIL information if you wish. You'll see the command switches at the end of the chapter.

Starting UnErase

If you need to recover files right now, before installing the utilities or adding any other data to your hard disk, insert the Norton Utilities Emergency diskette (#2 for 5.25" diskettes) in drive A: and enter the command A:UN-ERASE at the command prompt.

If the utilities are already installed, you can select **UnErase** from the Norton menu or enter the command UNERASE at the DOS prompt.

However you start it, the initial UnErase screen should appear, as shown in Figure 9-3. The dialog box in the middle lists all the erased files in the current directory. Key information from the directory entries is listed, along with a prognosis for recovery.

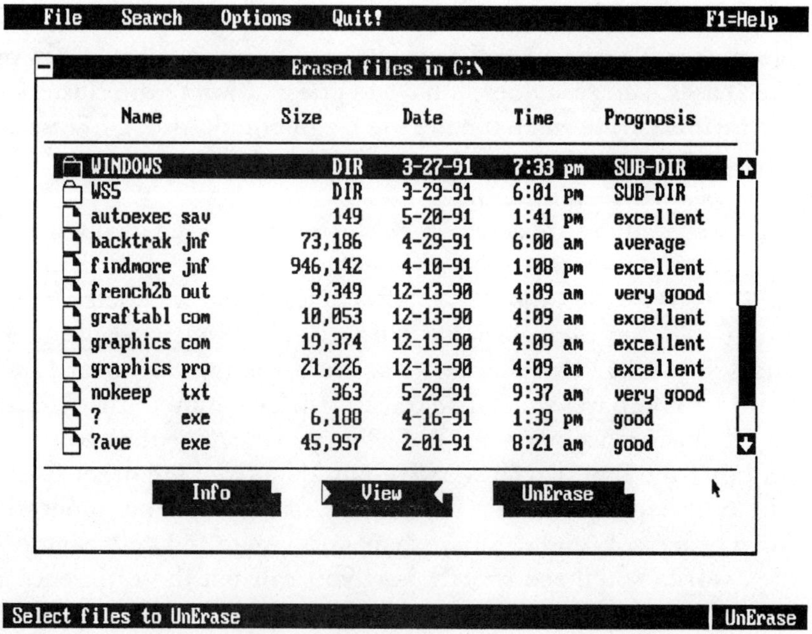

File	Search	Options	Quit!		F1=Help

Erased files in C:

Name		Size	Date	Time	Prognosis
WINDOWS		DIR	3-27-91	7:33 pm	SUB-DIR
WS5		DIR	3-29-91	6:01 pm	SUB-DIR
autoexec	sav	149	5-28-91	1:41 pm	excellent
backtrak	jnf	73,186	4-29-91	6:00 am	average
findmore	jnf	946,142	4-10-91	1:08 pm	excellent
french2b	out	9,349	12-13-90	4:09 am	very good
graftabl	com	10,053	12-13-90	4:09 am	excellent
graphics	com	19,374	12-13-90	4:09 am	excellent
graphics	pro	21,226	12-13-90	4:09 am	excellent
nokeep	txt	363	5-29-91	9:37 am	very good
?	exe	6,180	4-16-91	1:39 pm	good
?ave	exe	45,957	2-01-91	8:21 am	good

Info	View	UnErase

Select files to UnErase	UnErase

Figure 9-3   Initial UnErase Screen

You might be surprised at the number of unfamiliar filenames as well as the many duplicates. These result from applications such as word processors and spreadsheets freely making and deleting temporary working files and backup copies. The date and time fields can become important in deciding which of many duplicates to recover.

Locating Directories and Files

When you start UnErase, deleted files in the current directory are listed. Options on the **File** menu let you switch drives and directories while the **Options** menu lets you sort the list of files so that it is most convenient for your needs.

Changing Drives and Directories

To recover files on a different drive, select the **change Drive** option or press Alt-D. A dialog box lets you select the drive you want to work with. You will see the current directory on that drive.

To change directories, you can select **change diRectory** or press Alt-R and a dialog box lets you select the desired directory. But you don't always have to go through the dialog box. The current directory's subdirectories and parent directory (named ..) are all listed in the UnErase file list; their names are shown in all caps and their prognoses are shown as SUB-DIR. You can switch to any listed subdirectory by double-clicking on it or by highlighting it and pressing Enter.

Viewing All Directories

If you can't remember which directory the desired file was in, or if you want to recover files from several directories, try selecting **view All directories** (Alt-A). All deleted files on the current drive are listed. Instead of date and time information, each file's path is displayed.

Sorting the File List

If the file list is so long that you have difficulty finding the file(s) you need, sorting the list might help. Figure 9-4 shows the **Options** menu. You can sort the file list by filename (the default), extension, date and time (available when only one directory is displayed), size, directory (available only when all directories are displayed), or prognosis.

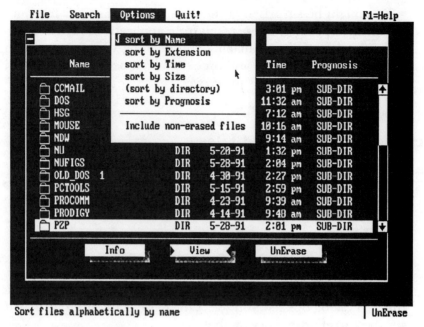

Figure 9-4   Options Menu

Including Nonerased Files

Sometimes it helps to see nonerased files in the list, which you can do by selecting **Include non-erased files**. Comparing file names, dates and times, sizes, and directories can help you identify the erased files you're looking for. You can view information on a non-erased file, and you can view the file itself. The prognosis **nonerased** identifies nonerased files in the list.

> **Note:** When you list nonerased files in all directories, you will see the entries in the TRASHCAN directory along with others, but the filenames look like @l30a40a.sav and @lj0a40j.sav. These are the names Erase Protect assigns to the files it preserves. Their original names and paths are recorded in Erase Protect's index.

Unerasing Files Preserved by Erase Protect

When Erase Protect is in effect, it captures erased files and stores them in a hidden directory called TRASHCAN for a while. As long as they are in TRASHCAN, files can be unerased with no problems.

Even though the files are stored in the TRASHCAN directory, they show up in the listing for the directory they were deleted from, as does FINDMORE.JNF in Figure 9-3 where it is listed under C:\. Look for these two characteristics for a TRASHCAN file:

- The first character of the filename is valid, not a question mark.
- The prognosis for recovery is "excellent."

In Figure 9-3, five files are preserved in TRASHCAN.

Checking the File

If you're not sure whether a file is the one you want, you can view information about it. Figure 9-5 shows the dialog box that appears when you select the **Info** button. The **Next** and **Prev** buttons show you the other files in the list.

If you're still not sure, try examining the file itself by selecting **View** or double-clicking on the file entry. A sample view is shown in Figure 9-6. The text view is shown; you can switch to hex view by selecting the **Hex** button. Use PageUp and PageDown and the Up and Down arrow keys to scroll through the file. The **Next** and **Prev** buttons show the other files in the current list.

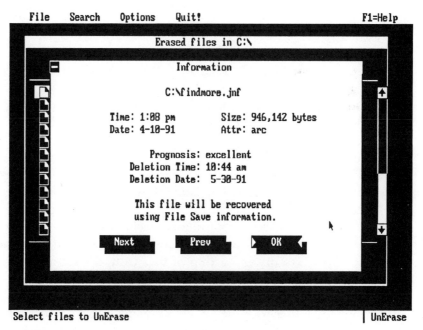

Figure 9-5   UnErase File Info

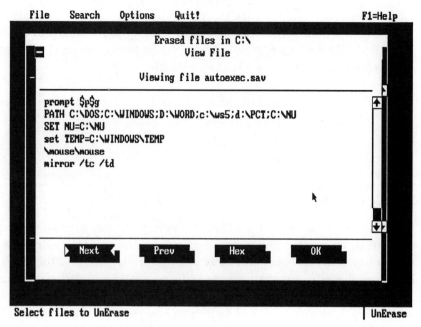

Figure 9-6   UnErase File Viewer

Recovering Files

To recover one file that's preserved in TRASHCAN, highlight it and select **UnErase**. The word RECOVERED appears in the prognosis column next to each file you recover.

You can recover several TRASHCAN files at once by tagging them first. To tag individual files, click right on each one or highlight each one in turn and press the Spacebar. You can untag a file again by repeating the same procedure.

The **File** menu, which is shown in Figure 9-7, can be used to tag groups of files using global filenames. The **select Group** option (or the gray + key on the numeric keypad) opens a dialog box where you can enter a global filename; all files matching that filename will be tagged.

You can also use the **Unselect group** option (or the gray – key on the numeric keypad) to untag a group of files from the set of tagged ones. For example, suppose you want to tag all the listed files except those with extension TMP. You would select *.*, then unselect *.TMP. You can also untag individual files with the Spacebar or the right mouse button.

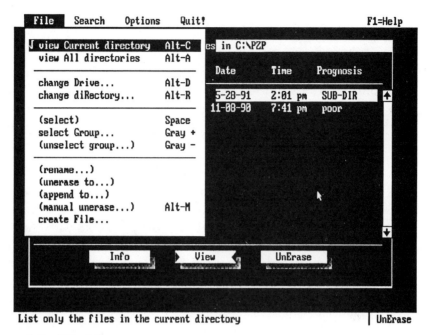

Figure 9-7   File Menu

Tip: When you use a global filename to tag a group of files, be sure to scroll through the entire file list to review all the files that have been tagged.

When all the desired files are tagged, select UnErase. A progress box shows what is happening as the files are unerased. As long as the tagged files are all TRASHCAN files, there will be no problem in recovering them. Each file is marked as RECOVERED in the **Prognosis** column after it is unerased.

Recovering Files from Delete-Tracking Information

If a file is not preserved by Erase Protect but has delete tracking information available for it, the filename is intact but the prognosis might be anything from "very good" to "poor." A "very good" prognosis means that all the file's clusters are still available. But that doesn't mean they still contain the same file's data. Another file might have used and released the clusters in the meantime. Lower prognoses mean that at least some of the file's clusters are currently in use by other files and cannot be recovered. A "poor" prognosis means that all the file's clusters are unavailable and the file cannot be recovered.

You can find out how UnErase interprets the prognosis by selecting the **Info** button. And you can use the **View** button to see what clusters will be recovered. If they contain the wrong data, you can be sure that the right data no longer exists, because there's no chance that UnErase has selected the wrong clusters when delete-tracking information is available. But all might not be lost; you could try to locate an earlier version of the file in the unused clusters using manual recovery techniques.

If you select the **UnErase** button for a delete-tracked file and nothing happens—that is, the prognosis does not change—the file was not recovered because the current directory already contains a file with the same name. You can use the **unerase To** option from the **File** menu to recover the file to a different directory. Or you can select **Include nonerased files**, find the file with the same name and the prognosis of "nonerased," and use the **Rename** option from the **File** menu to rename it. (You can't rename the erased file.)

Recovering Unprotected Files

You can recover files that haven't been preserved by Erase Protect or delete-tracked, but it can take a little more work and the results might not always be perfect. Even when the prognosis is good, UnErase could identify some incorrect clusters so that you may need to fix the file manually.

Tip: Binary files (program files with extensions EXE, COM, SYS, and BIN) are nearly impossible for the average human to read. If you try to unerase a binary file containing more than one cluster, there is no way for you to confirm the contents of the clusters. In most cases, you should restore a binary file by reinstalling the software from its original diskettes rather than trying to recover it.

Completing the Filename

Without Erase Protect or delete-tracking, the first character of the filename is lost. When you recover a file in this situation, UnErase asks you to supply the missing first character. It doesn't have to be the original first character; any character that's legal in a DOS filename will do. In Figure 9-3, the last two files in the window are not preserved by Erase Protect or Mirror.

UnErase won't let you duplicate a filename that already exists in the same directory. Suppose you delete SMARTSET.TBL and create a new one in the same directory. If you then recover the original one, you would have to give it a first character other than S.

> **Tip:** You could also recover it to another directory, which we'll cover in a few pages.

Unerasing "Good" or "Average" Files

For a file without delete-tracking information, a "good" prognosis means that the file's first cluster is available, and there are enough consecutive available clusters to hold the entire size of the file. For example, if a file started in cluster 1521 and required 13 clusters, and clusters 1521 through 1533 are available, the prognosis is "good." The file was *probably* contained in clusters 1521 through 1533, and those are the clusters that will be recovered if you select the **UnErase** button.

> **Tip:** Don't forget you can check the file using the **View** button to see if what's been found in the selected clusters is worth recovering.

An "average" prognosis means that the first cluster is available but there aren't enough consecutive clusters to recover the file in one chunk. UnErase is going to have to recover fragmented clusters, and the probability of getting the wrong clusters is high. You might have to manually adjust the file after recovery.

To unerase a file with a "good" or "average" prognosis, highlight it and select **UnErase**. A dialog box asks for the first character of the filename. (It might list unavailable letters; i.e., letters that would create duplicate filenames in the directory.) Then the file is unerased and the word "recovered" replaces the word "good" or "average" in the file list.

Since it's possible that some wrong clusters were recovered, you should view the recovered file to make sure it's okay. If it's not, you'll need to correct the problem, as explained in the next section.

> **Tip:** Don't be misled by nonsense data at the end of your recovered file. If the file's data seems intact, the nonsense at the end is just slack and can be ignored.

Correcting a Recovered File

Once you have recovered a file, you can manually adjust it by adding, deleting, and repositioning clusters. To start this process, highlight the file and select **aPpend to** from the **File** menu. Figure 9-8 shows the dialog box that appears.

> **Tip:** You can manually adjust any current file, not just unerased ones. Use the **Include nonerased files** option to add existing files to the UnErase screen. Then highlight the file you want to work with and select **aPpend to**. UnErase won't let you append a file just recovered from TRASHCAN or from delete-tracking information, but you can restart UnErase so the file looks like a nonerased file, then append it.

Viewing the File

As you work with the file, you might need to view it each time you add and remove clusters to see the results. The **view File** button displays the file in its current form on a screen that's similar to the general UnErase file viewer except that cluster numbers are identified.

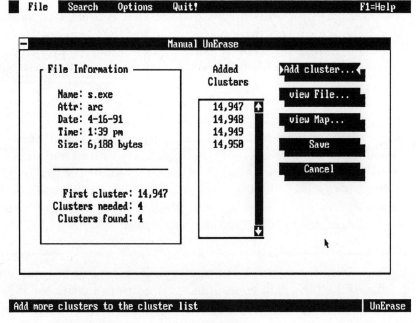

Figure 9-8   Manual UnErase Dialog Box

You can also select the **view Map** option to view a map showing the relationship of the current clusters to all the used and unused clusters on the drive.

Adding Clusters

To fix the file, you need to find and add the correct clusters, if they're available. Then go back and delete the unwanted clusters.

To find the necessary clusters, select **Add cluster**, which produces the dialog box shown in Figure 9-9. The **All clusters** option won't do any good after the file has already been recovered; UnErase has already added all the most likely clusters and won't add any more as a result of this option. But this option is very useful when manually building a file from scratch.

If you happen to know the numbers of the clusters you want, you can select the **Cluster number** option, which opens a dialog box where you can specify the desired cluster numbers.

But most likely, the **Next probable** option is the one you'll use when fixing an existing file. It adds the next available cluster to the file. Then you can view the file and decide if you want to keep the cluster.

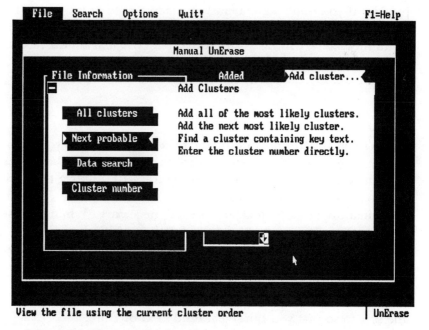

Figure 9-9   Add Clusters Dialog Box

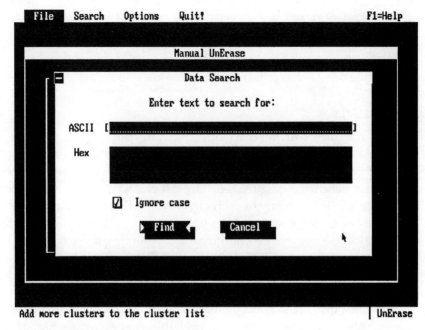

Figure 9-10   Data Search Dialog Box

> **Tip:** If you don't want a cluster, make a note of it but don't delete it
> until you have added at least one more cluster. If you delete a cluster
> immediately, UnErase will probably choose it again the next time you
> select **Next probable.**

Searching for Clusters

If you're having trouble finding the needed clusters and you know what data
you're looking for, you can speed things up with **Data Search,** which
produces the dialog box shown in Figure 9-10. Enter a text string such as
"Norton Utilities" or a hex string such as "E5 06 9F 12 FF"; you can use a
combination of both text and hex if necessary. When you select **Find,**
UnErase searches available clusters for the specified string.

Figure 9-11 shows the dialog box that opens when UnErase finds a cluster
containing the specified data. The found string is highlighted in the display
(in this case, it's "norton"). You can view the cluster and decide whether to
add it to the file or not. If you select **Add cluster,** the dialog box remains on
the screen so that you can select **Find next** or **Done.**

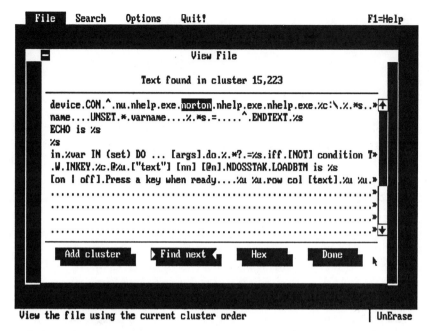

Figure 9-11   Found Cluster

If there are a lot of unused clusters on the drive, the search could take a long time. You can interrupt it by pressing any key or clicking any mouse button.

Even when the prognosis is good, don't be surprised if you can't find all the clusters belonging to a file. The first cluster might be intact, but a later cluster could have been overwritten.

Deleting Clusters

Once you have added all the necessary clusters, or as many as you can find, you might need to remove unwanted clusters. In the **Manual UnErase** dialog box (Figure 9-8), delete a cluster by highlighting its number in the **Added Clusters** box and pressing the Del key.

Rearranging Clusters

Sometimes you need to change the order of the clusters in the file. To move a cluster, highlight its number and press the Spacebar to tag it. Then use the Up and Down arrow keys to drag it to its new position. Press the Spacebar again to untag it. With the mouse, use the right button to drag it to its new position.

Saving the File

When the clusters are correct (or as near as possible), use the **Save** button to replace the existing file with the corrected one. A warning message advises you if you have selected more or fewer clusters than the file originally contained. The **File Information** box tells how many clusters the file contained when it was deleted and how many you have now. In the warning box, you can select **Resume** to work on the clusters some more or **Save anyway** to save the file as it is.

When you recover a file that's not in the TRASHCAN, you might get one or more clusters that used to belong to another erased file. If that other file is delete-tracked, you will see its prognosis drop to a lower rating immediately. If the other file is not delete-tracked but you took its first cluster, you'll see its prognosis drop to "poor." But if the other file is not delete-tracked and its first cluster is still available, its prognosis won't change.

If the clusters in question belong to the recovered file and you keep them there, the other file's prognosis will remain low, as it should—those clusters were never really available to it anyway. But if you release those clusters from the recovered file, the other file's prognosis will go back up again.

For this reason, when recovering several files not preserved by TRASHCAN, don't tag them as a group and recover them all at once. Recover one file at a time, viewing and adjusting its clusters before recovering the next one.

Unerasing "Poor" Files

A file's prognosis is "poor" when its former first cluster has been reused for another file. The condition of subsequent clusters is unknown if the file is not delete-tracked. You will not be able to recover the entire file, since at least its first cluster is gone, but you might be able to find some of its clusters. A delete-tracked file has a "poor" prognosis only when none of its clusters are available for recovery.

Such a file cannot be recovered automatically; the **UnErase** button produces an error message. You might be able to use a manual procedure on the file. To start the manual procedure, highlight the filename and select the **Manual unerase** option from the **File** menu. The resulting dialog box is just like the one in Figure 9-8 except that no sectors have been found and none are listed in the **Added clusters** box.

> **Note:** The **Manual unerase** option is not available for delete-tracked files since their clusters are known to be available or unavailable.

Suppose the file originally had ten clusters. The **All clusters** option adds the ten available clusters that follow the file's original first cluster. Once you have added the first set of clusters, you can continue to add, delete, and rearrange clusters as with good or average files.

You might prefer to use the **Data Search** or **Cluster number** options right from the start.

Recovering Files with No Directory Entries

So far, we've dealt with files whose directory entries appear in the UnErase file list. But you can also partially recover files whose directory entries have been overlaid and do not appear in the file list. You recover these files by constructing new files out of whatever clusters you can find. Since there is no file entry, you must create a new one by selecting **Create file** from the **File** menu. A dialog box asks for a new filename, which must be unique to the directory. You can specify a path, if desired; otherwise, the current path is used.

After the new file is named, the **Manual UnErase** screen appears, and you can begin finding and adding clusters just as you do in other manual recovery situations.

Recovering Directories

Suppose you had a subdirectory named C:\REALPROP, but you deleted all its files and removed the directory. Now you want to restore the directory and its files. After starting UnErase, you should select the C:\ directory. Since it was the parent directory, that is where REALPROP's directory entry should be. If REALPROP shows up in the list of erased files, you can recover it just like any other file. Otherwise, you'll probably need to reach the file by searching for lost names, which is explained shortly.

Once REALPROP is recovered, you should be able to switch to it and start recovering its files.

Recovering Files from Deleted Directories

Suppose you had a file named NIGHTSKY.DAT in a directory named ASTROGAM. Both the file and the directory were deleted and you can no

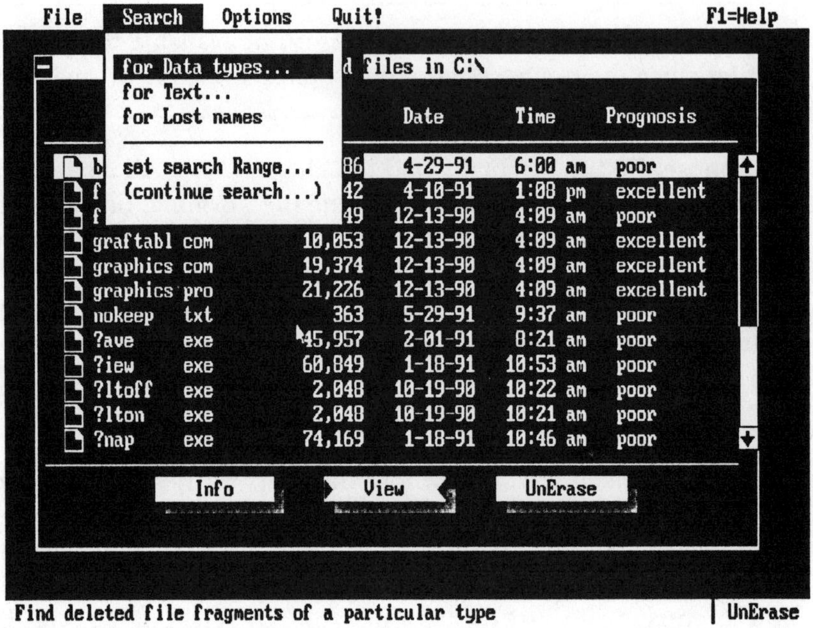

Figure 9-12   Search Menu

longer find the directory entries to recover them. How can you recover
NIGHTSKY.DAT?

Figure 9-12 shows the **Search** menu, which is used to find lost data (if it
still exists). Since your best chance of recovering NIGHTSKY.DAT is to find
its lost directory entry (which might still be on the disk in ASTROGAM
clusters, even though the ASTROGAM directory entry is gone), you should
try **Search for Lost names** first. This feature searches the unused clusters of
the current drive for any abandoned directories and lists all file entries it
finds. You can interrupt it when you see the name you're looking for appear
in the list. You then select files to recover just as you can on the erased files
list; they are recovered to the current directory. To return to the normal
erased files list, press Alt-C. To continue the search without having to restart
it, select **Continue search** from the **Search** menu.

If you don't locate NIGHTSKY.DAT's entry, then you can try one of the
other searches. The **Search for Data Types** option will let you select up to
four data types: normal text, Lotus 1-2-3 and Symphony, dBASE, and other
(that is, *not* text, Lotus 1-2-3, Symphony, or dBASE). Then UnErase searches
for unused clusters that match the designated data types. It lists found
clusters on a screen in the same format as the erased files list. Sometimes it
can link several clusters together in a chain. If it can't figure out the name of

the file that owned the chain, it creates a new name in the format FILE0001.*xxx* (where *xxx* indicates the type of data found). You can interrupt this process at any time, and you can view and recover any "file" in the list to the current directory.

> **Tip:** Incomplete Lotus 1-2-3, dBASE, and Symphony files might be usable if you use File Fix on them. (See Chapter 13 for File Fix.)

The **Search for Text** option lets you specify a text or hex string to search for. The **set search Range** option lets you enter cluster numbers to limit the area searched. But you can't force it to search used clusters. Only unused clusters are eligible for searching.

The **Continue search** option lets you continue an interrupted search without reentering the search parameters.

Unerasing to Another Directory

By default, UnErase places the recovered file in the same directory it was deleted from or the current directory if the original directory is no longer available. But there will be times when you want it in another directory. To accomplish that, select **Unerase to** from the **File** menu instead of the **UnErase** button. The first dialog box that opens asks which drive you want to use, and the next dialog box asks for the recovered file's path and name, suggesting a default.

The UNERASE Command

Suppose you erase the file named MSAFE.DOC and immediately change your mind. You really don't need to go through the UnErase screens to get it back. Simply enter this command at the DOS prompt:

```
UNERASE MSAFE.DOC
```

UnErase will examine the current directory for ?SAFE.DOC (MSAFE.DOC if Erase Protect or delete-tracking is in effect). If more than one exists, it will select the most recent one (according to the time and date stamp). If it is able to select and recover a file, it displays a message that the file was recovered.

If UnErase cannot recover the file because some of the clusters are no longer available, it will display a message to that effect. If it can't figure out which file to unerase or has any other problems, it displays the unerase screen, perhaps with several eligible files tagged.

A path and a global filename are both permitted in the UNERASE command.

UnErase also has three command switches. /IMAGE tells UnErase to use information in the IMAGE.DAT file, but not the MIRROR.FIL file. /MIRROR does the opposite; it causes UnErase to use the information in MIRROR.FIL but not IMAGE.DAT. As you might imagine, these two switches are mutually exclusive. The other switch, /NOTRACK, tells UnErase not to use delete-tracking information. You might use this switch if you want to manually recover a delete-tracked file, for example.

Looking Ahead

Now you know what to do if you accidentally erase a file or two (or change your mind after erasing them on purpose), but what if you accidentally reformat an entire disk? It's easy enough to do; all it takes is selecting the wrong drive or putting the wrong diskette in the right drive. All the files will be gone; so will their directories. You could manually recover each file (if the data still exists), but there's an easier way. The next chapter shows you how to use the UnFormat command to rescue all the files from a reformatted disk. Even if you don't need to do this right now, you might want to read the chapter anyway. It will make you a firm believer in Safe Format and Image.

10

UNFORMAT

If you've ever lost a set of files by accidentally reformatting the wrong disk, you'll appreciate what UnFormat can do for you. As long as the data has not actually been overwritten, UnFormat can recover the former directories and files. If an IMAGE.DAT or MIRROR.FIL file was saved as part of the formatting process, and if no subdirectories or files have been added to the disk since, then 100 percent of the data can be recovered. If subdirectories and files have been added to the disk since the reformatting, then UnFormat can recover the directories and files that haven't been overwritten. After unformatting, you might be able to rescue even more data with a manual UnErase (see Chapter 9).

UnFormat can also rescue the system area of a disk that has been corrupted by a virus, a runaway program, a power failure, or some other problem. If up-to-date Image or Mirror information is available, UnFormat can restore the Boot Record, FAT, and/or root directory as needed.

> **Tip:** UnFormat will treat FRECOVER.DAT (from Norton Utilities version 4.5 and earlier) just like IMAGE.DAT.

UnFormat can work without Image or Mirror information, but it does take longer and may not be as successful. (Sometimes it's actually more successful, as you will see.)

There are some situations in which UnFormat cannot rescue a formatted disk:

- The disk was physically reformatted. A physical format overwrites all the data in the clusters; all the directories and files are destroyed in the process. A physical format occurs when you run a DOS-style format on a diskette, or reformat a diskette using versions of DOS before 5.0. (Some format programs will do a physical format when reformatting a hard disk, too.) One reason for always using Norton Safe Format in safe mode or quick mode is that it does not physically reformat a disk. It does a logical format *only* on any disk that has already been physically formatted (see Chapter 3).

- The diskette was reformatted as a different capacity. If a diskette was originally formatted at 360K, for example, and you reformat it as 1.2M, then a physical format must be done, even by Safe Format.

- The disk was heavily reused after formatting. Every file and subdirectory you add to a disk takes up clusters that might hold former data. Restoring the former directory and FAT structure via UnFormat cannot bring back the clusters that have been overwritten. In fact, it can make a royal mess out of the disk. You are better off to manually unerase whatever former clusters you can find in this situation.

There are also several situations in which you will be able to recover part of the former information, but not all of it.

- You assigned a volume label while reformatting. The volume label takes up a directory entry, and the former contents of that entry are lost. No clusters will be overwritten, however.

- You made the disk bootable (and it wasn't bootable before). Making a disk bootable adds the system files and COMMAND.COM to the beginning of the disk, where they overwrite older directory entries and clusters. You'll lose whatever data was in the first few directory entries and clusters.

- You added files and/or subdirectories to the disk after reformatting. Every file or subdirectory you add overwrites a directory entry and at least one cluster.

You can get a perfect restoration of the former data only if all the following conditions are true:

- The disk was not physically reformatted.
- For a diskette, the capacity was not changed.

- If the disk was not bootable before, it was not made bootable while reformatting.
- A label was not added to the disk during reformatting.
- No files or subdirectories were added to the disk after reformatting.

Even if you can't get a perfect restoration, you can often restore some or most of the former data.

Starting UnFormat

If you need to unformat a hard disk before installing the Norton Utilities, insert the Emergency Diskette (#1 in the 5.25" format) into drive A: and enter these commands:

```
A:
UNFORMAT
```

If the Norton Utilities are already installed, you can start UnFormat by entering the UNFORMAT command at the DOS prompt or by selecting **UnFormat** from the Norton menu (**Recovery** section).

Note: If the UNFORMAT command results in the message "Invalid or unspecified drive," you've reached DOS 5.0's Unformat program instead of Norton's. Switch to the directory containing the Norton Utilities and try again. Or better yet, rename DOS's UNFORMAT.EXE to XXUFORMT.EXE.

Searching for IMAGE.DAT

UnFormat asks which drive to unformat. Then it opens the dialog box shown in Figure 10-1. Your answer to this question determines whether or not UnFormat will search for an image file.

Since recovery will be much better if an up-to-date image file is available, you should always answer yes to this question unless you're positive that no image information exists or that it's out of date. Recall that image information might have been saved by Safe Format, by Speed Disk, or by an Image or Mirror command. It doesn't do any harm to answer yes and have it turn out that there is no image file; it just takes a little time while UnFormat searches unsuccessfully for the file.

After you close this dialog box, UnFormat asks you if you're sure that you want to unformat the disk. If you answer **Yes**, it begins the search for an

Figure 10-1   Image Information Dialog Box

image file if you said there was one. A disk map appears so that you can watch the progress of the search.

When UnFormat finds the image file, it opens the dialog box in Figure 10-2. Now is the time for some intelligent consideration. Is the image file so out of date that you don't want to use it? Let's look at what happens when you use an image file. UnFormat copies the Boot Record, FAT, and root directory from the image file to the disk, overlaying the current ones. It makes no effort to coordinate the current contents of the clusters with these system areas. As long as nothing new has been written to the clusters since the image information was captured, it will work out perfectly. But if the clusters have changed, then the data in the image file will make the root directory and FAT out of sync with the actual contents of the clusters. If only a few clusters have changed—for example, if you made the diskette bootable or added only a couple of files after reformatting—then only a few restored files will be wrong and the unformat is probably worth it; it will rescue most of your files and subdirectories. But if the clusters have changed a lot since the image information was captured, then you should not use it in unformatting. You're better off letting UnFormat rebuild the disk from scratch.

Recall that Image will save the previous IMAGE.DAT as IMAGE.BAK if you wish. Mirror will save the previous MIRROR.FIL as MIRROR.BAK. If

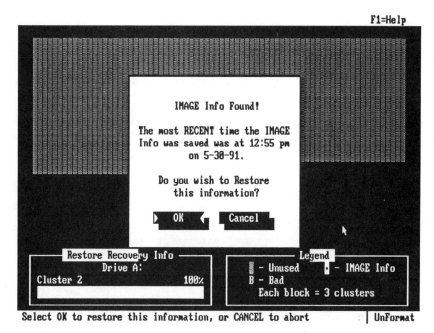

Figure 10-2   IMAGE.DAT Found Dialog Box

UnFormat finds multiple files, it opens a dialog box like the one in Figure 10-3. Here again, you need to make an intelligent decision about which image file to use, if any. You want the version that was saved when the disk was reformatted, or if that wasn't done, the most recent version before the disk was reformatted. Ordinarily, that will be the version saved in IMAGE.DAT or MIRROR.FIL. But if you've run Image or Mirror on the disk since reformatting it, either intentionally or inadvertently (e.g., by rebooting), then you would need to use an earlier file to unformat the disk.

Tip: Image will not record image information immediately after reformatting a nonbootable disk because the root directory and FAT are empty. Therefore, if you capture an image during reformatting, then run Image on the disk immediately (perhaps by rebooting), the second image will not be captured and IMAGE.DAT will still be valid. But if you reformat the disk to be bootable, the root directory and FAT contain entries for the system files and an Image command would capture a new IMAGE.DAT.

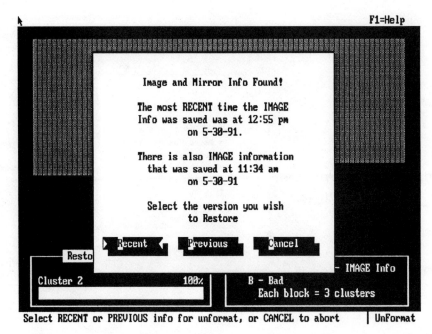

F1=Help

```
                Image and Mirror Info Found!

               The most RECENT time the IMAGE
               Info was saved was at 12:55 pm
                       on 5-30-91.

               There is also IMAGE information
                  that was saved at 11:34 am
                       on 5-30-91

                 Select the version you wish
                        to Restore

      ▶ Recent ◀      Previous       Cancel
```

Resto...

Cluster 2   100%   B - Bad
                                   Each block = 3 clusters

Select RECENT or PREVIOUS info for unformat, or CANCEL to abort | UnFormat

Figure 10-3   Two Image Files Found

If you're trying to recover from damage to your system areas by a virus or other problem, as opposed to reformatting, then you need to use the image file that was saved immediately before the damage was done, if one exists.

Full or Partial Restoration

After you deal with the image file, UnFormat gives you one last chance to change your mind by asking if you're *absolutely* sure you want to unformat the designated drive. Then the dialog box in Figure 10-4 opens.

A **Full** restoration replaces the Boot Record, root directory, and FAT, while a **Partial** restoration lets you choose which of these items to restore. If you're trying to undo a reformatting, you should do a full restoration. A partial restoration is appropriate if you're trying to recover a corrupted item, but if you're not sure what to do, you should probably do the full restoration.

Rebuilding the Disk from Scratch

When image data is not available, UnFormat must rebuild the root directory and FAT by examining the data in the clusters. It's fairly easy to reconstruct

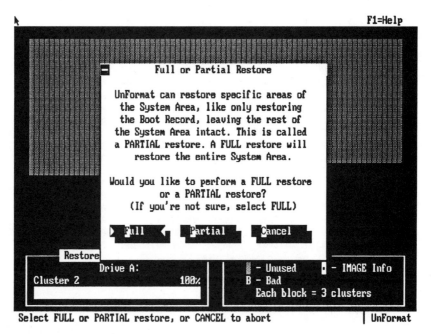

Full or Partial Restore

UnFormat can restore specific areas of
the System Area, like only restoring
the Boot Record, leaving the rest of
the System Area intact. This is called
a PARTIAL restore. A FULL restore will
restore the entire System Area.

Would you like to perform a FULL restore
or a PARTIAL restore?
(If you're not sure, select FULL)

Full   Partial   Cancel

Restore
Drive A: ▌ - Unused   ▪ - IMAGE Info
Cluster 2   100%   B - Bad
                             Each block = 3 clusters

Select FULL or PARTIAL restore, or CANCEL to abort   │ UnFormat

Figure 10-4   Full or Partial Dialog Box

the subdirectory structure. UnFormat can recognize directory entries in a cluster, and since the second entry in every subdirectory refers to its parent directory, the relationships can be determined. When the subdirectories are intact, all files in subdirectories can be reconstructed in the FAT. (As with UnErase, the reconstruction might not always be perfect, however.)

The entries in the root directory are another matter. When Safe Format reformats a disk with existing files and subdirectories, it does not lay down a new root directory. Instead, it simply deletes the entries in the existing directory so that they can be recovered if necessary. But without image information, UnFormat can't recover them.

Figure 10-5 shows an example of a root directory before and after un-formatting. You can see that UnFormat left the first two entries alone. You will be able to recover these files with UnErase if you want them.

UnFormat found some subdirectories in the clusters, so it created entries for them starting in the third position, calling them DIR0 and DIR1. You can easily view these directories to determine their real names. Chapter 16 shows you how to use Norton Change Directory to rename directories.

After the last subdirectory entry, UnFormat considers the rest of the former root directory to be invalid. So it replaces the hex E5 at the beginning

```
    Object   Edit   Link   View   Info   Tools   Quit                    F1=Help
   Name     .Ext   Size    Date        Time    Cluster Arc R/O Sys Hid Dir Vol
   Sector 15                                                                    ↑
   ⌐AMES7    CHP    1298   5-30-91    2:42 pm     442  Arc
   ⌐AMES7    CIF     128   5-30-91    2:42 pm     445  Arc
   ⌐REEINFO  NCD     123   7-30-91    2:33 pm     446  Arc
   ⌐REE4     PRT     380  12-12-90    8:21 am     447  Arc
   ⌐REE5     PRT     380  12-12-90    8:21 am     448  Arc
   ⌐REE6     PRT     283  12-12-90    8:21 am     449  Arc
   ⌐CHED     BAK    5632   3-06-91    6:24 am     450  Arc
   ⌐CHED     DOC    5632   3-06-91    6:34 am     461  Arc
   ⌐CHNAME   BAK    4608   2-28-91    4:03 am     472  Arc
   ⌐CHNAME   DOC    6144   2-28-91    5:31 am     481  Arc
   ⌐CHEDFUL  BAK    5632   3-03-91    5:14 am     493  Arc
   ⌐CHEDFUL  DOC    8704   3-03-91    5:20 am     504  Arc
   ⌐AMES7    BAK    5632   3-06-91    6:25 am     521  Arc
   ⌐AMES7    DOC    9216   3-06-91    6:33 am     532  Arc
   ⌐OLCENT   BAK    2048   3-06-91    8:14 am     550  Arc
   ⌐OLCENT   DOC    2048   3-06-91    8:41 am     554  Arc
   Sector 16
   ⌐EMP               69   6-06-91   12:25 pm     558  Arc
   ⌐CREEN00  PCX    3713   5-17-91   10:26 am     559  Arc                      ↓
      Root Directory                                       Sector 15   ▲
      A:\                                               Offset 0, hex 0 ▼
   Press ALT or F10 to select menus                       | Disk Editor
```

(a)   Before Recovery

```
    Object   Edit   Link   View   Info   Tools   Quit                    F1=Help
   Name     .Ext   Size    Date        Time    Cluster Arc R/O Sys Hid Dir Vol
   Sector 15                                                                    ↑
   ⌐AMES7    CHP    1298   5-30-91    2:42 pm     442  Arc
   ⌐AMES7    CIF     128   5-30-91    2:42 pm     445  Arc
   DIR0               0   8-12-91    1:33 pm     719               Dir
   DIR1               0   0-00-80   12:00 am     576               Dir
             Unused directory entry
             Unused directory entry
             Unused directory entry
             Unused directory entry
             Unused directory entry
             Unused directory entry
             Unused directory entry
             Unused directory entry
             Unused directory entry
             Unused directory entry
             Unused directory entry
             Unused directory entry
   Sector 16
             Unused directory entry
             Unused directory entry                                            ↓
      Root Directory                                       Sector 15   ▲
      A:\                                               Offset 0, hex 0 ▼
   Press ALT or F10 to select menus                       | Disk Editor
```

(b)   After Recovery (Directory View)

Figure 10-5   Effect of UnFormat

```
     Object   Edit  Link   View   Info   Tools   Quit                F1=Help
   Sector 15
   00000000:  E5 41 4D 45 53 37 20 20 - 43 48 50 20 00 00 00 00  ªAMES7 CHP ....
   00000010:  00 00 00 00 00 00 56 75 - BE 16 BA 01 12 05 00 00  ......Vu⌐_∥θ‡...
   00000020:  E5 41 4D 45 53 37 20 20 - 43 49 46 20 00 00 00 00  ªAMES7 CIF ....
   00000030:  00 00 00 00 00 00 56 75 - BE 16 BD 01 80 00 00 00  ......Vu⌐_∥θ¢...
   00000040:  44 49 52 30 20 20 20 20 - 20 20 20 10 00 00 00 00  DIR0       ▶....
   00000050:  00 00 00 00 00 00 3B 6C - 0C 17 CF 02 00 00 00 00  ......;l♀↨╧θ....
   00000060:  44 49 52 31 20 20 20 20 - 20 20 20 10 00 00 00 00  DIR1       ▶....
   00000070:  00 00 00 00 00 00 00 00 - 00 00 40 02 00 00 00 00  ..........@θ....
   00000080:  00 52 45 45 35 20 20 20 - 50 52 54 20 00 00 00 00  .REE5   PRT ....
   00000090:  00 00 00 00 00 00 B0 42 - 8C 15 C0 01 7C 01 00 00  ......░Bî.└θ|θ..
   000000A0:  00 52 45 45 36 20 20 20 - 50 52 54 20 00 00 00 00  .REE6   PRT ....
   000000B0:  00 00 00 00 00 00 B5 42 - 8C 15 C1 01 1B 01 00 00  ......Bî.└θ←θ..
   000000C0:  00 43 48 45 44 20 20 20 - 42 41 4B 20 00 00 00 00  .CHED   BAK ....
   000000D0:  00 00 00 00 00 00 07 33 - 66 16 C2 01 00 16 00 00  ......•3f_┬θ.—..
   000000E0:  00 43 48 45 44 20 20 20 - 44 4F 43 20 00 00 00 00  .CHED   DOC ....
   000000F0:  00 00 00 00 00 00 48 34 - 66 16 CD 01 00 16 00 00  ......H4f_═θ.—..
   00000100:  00 43 48 4E 41 4D 45 20 - 42 41 4B 20 00 00 00 00  .CHNAME BAK ....
   00000110:  00 00 00 00 00 00 64 20 - 5C 16 D8 01 00 12 00 00  ......d \_.Øθ.‡..
   00000120:  00 43 48 4E 41 4D 45 20 - 44 4F 43 20 00 00 00 00  .CHNAME DOC ....
   00000130:  00 00 00 00 00 00 71 2E - 5C 16 E1 01 00 18 00 00  ......q.\_ßθ.↑..
   Root Directory                                      Sector 15  ▲
   A:\                                            Offset 0, hex 0  ▼
   Press ALT or F10 to select menus                        | Disk Editor
```

(c)   After Recovery (Hex View)

Figure 10-5   Effect of UnFormat

of each entry with hex 00, marking the entry as "unused." You can see in the directory view that all the entries after DIR1 are unused. But look at the hex view—the entry information is still there! You can still recover any files you need. In order to make UnErase "see" their entries, you must use Disk Editor to change each initial hex 00 back to hex E5. (Chapter 14 shows you how to make these kinds of changes with Disk Editor.)

Tip: Many experienced users place *all* their files in subdirectories except for those required for booting on the boot drive (the two system files, COMMAND.COM, AUTOEXEC.BAT, and CONFIG.SYS). This practice has two advantages. It saves space in the root directory, which has a limited number of entries (the number depends on the size of the disk), whereas subdirectories are unlimited. It also avoids having to find and unerase files in the root directory after unformatting a disk.

The UNFORMAT Command

When you start UnFormat from the DOS prompt, you can include a drive name on the command, as in the following example:

```
UNFORMAT D:
```

This will bypass the drive selection dialog box and go straight to the image question. You can add a /IMAGE switch to use Image information only (no Mirror information), or a /MIRROR switch to do the opposite.

Looking Ahead

The last thing UnFormat suggests is that you run Norton Disk Doctor to fix up any problems on the disk. Disk Doctor can diagnose and fix many types of disk problems. You should use it not only when a disk is giving you trouble, but also periodically as a preventive measure. The next chapter shows you how it works.

11

NORTON DISK DOCTOR

Once upon a time, if a disk started to go bad or if errors crept into the system areas, there was very little you could do to rescue your data. But now, Norton Disk Doctor (NDD) gives you tremendous power to test your disks for problems and correct any problems found.

NDD looks for problems in the Partition Table, Boot Record, root directory and all subdirectories, and the FAT. If you wish, it also tests every sector on the disk, rescues as much data as possible from bad sectors, and marks them as bad in the FAT so they can't be used anymore. It also issues a detailed report so that you can build documentary evidence of a hard disk's problems, if necessary.

You should use Disk Doctor on a regular (i.e., daily) basis for early diagnosis of developing hard-disk problems. You should also use it whenever you experience problems with a hard disk or diskette.

You might first realize that a problem exists when DOS reports a read or write error. Several of the Norton Utilities, such as Disk Editor and Speed Disk, will also identify and report problems they spot. If data drops in or out of a file or if a program suddenly starts behaving erratically, there might be a FAT error; Disk Doctor will find it and perhaps even fix it.

When a sector goes bad on a disk, you stand to lose the whole file; DOS will report a read error and refuse to give you any data from the file, even though many of its sectors are in good shape. Disk Doctor, on the other hand, will rescue as much of the file as possible; you might lose only a few bytes. If the file is a spreadsheet, drawing, word-processing document, and the like, you can probably inspect it and restore the missing data.

Starting Disk Doctor

To start Disk Doctor, select **Disk Doctor** from the Norton menu or enter NDD at the DOS prompt. You can also start it from the Emergency diskette (#1 on the 5.25" version) if you have not yet installed the utilities or if your hard disk is currently unavailable. No matter which technique you use to start it, the first screen looks like the one in Figure 11-1.

Diagnosing (and Correcting) Disks

The overall process of diagnosing and correcting disks follows these general steps:

- You select the **Diagnose** button.
- You select the drives to be diagnosed.

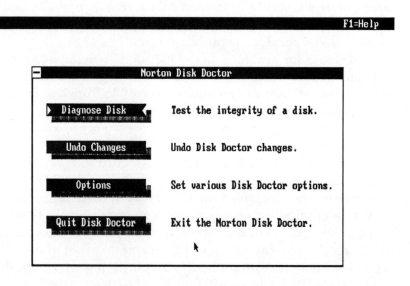

Figure 11-1   Norton Disk Doctor Initial Screen

- CMOS information is analyzed. (CMOS is a small, battery-powered memory chip that stores vital startup information about your system including the type of hard disk you have.)
- The hard disk's partition layout is analyzed.

For each selected drive:

- The Partition Table is analyzed.
- The Boot Record is analyzed.
- The File Allocation Table is analyzed.
- The directory structure is analyzed.
- The file structure is analyzed.
- The FAT is examined for lost and cross-linked clusters.
- (optional) The surface is tested for bad sectors.
- A summary of the results is displayed.
- (optional) You can display or print a detailed report of what happened.

If a problem is found, a dialog box explains the problem and gives you the option of fixing it, not fixing it and continuing, or canceling the test. If you choose to fix it, you have the option of saving undo information on another drive so that you can undo the fixup later if desired.

The following sections explain each step in more detail. During the first analyses, the dialog box shown in Figure 11-2 appears on the screen. Each analysis is highlighted as it is performed and checked off afterward.

Partition Table Analysis

A hard disk's Partition Table is crucial to DOS's ability to access the disk. If it gets damaged, you could lose contact with all the data on the hard disk until it gets fixed again. Norton Disk Doctor does its first examination of the Partition Table as soon as you select the drive. If it has been corrupted by a virus or some other problem, Disk Doctor will display appropriate (and somewhat frightening) messages. It might even ask you if you have been having trouble accessing the disk.

Disk Doctor will offer to fix the Partition Table, and you should let it if you have no other recourse. If the table is badly damaged, Disk Doctor might have to guess at values, which can be less than perfect.

F1=Help

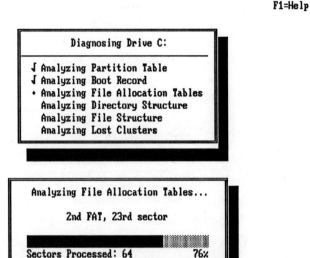

Figure 11-2   Analysis Progress Box

Tip: In the next chapter, you'll learn how to make a backup copy of your Partition Table and other vital areas so that you can restore them if need be. If you have a backup copy (called a *rescue disk*), then you don't need to let Disk Doctor fix the Partition Table. You also might be able to restore it using UnFormat and an Image or Mirror file.

Boot Record Analysis

Disk Doctor checks the Boot Record for reliability and valid contents. Figure 11-3 shows a typical error message resulting from an error in the Boot Record. You would select **Yes** to fix the boot record, **No** to continue the diagnosis without fixing the boot record, and **Cancel** to discontinue the diagnosis.

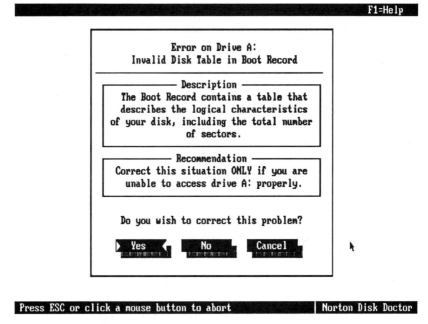

Figure 11-3   Typical Error Message

FAT Analysis

During the FAT analysis, Disk Doctor verifies the authenticity of the FAT by looking for invalid entries, including a comparison of the two FATs. A typical error message at this point would be:

Media Descriptor Byte is invalid

This message means that the code identifying the disk type, which is stored in the FAT, is invalid and could cause problems in accessing the disk. Disk Doctor will fix the Media Descriptor Byte if you request it.

Disk Doctor will return to the FAT to look for lost and cross-linked clusters after it verifies the directory and file structures.

Directory Structure Analysis

During the directory structure analysis, Disk Doctor examines every directory in the tree to make sure that it contains valid entries. It also checks the validity of the entries for the directory itself and its parent.

File Structure Analysis

Disk Doctor compares each file's directory entry with its FAT entries and reports on any inconsistencies. For example, if a file's size indicates that it needs five clusters, but its FAT chain contains only four clusters, a problem is identified.

Lost Cluster Analysis

After the FAT and directories have been generally validated, Disk Doctor examines the FAT for lost clusters (clusters that are marked as used but are not part of a complete chain) and cross-linked clusters (clusters that belong to more than one chain). A typical error message would be:

There are 7 lost clusters in 3 chains

The reason the chains are lost is because they have no beginning in a directory entry; it's therefore impossible to tell what file they belong to, if any. In most cases, lost clusters belong to deleted files, but something (such as a power fluctuation) interrupted DOS before it finished zeroing the FAT chain. Since lost clusters take up disk space, you should fix them. You have the choice between saving them as files or deleting them. If you delete chains, Disk Doctor simply zeros the FAT entries, making those clusters once more available to receive new data. If you save them as files, Disk Doctor devises generic filenames in the format FILE*nnnn*._DD. When you're done with Disk Doctor, you can inspect those files using Disk Editor and decide whether to keep or delete them.

Surface Test

Let's assume for a moment that no problems were found in the previous tests and Disk Doctor goes on to the surface test, which retests the disk surface for bad sectors. This test takes much longer than all the other analyses combined, and it is optional. When the lost cluster analysis is finished, the dialog box shown in Figure 11-4 opens. You set up the surface analysis in this dialog box, if desired, or cancel it if you don't want to take the time to test the disk surface now.

Test

The **Test** control group lets you choose how extensively you want to test. If you choose **Disk Test** (which is the default), every sector on the disk or

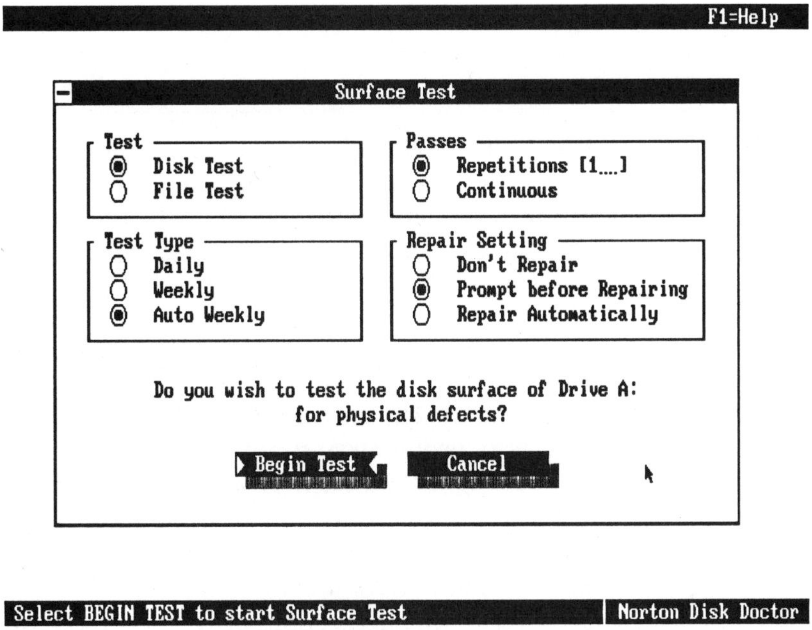

F1=Help

```
┌─────────────────────────────────────────────────────────────┐
│ ■                        Surface Test                         │
│                                                               │
│   ┌─ Test ──────────────────┐  ┌─ Passes ──────────────────┐ │
│   │  ◉  Disk Test           │  │  ◉  Repetitions [1....]    │ │
│   │  ○  File Test           │  │  ○  Continuous            │ │
│   └─────────────────────────┘  └───────────────────────────┘ │
│                                                               │
│   ┌─ Test Type ─────────────┐  ┌─ Repair Setting ──────────┐ │
│   │  ○  Daily               │  │  ○  Don't Repair          │ │
│   │  ○  Weekly              │  │  ◉  Prompt before Repairing│ │
│   │  ◉  Auto Weekly         │  │  ○  Repair Automatically  │ │
│   └─────────────────────────┘  └───────────────────────────┘ │
│                                                               │
│          Do you wish to test the disk surface of Drive A:     │
│                     for physical defects?                     │
│                                                               │
│              ▶ Begin Test ◀        Cancel                  ▶  │
│                                                               │
└─────────────────────────────────────────────────────────────┘
```

Select BEGIN TEST to start Surface Test   Norton Disk Doctor

Figure 11-4   Surface Test Dialog Box

partition is tested. If you choose **File Test**, only the used sectors are tested, which can take much less time.

Test Type

The **Daily** test does a quick scan of the sectors but doesn't actually read and check them in detail. The **Weekly** test, which takes much longer, thoroughly checks every sector to be tested. The **Auto Weekly** test is a compromise: If you run it on a Friday, the weekly test is done, but on any other day, the daily test is done. **Auto Weekly** is most useful when you run Norton Disk Doctor from your AUTOEXEC.BAT file.

Passes

Most surface problems will be caught on the first run, but some intermittent problems might require several passes to be located. If you're not satisfied that the error you are trying to locate was found, set the test up to run several times by entering a number larger than 1 next to **Repetitions**. If you're still not satisfied, select **Continuous** and let the test run until the problem is located or you are convinced that there is no problem. (Many people let the test run overnight—in which case you probably ought to select **Repair automatically** in the next section.)

Tip: Disk Doctor's surface analysis can find and fix many bad sectors, but it is not as rigorous a test as Calibrate's. When in doubt, use Calibrate (which is explained in Chapter 5).

Repair Setting

Disk Doctor repairs a sector problem by moving as much data as possible to good sectors and marking the cluster containing the faulty sector as BAD. If you prefer to just identify problems and not fix them, select **Don't Repair**. If you want to see a message about each problem sector and decide on the spot whether to fix it or not, select **Prompt before Repairing**. To let Disk Doctor do its thing, select **Repair Automatically**. No matter which option you choose, you can maintain undo information to undo the repairs later, if need be, and you can get a detailed report of which sectors were found to be bad and which ones were repaired, so you won't lose out on any documentary evidence by letting Disk Doctor repair the sectors automatically.

Warning: A few bytes lost from a program file can make it malfunction so that it might damage your data files. Don't keep a program file that has been rescued from a bad sector by Disk Doctor. Reinstall the program from its original diskettes instead.

Running the Surface Analysis

When you select the **Begin Test** button, a disk map appears that is nearly identical to the maps displayed by Disk Editor and Speed Disk. Disk Doctor animates the map so that you can see which sector is currently being tested and which ones are complete for the current pass. The screen also displays a progress box that shows a time estimate, the time elapsed so far, the percent complete, the current sector number, the total number of sectors, and the pass number. You can cancel the surface test by pressing Enter or by clicking either mouse button.

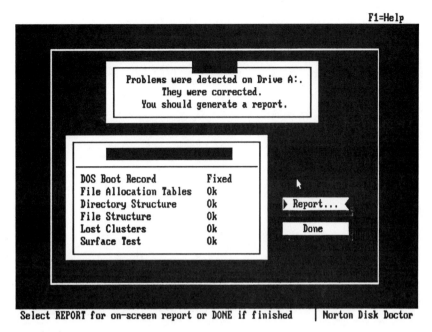

Figure 11-5 Summary Dialog Box

The Diagnosis Summary

When the diagnosis and repair are complete, a summary box like the one shown in Figure 11-5 appears. If no problems are indicated, you can select **Done** to terminate Disk Doctor.

If the summary shows that problems were found in any area of a hard disk, you should generate a report that you can keep on file. A good audit trail of developing hard-disk problems can warn you that a repair is needed and can help the repair technician identify and fix the problem. It's not as important to keep evidence of diskette problems since most people just throw diskettes away when they become unreliable.

The Disk Doctor Report

Figure 11-6 shows an example of a report generated by Disk Doctor after diagnosing and repairing a disk with a couple of problems. As you can see, the report details the disk's physical and logical information as well as the results of each diagnostic test that was performed.

```
                     Norton Disk Doctor II
                     Norton Utilities, 5.0
               Saturday, February 23, 1991 2:28 pm

                  ***************************
                  *   Report for Drive A:   *
                  ***************************

                          DISK TOTALS
          - - - - - - - - - - - - - - - - - - - - - - - - - - - - -
            1,213,952 bytes Total Disk Space
                9,728 bytes in 7 User Files
                1,024 bytes in 2 Directories
            1,203,200 bytes Available on the Disk

                    LOGICAL DISK INFORMATION
          - - - - - - - - - - - - - - - - - - - - - - - - - - - - -
                 Media Descriptor:  F9
                  Large Partition:  No
                         FAT Type:  12-bit
                    Total Sectors:  2,400
                   Total Clusters:  2,371
                 Bytes Per Sector:  512
               Sectors Per Cluster: 1
                 Bytes Per Cluster: 512
                   Number of FATs:  2
                First Sector of FAT: 1
          Number of Sectors Per FAT: 7
          First Sector of Root Dir:  15
      Number of Sectors in Root Dir:  14
      Maximum Root Dir File Entries:  224
          First Sector of Data Area:  29

                    PHYSICAL DISK INFORMATION
          - - - - - - - - - - - - - - - - - - - - - - - - - - - - -
                     Drive Number:  0
                            Heads:  2
                        Cylinders:  80
                 Sectors Per Track: 15
                    Starting Head:  0
                Starting Cylinder:  0
                  Starting Sector:  1
                      Ending Head:  1
                  Ending Cylinder:  79
                    Ending Sector:  15

                     SYSTEM AREA STATUS
          - - - - - - - - - - - - - - - - - - - - - - - - - - - - -

               Invalid Disk Table in Boot Record
                      Status: Corrected

                    FILE STRUCTURE STATUS
          - - - - - - - - - - - - - - - - - - - - - - - - - - - - -

  ******************* Errors Processing Directories ********************
```

Figure 11-6   Sample Disk Doctor Report *(continued)*

```
                      \DIR0
           Illegal Directory; Corrected


                 SURFACE TEST STATUS
     - - - - - - - - - - - - - - - - - - - - - - - - - - - -
                   Test Settings
                 - - - - - - - - - - - - - -
               Test:  Disk Test
          Test Type:  Daily
     Repair Setting:  Prompt before Repairing
    Passes Requested:  5
    Passes Completed:  5
       Elapsed Time:  5 minutes, 31 seconds

     No Errors encountered in Surface Test
```

Figure 11-6

To obtain the report, select **Report** on the summary screen. The next dialog box shows the report on your screen and includes **Print** and **Save as** buttons. To view the report on your screen, just page through it. If you want a paper copy, select **Print**. Or you can store it in a disk file by selecting **Save as**, in which case a dialog box asks for the name of the file to use.

Undoing Changes

Whenever Disk Doctor repairs a problem, you have the option of saving the information necessary to undo the repair. Most of the time, you won't need to undo repairs, but you might as well save the information anyway, just in case. You can always delete it later.

When you tell Disk Doctor that you want to save the information, you must select a *different* drive, preferably a drive that you know has no problems itself. Disk Doctor recommends a diskette, but if you're repairing a diskette, you might want to save the information on your hard drive. Disk Doctor creates a file named NDDUNDO.DAT on the root directory of the indicated drive or diskette. Keep a copy of the Disk Doctor report with the undo disk so that you can see exactly what changes will be undone, if necessary.

Tip: If you're going to undo changes, do so immediately, never after you have made additional changes to the disk. You might restore something that is no longer valid, throwing the entire disk out of whack. For example, you might restore FAT entries for files that no longer exist, overlaying new FAT entries that were valid.

To undo the repair, start Disk Doctor and select **Undo Changes** on the initial screen, which opens the dialog box shown in Figure 11-7. If you still want to undo the changes after reading the dialog box, you would select **Yes**.

The next dialog box asks you to select the drive where the UNDO file was stored. Disk Doctor then finds the UNDO file and shows you the time and date when it was saved. You get one more chance to indicate that you are *sure* you want to undo the changes.

> **Warning:** Check the time and date carefully. If you use the wrong UNDO file, severe damage could be done.

Undo always undoes all the changes included in the undo file; you have no way to select the drive to treat or the changes to undo. If you diagnosed and fixed several disks in one run, don't undo changes if you have made subsequent changes to any one of them. (Check the report to find out which drives were treated.)

A progress box keeps you informed while the changes are being undone, and a dialog box advises you when Undo is complete. It would be wise to delete the undo file at this time so that you don't accidentally use it again.

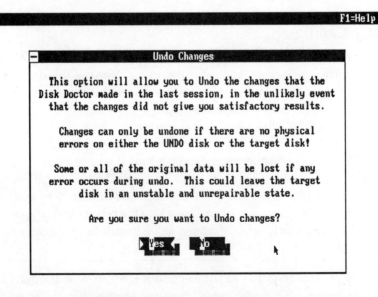

Figure 11-7   Undo Dialog Box

Setting Up NDD Options

So far, you have seen the default setup for Norton Disk Doctor. But you do have some control over which tests are performed, the default surface test options, and the messages that appear when a problem is found. Figure 11-8 shows the dialog box that opens when you select **Options** from the initial Disk Doctor screen.

After you set up the various options the way you want them, you would select **Save Settings** to make them permanent. If you want to use them for this Disk Doctor session only, select **OK** instead.

The settings are saved in a file named NDD.INI. From then on, whenever you start Norton Disk Doctor (even if you start it from a diskette), it will find NDD.INI and use those settings. But if you delete or rename NDD.INI, Disk Doctor will go back to its default settings.

> **Tip:** If you are setting up Disk Doctor for end users, simply copy the NDD.INI files to their drives.

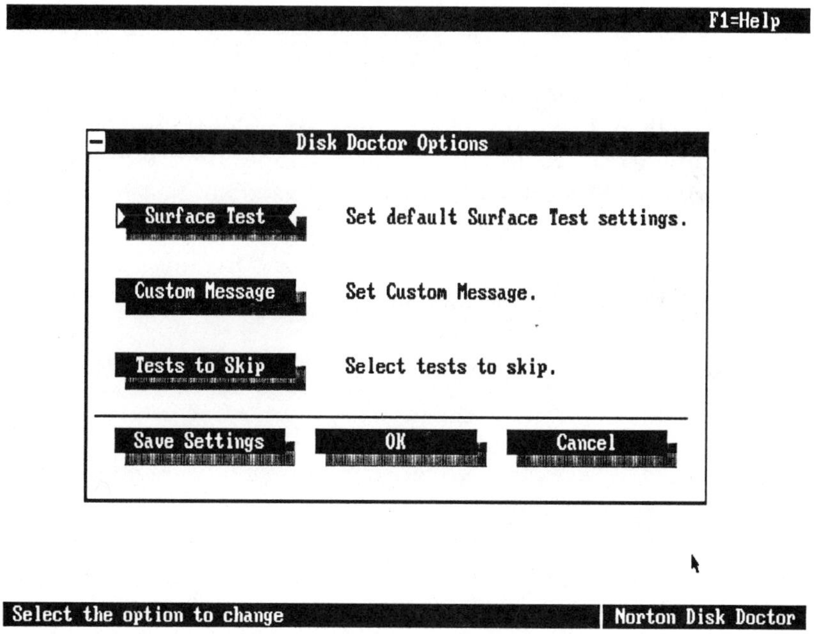

Figure 11-8   Disk Doctor Options Dialog Box

Surface Test Defaults

The **Surface Test** button opens a dialog box nearly identical to the one shown in Figure 11-4, except that the message at the top says "Select the default settings for the Surface Test." When the dialog box appears, the current default settings are shown. All you have to do is select the ones you want and close the dialog box again.

Custom Messages

You might not want others who use your computer to fix errors on your disk without your knowledge. Or you might want to prevent end users from fixing errors. The **Custom Message** option lets you set up a special message to be displayed if NDD finds any problem. For example, you might want to say:

> **Please notify Larry Edwards (ext. 1049) that a problem has been found. Do not use this computer until it has been fixed.**

With this facility in force, users cannot continue with the test. When they close the custom message box, they are returned to the initial screen.

The custom message appears only during the initial tests. It does not affect the surface test.

Figure 11-9 shows the dialog box that opens when you select **Custom Message**. To set up a custom message, you must do two things: Check the **Prompt with Custom Message** box and type the message in the text box.

You can dress up your message with attributes such as bold and underlined text. Simply press F2 to change the attribute before typing the text to use that attribute. F2 cycles through the text attributes in this order: reverse video, bold, underlined, normal; the message "Current attribute is ..." next to the text box tells you which attribute is currently selected. For example, suppose you want to type this message:

> **Do not** continue with this test.

You would press F2 twice to get to the bold attribute, then type "Do not". Then you would press F2 two more times to get back to normal before typing the rest of the message.

If someone reports a problem to you, you can run Disk Doctor without the custom message by starting Norton Disk Doctor, selecting **Options**, selecting **Custom Message**, and removing the check mark from the **Prompt with Custom Message** option. The message itself will stay in the text box so that you can easily reestablish it after you have fixed the disk.

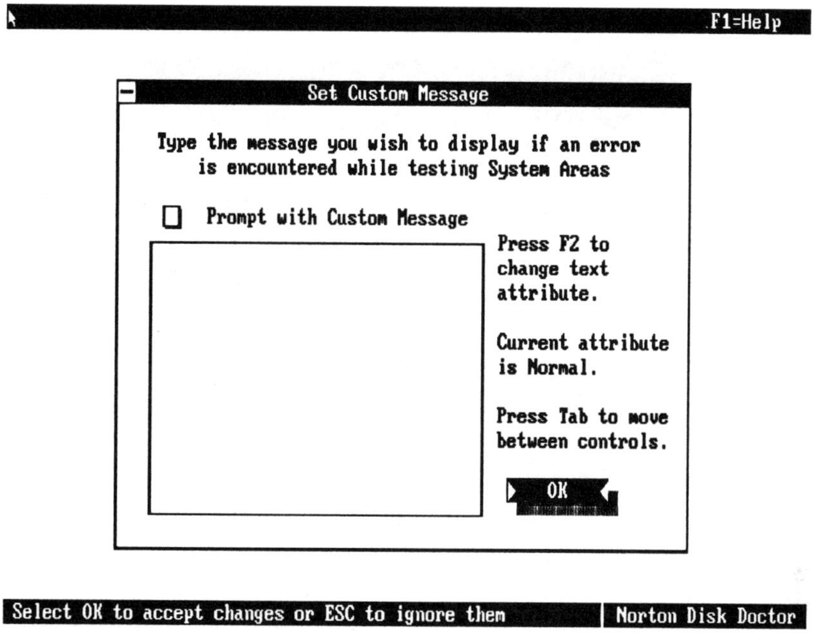

```
                                                         F1=Help

        ┌─────────────────────────────────────────────┐
        │ ─         Set Custom Message                 │
        │                                              │
        │  Type the message you wish to display if an error │
        │     is encountered while testing System Areas     │
        │                                              │
        │  ☐  Prompt with Custom Message               │
        │  ┌────────────────────────┐  Press F2 to     │
        │  │                        │  change text     │
        │  │                        │  attribute.      │
        │  │                        │                  │
        │  │                        │  Current attribute │
        │  │                        │  is Normal.       │
        │  │                        │                  │
        │  │                        │  Press Tab to move │
        │  │                        │  between controls. │
        │  │                        │                  │
        │  │                        │     ▶   OK   ◀    │
        │  │                        │                  │
        │  └────────────────────────┘                  │
        │                                              │
        └─────────────────────────────────────────────┘

    ┌───────────────────────────────────────────┐┌─────────────────┐
    │ Select OK to accept changes or ESC to ignore them ││ Norton Disk Doctor │
    └───────────────────────────────────────────┘└─────────────────┘
```

Figure 11-9   Custom Message Dialog Box

Skipping Tests

Disk Doctor lets you skip certain tests if they are not compatible with your computer. You will know the first time you run Disk Doctor if your system has incompatibilities with it. Figure 11-10 shows the dialog box that opens when you select **Tests to Skip** from the initial screen.

In addition to being able to skip the partition tests and the CMOS tests, if necessary, you can also choose to permanently skip the surface test. This saves a little time when running Disk Doctor by not displaying the **Surface Test** dialog box.

The last option, labeled **Only 1 Hard Disk**, helps you out of a rare situation where Disk Doctor sees more hard disks than you actually have. If Disk Doctor is having trouble identifying your hard disk, check this option.

> **Tip:** If Disk Doctor is having trouble with your hardware configuration, try checking all the boxes on this dialog box. If that works, uncheck them one at a time until you find the ones that need to be checked. If you can't solve the problem yourself, you can call the Norton technical support hotline for help.

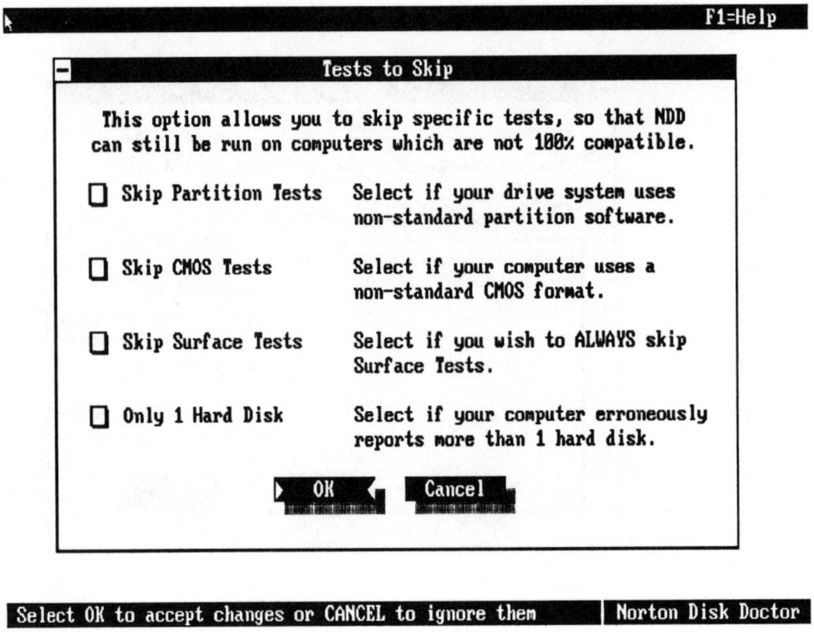

Figure 11-10   Tests to Skip

The NDD Command

You can run Norton Disk Doctor from the DOS command prompt using this command format:

```
NDD [drivenames] [switches]
```

Table 11-1 shows the switches. You must specify either /COMPLETE or /QUICK in order to bypass the initial Disk Doctor screen and go right into the tests. The other switches can be specified along with /COMPLETE or /QUICK.

If you don't specify any drive names, the current drive is tested. If you don't specify one of the report switches, no report is generated.

The Norton Utilities installation program offers the option of inserting NDD /QUICK into AUTOEXEC.BAT. You might want to check your AUTOEXEC.BAT to see if it is there. If not, consider adding it so that your hard disk is checked out every time you boot, adapting it to test all your hard drives, not just the current one. You might also want to add an /R switch to generate a report file, which you can check later if you suspect problems with the disk.

Table 11-1   NDD Command Switches

/QUICK	Test the system area but not the data area
/COMPLETE	Test both areas
/R: *file*	Store the report in *file*
/RA: *file*	Append the report to *file*

Tip: If you are going to generate the report during booting, be sure to use /R instead of /RA. /RA appends the new report to the end of whatever file you name. If you let this happen for (say) 100 days in a row, the file would contain 100 reports. You could end up building a huge file on your disk with /RA.

Looking Ahead

Disk Doctor can be a great help in rescuing your disk from a variety of ills, but in some cases you can do better using Disk Tools—a collection of utilities that not only can fix certain types of problems, but can actually prevent some. The next chapter shows you how to use Disk Tools.

12

DISK TOOLS

We now come to a group of facilities that can both prevent and correct disk errors, even some catastrophic ones. The main Disk Tools screen, shown in Figure 12-1, lists the six features included in this package. **Make a Disk Bootable** can install or correct those portions of a disk that are necessary for booting. **Recover from DOS's RECOVER** undoes the damage done by DOS's notorious RECOVER program.

Revive a Defective Diskette redoes the physical formatting on a diskette much as Calibrate does with a hard disk. **Mark a Cluster** marks a good cluster as bad and vice versa. **Create Rescue Disk** copies your hard disk Partition Tables, Boot Records, and CMOS values to a diskette for safekeeping. **Restore Rescue Disk** copies them back to the hard disk again to help you recover from a virus attack or other problem.

To start Disk Tools, enter the command DISKTOOL at the DOS prompt or select **Disk Tools** from the Norton menu (**Recovery** section). The screen shown in Figure 12-1 should appear after an introductory screen.

Make a Disk Bootable

To boot from a disk, it must have several characteristics:

- It must have the correct boot record, which contains the actual boot program.

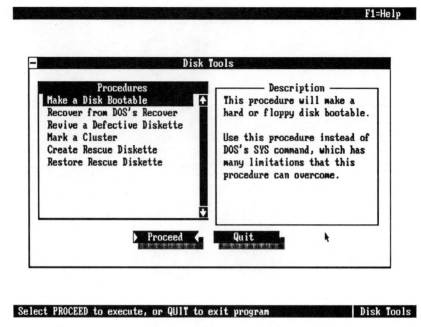

Figure 12-1   Disk Tools Main Menu

- The first files on the disk must be the two DOS system files; their names vary from one DOS version to another, but they generally take the form *xxx*IO.*xxx* and *xxx*DOS.*xxx*. They must not only occupy the first directory entries on the disk but also the first clusters.

- The correct version of COMMAND.COM must be somewhere in the root directory.

- For a hard disk, the partition table must indicate which partition is bootable; only one partition can be so designated. (Otherwise, your system wouldn't know which partition to boot from.)

You can make a disk bootable while logically formatting it; the format program will put the correct boot record, system files, and COM-MAND.COM in place. For a hard disk, you must also use FDISK (the partitioning program) to indicate which partition is bootable.

The problem arises when you need to make a disk bootable after it has been formatted, assuming that you don't want to reformat it. For example, suppose a virus corrupted the boot record on your hard disk or you accidentally deleted a system file. Or suppose your hard disk isn't set up for booting, and now you want to be able to boot from it.

DOS includes a program called SYS that copies the necessary boot record and system files to a disk, but that falls short of making the disk bootable. It doesn't copy COMMAND.COM and it doesn't make the necessary entry in the partition table. Furthermore, if the disk already contains files where the system files should go, earlier versions of SYS (before DOS 5.0) give up and display the message "No room for system on destination disk."

The **Make a Disk Bootable** tool will take all the steps necessary to make a disk bootable, including moving existing files around to make room for the system files. Figure 12-2 shows before and after views of a diskette's root directory as seen by Disk Editor. You can see for yourself what **Make a Disk Bootable** does. Before, the file starting in cluster 2 was FIGS03.CIF; **Make a Disk Bootable** moved it to cluster 72; it also moved its directory entry. Similarly, it moved FIGS03.CAP out of the second directory entry, and it added IO.SYS, MSDOS.SYS, and COMMAND.COM to the disk. What you can't see in this view is that it also installed a new, bootable boot record.

Requirements to Make a Disk Bootable

In order to make a disk bootable, it must have room somewhere on the disk for the system files and COMMAND.COM and it must have at least three available entries in the root directory. You might have to delete some files to make enough room. To make a hard-disk partition bootable, it must be a DOS partition, and no other partition on the hard disk (DOS or otherwise) can currently be designated as bootable.

Using Make a Disk Bootable

To use **Make a Disk Bootable**, simply select it from the Disk Tools main menu. A dialog box lets you select the drive to work on. Then a series of message boxes shows you what's happening. If **Make a Disk Bootable** must move files out of the way, it could take a few minutes, so be patient.

> **Tip:** You can safely interrupt **Make a Disk Bootable** by pressing any key. It finishes moving whatever file it was working on before quitting.

Recover from DOS's RECOVER

No, it's not a joke. DOS's RECOVER program was meant to rescue data from bad sectors, but it can leave your disk looking like a cyclone struck it. If you

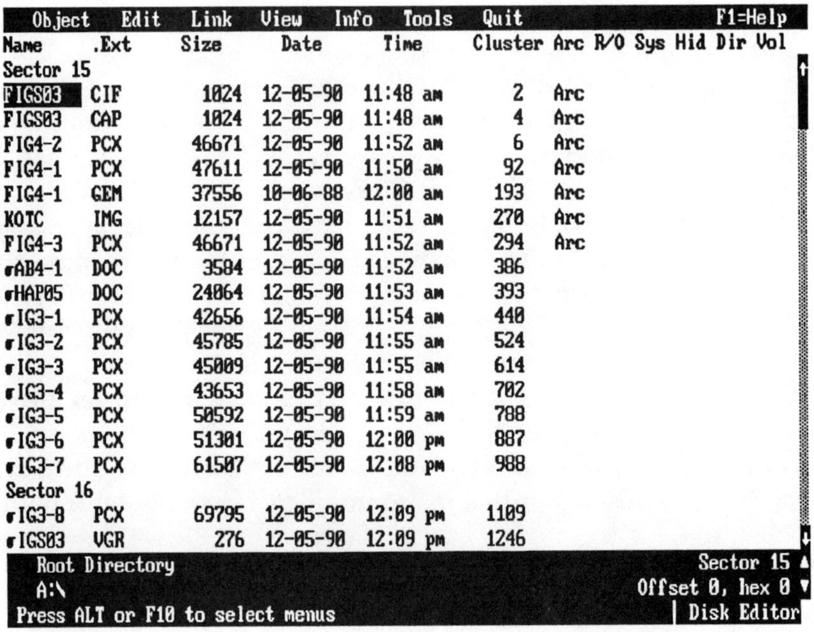

```
  Object  Edit   Link    View    Info   Tools   Quit                      F1=Help
Name       .Ext   Size    Date        Time    Cluster Arc R/O Sys Hid Dir Vol
Sector 15
FIGS03     CIF     1024  12-05-90  11:48 am       2   Arc
FIGS03     CAP     1024  12-05-90  11:48 am       4   Arc
FIG4-2     PCX    46671  12-05-90  11:52 am       6   Arc
FIG4-1     PCX    47611  12-05-90  11:50 am      92   Arc
FIG4-1     GEM    37556  10-06-88  12:00 am     193   Arc
KOTC       IMG    12157  12-05-90  11:51 am     270   Arc
FIG4-3     PCX    46671  12-05-90  11:52 am     294   Arc
•AB4-1     DOC     3504  12-05-90  11:52 am     386
•HAP05     DOC    24064  12-05-90  11:53 am     393
•IG3-1     PCX    42656  12-05-90  11:54 am     440
•IG3-2     PCX    45785  12-05-90  11:55 am     524
•IG3-3     PCX    45009  12-05-90  11:55 am     614
•IG3-4     PCX    43653  12-05-90  11:58 am     702
•IG3-5     PCX    50592  12-05-90  11:59 am     788
•IG3-6     PCX    51301  12-05-90  12:00 pm     887
•IG3-7     PCX    61507  12-05-90  12:08 pm     988
Sector 16
•IG3-8     PCX    69795  12-05-90  12:09 pm    1109
•IGS03     VGR      276  12-05-90  12:09 pm    1246
  Root Directory                                          Sector 15 ▲
  A:\                                              Offset 0, hex 0 ▼
  Press ALT or F10 to select menus                      | Disk Editor
```

(a)   Before

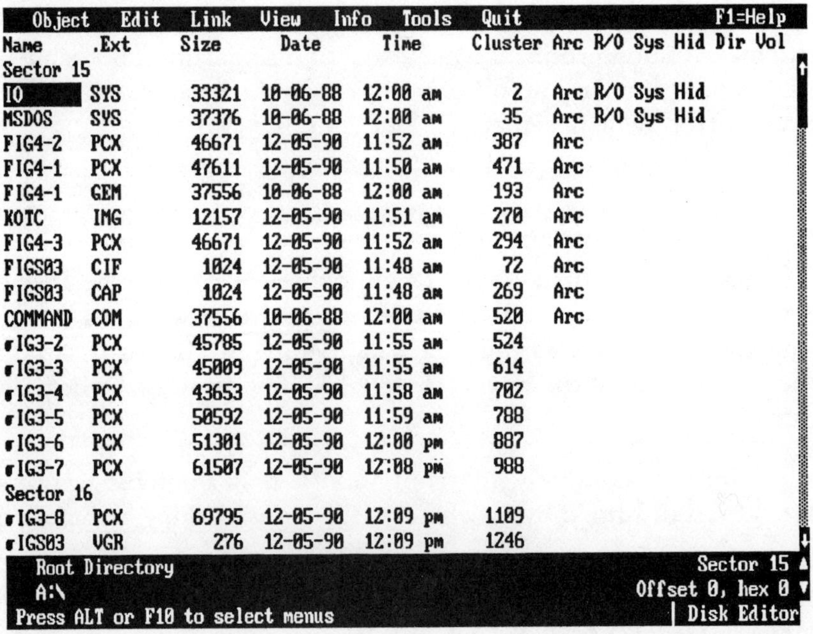

```
  Object  Edit   Link    View    Info   Tools   Quit                      F1=Help
Name       .Ext   Size    Date        Time    Cluster Arc R/O Sys Hid Dir Vol
Sector 15
IO         SYS    33321  10-06-88  12:00 am       2   Arc R/O Sys Hid
MSDOS      SYS    37376  10-06-88  12:00 am      35   Arc R/O Sys Hid
FIG4-2     PCX    46671  12-05-90  11:52 am     387   Arc
FIG4-1     PCX    47611  12-05-90  11:50 am     471   Arc
FIG4-1     GEM    37556  10-06-88  12:00 am     193   Arc
KOTC       IMG    12157  12-05-90  11:51 am     270   Arc
FIG4-3     PCX    46671  12-05-90  11:52 am     294   Arc
FIGS03     CIF     1024  12-05-90  11:48 am      72   Arc
FIGS03     CAP     1024  12-05-90  11:48 am     269   Arc
COMMAND    COM    37556  10-06-88  12:00 am     520   Arc
•IG3-2     PCX    45785  12-05-90  11:55 am     524
•IG3-3     PCX    45009  12-05-90  11:55 am     614
•IG3-4     PCX    43653  12-05-90  11:58 am     702
•IG3-5     PCX    50592  12-05-90  11:59 am     788
•IG3-6     PCX    51301  12-05-90  12:00 pm     887
•IG3-7     PCX    61507  12-05-90  12:08 pm     988
Sector 16
•IG3-8     PCX    69795  12-05-90  12:09 pm    1109
•IGS03     VGR      276  12-05-90  12:09 pm    1246
  Root Directory                                          Sector 15 ▲
  A:\                                              Offset 0, hex 0 ▼
  Press ALT or F10 to select menus                      | Disk Editor
```

(b)   After

Figure 12-2   Results of Make a Disk Bootable

run RECOVER without specifying a filename, it "recovers" every file on the disk into the root directory, assigning generic filenames of FILE0001.REC, FILE0002.REC, and so on. There might be hundreds of them—text, programs, graphics, databases all jumbled together—you won't know which is which. It could take many long hours to inspect each file and decide whether to rename or delete it.

Figure 12-3 shows the root directory of a diskette before and after running RECOVER; imagine what would have happened if it had been a hard disk with many hundreds of files.

Recover from DOS's RECOVER actually has two functions. The first is to undo the damage done by RECOVER. Figure 12-4 shows the root directory of the same diskette as in Figure 12-3 after it has been rescued by **Recover from DOS's RECOVER**. It's not perfect, but it's much better. The previous file and subdirectory names couldn't be recovered, but at least the subdirectory structure has been restored and many file types have been identified. Compare the directory in Figure 12-4 to the original directory in Figure 12-3 (you can match up files by their starting cluster numbers) and you will see that COM, EXE, DOC (Microsoft Word documents), and WK1 (Lotus 1-2-3 spreadsheets) have been correctly identified. The two SYS files have also been identified as COM files, but you will be able to readily spot those two files: they're always the first two files on a bootable disk.

> **Note:** The file sizes are larger in the rescued directory because the entire last cluster is counted. **Recover from DOS's RECOVER** cannot tell where the file ends and slack begins. For this reason, you should not trust any program files that have been recovered. Reinstall all programs from their original diskettes.

The two subdirectories have also been correctly identified. The filenames in the subdirectories will be perfect (unless a bad sector was encountered) because **Recover from DOS's RECOVER** found the subdirectory clusters and relinked them to the root directory. Only the root directory entries have been reconstructed.

> **Tip:** This is another good reason to keep all files in subdirectories (except for those files necessary for booting).

The second function of **Recover from DOS's RECOVER** is to provide a substitute for DOS's RECOVER in one situation: where the root directory

Object	Edit	Link	View	Info	Tools	Quit						F1=Help

Name	.Ext	Size	Date	Time	Cluster	Arc	R/O	Sys	Hid	Dir	Vol
Sector 15											
IO	SYS	33321	10-06-88	12:00 am	2	Arc	R/O	Sys	Hid		
MSDOS	SYS	37376	10-06-88	12:00 am	68	Arc	R/O	Sys	Hid		
COMMAND	COM	37556	10-06-88	12:00 am	346	Arc					
EGATEST	COM	6563	7-24-87	7:16 pm	420	Arc					
FARGO-ND		0	2-23-91	12:40 pm	141					Dir	
CHAP08	DOC	16384	11-19-90	9:28 am	236	Arc					
JELLS-ID		0	2-23-91	12:40 pm	142					Dir	
ACCTG	WK3	2186	8-30-90	1:23 am	325	Arc					
ᴨATA	WK3	3199	8-30-90	1:23 am	330						
EMPFILE	DBF	666	8-30-90	1:23 am	337	Arc					
EXPENSES	WK1	2315	8-30-90	1:23 am	339	Arc					
ᴨLQ		9	5-16-89	9:28 am	344						
AMCDOC	STY	2048	12-11-90	6:19 am	345	Arc					
MACRO	GLY	32768	8-15-90	7:57 pm	436	Arc					
ᴨPUP	CMP	276	12-18-90	11:57 am	573						
DUMPFILE	DBF	666	8-30-90	1:23 am	453	Arc					
Sector 16											
PROCOMM	IMG	30379	1-03-80	7:19 am	455	Arc					
ᴨVUP	CMP	100	1-18-91	7:39 am	574						

Root Directory   Sector 15 ▲
A:\   Offset 192, hex C0 ▼
Press ALT or F10 to select menus | Disk Editor

(a)   Before

Object	Edit	Link	View	Info	Tools	Quit						F1=Help

Name	.Ext	Size	Date	Time	Cluster	Arc	R/O	Sys	Hid	Dir	Vol
Sector 15											
FILE0001	REC	33792	2-23-91	12:45 pm	2						
FILE0002	REC	37376	2-23-91	12:45 pm	68						
FILE0003	REC	512	2-23-91	12:45 pm	141						
FILE0004	REC	512	2-23-91	12:45 pm	142						
FILE0005	REC	512	2-23-91	12:45 pm	143						
FILE0006	REC	37376	2-23-91	12:45 pm	144						
FILE0007	REC	512	2-23-91	12:45 pm	217						
FILE0008	REC	16384	2-23-91	12:45 pm	236						
FILE0009	REC	37888	2-23-91	12:45 pm	218						
FILE0010	REC	2560	2-23-91	12:45 pm	325						
FILE0011	REC	2048	2-23-91	12:45 pm	324						
FILE0012	REC	1024	2-23-91	12:45 pm	337						
FILE0013	REC	2560	2-23-91	12:45 pm	339						
FILE0014	REC	37888	2-23-91	12:45 pm	346						
FILE0015	REC	6656	2-23-91	12:45 pm	420						
FILE0016	REC	2048	2-23-91	12:45 pm	345						
Sector 16											
FILE0017	REC	1024	2-23-91	12:45 pm	453						
FILE0018	REC	30720	2-23-91	12:45 pm	455						

Root Directory   Sector 15 ▲
A:\   Offset 0, hex 0 ▼
Press ALT or F10 to select menus | Disk Editor

(b)   After

Figure 12-3   Impact of RECOVER

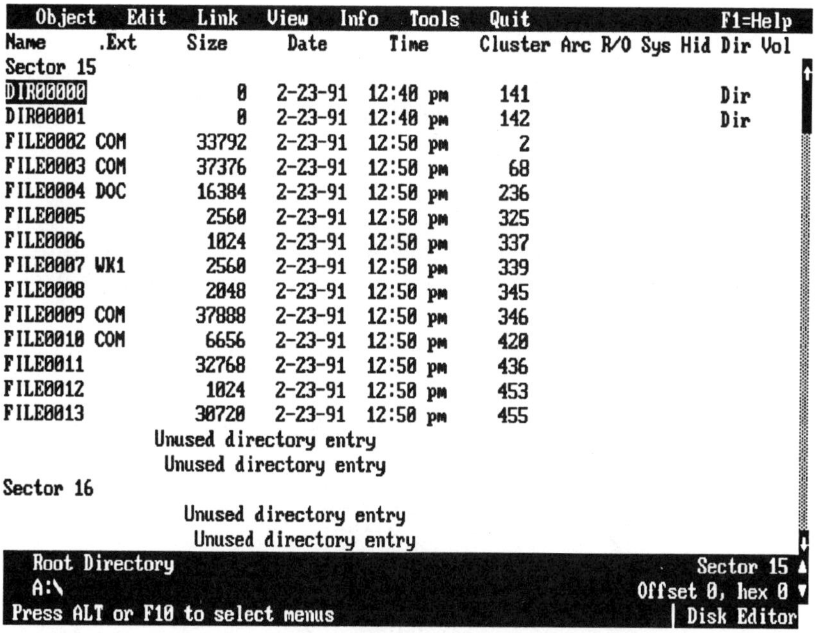

```
 Object   Edit   Link   View   Info   Tools   Quit                    F1=Help
Name     .Ext    Size      Date      Time    Cluster Arc R/O Sys Hid Dir Vol
Sector 15
DIR00000            0    2-23-91   12:40 pm    141                     Dir
DIR00001            0    2-23-91   12:40 pm    142                     Dir
FILE0002 COM    33792    2-23-91   12:50 pm      2
FILE0003 COM    37376    2-23-91   12:50 pm     68
FILE0004 DOC    16384    2-23-91   12:50 pm    236
FILE0005         2560    2-23-91   12:50 pm    325
FILE0006         1024    2-23-91   12:50 pm    337
FILE0007 WK1     2560    2-23-91   12:50 pm    339
FILE0008         2048    2-23-91   12:50 pm    345
FILE0009 COM    37888    2-23-91   12:50 pm    346
FILE0010 COM     6656    2-23-91   12:50 pm    420
FILE0011        32768    2-23-91   12:50 pm    436
FILE0012         1024    2-23-91   12:50 pm    453
FILE0013        30720    2-23-91   12:50 pm    455
              Unused directory entry
              Unused directory entry
Sector 16
              Unused directory entry
              Unused directory entry
  Root Directory                                              Sector 15
  A:\                                                    Offset 0, hex 0
  Press ALT or F10 to select menus                          Disk Editor
```

Figure 12-4   Result of Recover from DOS's RECOVER

itself has been damaged. In all other situations, you should use Norton Disk Doctor to rescue data from bad sectors. But if the root directory is destroyed, then **Recover from DOS's RECOVER** will do a better job.

How Recover from DOS's RECOVER Works

Recover from DOS's RECOVER searches the disk for subdirectory clusters and uses them to restore the disk's directory tree. Since the original names are unavailable in the root directory (because RECOVER nuked them or because the root directory is damaged), it must generate names (DIR00001, DIR00002, etc.) for the subdirectories that branch off the root directory. But all lower-level directories and their files have their real names.

Restoring the subdirectories similarly restores their files. Then **Recover from DOS's RECOVER** can determine which file chains in the FAT must belong to the root directory. Here again it must generate names for these files because the originals have been lost, naming them FILE0001, FILE0002, etc. (If working on a partially damaged root directory, it renames only those filenames that have been damaged.)

> **Note:** If the root directory contains a bad sector and/or the FAT is damaged, **Recover from DOS's RECOVER** cannot rescue the disk. It displays an appropriate message, suggesting that you run Norton Disk Doctor, and quits.

Recover from DOS's RECOVER, like UnErase, has the ability to recognize certain types of files by inspecting their data: COM, EXE, Lotus 1-2-3, and Microsoft Word. When generating filenames, it will assign appropriate extensions wherever possible. This can help you in trying to identify what each file is and what to do with it. For the rest of the directory entry, it uses the current date and time and sets no attributes (except directory).

Running Recover from DOS's RECOVER

To execute **Recover from DOS's RECOVER**, select it from the main Disk Tools menu. You will be asked to identify the drive to be recovered. You will also need to respond to several dialog boxes warning you about what's going to happen. Finally, you can watch the recovery process on an animated map.

Recovering from Recover from DOS's RECOVER

After **Recover from DOS's RECOVER** terminates, you'll have to deal with the unknown files and subdirectories in your root directory. The subdirectories are easy. Use Norton Change Directory (explained in Chapter 16) to view each one, decide what its real name is, and rename it.

The executable files (COM and EXE) are also easy—you should delete them. Never run a program that might be corrupted; it could run away and damage data on your disk. Don't even run it once to see what it is. Reinstall any needed software from its original diskettes.

The rest of the files do need to be examined. If a file has no extension, try viewing it in Disk Editor (hex or text view). If you're still not sure what it is, try opening it under your word processor, desktop publisher, spreadsheet, database manager, drawing program, or whatever other applications you have. You might have to rename it with appropriate extensions to force an application to try to open it. For example, to try to open a file under Lotus 1-2-3, you would have to give it the extension WK1, WKS, or WK3. As you figure out what each mystery file is, rename it appropriately.

If you still haven't figured out what a particular file is, leave it on the disk for a few days. You might realize later which file is missing.

It could take a long time to identify and deal with the mystery files in your root directory. Just keep reminding yourself how long it would have taken if every file on the disk had been renamed and placed in the root directory.

Revive a Defective Diskette

You saw in Chapter 5 that sometimes a disk needs to have its low-level (physical) format redone. Calibrate will do this for a hard disk. For a diskette, use **Revive a Defective Diskette**. Sometimes this is all you need to fix a malfunctioning diskette. **Revive a Defective Diskette** will even work on a physically damaged diskette, reviving whatever sectors it can.

When to Use Disk Doctor and When to Use Revive a Defective Diskette

Norton Disk Doctor can correct many diskette problems, but its solution to a defective sector (discovered during surface testing) is to mark the sector as bad, making it unavailable for future use. Any time a diskette is experiencing read-write errors, you should run **Revive a Defective Diskette** first, because it might be able to fix the sector without marking it as bad. If **Revive a Defective Diskette** can't fix the sector, it will advise you to run Norton Disk Doctor.

How to Run Revive a Defective Diskette

To run **Revive a Defective Diskette**, select it from the main Disk Tools menu. You'll have to identify the diskette drive. Then a progress box keeps you informed as the work progresses, which takes only a few minutes.

After **Revive a Defective Diskette** is finished, it's a good idea to run Disk Doctor (including a surface test) just for safety's sake.

Mark a Cluster

The **Mark a Cluster** function lets you change a cluster marking in the FAT from good to bad or vice versa. When it marks a cluster as bad, **Mark a Cluster** checks to see if the cluster belongs to a file; if so, it copies the file's data to another cluster and revises the FAT chain accordingly. You don't lose any data by marking a cluster as bad.

Mark a Cluster lets you manually solve an intermittent data problem. If you occasionally get sector errors but neither Disk Doctor, Calibrate, nor

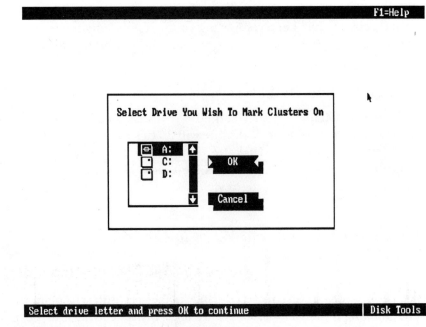

Select Drive You Wish To Mark Clusters On

A:
C:
D:

OK

Cancel

Select drive letter and press OK to continue   Disk Tools

Figure 12-5   Mark Cluster Dialog Box

Revive a Defective Diskette solves the problem, you can frequently eliminate the problem by marking the cluster as bad. You can also prevent future problems by creating buffer zones around known bad clusters if you're a particularly cautious person. That is, for each bad cluster on a disk, you can mark its neighboring clusters as bad, too. (View the FAT under Disk Editor to find the known bad clusters; they're marked with the word BAD.)

Mark a Cluster can also be used to change a cluster marking from bad to good. This lets you undo the mistake if you accidentally marked the wrong cluster as bad.

Using Mark a Cluster

To use **Mark a Cluster**, select it from the main Disk Tools menu. A dialog box lets you select the desired drive. Then the dialog box shown in Figure 12-5 opens. Enter the cluster number (you can do only one at a time) and select **Good** or **Bad**. When you select **OK**, progress boxes show you what is happening.

Rescue Disks

An old adage says that an ounce of prevention is worth a pound of cure. Creating a rescue disk now can save you a lot of trouble later on. The **Create Rescue Disk** function copies your hard disk's Partition Tables, Boot Records, and CMOS values to a diskette. If any of those items are damaged by a head crash, virus, runaway program, or hardware malfunction, **Restore Rescue Disk** can restore them from the rescue disk you so wisely made in advance.

The rescue disk has a couple of advantages over Norton Disk Doctor when you need to fix a corrupted disk. It has the correct CMOS values on it, whereas Norton Disk Doctor can't restore those values. And because it has the real Partition Table and Boot Record values on it, it is somewhat more reliable in these cases than Norton Disk Doctor, which can only make an educated guess at the correct values.

Creating the Rescue Disk

To create a rescue disk, select **Create Rescue Disk** from the main Disk Tools menu. Then select the disk drive to store the rescue information on. Everything else is automatic. Label the rescue disk and put it away in a safe place.

Tip: Create a rescue disk NOW!

Any time you change your hard disk's CMOS values (with the SETUP program), its hard-disk partitioning (with the FDISK program), or its Boot Records (with the FORMAT program), you should create a new rescue disk and eliminate the old one.

Restoring from the Rescue Disk

To restore the hard disk, place the rescue diskette in the appropriate drive and select **Restore Rescue Disk** from the Disk Tools menu. First you must select the drive containing the rescue disk. Then a dialog box lets you select the item(s) you want to restore.

> **Warning:** Don't restore your hard drive from an out-of-date rescue disk. You could cause the system information to be out of sync with what's actually on the disk, making the disk and its data unusable.

Looking Ahead

Sometimes when you unerase, unformat, or otherwise rescue a spreadsheet or database file, you still can't use it because its header information is damaged or missing. The next chapter shows you how to use File Fix to restore headers in these types of files, so that the data can be recovered.

13

FILE FIX

Losing a word-processor file is inconvenient but not usually disastrous, even if it takes you several days to rewrite it. But if you lose a worksheet or database, you might not be able to replace it; you might not be able to recall or regenerate the essential information. Of course, using the full powers of the recovery utilities, you can usually rescue most of the data from a damaged or deleted file. But unfortunately, that alone may not be enough to make a worksheet or database accessible again.

The initial record in both worksheet and database files, called the *header*, contains crucial information about the structure of the file. For a worksheet, the header contains such information as column widths and ranges. Database headers contain field definitions, without which the database is useless. And both types of file headers contain the signature of the software that created the file. If a file's header record is damaged, you won't be able to load it into the spreadsheet or database manager that created it, and therefore, you won't be able to access its data.

Even if the header record is intact, you might not be able to access all the records or cells in the file. Both spreadsheets and databases depend on the data's being stored in a strict layout. For example, in a database, every record must be exactly the same size; if one record is off by as much as one byte, the rest of the records are thrown off, even though they are the correct size.

When you rescue a worksheet or database via UnErase, UnFormat, and the other recovery utilities, it might still contain problems that make it inaccessible under its own software. But File Fix can often restore a damaged

267

header and rescue all undamaged cells and records, making the file accessible again. The only data you need to replace are cells and records that were so badly damaged they couldn't be rescued.

The dBASE program includes a Zap facility that deletes all the records in a database. It can be handy when used correctly, but it's dangerous to misuse it. FileFix also includes a facility to unzap databases.

How File Fix Works

With a worksheet, File Fix operates fairly automatically. You have the choice of rescuing the entire file, which would include all the range information, headers, footers, and other fields that are stored at the beginning of the file, or just the cells themselves (cells can include data, formulas, labels, and formats). Of course, you should try rescuing the whole file first. But if that doesn't work, you can then try rescuing just the cells. (It's a lot easier to redo the up-front information than to redo the cells.)

For databases, File Fix will help you replace a damaged header. You can copy it from another database that has an identical structure, you can redefine the fields if you know what the correct definitions are, or you can actually view and manipulate the data from the first few records until you discover the correct field definitions.

Once the header is fixed, the records themselves must be examined. File Fix does this automatically if you wish, rejecting any record containing invalid data (such as an X in a numeric field or a 5 in a logical field). Or it shows you the records and let you decide whether to accept or reject them.

In any case, File Fix generates a detailed report showing you exactly what was copied to the fixed file and what was rejected. From the report you can determine whether the repair was good enough or whether it needs to be rerun with other options.

Starting File Fix

You can start File Fix by selecting it from the Norton menu (**Recovery** section) or by entering the FILEFIX command at the DOS prompt. The first screen you see, which is shown in Figure 13-1, lets you choose the type of file you want to rescue.

Spreadsheets

File Fix can work on files originally created by Lotus 1-2-3 versions 1, 1A, and 2; Symphony versions 1.0 and 1.1; and other spreadsheet packages that use the same formats.

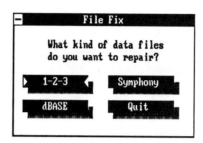

Figure 13-1   File Fix Main Menu

To fix a spreadsheet file, select either 1-2-3 or Symphony from the main File Fix menu. When the dialog box shown in Figure 13-2 opens, find and select the file you want to repair.

Figure 13-3 shows the next dialog box. At the top, you must supply a filename for the repaired file. File Fix does not repair in place but always creates a new file to contain the data salvaged from the damaged file. This gives you the opportunity to try other types of repairs on the damaged file if the first attempt isn't good enough. But it also means the new file will overwrite clusters that you might have wanted to unerase. If there's any chance that you might later need to unerase data from the drive you're working on, store the repaired file on a diskette (unless it's too large) by putting A: or B: in front of the filename, as in A:FIXED.WK3.

The default repair mode attempts to recover all the data in the file: headers and footers, ranges, dimensions, column widths, and so on, in addition to cell data. You should always try this option first; it does no harm if it fails, and it might succeed at least partially. If it fails, you can run the job again using the **Recover cell data only** option.

When you select **Begin**, File Fix goes to work. First, it checks the FAT and directories of the target drive, somewhat like Disk Doctor, to make sure no problems exist. You'll see the message "Checking drive *x:* allocation integ-

F1=Help

```
┌─────────────────────────────────────────────────────────┐
│─          Choose File to Repair                          │
├─────────────────────────────────────────────────────────┤
│ File name: [*.wk*...........................]            │
│                                                          │
│ Directory: A:\                                           │
│                                                          │
│      Files            Dirs              Drives           │
│  ┌──────────┐    ┌──────────┐     ┌──────────┐          │
│  │ acctg.wk3 ▲│   │ PROCOMM  ▲│    │⊞ A:     ▲│          │
│  │ data.wk3  │   │          │     │  C:      │          │
│  │ expenses.wk1│ │          │     │  D:      │          │
│  │ prctg.wk3 │   │          │     │          │          │
│  │ prenses.wk1│  │          │     │          │          │
│  │ prfix.wk1 ▼│  │          ▼│    │         ▼│          │
│  └──────────┘    └──────────┘     └──────────┘          │
│                                                          │
│         ▶ OK  ◀          Cancel                          │
│                                                          │
└─────────────────────────────────────────────────────────┘
```

File Fix

Figure 13-2   Choose File to Repair Dialog Box

F1=Help

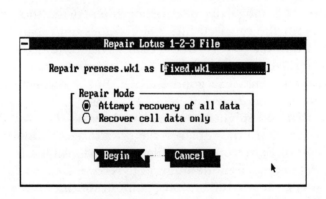

File Fix

Try ALL DATA first; use CELL DATA ONLY for badly damaged files

Figure 13-3   Repair Lotus 1-2-3 File Dialog Box

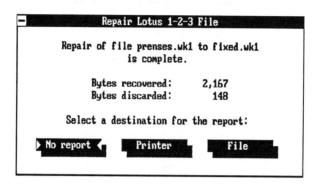

Figure 13-4   Report Dialog Box

rity." If it finds a problem, it displays an error message and terminates. You must correct the problem with Disk Doctor before you can continue with File Fix.

Next you will see a progress box while the file is being fixed. When File Fix has done all it can, the dialog box shown in Figure 13-4 appears. The report contains details about which cells were saved and which were corrupted. It can help you identify areas you need to fix when you reopen the spreadsheet. You should either print the report or save it as a disk file.

After File Fix is finished, you can try to load the repaired file with your spreadsheet software and see what you have. If it's still unusable, you can return to File Fix and try recovering only the cell data. You'll have to redo your ranges and so on, but that's better than losing everything.

Databases

File Fix can repair database files originally created by dBASE II, III, III+, or IV, Clipper, FoxBase, and compatible packages. Start by selecting dBASE on the main File Fix menu. The dialog box shown in Figure 13-2 lists files with extension DBF this time. After you identify the file you want, the dialog box shown in Figure 13-5 opens.

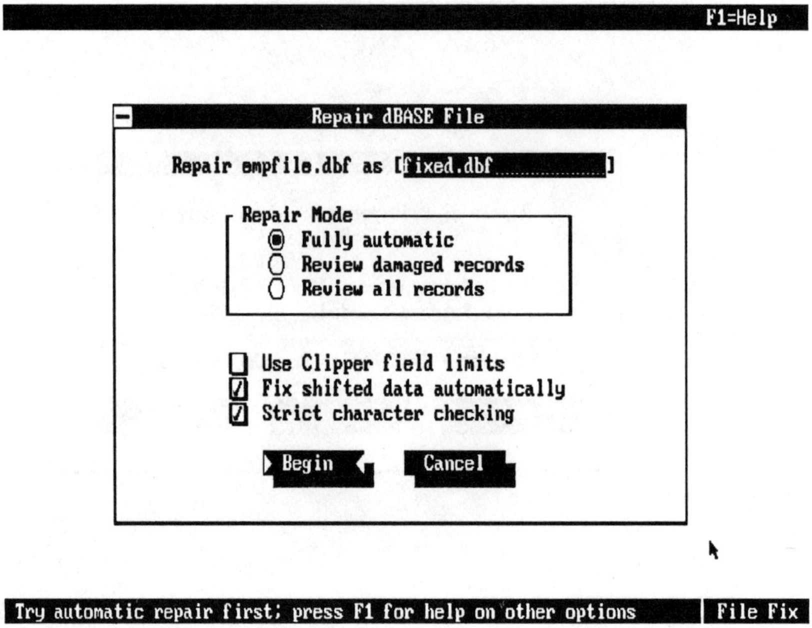

Figure 13-5   dBASE File Repair Dialog Box

At the top of this dialog box, enter the name of the file to be created, being sure to assign it to another drive if you might need to unerase files from this drive.

Repair Modes

You can select from three repair modes that control which database records are copied from the damaged file to the fixed file.

Fully automatic mode automatically accepts or rejects records based on whether they contain invalid data. Most of its decisions are good, but you might find that it accepts records you don't want and rejects records you could have easily fixed. For example, it would reject this record because of the X in a numeric field:

LASTNAME (character)	FIRSTNAME (character)	AGE (numeric)	SCHOOL (character)
FERNANDEZ	DAVIDA	1X	SANTA MARIA

On the other hand, it would accept this record because all the values are valid, if meaningless:

LASTNAME	FIRSTNAME	AGE	SCHOOL
(character)	(character)	(numeric)	(character)
56*29	---1-	01	GRX2,C7aa

Review damaged records mode automatically accepts all records containing valid data but displays invalid ones in a dialog box. You have the choice of accepting or rejecting each invalid record. If you accept it, the invalid data is replaced with a default value so that the database won't reject the record.

Review all records mode displays every record in the database so that you can accept or reject it, giving you complete control over the contents of the database.

> **Tip:** Try **Review damaged records** mode first. It lets you salvage the maximum number of records without having to review every one. (Records containing nonsense values can be deleted or fixed later.)

File Repair Options

Three options appear at the bottom of the Repair dBASE File dialog box (Figure 13-5). **Use Clipper field limits** should be checked for Clipper files and not checked for all other types of databases. (Clipper allows larger fields than the other database packages.)

Fix shifted data automatically corrects data that has gotten out of alignment with the fields. By default, this option is checked, and you should leave it checked unless you *know* that all the database fields are aligned properly. (That is, every field starts and ends in the correct place within every record.) If you uncheck it, File Fix can work faster, but more records might be rejected if any fields are shifted.

Strict character checking considers extended characters (i.e., characters above hex 127 such as é and ¢) to be invalid in character fields. It's a pretty good indication that the field has been corrupted, but if your database has fields where extended characters would be legitimate—for example, if it contains names like Üta Thølm—then you should uncheck this option. If you're reviewing records with this option checked, File Fix shows you any records containing extended characters and lets you decide what to do. But if the automatic repair mode is in effect, File Fix accepts the record but replaces the extended characters with spaces.

Reviewing and Correcting Field Definitions

File Fix essentially works in two phases. First it deals with the database header, then with the records themselves.

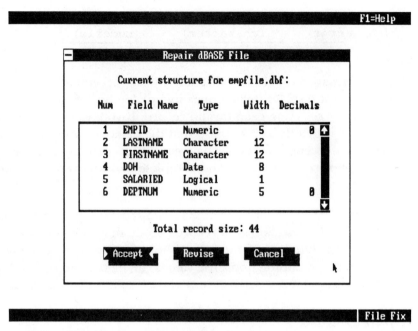

Figure 13-6   Current Structure Dialog Box

In the first phase, File Fix examines the file's header. If it's damaged, you might have to supply the dBASE version number for the header. Then you will be asked to review the field structure, as the field definitions may be either missing or corrupted.

When the header is in perfect condition, a dialog box tells you it found no errors in the header, but you still have the option of reviewing the field structure before going on to the second phase. This is generally a good idea.

Several dialog boxes will lead you through the process of reviewing and correcting the field definitions. Figure 13-6 shows the first of these, which shows File Fix's best guess at the field definitions. If they are correct, you can select **Accept** to go on to the second phase. If the field definitions are incorrect, or if you're not sure, select the **Revise** button.

Figure 13-7 shows the dialog box that allows you to revise the field definitions. The easiest way to define the structure of a database here is to copy (import) the header from another database that has the exact same structure. It might even be an earlier version of the now-damaged database; as long as its header is intact and contains the desired field definitions, you can use it. When you select the **Import** button, a dialog box asks for the name of the database to import from. Then the **Current Structure** dialog box

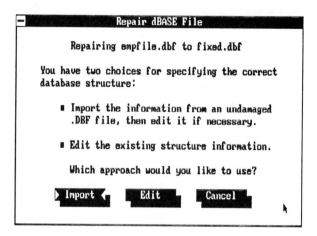

Figure 13-7   Import or Edit Dialog Box

(Figure 13-6) reappears, showing the new structure for you to accept or revise.

Editing the Field Definitions

If you can't import the header from another database, you'll have to edit the existing structure. When you select **Edit**, the dialog box in Figure 13-8 appears.

The first thing File Fix needs to know is where the first record starts. It shows the beginning of the file in the center window, and all you have to do is press Right arrow and Left arrow to shift the data until the first character of the first record is aligned in the upper-left corner of the window. Don't worry yet about how the rest of the data lines up. If you have a mouse, you can drag the data left and right; just grab any character inside the window.

In the example in Figure 13-8, the first record starts with "67543" so we would press Left arrow eight times to shift that field to the upper left corner.

In the next dialog box (Figure 13-9), you establish the record size. The beginning of the data area appears in the central window. As you press Left arrow and Right arrow, the window shrinks and expands until you reach the right record size; each record will start at the beginning of a line and the

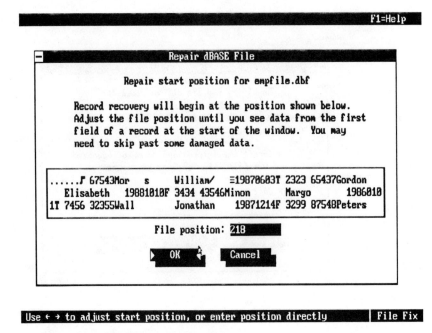

Figure 13-8   Start Position Dialog Box

fields will be stacked in neat columns. Alternatively, you can drag the window border with the mouse or just type the **Record size** if you know it.

Figure 13-10 shows the next dialog box, in which you establish the field sizes. File Fix's best guesses as to field names, types, and sizes are shown, along with data from the first record.

First, make sure the correct number of fields are shown. If there are too many fields, highlight unwanted ones and press Del to delete them. If you need more fields, highlight a field and press Ins to insert a field after it. You can change the location of a field by tagging it (press the Spacebar) and dragging it to the new location. Or you can hold the right mouse button down and drag the field to another location. Only the field definition moves; the data stays where it is.

When the correct number of fields are shown, you're ready to work on the field sizes. Highlight the first field and press Left arrow and Right arrow until its width is correct (the second field will now start in the correct position). You can also drag the end of the field highlight right or left with the mouse. Continue working down the column until all the field widths are correct.

Below the work area, six data items keep you informed about the currently highlighted field as well as the record size. They keep up with the changes you make.

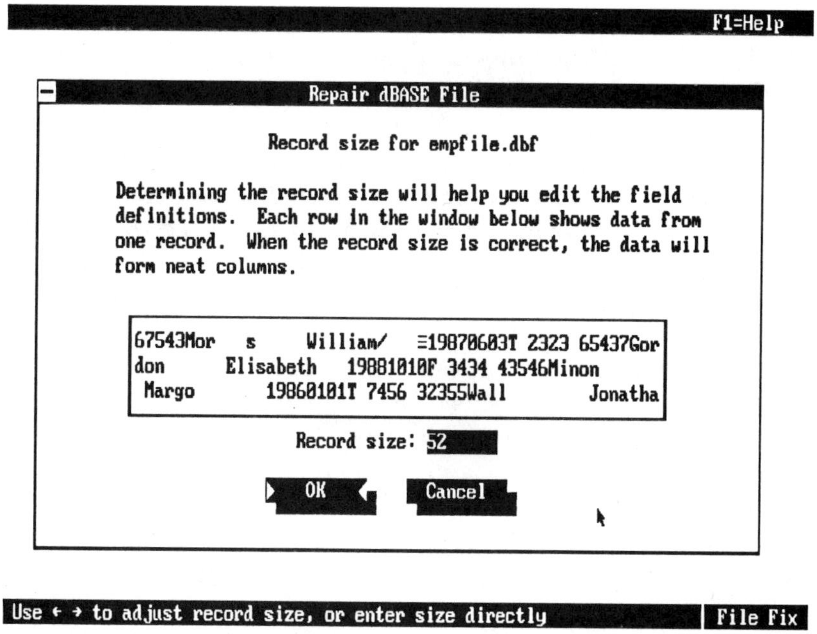

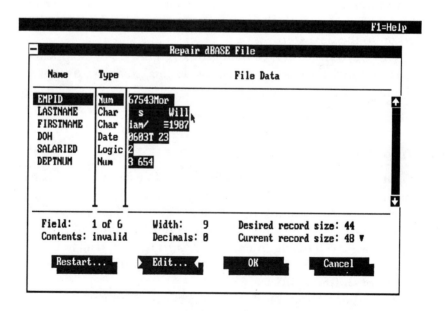

Figure 13-9   Record Size Dialog Box

Figure 13-10   Field Definition Dialog Box

Another way to redefine a field is to highlight it and select the **Edit** button. A dialog box appears in which you can specify the field name, width, type, and number of decimal places. This is often easier than shifting the sample data around as long as you know what the correct values are. And it's the only way to redefine the field type and number of decimal places.

Two statistics shown on the screen are **Desired record size** (determined from the dialog box in Figure 13-9) and **Current record size** (the sum of all the field widths). You need to keep working on the fields until these two numbers match. A down arrow next to the **Current Record Size** means that you need to make the record smaller; an up arrow, larger. If at any time you decide that you made a mistake on a previous screen, the **Restart** button returns you to the **Start Position** dialog box (Figure 13-8) so you can review and revise your work. (You can also revise the start position on-the-fly by pressing Ctrl-Right arrow and Ctrl-Left arrow.)

When you are satisfied with the field definitions, select **OK**. You will see a warning message if the total field widths don't match the defined record size; you have the chance to go back and try again or accept the definitions as-is and continue.

You will also see a warning message if the data in the first record doesn't match the field definitions. This usually results from a type mismatch and can be the result of a corrupted first record. If you know that the field definitions are correct and the first record contains invalid data (you should have been able to see that while working on the field definitions), you can go on to the next step.

The **Current Structure** dialog box (Figure 13-6) reappears showing the database structure as you have now defined it. Select **Accept** to continue to the next phase.

Accepting/Rejecting Records

Figure 13-11 shows the dialog box that File Fix uses to display individual records for you to accept or reject. You can see how many fields are considered to be damaged; damaged fields are also tagged in the display.

You have two options in addition to **Accept** and **Reject** in this dialog box. If the data is out of alignment, select **Shift** to let you align it with Right arrow and Left arrow. You can see how many characters you have shifted in the **Amount shifted** field.

The other button, **Mode,** lets you switch from your current review mode to one of the other review options. For example, suppose you are currently

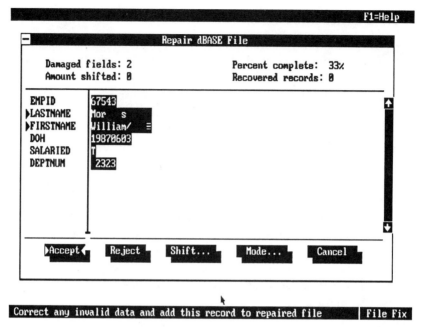

Figure 13-11   Review Record Dialog Box

reviewing every record and you can see that File Fix would accept and reject the same records that you would. You can select Fully automatic mode to discontinue reviewing records, or you could select Review damaged records to see damaged records only.

Unzapping a Database

The dBASE application lets you *zap* a database: this keeps the header but deletes all the records. But suppose you zap the wrong database or change your mind after zapping one. You can't unzap it with dBASE, but you can with (guess what) File Fix.

To unzap a database, follow the same procedure that you use to fix a damaged database file. When File Fix examines the selected database and sees that it is zapped, it will ask if you want to unzap it. When you say yes, File Fix searches the unused clusters for dBASE-style data and recovers it. As with any recovery process, the results might not be 100 percent accurate, especially if any clusters were reused, but you might be able to rescue at least some of your former data.

The File Fix Report

When File Fix has finished fixing the worksheet or database, it offers you the option of creating a detailed report of what was and was not saved. You can either print the report or save it in a file on disk.

Figure 13-12 shows portions of a report for a worksheet. The beginning of the report shows general information about the repair job. Then every location in the worksheet is listed so that you can see exactly what was recovered and what was lost. (The list can be very long, even for a small worksheet; we cut most of it out of the example.)

Figure 13-13 shows a fixed database report. You can see which options were used and that the header record was repaired manually. Out of 10 records, 8 were recovered unchanged and 2 were recovered manually. One 225-byte section (the old header record) was not recovered. In the list of records at the end of the report, you can see the beginning data of the two records that were replaced; discarded records would also be listed here. This list can help you determine which records need to be examined and/or replaced manually.

The FILEFIX Command

You can skip the first two dialog boxes of File Fix by including the filename of the file you want to fix in the FILEFIX command, as in these examples:

```
FILEFIX MEMBERS.DBF
FILEFIX D:\LOTUS\PROJSUM.WK3
```

Looking Ahead

If you've been reading straight through this book, you've already seen several references to things you can do with Disk Editor's editing mode: changing file attributes, fixing up directory entries zeroed by UnFormat, and so on. The next chapter, which returns to the subject of Disk Editor, shows you how to do these things and much more.

```
                    File Fix Lotus 1-2-3 Repair
                          Norton Utilities
                  Wednesday, January 16, 1991 7:38 am


                 ***********************************
                 *  Report for File A:\prenses.wk1  *
                 ***********************************


                      Repair mode: All data
                    Corrected file: fixpren.wk1


                Numeric cells recovered:          3
                  Label cells recovered:         11
                Formula cells recovered:          0
                  Blank cells recovered:          0
                                            ----------
                    Total cells recovered:        14


                       Recovered bytes:       2,167
                     Unrecovered bytes:         148
                   Unrecovered sections:          8


      File
   Location   Cell    Type                        Contents
   --------   ------  ----------   ------------------------------------------------
   ...        ...     ...          .....
   ...        ...     ...          .....
   ...        ...     ...          .....
      2,043   A1      Label        'Office Expenses
      2,069           *******      *** DAMAGE: 11 bytes unrecovered ***
      2,080   C3      Integer      32174
      2,091   D3      Integer      32203
      2,102   E3      Integer      32234
      2,113           *******      *** DAMAGE: 12 bytes unrecovered ***
      2,125   C4      Label        \-
      2,137   D4      Label        \-
      2,149   E4      Label        \-
      2,161           *******      *** DAMAGE: 23 bytes unrecovered ***
      2,184   A6      Label        'Telephone
      2,204   A7      Label        'Supplies
      2,223           *******      *** DAMAGE: 24 bytes unrecovered ***
      2,247   B9      Label        \-
      2,259   C9      Label        \-
      2,271   D9      Label        \-
      2,283   E9      Label        \-
      2,295   A10     Label        'TOTAL
      2,311           EOF
```

Figure 13-12   Worksheet Report

```
                     File Fix dBASE Repair
                        Norton Utilities
              Saturday, February 23, 1991 1:47 pm


          ****************************************
          *  Report for File B:\dumpfile.dbf  *
          ****************************************

                     Repair mode: Fully automatic
            Use Clipper field limits: Off
       Fix shifted data automatically: On
            Strict character checking: On
                   Corrected file: fixed.dbf



              Header errors corrected manually

       Physical records (based on file size):      10

              Records recovered unchanged:           8
           Records recovered with repairs:           2
                                              -----------
                    Total records recovered:         10


                       Recovered bytes:      425
                       Replaced bytes:        16
                     Unrecovered bytes:      225
                  Unrecovered sections:        1


     File     Physical   Recovered    Recovery    Number of
   Location    Record     Record       Action       Bytes       File Data
   --------   --------   --------   ------------   --------   --------------------
        0                            discarded       225    ..........,..........
      225         1          1       replaced          8    .67543Mo
      269         2          2       replaced          8    .65437Go
      313         3          3       saved recs      352
```

Figure 13-13   Database Report

CHAPTER

14

DISK EDITOR AS AN EDITOR

You've seen how to use Disk Editor in read-only mode, and perhaps you've even used it to examine the effects of some of the utilities you've read about. But you can also make changes to your disk with Disk Editor, to fix errors, rescue data from unused areas (even areas outside the DOS partitions), wipe a specific block of data, and handle many other tasks.

Putting Disk Editor into Edit Mode

By default, Disk Editor is in read-only mode, meaning that you can't make any changes to objects. To switch to edit mode, start Disk Editor and select the **cOnfiguration** option from the **Tools** menu, which opens the dialog box shown in Figure 14-1. Uncheck the **Read Only** box, then select **OK** to stay in edit mode for this session only or **Save** to make edit mode the default mode from now on. You won't see any immediate difference on the Disk Editor screen, but you can now edit the data that you see.

> **Tip:** It's safer to keep read-only mode as the default, switching to edit mode only when you need to.

To start up Disk Editor in edit mode for one session only, you can add a /W (for Write-able) Switch to the DISKEDIT command line.

283

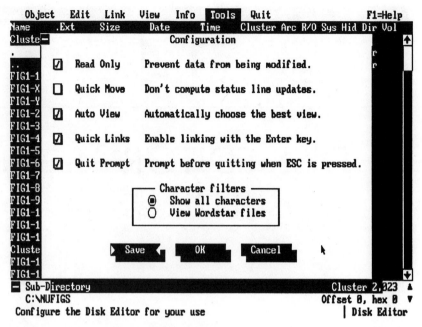

Figure 14-1   Configuration Dialog Box

Special Editing Facilities

The **Edit** menu, shown in Figure 14-2, contains several options that help you in editing objects.

Marking Blocks

Depending on the viewer you're working in, you usually edit data one byte at a time or one field at a time (such as the size field in a directory entry). But some operations can be performed on a *block* of data: a string of bytes, for example, or several adjacent entries in a directory.

To identify a block, place the cursor at one end of the block and select **Mark** (Ctrl-B). As you move the cursor to the other end of the block, a highlight stretches to mark the block. If you have a mouse, you don't have to select **Mark**; just drag the pointer over the desired block (while holding the button down).

Once a block is marked, you can copy it or fill it. These operations are explained in the following sections. You can unmark a block by clicking anywhere or by selecting **Mark** again.

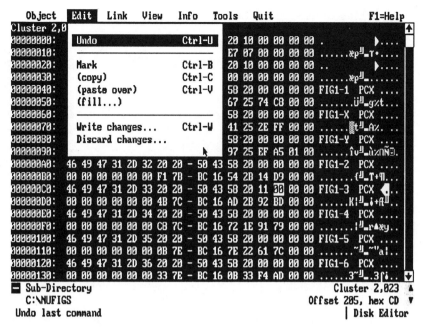

Figure 14-2   Edit Menu

Using the Clipboard

A clipboard facility lets you copy blocks from one location to another. The clipboard can hold up to 4096 bytes (eight sectors). First mark the block; then select **Copy** (Ctrl-C), which copies the block to the clipboard. (An error message tells you if the block is too large; if it works, there is no message.)

Once the block is on the clipboard, switch to the object that should receive the block, if necessary. Position the cursor where the first byte of the block should go, then select **Paste Over**. The block will be copied from the clipboard to the indicated location. Every byte or field that was changed will be highlighted so that you can see the effect.

If you change your mind, you can undo a paste-over by selecting **Undo** (Ctrl-U), as long as only one sector was affected. A warning message tells you when a paste-over crossed a sector boundary and cannot be undone.

You can view and edit the clipboard. Whenever it contains data, the **cLipboard** option is available on the **Object** menu. If you paste from the clipboard after editing it, the edited version is pasted.

A block stays on the clipboard until you use the **Copy** option again, which replaces it with another block, or until you terminate Disk Editor. Once a block is on the clipboard, you can edit and paste it several times if desired.

Filling a Block

You can fill a block with a single repeated character, much like wiping the block. After marking the block, select **Fill** from the **Edit** menu. In the resulting dialog box, you select the fill character. When you close the dialog box, the fill takes place.

There is no limit on the size of a block to be filled; you could fill an entire hard disk if desired. When the selected block resides within one sector, the fill can be undone; you must write it to the disk to make it permanent. But if it crosses a sector boundary, it is done directly on the disk and cannot be undone. A strong warning appears in the dialog box in which you select the fill character when the block crosses a sector boundary.

Writing to Another Location

Any time you are going to edit a vital area—such as a system area—you would be wise to make a backup copy first so you can restore the original in case your editing doesn't work.

To make a copy of the current object, select **Write to** from the **Tools** menu, which opens the dialog box shown in Figure 14-3. It's probably easiest (and safest) to save the object in a file on a diskette. When you select **to a File**, dialog boxes ask for the drive and filename.

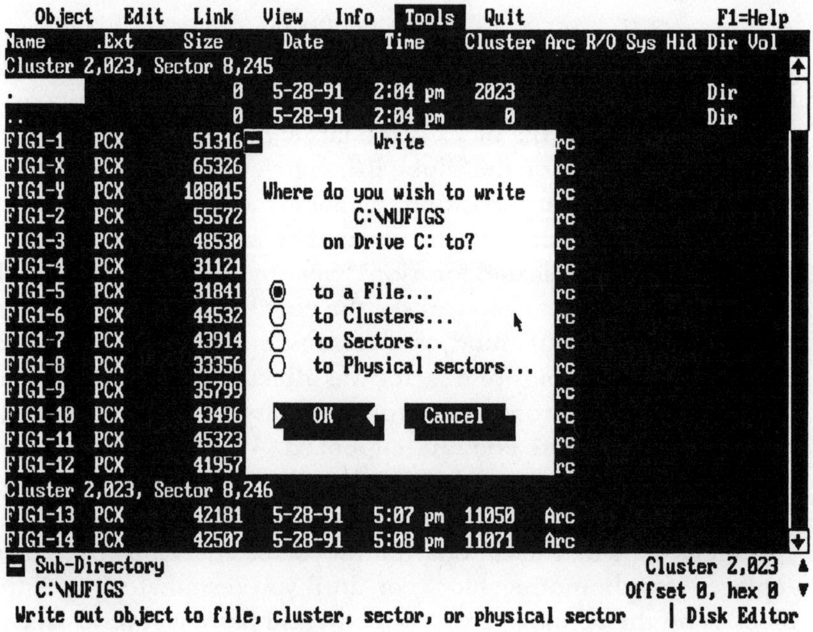

Figure 14-3   Write To Dialog Box

For example, suppose you plan to edit the root directory on drive C:. After you have loaded the root directory as an object, select **Write to,** then select drive A: as the target drive and assign a filename such as ROOTDIRC.SAV. Also, write down the starting sector number of the root directory so that you know where to restore it, if necessary.

To restore the root directory on C: again, load A:ROOTDIRC.SAV as an object. Then select **Write to,** and select **to Sectors** in the resulting dialog box. In the next dialog boxes, select drive C: and enter the correct sector number for the root directory on drive C:, which you wrote down and saved earlier.

Write to can also be used for copying objects from one location to another. For example, you could load clusters 500-525 as an object, then write them to a location on the same drive or on another drive. You can even make a file out of them by selecting **to a File** in the **Write to** dialog box.

Warning: Select the target location of a **Write to** operation carefully. Any previous data in that location is overwritten and cannot be recovered. Pay attention to how large the object to be saved is, and make sure the *entire* target location contains no valuable data. This operation could overwrite a crucial system area or directory.

Editing in Hex View

Figure 14-4 shows a typical object in hex view. You make changes by overtyping bytes in the hex or the ASCII section. You cannot delete or insert bytes; you can only overtype what's already there.

In edit mode, the hex section and the ASCII section each have a cursor, but only the *active* cursor is blinking. Your changes take place at the active cursor and are reflected at the other cursor. The Tab key moves the active cursor from one section to the other. Or you can click on whatever location you want to move the cursor to.

The data you type depends on which section is active. For example, suppose you want to enter a "w" (hex 77) in a byte. If the ASCII section is active, you would type the letter "w" on your keyboard, but in the hex section you would type the two hex digits "77".

Entering Keyboard Characters

It's easiest to enter keyboard characters such as "w" in the ASCII section. Tab the active cursor to the ASCII section if necessary, position it on the byte you want to replace, and type the desired new character. You will see its hex

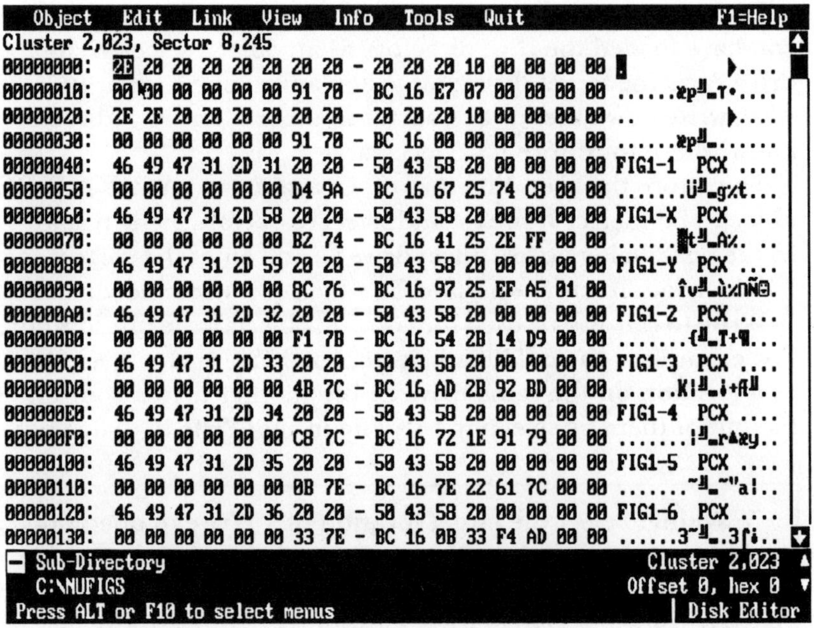

```
 Object   Edit   Link   View   Info   Tools   Quit              F1=Help
Cluster 2,023, Sector 8,245
00000000: 2B 20 20 20 20 20 20 20 - 20 20 20 10 00 00 00 00 █         ▶....
00000010: 00 ↘00 00 00 00 00 91 70 - BC 16 E7 07 00 00 00 00 ......xpⁿ⌐T•....
00000020: 2E 2E 20 20 20 20 20 20 - 20 20 20 10 00 00 00 00 ..        ▶....
00000030: 00 00 00 00 00 00 91 70 - BC 16 00 00 00 00 00 00 ......xpⁿ▬......
00000040: 46 49 47 31 2D 31 20 20 - 50 43 58 20 00 00 00 00 FIG1-1  PCX ....
00000050: 00 00 00 00 00 00 D4 9A - BC 16 67 25 74 C8 00 00 ......ü╨_g%t...
00000060: 46 49 47 31 2D 58 20 20 - 50 43 58 20 00 00 00 00 FIG1-X  PCX ....
00000070: 00 00 00 00 00 00 B2 74 - BC 16 41 25 2E FF 00 00 ......▓tⁿ_A%. ..
00000080: 46 49 47 31 2D 59 20 20 - 50 43 58 20 00 00 00 00 FIG1-Y  PCX ....
00000090: 00 00 00 00 00 00 8C 76 - BC 16 97 25 EF A5 01 00 ......î√ⁿ_ù%ñÑ☺.
000000A0: 46 49 47 31 2D 32 20 20 - 50 43 58 20 00 00 00 00 FIG1-2  PCX ....
000000B0: 00 00 00 00 00 00 F1 7B - BC 16 54 2B 14 D9 00 00 ......±{ⁿ_T+¶...
000000C0: 46 49 47 31 2D 33 20 20 - 50 43 58 20 00 00 00 00 FIG1-3  PCX ....
000000D0: 00 00 00 00 00 00 4B 7C - BC 16 AD 2B 92 BD 00 00 ......K|ⁿ_ñ+Æⁿ..
000000E0: 46 49 47 31 2D 34 20 20 - 50 43 58 20 00 00 00 00 FIG1-4  PCX ....
000000F0: 00 00 00 00 00 00 C8 7C - BC 16 72 1E 91 79 00 00 ......╚|ⁿ_r▲æy..
00000100: 46 49 47 31 2D 35 20 20 - 50 43 58 20 00 00 00 00 FIG1-5  PCX ....
00000110: 00 00 00 00 00 00 0B 7E - BC 16 7E 22 61 7C 00 00 ......♂~ⁿ_~"a|..
00000120: 46 49 47 31 2D 36 20 20 - 50 43 58 20 00 00 00 00 FIG1-6  PCX ....
00000130: 00 00 00 00 00 00 33 7E - BC 16 0B 33 F4 AD 00 00 ......3~ⁿ_♂3⌠ñ..
─ Sub-Directory                                     Cluster 2,023 ▲
  C:\NUFIGS                                          Offset 0, hex 0 ▼
  Press ALT or F10 to select menus                 │  Disk Editor
```

Figure 14-4　Hex View

equivalent appear at the same position in the hex section. Both changes will be highlighted.

Entering Nonkeyboard Characters

Entering characters that don't appear on the keyboard is somewhat more difficult. You can look up the character in the **ASCII Table** dialog box (**Tools** menu) to find out its decimal and hex equivalents. For example, the character Γ is expressed in decimal as 226 and hexadecimal as E2. To enter the character in the ASCII section, hold down Alt while you type its decimal number on the numeric keypad. When you release Alt, the character will appear in the ASCII section and its hex equivalent will appear at the same location in the hex section. To type the character in the hex section, just type its two-digit hex equivalent; the character will also appear in the ASCII section. Both versions will be highlighted.

Pressing the Enter key causes a quick link to another object, so how can you type a carriage return in the object? You have to use the hex section. The two bytes 0D 0A represent a carriage return.

When using the ASCII table, keep in mind that the characters below decimal 32 (hex 20) and above decimal 127 (hex 7F) are not standardized.

The characters you see in the table are the ones that the Norton Utilities display on your monitor when that value is encountered, but they might have different effects with other software and when sent to a printer. The characters below decimal 32 (hex 20), in particular, might act as printer control characters rather than printable characters; that is, they might ring the printer's bell, roll the carriage down, eject a page, or have some other effect. You should check your printer documentation to find out which characters have what effect.

Entering Noncharacter Data

Many files and system areas contain noncharacter data. Numeric values, for example, are often stored in a much more efficient format than ASCII characters allow. But you can't read them or edit them unless you know exactly how to interpret the formats. If you are going to edit noncharacter data, you will find the hex section much easier to use than the ASCII section. Disk Editor will attempt to interpret each byte as a character in the ASCII section, but those characters can be ignored.

Undoing Changes

When you make changes in either section, they are made in memory only. The disk still contains the original, unchanged object until you actually *write* the changes. As long as changes have not been written to disk, they are highlighted on your screen, and they can be undone.

Disk Editor includes an undo feature that remembers every change you make up to one segment's worth (512 bytes) and lets you undo them in reverse order. That is, it undoes the most recent change first, then the next most recent change, and so on. Suppose you overtype "Ruth" with "Judi." If you select undo, the "i" is changed back to an "h" since that was the last byte changed; the next undo changes "d" back to "t"; the third undo changes "J" back to "R." The "u" was not changed (even if you overtyped it) and so is not in the undo buffer.

In addition to using the **Undo** option, you can undo changes in hex view by backspacing over the change to be undone. In fact, in the hex section, you can undo half a byte this way; in all other settings, changes are undone a whole byte at a time.

Writing Changes

When you're sure that you want to record the changes you have made, you can use the **Write changes** option from the **Edit** menu (Ctrl-W), which writes all highlighted changes to disk. When changes are written to disk, the highlights disappear and the undo buffer is cleared.

Discarding Changes

Sometimes you need to undo all the changes you have made for some reason. You can undo them all at once with the **Discard changes** option, which is easier than pressing Ctrl-U until they're gone.

Crossing Sector Boundaries

In any event, you must either write or discard changes when you cross a sector boundary. Whenever you make a move that would cross a sector boundary, such as moving the cursor to the next sector or selecting a different object, a dialog box asks if you want to write, discard, or review changes. Selecting **Write** or **Discard** takes the designated action, then completes the requested sector change. Selecting **Review** returns you to the original sector for more editing. (This dialog box may also appear when you change views.)

Checking Your Work

After you have saved changes to disk, you might want to try them out without exiting Disk Editor. Recall that you can select **Shell to DOS** from the **Exit** menu to get to a DOS prompt and enter a command without losing your place in Disk Editor.

For example, suppose you have fixed up a damaged directory entry in the root directory of drive A: and you want to see if it works. Select **Shell to DOS**, enter the command DIR A:, and view the results. Then type EXIT to return to Disk Editor.

A Word to the Wise

Be very, very cautious of any changes you make to your system areas in hex view or one of the other views. You not only might make individual files inaccessible (with illogical values in directories or the FAT, for example), you could possibly make the whole disk inaccessible (with illogical values in the Partition Table or Boot Record).

Be sure to back up objects that you are going to change so that you can restore the original, if necessary. You have already learned how to use **Create rescue disk** to make copies of your Partition Table and Boot Record from which you can restore your hard disk if necessary. Certainly you should do this before editing those objects.

You can also copy the current object to any specified location using the **Write to** option from the **Tools** menu.

Editing in Other Views

Editing in the other views has similarities to editing in the hex view, but there are also differences. You still overtype existing data to make changes; unsaved changes are highlighted and can be undone in reverse order; you can save changes to disk with the **Write changes** option or discard them with **Discard changes**; you must write or discard changes when crossing sector boundaries. On the other hand, each view contains only one cursor, and it is always active. All the viewers except the hex viewer prevent you from entering invalid values in fields (although you can enter illogical ones); if you type an invalid value, it simply disappears and the former value is still there. If for some reason you need to enter an invalid value, you have to do it in the hex editor. (That's how we forced some of the disk errors that you have seen as examples in chapters such as Disk Doctor.)

In some fields, you can appear to insert or delete characters. For example, you could change the date in a directory entry from 5-10-92 to 10-10-92, or you could change a cluster number from 100 to 1050. But in all those cases, you are not working on character data and you are not really changing the size of the field as it is stored on the disk. If you examine your work in hex view, you will see that the field contains the same number of bytes before and after the change.

In addition to the above differences from hex view, some of the views have special editing facilities, which you'll see as we discuss each view.

> **Reminder:** You cannot edit in text view. Use a text editor or a word processor to change a text file. Or you can do it in the ASCII section of hex view.

Directory View

Editing directory entries under Disk Editor is a handy way to change attributes such as System and Hidden that can't be manipulated by DOS commands (before DOS 5.0), to change the date/time stamps of a file, and to fix corrupted filenames. Don't try to erase or unerase a file by just changing the first character of the filename; the FAT must also be changed when erasing and unerasing files. Also, don't change a file's size or cluster number unless you know exactly what you are doing.

```
  Object   Edit   Link   View   Info   Tools   Quit                F1=Help
 Name     .Ext    Size    Date      Time    Cluster Arc R/O Sys Hid Dir Vol
 Cluster 2,023, Sector 8,245                                                ▲
 .                        0     5-28-91   2:04 pm   2023              Dir
 ..                       0     5-28-91   2:04 pm      0              Dir
 FIG1-1   PCX    51316    5-28-91   7:22 pm   9575   Arc
 FIG1-X   PCX    65326    5-28-91   2:37 pm   9537   Arc
 FIG1-Y   PCX   100015    5-28-91   2:52 pm   9623   Arc
 FIG1-2   PCX    55572    5-28-91   3:31 pm  11092   Arc
 FIG1-3   PCX    48530    5-28-91   3:34 pm  11181   Arc
 FIG1-4   PCX    31121    5-28-91   3:38 pm   7794   Arc
 FIG1-5   PCX    31841    5-28-91   3:48 pm   8830   Arc
 FIG1-6   PCX    44532    5-28-91   3:49 pm  13067   Arc       ▶
 FIG1-7   PCX    43914    5-28-91   7:23 pm   9700   Arc
 FIG1-8   PCX    33356    5-28-91   5:00 pm   3579   Arc
 FIG1-9   PCX    35799    5-28-91   5:01 pm   1600   Arc
 FIG1-10  PCX    43496    5-28-91   5:03 pm   3615   Arc
 FIG1-11  PCX    45323    5-28-91   5:04 pm  10643   Arc
 FIG1-12  PCX    41957    5-28-91   5:06 pm  10908   Arc
 Cluster 2,023, Sector 8,246
 FIG1-13  PCX    42181    5-28-91   5:07 pm  11050   Arc
 FIG1-14  PCX    42507    5-28-91   5:08 pm  11071   Arc                     ▼
 ─ Sub-Directory                              Cluster 2,023    ▲
   C:\NUFIGS                                  Offset 0, hex 0  ▼
   Press ALT or F10 to select menus          │ Disk Editor
```

Figure 14-5   Directory View

Figure 14-5 shows an example of the directory view. You can enter any value you want in the filename, extension, and size fields, but Disk Editor will ignore invalid dates, times, and cluster numbers.

You can't type any values at all in the am/pm field or in any of the attribute fields. These fields are all toggle switches activated by highlighting them and pressing the Spacebar. For example, suppose you want to change the time for FIG1-1.PCX from 7:22 pm to 10:15 am. Three separate fields are involved: the hours, the minutes, and the am/pm toggle. First you would tab to or click on the hour field and overtype 7 with 10. Then you would tab to or click on the minutes field and overtype 22 with 15. Finally you would tab to the am/pm field and press the Spacebar to toggle it from pm to am.

Suppose you want to assign the Hidden attribute to FIG1-X.PCX. You would tab to the Hid field and press the Spacebar to toggle the attribute on.

The Set Date/Time Function

Suppose you're ready to ship a group of 20 files to a client and you want them all to show a uniform date/time stamp—say 12:00 noon on the day of shipment. You could set each file's date/time stamp individually, or you could set them all at once with the **set Date/time** option from the Tools menu.

First, you need to make a block out of all the files to be changed. If all 20 files do not have adjacent entries, you might have to repeat this procedure a few times to set them all. When you select **set Date/time**, a dialog box asks for the new date and time. All highlighted file entries are changed when you close the dialog box.

The Set Attributes Function

Suppose you also want to make the 20 files read-only, and their Archive and Hidden attributes should be turned off, but their system attributes should be left alone since two of the files are system files and should stay that way. Block the adjacent file entries to be affected, then select the **set aTtributes** option from the Tools menu, which opens the dialog box shown in Figure 14-6. You would check the box for **Read only** under **Set**. For **Archive** and **Hidden** you would check **Clear**. You would leave both boxes blank for **System** so that attribute will not be changed.

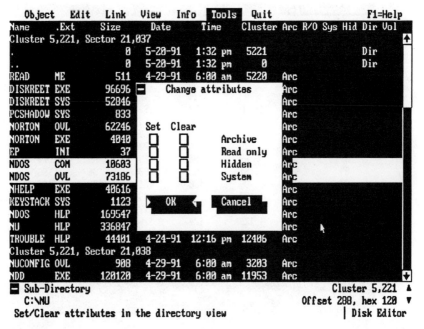

Figure 14-6   Set Attributes Dialog Box

Boot Record View

You can edit in the Boot Record view, but you must be extremely careful not to do more harm than good. If your Boot Record has become corrupted, you're better off restoring it from the rescue disk. If you don't have a rescue disk (tsk! tsk!), use Disk Doctor to identify and fix the problem.

If you feel you must edit the Boot Record, save a current copy as a file on another drive so you can restore it if necessary.

FAT View

Figure 14-7 shows an example of a FAT view. You can overtype any entry with a cluster number, as long as it's legitimate, with E for EOF (end-of-file), or with B for BAD. Use this method of marking a bad cluster only if the current entry is 0, meaning the cluster is unused. For used clusters, use the **Mark a Cluster** function of Disk Tools, which will move the file data to another cluster and revise the FAT chain.

Be very careful in changing FAT entries. You could end up making orphans out of clusters (that is, you can't trace their chains back to a directory entry) or cross-linking clusters (that is, more than one chain leads to the same

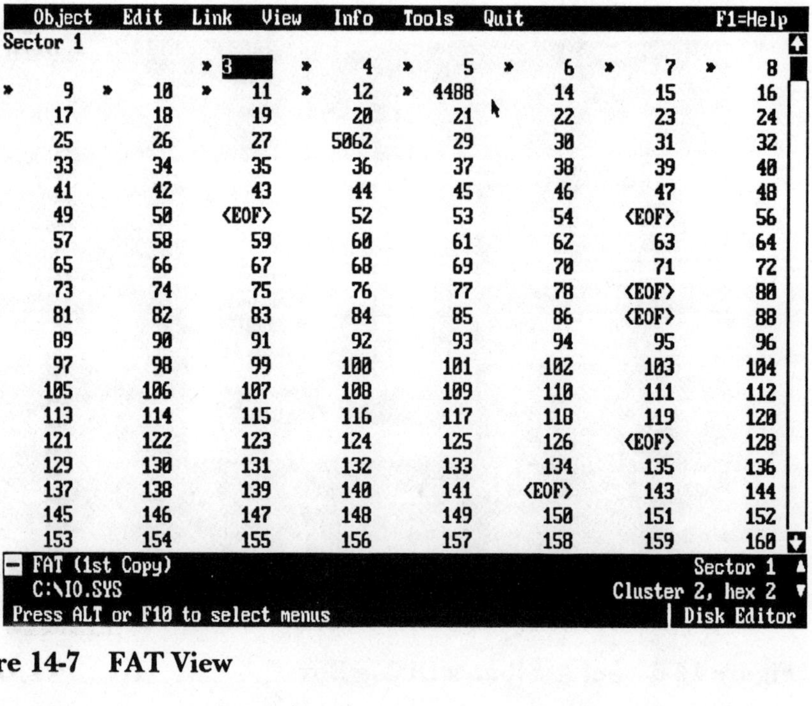

```
  Object   Edit   Link   View   Info   Tools   Quit                    F1=Help
  Sector 1
                       »  3        »   4  »   5  »   6  »   7  »   8
   »   9  »   10  »   11  »  12  » 4488      14      15      16
       17      18      19      20      21 ▶    22      23      24
       25      26      27    5062      29      30      31      32
       33      34      35      36      37      38      39      40
       41      42      43      44      45      46      47      48
       49      50    <EOF>    52      53      54    <EOF>    56
       57      58      59      60      61      62      63      64
       65      66      67      68      69      70      71      72
       73      74      75      76      77      78    <EOF>    80
       81      82      83      84      85      86    <EOF>    88
       89      90      91      92      93      94      95      96
       97      98      99     100     101     102     103     104
      105     106     107     108     109     110     111     112
      113     114     115     116     117     118     119     120
      121     122     123     124     125     126    <EOF>   128
      129     130     131     132     133     134     135     136
      137     138     139     140     141    <EOF>   143     144
      145     146     147     148     149     150     151     152
      153     154     155     156     157     158     159     160
  ─ FAT (1st Copy)                                       Sector 1
    C:\IO.SYS                                        Cluster 2, hex 2
    Press ALT or F10 to select menus                 | Disk Editor
```

Figure 14-7   FAT View

cluster). If your FAT is corrupted, let Disk Doctor fix it. If Disk Doctor doesn't clear it up and you feel you must edit it yourself, store a backup copy before you start. Also, use two Disk Editor windows and compare the 1st FAT to the 2nd FAT. Very often, only the 1st FAT is corrupted; you can find out the correct entries from the 2nd FAT.

If you feel very confident that you know what you're doing, you can edit the FAT to hide data in "bad" clusters, unhide it again, concatenate two or more files into one or split a file into two (don't forget to fix the directory entries also), move clusters from one file to another, and so on.

When you write changes to the FAT, a dialog box asks if you want to update the other copy of the FAT also, which you should, of course, except in very unusual circumstances. Then you are asked if you want to rescan the disk; if you say yes, Disk Editor rereads the directories and FAT and notifies you if it finds any inconsistencies.

Partition Table View

Figure 14-8 shows an example of the Partition Table view. (The fields are explained in Chapter 2.) As with the other system areas, you should edit the Partition Table with Disk Editor only as a last resort. Use your rescue disk to replace a damaged Partition Table, or use Disk Doctor to repair it. To alter the partition definitions, use the DOS FDISK program (or whatever program created the Partition Table). Edit the Partition Table under Disk Editor only in situations where these solutions are inadequate, such as viewing and repairing a non-DOS partition.

You can enter any appropriate value in the **System** column. The **Boot** column is a toggle; press the Spacebar to toggle it between No and Yes. (Only one partition should say Yes.) The sector addresses and counts can be overtyped as needed.

No, you don't have to figure out how many sectors are in a partition. Disk Editor includes a facility to calculate partition data for you. You give it two values from an entry and it will calculate the other two. For example, suppose you want the partition to start at sector 4,5,10 and end at sector 6,480,17. Enter those two values and overtype **Relative Sectors** and **Number of Sectors** with zeros (very important—this is how Disk Editor knows which fields you want calculated). Highlight the entire table entry and select **Recalculate Partition** from the **Tools** menu. You'll see the new sector values immediately.

You can likewise enter the **Relative Sectors** and **Number of Sectors** and ask Disk Editor to calculate the starting and ending sector numbers. Or you could enter the starting sector and number of sectors and calculate the other two values.

```
 Object   Edit   Link   View   Info   Tools   Quit                    F1=Help

       |    | Starting Location   | Ending Location      | Relative |Number of
 System|Boot|Side Cylinder Sector |Side Cylinder Sector  | Sectors  |Sectors    ↑
 DOS-16| Yes| 1      0      1      | 4    770     17       |       17 |   65518
 EXTEND| No | 0     771     1      | 4    975     17       |    65535 |   17425
 unused| No | 0      0      0      | 0     0       0       |        0 |       0
 unused| No | 0      0      0      | 0     0       0       |        0 |       0   ↓



                              ▶

 ▬ Partition Table                         Cyl 0, Side 0, Sector 1   ▲
   Hard Disk 1                             Offset 450, hex 1C2        ▼
   Press ALT or F10 to select menus        | Disk Editor
```

Figure 14-8   Partition Table View

Warning: You can lose access to all the data on a disk by editing the
Partition Table incorrectly.

The DISKEDIT Command

Table 14-1 shows the complete format of the DISKEDIT command. If you
want to use some of the parameters, you can add them to the command in
the text box at the bottom of the Norton menu, or you can enter your own
DISKEDIT command at the DOS prompt.

If you specify a drive, path, or filename, the specified object is the initial
object displayed. Suppose you want to examine the file named BACKPACK
which is in C:\SOFTSPRT. Rather than going through the menus and dialog
boxes to select that object, you could just enter this command:

```
DISKEDIT C:\SOFTSPRT\BACKPACK
```

Table 14-1   DISKEDIT Command Reference

Format:

DISKEDIT [*d:*] [*path*] [*filename*] [*switches*]

Switches:

/M	Starts up Disk Editor in maintenance mode
/W	Read-only off (Write-able mode)
/X:[*drives*]	Excludes the specified drive(s) from processing (necessary for some systems to eliminate allocated but nonexistent drives)

If you want to examine drive A: as a physical disk, you could enter this command:

    DISKEDIT A: /M

Looking Ahead

We've finished our discussion of tools and techniques for rescuing data. By now, you should be able to get yourself out of most of the everyday problems that you experience with your computer and its data. And when you encounter a problem that you can't handle yourself, you'll be able to discuss it with your repair technician without feeling as if you just entered the Twilight Zone.

Have you ever wondered exactly how many tracks your hard disk has or what type of math coprocessor your computer has, if any? Have you ever called a hardware or software technician for help and been unable to answer technical questions about your machine? For that matter, have you ever tried to unload TSRs but not been able to figure out the correct order? The next chapter shows you how to use the System Information utility, which probably tells you much more about your hardware and software than you ever wanted to know.

15

SYSTEM INFORMATION

The System Information utility gives you detailed technical reports on the various parts of your system. Unless you're a hardware/software techie, at least some of the information will be meaningless to you. But on the other hand, some of it is useful to even the most casual of users.

System Information will display, save in disk files, and/or print reports on your system's disk drives, monitor, memory use, serial and parallel ports, and other hardware/software features. It will even test your system's speed and compare it to several popular brands; this is called a *benchmark* test.

System Information lets you page through the entire set of reports or go straight to a specific one. You can also print (or save) the whole set or just the ones you want.

We won't attempt to explain the meaning of all the items in all the reports; that would take a book of its own. But we will show you what's available and how to get the information you need. We'll also explain some of the handier items that you might not be familiar with.

Starting System Information

You start System Information by selecting **System Info** on the Norton menu (**Tools** section) or by entering either SYSINFO or SI at the DOS prompt (depending on how your utilities were installed). The dialog box shown in Figure 15-1 appears first. This box shows a summary the information available from the **System** menu. You can page through all the reports on

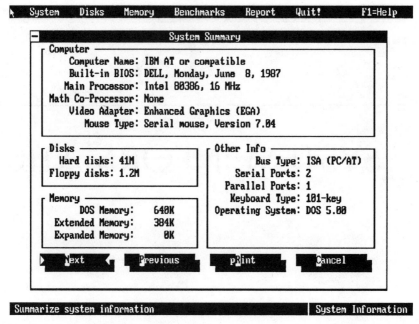

Figure 15-1   System Summary

your screen by repeatedly selecting the **Next** button, or you can use the menus to select specific reports.

The System Summary

The system summary gives you general information about your system. You can find out what type of main processor you have, whether you have a math coprocessor, whether you have extended and/or expanded memory, and so on. It's also useful for making sure all your hardware is installed correctly. For example, suppose you installed a math coprocessor but forgot to set the necessary internal switches to make the system recognize it. The system summary would tell you that the system sees no math coprocessor.

The Full Report (Except Interrupts)

Figure 15-2 shows a nearly complete System Information report in print format, which takes several pages. This is the same information that is in all the dialog boxes, although the on-screen format is slightly different.

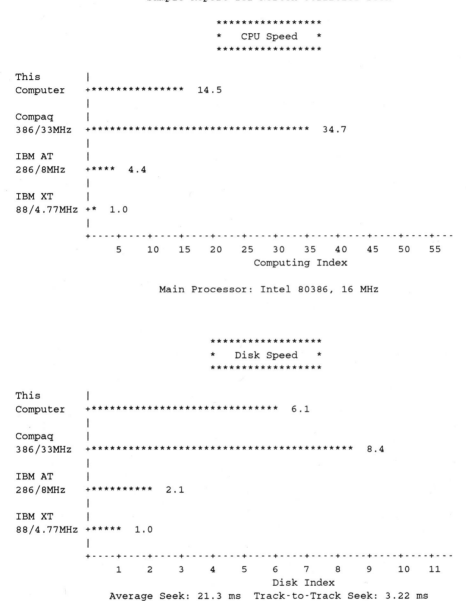

```
                    System Information 6.00
                         System Report
                  Friday, May 31, 1991 12:05 pm
               Sample Report for Norton Utilities Book


                    *****************
                    *   CPU Speed   *
                    *****************


This         |
Computer     +***************  14.5
             |
Compaq       |
386/33MHz    +*********************************  34.7
             |
IBM AT       |
286/8MHz     +****  4.4
             |
IBM XT       |
88/4.77MHz   +*  1.0
             |
             +----+----+----+----+----+----+----+----+----+----+----+---
                  5    10   15   20   25   30   35   40   45   50   55
                                  Computing Index

                 Main Processor: Intel 80386, 16 MHz




                    *****************
                    *  Disk Speed   *
                    *****************


This         |
Computer     +*****************************  6.1
             |
Compaq       |
386/33MHz    +******************************************  8.4
             |
IBM AT       |
286/8MHz     +**********  2.1
             |
IBM XT       |
88/4.77MHz   +*****  1.0
             |
             +----+----+----+----+----+----+----+----+----+----+----+---
                  1    2    3    4    5    6    7    8    9    10   11
                                   Disk Index
            Average Seek: 21.3 ms  Track-to-Track Seek: 3.22 ms
                 Data Transfer Rate: 698.8 Kilobytes/Second
```

Figure 15-2   System Report *(continued)*

```
                    *********************************
                    *   Overall Performance Index   *
                    *********************************

This          |
Computer      +************  11.6
              |

Compaq        |
386/33MHz     +************************  25.9
              |

IBM AT        |
286/8MHz      +****  3.7
              |

IBM XT        |
88/4.77MHz    +*  1.0
              |
              +----+----+----+----+----+----+----+----+----+----+---
                   5   10   15   20   25   30   35   40   45   50   55
                            Overall Performance Index




                    *********************
                    *   System Summary   *
                    *********************

          -------------------- Computer --------------------
            Computer Name: IBM AT or compatible
            Built-in BIOS: DELL, Monday, June  8, 1987
           Main Processor: Intel 80386, 16 MHz
        Math Co-Processor: None
            Video Adapter: Enhanced Graphics (EGA)
               Mouse Type: Serial mouse, Version 7.04

          -------------------- Disks --------------------
        Hard disks: 41M
      Floppy disks: 1.2M

          -------------------- Memory --------------------
            DOS Memory:     640K
       Extended Memory:     384K
       Expanded Memory:     608K

          -------------------- Other Info --------------------
               Bus Type: ISA (PC/AT)
            Serial Ports: 2
          Parallel Ports: 1
          Keyboard Type: 101-key
        Operating System: DOS 5.00
```

Figure 15-2   *(continued)*

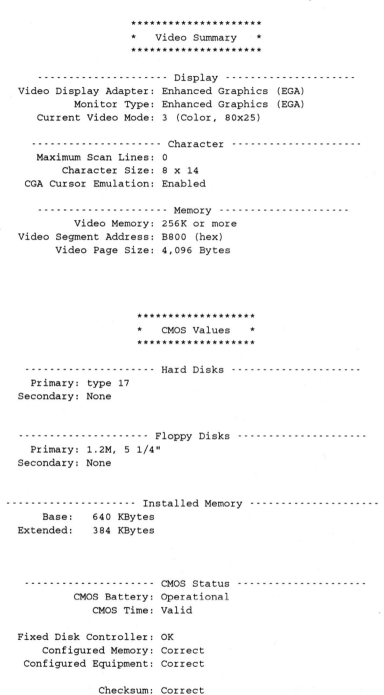

```
                    *********************
                    *   Video Summary   *
                    *********************


           -------------------- Display --------------------
Video Display Adapter: Enhanced Graphics (EGA)
          Monitor Type: Enhanced Graphics (EGA)
     Current Video Mode: 3 (Color, 80x25)


           -------------------- Character --------------------
   Maximum Scan Lines: 0
        Character Size: 8 x 14
CGA Cursor Emulation: Enabled


           -------------------- Memory --------------------
          Video Memory: 256K or more
Video Segment Address: B800 (hex)
       Video Page Size: 4,096 Bytes




                    *******************
                    *   CMOS Values   *
                    *******************


        -------------------- Hard Disks --------------------
     Primary: type 17
   Secondary: None


        -------------------- Floppy Disks --------------------
     Primary: 1.2M, 5 1/4"
   Secondary: None


   -------------------- Installed Memory --------------------
       Base:   640 KBytes
   Extended:   384 KBytes




        -------------------- CMOS Status --------------------
          CMOS Battery: Operational
             CMOS Time: Valid

Fixed Disk Controller: OK
    Configured Memory: Correct
Configured Equipment: Correct

              Checksum: Correct
```

Figure 15-2 *(continued)*

```
                    ************************
                    *   Memory Summary    *
                    ************************


         -------------------- DOS Usage --------------------
         DOS reports 640 K-bytes of memory:
            56 K-bytes used by DOS and resident programs
           584 K-bytes available for application programs


         -------------------- Overall --------------------
         A search for active memory finds:
           640 K-bytes main memory      (at hex 00000-0A000)
            32 K-bytes display memory    (at hex 0B800-0C000)
           384 K-bytes extended memory   (at hex 10000-16000)
           608 K-bytes expanded memory

         -------------------- BIOS Extensions --------------------
         ROM-BIOS Extensions are found at hex paragraphs:
         C000



                  ****************************
                  *   Expanded Memory (EMS)  *
                  ****************************


            EMM Version:  LIM 4.0

      Total EMS Memory:       608K
     Reserved By System:  -   384K
             Allocated:   -    96K
                          --------
              Available:  =   128K


             Page Frame:  D000
         Mappable Pages:  40


                      Total    Free
            Handles:     64      62
          Raw Pages:     38       8
     Standard Pages:     38       8


     Handle  Pages   Size   Name
        0      24     384K   System
        1       6      96K   NDOS:000



                  ****************************
                  *   Extended Memory (XMS)  *
                  ****************************


     Total XMS Memory:       320K
             Allocated:  -    320K
                          --------
              Available:  =     0K
```

Figure 15-2   *(continued)*

```
              XMS Version:  2.00
          Driver Revision:  2.76
        Available Handles:  31

        High Memory Area:  Allocated
                A20 Line:  Enabled

              UMB Server:  None
          Available UMBs:     0K
        Largest Free UMB:     0K


Handle   Block      Size  Locks
42,774       0      320K      0



              *************************
              *   DOS Memory Blocks   *
              *************************

    026F   17,360  DOS System Area      Data
    06AD       64  DOS System Area      Data
    06B2    2,784  COMMAND.COM          Program
    0761      512  COMMAND.COM          Environment
    0782      160  MOUSE.COM            Environment
    078D   12,192  MOUSE.COM            Program
    0A88      160  Free memory          Environment
    0A93    6,544  MIRROR               Program
    0C2D    8,208  FILESAVE.EXE         Program
    0E2F  182,080  Free memory          Program
    3AA4  415,152  Free memory          Data



              *********************
              *   TSR Programs   *
              *********************

Address   Size  Owner                Hooked Interrupt Vectors
-------------------------------------------------------------------
    0008   17,424  DOS System Area    00 01 02 03 04 08 09 0A 0B ...
    06B3    3,296  COMMAND.COM        22 24 2E
    078E   12,352  MOUSE.COM          0B 10 ED FA
    0A94    6,544  MIRROR             19 EB
    0C2E    8,208  FILESAVE.EXE       21
    0E30  597,392  Free memory



              **********************
              *   Device Drivers   *
              **********************

   Address    Name     Description
-------------------------------------------------------------------
   011E:0048  NUL      NUL device
   04BE:0000  EGA$     Unrecognized Device
```

Figure 15-2   *(continued)*

```
02BC:0000   EMMXXXX0   Expanded Memory Manager (EMS)
0271:0000   XMSXXXX0   Extended Memory Manager (XMS)
0072:0007   CON        Console keyboard/screen
0073:0009   AUX        First Serial Port
0074:000B   PRN        First Parallel Printer
0075:000D   CLOCK$     System Clock Interface
0076:000F   A: - D:    DOS Supported Drives
0077:000F   COM1       First Serial Port
0079:0001   LPT1       First Parallel Printer
007A:0003   LPT2       Second Parallel Printer
007B:0005   LPT3       Third Parallel Printer
007C:0007   COM2       Second Serial Port
007D:0009   COM3       Third Serial Port
007E:000B   COM4       Fourth Serial Port



            ********************
            *   Disk Summary   *
            ********************


Drive   Type          Size          Default Directory
-------------------------------------------------------------
A:   1.2M, 5 1/4"   1.2M
B:   Phantom Drive
C:   Hard Disk 1    33M
D:   Hard Disk 1    9M
E:   Available
F:   Available
G:   Available
H:   Available
I:   Available
J:   Available
K:   Available
L:   Available
M:   Available
N:   Available
O:   Available
P:   Available
Q:   Available
R:   Available
S:   Available
T:   Available
U:   Available
V:   Available
W:   Available
X:   Available
Y:   Available
Z:   Available
```

Figure 15-2   *(continued)*

```
****************************
*   Disk Characteristics   *
****************************


------------------- Drive A: --------------------
              No disk in drive
              No physical information


------------------- Drive C: --------------------
                LOGICAL CHARACTERISTICS

        Bytes per sector: 512
      Sectors per cluster: 4
       Number of clusters: 16,339
      Sectors per cluster: 4
       Number of clusters: 16,339
          Number of FAT's: 2
                 FAT type: 16-bit
   Media Descriptor Byte: F8 Hex
         FAT start sector: 1        Sectors Occupied 128
    Root Dir start sector: 129      Sectors Occupied 32
        Data start sector: 161      Sectors Occupied 65,360

                PHYSICAL CHARACTERISTICS

                   Sides: 5
                  Tracks: 771
        Sectors per track: 17
             Drive number: 80 Hex


------------------- Drive D: --------------------
                LOGICAL CHARACTERISTICS

        Bytes per sector: 512
      Sectors per cluster: 8
       Number of clusters: 2,170
      Sectors per cluster: 8
       Number of clusters: 2,170
          Number of FAT's: 2
                 FAT type: 12-bit
   Media Descriptor Byte: F8 Hex
         FAT start sector: 1        Sectors Occupied 14
    Root Dir start sector: 15       Sectors Occupied 32
        Data start sector: 47       Sectors Occupied 17,368

                PHYSICAL CHARACTERISTICS

                   Sides: 5
                  Tracks: 205
        Sectors per track: 17
             Drive number: 80 Hex
```

Figure 15-2   *(continued)*

```
************************
*   Partition Tables   *
************************
```

			Starting			Ending		Relative	Number of
System	Boot	Side	Track	Sector	Side	Track	Sector	Sectors	Sectors
DOS-16	Yes	1	0	1	4	770	17	17	65,518
DOS-12	No	1	771	1	4	975	17	17	17,408

```
************************************
*   AUTOEXEC.BAT file from drive C:   *
************************************
```

```
prompt $p$g
PATH C:\DOS;C:\WINDOWS;D:\WORD;c:\ws5;d:\PCT;C:\NU
SET NU=C:\NU
set TEMP=C:\WINDOWS\TEMP
\mouse\mouse
mirror /tc /td
ep /on
```

```
************************************
*   CONFIG.SYS file from drive C:   *
************************************
```

```
FILES=30
buffers = 30
DEVICE=C:\DOS\himem.sys
device=c:\dos\emm386.exe 512
rem device=c:\dos\smartdrv.sys 320
DEVICE=C:\DOS\ega.sys
SHELL = C:\NDOS.COM C:\DOS\ /P
DOS=umb,HIGH
```

```
******************
*   User Notes   *
******************
```

Computer #105

Figure 15-2

We have omitted two sections of the report, hardware and software interrupts, because they're very long and only die-hard systems types would be interested in them. (If you want to see them, you can view them by selecting the **Hardware interrupts** and **Software interrupts** options from the **System** menu.)

Report Sections

The report contains the sections described below.

Benchmark Tests

The three charts at the beginning of the report show the results of the CPU speed, hard-disk speed, and the overall performance benchmark tests. These three options appear on the **Benchmarks** menu. If you're on a network, a fourth report, network performance speed, is also available.

System Summary

The printed system summary contains the same information as the **System Summary** dialog box, although in a different format. You can display and print the system summary from the **System summary** option on the **System** menu.

Video Summary

This section tells you about your monitor. Most of this information is fixed, but you can change the current video mode using Norton Control Center (see Chapter 16 for details). Use the **Video summary** option on the **System** menu to get this report.

CMOS Values

This section tells you what system information your CMOS contains. It also reports on the status of your CMOS. A CMOS must have a battery to retain its information when the system is off. When the battery runs down, you won't be able to boot normally. Instead, you'll get a message to run the SETUP program—a built-in program which sets the CMOS values. (Check your hardware manuals to find out how to run SETUP; it's usually triggered by an unusual hotkey such as Ctrl-Alt-\.) As you can see in the **CMOS Status** section, System Information checks out the CMOS battery, the system time (the CMOS chip is also your clock/calendar), the fixed disk controller, the memory and equipment configuration. It also verifies a checksum maintained by CMOS as a diagnostic tool. Choose the **CMOS status** option on **System** menu to get this report.

Memory Summary

This report shows you how your memory is currently being used (which includes the System Information program). You can see this report by selecting the **memory Usage summary** option from the **Memory** menu.

Expanded and Extended Memory

These reports show how much of each type of memory you have and how it's being used. You won't see exactly what programs are using the space, but you can find out how much is being used and how much is available.

DOS Memory Blocks

This report shows you details of what programs are loaded at what addresses in DOS conventional memory. Use the **memory Block list** option from the **Memory** menu to see this report.

TSR Programs

This report shows you what TSRs are currently loaded. If you need to uninstall TSRs and aren't sure in what order they were loaded, this report shows the correct order. When you look at this report on screen, you can highlight a TSR to find out the path and name of the program that installed it as well as what options were used in the startup command (the startup options are not always available). To see the report, use the **TSR programs** option from the **Memory** menu.

Device Drivers

A device driver is a program that controls a hardware device. As you can see from the list in the sample report, it takes a lot of device drivers to service all your hardware. Select the **Device drivers** option on the **Memory** menu to see this report.

Disk Summary

This report shows what is assigned to every possible drive name. You can see it by selecting **Disk summary** from the **Disks** menu.

> **Note:** Drive B: will show up as a phantom drive if you have only one diskette drive. You can actually reference the phantom drive B: in DOS commands when two diskette drives are necessary, as in copying a file from one diskette to another.

Disk Characteristics

This report shows you many details about your disk drives, including the locations of your FAT, root directory, and data areas. Select **disk Characteristics** from the **Disks** menu to see this report.

Partition Tables

The Partition Tables should look familiar to you (if you read the chapters on Disk Editor). To see this information for your computer, select the **Partition Tables** option from the **Disks** menu.

AUTOEXEC.BAT and CONFIG.SYS

These two reports simply list your two startup files. Use the **view AUTOEXEC.BAT** and **view CONFIG.SYS** options from the **Report** menu to see them.

Printing the Full Report

To print or save a full report such as the one shown in Figure 15-2, select the **Print report** option from the **Report** menu. Figure 15-3 shows the dialog box that appears. By default, all the items are selected. You can uncheck the ones you don't want, as we did with **Hardware interrupts** and **Software interrupts** before printing the report in Figure 15-2.

If you check **Report header** and **Notes at end of report**, two additional dialog boxes let you enter your own messages for the beginning and end of the report. We used these features to put the message "Sample Report for Norton Utilities Book" at the beginning and "Computer #105" in the **User Notes** section at the end.

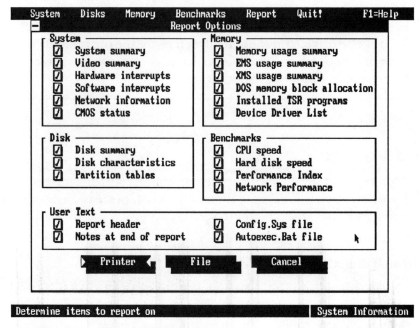

Figure 15-3   Print Report Dialog Box

System Information Command Options

The SYSINFO command can include several switches, as shown in Table
15-1. You can cycle automatically through all the on-screen reports with the
/AUTO:*n* switch, where *n* specifies the number of seconds to display each
screen. You can change to the next screen without waiting for it to time out

---

Table 15-1   SYSINFO Command Reference

Format:

SYSINFO [*drive:*] [*switches*]

Switches:

/AUTO:*n*	Automatic mode; display each screen for *n* seconds
/DEMO	Demonstration mode
/DI	Display Drive Information summary only
/SOUND	Beep between CPU tests
/SUMMARY	Display system summary only
/TSR	Display TSR list only
/N	Bypass live memory probe

---

by pressing Enter. To terminate the display and return to the DOS prompt or Norton menu, press Esc. All other keys are ignored.

The /DEMO mode is similar, but shows only system summary and bench-mark reports. It also responds to Enter and Esc.

If all you're interested in is finding out which TSRs are loaded and in what order, use the TSR switch, which simply lists the current TSRs on the DOS screen without going into System Information's normal menus and dialog boxes.

Looking Ahead

The next chapter covers some utilities that you will probably use every day—especially if you have been struggling with DOS commands such as MODE. As a sneak preview, Norton Control Center lets you set up your hardware by selecting items from a dialog box (instead of entering a complex and confusing MODE command). Norton Change Directory makes it a snap to create and remove directories, and you can change to a directory by entering just the first letter of its name—you don't have to specify the entire path! FileFind helps you locate lost files—either by name or by contents. And DS sorts the entries in a directory.

16

IMPROVING ON DOS

As you have seen in previous chapters, many of the utilities improve on what DOS provides, but you'll find the utilities covered in this chapter particularly useful. Norton Control Center lets you change your hardware settings without having to go through the MODE command. Norton Change Directory gives you a much easier facility to control directories and volume labels than the comparable DOS commands (MD, CD, RD, VOL, and LABEL). FileFind searches all your disks if necessary looking for files that meet specified characteristics. And DS (directory sort) sorts the entries in a directory.

Norton Control Center

Your personal computer has several variable settings, such as monitor colors, video mode, and mouse speed. DOS gives you commands to control these settings, but they're difficult commands and many people don't know how to use them. Norton Control Center gives you a much simpler method of changing these settings.

Starting Norton Control Center

To start Norton Control Center, select **Control Center** on the Norton menu (**Tools** section) or enter the command NCC at the DOS prompt. The initial

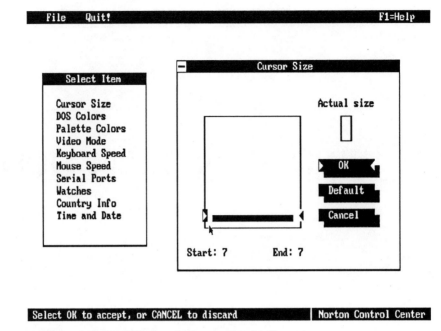

Figure 16-1   Norton Control Center Main Screen

screen, which is shown in Figure 16-1, lists all the settings that you can view and change.

Cursor Size

By default, the cursor is a single underline. If it doesn't show up well on your screen, you can make it larger. Figure 16-1 shows the dialog box (on the right) that you use. Use the Up arrow and Down arrow keys to adjust the size of the cursor (shown in the **Actual size** box) until you find a size you like. Then select **OK**.

Colors

If you have a color monitor, you don't have to live with a black-and-white DOS screen. You can change its colors with Norton Control Center. A dialog box displays all the available colors and lets you select the ones you want for foreground and border. You can also select bright or blinking for the background color. A sample block of text shows you the result.

The **Palette Colors** option, which is available only with EGA and VGA adapters, lets you choose the 16 colors (out of 64 possible) that are available for DOS colors. You'll refer to these colors as red, green, black, bright red, bright green, bright black, and so on, no matter what color they actually produce.

Video Mode

Most video monitors are capable of more than one mode. For example, if you have a VGA monitor, it can display 25 (the default), 40, or 50 lines per screen, in color or in black and white. The **Video Mode** option shows you the options available for the monitor so that you can select the ones you want. You will see the results as soon as you select **OK**.

Keyboard Speed

The **Keyboard Speed** option, which works with machines containing 80286 or higher processors (that is, ATs or more advanced machines), lets you control how quickly a key repeats. Figure 16-2 shows what the screen looks like when you choose this item.

The first control group determines how fast a key repeats; that is, the number of characters per second. You set this factor by moving the slide on

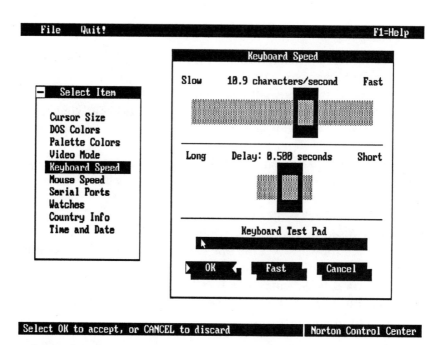

Figure 16-2   Keyboard Speed

the bar to the left for a slower rate or the right for a faster one. You can move the slide with the Left and Right arrow keys or press Home or End to jump to the extreme limit. Or you can drag the slide with the mouse.

The middle control group determines how long you hold a key down before it starts repeating. By default, it is .5 second. You can make it shorter if you want your keys to appear more sensitive, or make it longer if you want more time to release keys before they start repeating.

The text box at the bottom of the dialog box gives you a test pad to try out the current rate. Hold down any character key and see how quickly it repeats. You can continue to adjust the rates until you find those that you like.

If you want to use the fastest possible speeds, you don't have to use the slides. Just select the **Fast** command button.

Mouse Speed

This feature, which is available only when you have a Microsoft-compatible mouse, lets you control how sensitive the mouse is. The faster the speed, the farther the pointer moves when you move the mouse. This is set by a slide much like the one in **Keyboard Rate**. All you have to do is move your mouse pointer to try it out.

Serial Ports

The **Serial Ports** option lets you set the communications characteristics of your serial ports, which you must do in order to use serial-interface equipment. Figure 16-3 shows the screen when this option is selected. You will have to look in your hardware manuals to find out what the appropriate settings are for the equipment that is connected to your serial ports.

The **Baud** rate determines how fast data is transferred to and from the designated port. For example, you might have a laser printer on COM1 that requires a baud rate of 9600 (that's approximately 960 characters per second) and a modem on COM2 that requires 2400 baud.

The **Parity** check indicates what method will be used to identify faulty data (usually caused by noise in the cables or telephone lines). All the possible schemes are shown; select the one that is correct for the equipment you have installed or the software that uses it.

The **Data Bits** indicates whether the data to be transferred contains eight or fewer bits (binary digits) per byte. Select the one that is correct for your equipment or software.

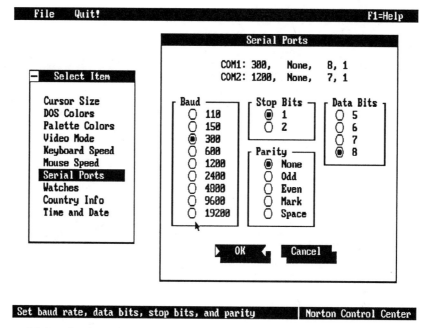

Figure 16-3   Serial Port Options

The **Stop Bits** indicates how many bits identify the end of a byte. All the possible values are shown. Select the one that is right for your equipment.

Watches

Norton Control Center makes four stopwatches available so that you can time various tasks as you work. Figure 16-4 shows the Norton Control Center screen with the **Watches** option chosen.

Suppose you are working on three different projects throughout the day, for which you need to keep accurate time records. When you start on the first task, start the first watch. After it's started, the **Start** button changes to a **Pause** button when that watch is selected. When you put that task aside, pause the first watch. Do the same with your second and third tasks. Whenever you return to a task, restart its watch. Whenever you put it aside, pause it. When you're ready to quit for the day, stop all three watches. If you've been assiduous about pausing and restarting the watches, you will have an accurate display, to the nearest tenth of a second, of the time you have spent on each project.

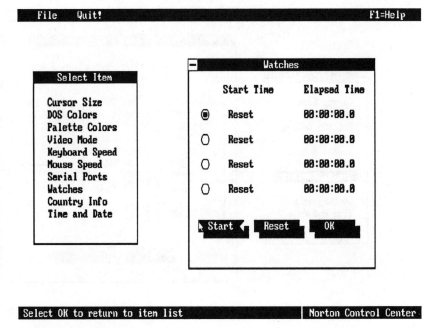

Figure 16-4   Watches

You can stop a watch and reset it to zero by selecting it and selecting **Reset**. You can run all four watches at once, if desired.

Country Info

DOS gives you the ability to change the formats that are used for dates, times, and monetary values. Your system will have default formats that depend on where you bought it, but you can change to any other available format.

In order to change to another country setting, you must have loaded the correct country data in CONFIG.SYS and you must have started a DOS program called NLSFUNC. For example, to use the country information included with your DOS package, you would place this command in CONFIG.SYS:

```
DEVICE=C:\DOS\COUNTRY.SYS
```

In addition, you would enter this command at the DOS prompt (or place it in AUTOEXEC.BAT):

```
NLSFUNC C:\DOS\COUNTRY.SYS
```

> **Note:** See page 172 for instructions on editing CONFIG.SYS and AUTOEXEC.BAT.

Once you have established the prerequisites, you can change to another country's format by selecting the **Country Info** option on the Norton Control Center screen. All the formats that your country file makes available are listed, and all you have to do is choose the one you want.

Time and Date

The last option on the Norton Control Center screen lets you set the system's time and date. A dialog box shows the current time and date and lets you overtype them. (You can also change them with the gray + and – keys on the numeric keypad, but overtyping them is easier.)

Saving the Current Settings

Once you have set your system up the way you like it, you can save the settings in a file that can be recalled when you want to use those same settings again. To save the settings, select the **Save settings** option from the **File** menu. A dialog box asks for the name of the file to be saved.

To restore the settings from a file, select the **Load settings** option from the **File** menu. A dialog box asks for the name of the file to use.

The NCC Command

The NCC command has quite an extensive set of parameters, as shown in Table 16-1, so that you can accomplish many of the functions from the command prompt. This lets you include the desired commands in AUTOEXEC.BAT to set up your system the way you like it when you boot.

Restoring Settings from an NCC File

The easiest way to set up your system is to start up NCC, use the dialog boxes to establish whatever settings you want, then save all the settings in a file using the **Save settings** option (**File** menu). You can restore the settings from that file with an NCC command. If the file is named C:\MYSETUP.NCC, you would use this command:

```
NCC C:\MYSETUP.NCC /SET
```

Table 16-1   NCC Command Reference

To start up Norton Control Center:

NCC

To restore settings from an NCC file:

NCC *filespec* [/CURSOR | /DOSCOLOR | /PALETTE | /SET]

/CURSOR	Sets cursor only from NCC file
/DOSCOLOR	Sets DOS colors only from NCC file
/PALETTE	Sets palette colors only from NCC file
/SET	Sets all settings from NCC file

To set up video and keyboard:

NCC [/FAST] [/BW80 | /CO80 | /*nn*]

/FAST	Sets keyboard to fastest rates
/BW80	Sets monitor to black and white, 25 x 80
/CO80	Sets monitor to color, 25 x 80

/*nn*	Sets monitor to *nn* lines:
	    EGA: 25, 35, or 43
	    VGA: 25, 40, or 50

To start and stop watches:

NCC [/START[:*n*]] [/STOP[:*n*]] [/C:"*comment*"] [/L] [/N]

/START[:*n*]	Starts watch *n*; default is 1
/STOP[:*n*]	Displays current value of watch *n*; default is 1; does not stop the watch
/C:"*comment*"	Includes *comment* in output messages
/L	Displays output on left instead of right
/N	Supresses time and date in output messages

If you don't want to restore all the settings, you could use /CURSOR, /DOSCOLORS, or /PALETTE to set just one feature.

> **Tip:** To set up your system automatically during booting, place the appropriate NCC command(s) in your AUTOEXEC.BAT file.

Setting Up the Monitor and Keyboard

If all you want to do is set up your monitor and/or keyboard speed, you might not need to create an NCC file. You can set the monitor to black and white or color with one of these commands:

```
NCC /BW80
```

or

```
NCC /CO80
```

You can set the number of lines on the monitor with a command like this:

```
NCC /40
```

You can't set specific keyboard rates without opening the NCC dialog box or using an NCC file, but you can set the fastest rates with this command:

```
NCC /FAST
```

You can combine /FAST with monitor switches, as in:

```
NCC /CO80 /FAST
```

Using the Watches

When you start or stop a watch from the command line, NCC displays the current time and date, the elapsed time, and any comment you specify.

You can redirect these messages to the printer or a file for a permanent record. For example, suppose you simply track all your computer time for tax purposes. You could place the following command in AUTOEXEC.BAT:

```
C:\NU\NCC /START /C:"Starting up at..." >> C:\TAXTRACK.IRS
```

The /START switch starts up watch number 1 since no watch number is specified. The output message looks like this:

```
Starting up at...5:06 pm Friday, December 9, 1992
```

The phrase at the end of the command line (>> C:\TAXTRACK.IRS) redirects the output message from the monitor to a disk file named

C:\TAXTRACK.IRS. They are appended to the end of the file so you have a running record of every time you booted the computer.

Tip: Put the NCC command at the beginning of AUTOEXEC.BAT so the time to process the remaining startup commands is counted. In our example, we included the path at the beginning of the command because it's executed before a search path has been established by a PATH command in AUTOEXEC.BAT.

You would also need to enter an NCC command right before shutting down to record the stop time and duration. You could use a command like this:

```
NCC /STOP /C:"Shutting down at..." >> C:\TAXTRACK.IRS
```

This command adds a message similar to the following to the end of the TAXTRACK.IRS file:

```
Shutting down at...9:22 pm Friday, December 11, 1992
                    4 hours, 16 minutes, 2 seconds
```

The elapsed time comes from watch number 1 because no watch number is specified.

Note: If you put this command in the same batch file with a park command, put the park command *last*. Since the NCC command writes to disk, it would unpark the heads if it followed the park command.

The /STOP switch doesn't actually stop or pause the specified watch. It reports the current setting, but the watch keeps right on ticking. To pause a watch, you must use the **Pause** button in the NCC dialog box. You can reset a watch from the command line using the /START switch.

To start the third stopwatch, enter this command:

```
NCC /START:3
```

To stop stopwatch 3 from the DOS prompt and display the comment "Time spent on AMT project," along with the time, date, and value of stopwatch 3, enter this command:

```
NCC /STOP:3 /C:"Time spent on AMT project"
```

The output of the above command would look like this:

```
Time spent on AMT project 5:06 pm Friday, December 4, 1992
                          2 hours, 3 minutes, 23 seconds
```

If you include the /L switch, then the output looks like this:

```
Time spend on AMT project 5:06 pm Friday, December 4, 1992
2 hours, 3 minutes, 23 seconds
```

The /N switch suppresses the current time and date from these messages.

Norton Change Directory

Norton Change Directory makes it easy for you to manage your directories. It provides a graphic display of the directory tree and lets you select the directory you want to work with. It includes all the DOS directory functions for creating, changing to, and removing a directory. In addition, it includes functions to print, speed search, and rename directories. You can also manipulate volume labels with this command.

Start Norton Change Directory by selecting **Norton CD** from the Norton menu (**Tools** section) or by entering the NCD command at the DOS command prompt. Figure 16-5 shows an example of the initial screen, in which the directory tree of the default drive is displayed. The layout clearly depicts the parent-child relationships among the directories. The current directory is highlighted.

Directory Functions

To make a directory the default directory, highlight it and press Enter or double-click on it. You will be returned to the command prompt or the Norton menu with the selected directory active. All other directory functions appear on the **diRectory** menu, which is shown in Figure 16-6.

Print Tree opens a dialog box with three options. If your printer can handle graphics characters, then **Tree, Graphic chars** will reproduce the tree much as it appears on the screen. If graphic characters come out as text

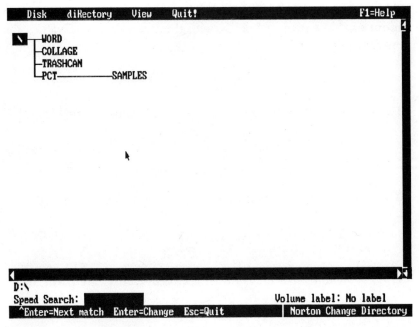

Figure 16-5   Initial NCD Screen

Figure 16-6   Directory Menu

characters (Cs, Ds, and so on), then try the **Tree, Non-graphic chars** option. It draws the tree using + | and – to create a graphic effect. Or you can leave out the graphic effect altogether with the **List** option, which simply lists the directories.

At the top of the dialog box is a text box containing the default name PRN (DOS's name for your printer). You can change that name to a filename to save the tree in a disk file instead of printing it.

The **Rename** option opens a dialog box that lets you specify a new name for the highlighted directory. You will see the name change as soon as you close the dialog box.

The **Make** option lets you create a new subdirectory. Highlight the desired parent first. When you select **Make**, a dialog box asks for the name of the new subdirectory. It is automatically attached to the highlighted directory.

The **Delete** option is much more powerful than DOS's RD (Remove Directory) command. You cannot delete a directory that contains any files or subdirectories. If you try with RD, DOS will simply refuse to delete the directory. But NCD will display the list of files and, if you want, delete them and the directory in one operation. But it won't delete a subdirectory or a read-only file when it is clearing out a directory before removing it. You must use the **remove Tree** option to delete an entire subtree.

The **tree Size** option displays the total size of all the files in the tree.

Three of the options—**Copy tree**, **remove Tree**, and **prune & Graft**—are unavailable by default. If you want to use one of them, you must enable it from the dialog box opened by the **Configure** option.

Copy tree copies an entire tree, with files, to a new location, which can be another drive or another parent. You can choose to delete the original after the copy is completed. The **remove Tree** option deletes an entire tree and its files.

The **prune & Graft** option moves a subtree from one parent to another. This has the same effect as copying the subtree, then deleting the original, but it's faster. When you select **prune & Graft**, the currently highlighted subtree begins flashing. Click on the new parent or highlight it and press Enter.

Warning: Be extremely careful when you use **remove Tree** or **prune & Graft**. It's difficult to recover files and directories deleted this way, and you might not be able to recover all of them successfully. You can't use **prune & Graft** on some network drives.

If you use the **Configure** option to enable any of these functions, it will stay enabled until you disable it again. It's wise to keep them disabled until you specifically need one, enable it only as long as you need it, then disable it immediately.

Finding the Directory You Want

If your tree is small enough, you will be able to see all the directories on the screen at once. But with very large trees, some directories might be off the screen. You can use several techniques to find the directory you want.

> **Note:** The entire tree is always printed or saved on disk no matter how much appears on the screen.

If you have an EGA or VGA monitor with good resolution, the **View** menu provides the best solution to seeing all the directories. It lets you display more lines per screen, reducing the size of the tree so that it might fit. This option affects only the NCD screen.

If **View** doesn't work for you, another alternative is to try **Speed Search**. Type the first few letters of the desired directory's name. With each letter you type, the highlight will jump to the next directory starting with that combination of letters. Use Ctrl-Enter to jump to the next directory starting with the same combination.

If the directory is on another drive, use the **Change disk** option from the **Disk** menu, which opens a dialog box where you can select the desired drive.

Rescanning the Disk

The first time you use Norton Change Directory on a drive, it scans the directory structure on that drive and stores it in a disk file named TREEINFO.NCD. (On a network drive, it places TREEINFO.NCD in a directory named NCDTREE.) From then on, it updates TREEINFO.NCD with every directory change you make through NCD. It does not rescan the drive, which can be time-consuming, unless you force it to.

If you make any changes to the drive's directory structure using DOS, NDOS, or application commands instead of NCD, NCD won't know about them and won't update TREEINFO.NCD, which will then be out of sync with the actual directory tree. You can avoid this situation by always using NCD commands to make any changes to your directory tree. But if you do make some changes through DOS or other software, you can force NCD to rescan the drive by selecting the **Rescan disk** option from the **Disk** menu.

> **Note:** NCD doesn't bother saving tree information for a tree with fewer than five directories. With such small trees, it can take just as long to save and keep TREEINFO.NCD up to date as to rescan the disk every time.

Volume Label

The **Disk** menu also contains a **Volume label** option, which lets you view, add, change, or delete the current drive's volume label.

NCD Command

Many of NCD's directory functions can be done directly from the DOS prompt and should be used in place of the DOS MD and RD commands so that TREEINFO.NCD is kept up to date. Table 16-2 shows the format of the NCD command.

Table 16-2   NCD Command Reference

Format:

NCD [*directory*] [*command*] [*switches*]

directory	Switches to the indicated directory (You need only specify enough of the directory name to be unique)

Commands:

MD [*path*]*directory*	Creates a directory
RD [*path*]*directory*	Removes (deletes) a directory
SIZE [*path*]*directory*	Displays total size of all directories and files in subtree
COPY *source destination* [/DELETE]	Copies subtree
GRAFT *source destination* [/NET]	Moves subtree
RMTREE [*path*]*directory* [/BATCH]	Removes subtree

Switches:

/R	Rescan the drive
/N	Don't update TREEINFO.NCD
/L[:*filespec*]	Lists tree on command prompt screen or saves it in a file

(continued)

Table 16-2   *(continued)*

/G	Uses graphic characters to list tree (used with /L)
/NG	Uses nongraphic characters to list tree (used with /L)
/A	Lists or saves all trees except diskettes (used with /L)
/P	Pauses after pages (used with /L)
/V:*label*	Adds or changes volume label
/T	Displays number and total size of files in subtree
/DELETE	Deletes source after copy (used with COPY)
/NET	Does network-style move (used with GRAFT)
/BATCH	Skips prompts

Creating, Changing, and Removing Directories

To change directories from the DOS prompt, specify the name of the directory you want, as in:

```
NCD REGCOMM
```

You don't even have to specify the path unless the directory name is not unique. In fact, you don't even have to specify the complete directory name. If you enter this command:

```
NCD S
```

NCD will change to the next directory starting with the letter S. If two or more directories in this tree start with S, you might want to be more specific and use SC or SP.

To make or delete a directory, use an MD or RD command, including the path if necessary, as in:

```
NCD MD NUFIGS
```

and

```
NCD RD NUFIGS
```

These commands create a new directory as a child of the current directory and then delete that same directory. You can specify a full path if necessary, as in:

```
MD D:\TOOLKIT\PROGS
```

This command creates a new directory called PROGS under the existing directory TOOLKIT on drive D.

The /R switch forces NCD to rescan the drive. The /N switch prevents NCD from updating TREEINFO.NCD; it is used in conjunction with other parameters when the drive in question is write-protected. For example, suppose you want to change directories on a write-protected diskette. You would enter this command:

```
NCD TALLIES /N
```

Copying, Moving, and Deleting Subtrees

The COPY, GRAFT, and RMTREE parameters won't work unless the associated functions are enabled in the **Configure** dialog box. Suppose you want to copy the subtree headed by C:\MYDOCS to drive A:. You could use this command:

```
NCD COPY C:\MYDOCS A:\
```

The entire directory structure, including files, subdirectories, and their files and subdirectories, is copied to drive A:. Add the /DELETE switch to the command to delete the original subtree after it is copied.

Tip: Use the command NCD SIZE C:\MYDOCS first to make sure the whole structure will fit on A:.

If you prefer, you can use the GRAFT parameter to move a subtree, as in:

```
NCD GRAFT C:\MYDOCS A:\
```

Add the /NET switch if the source or target is on a network drive. /NET makes GRAFT work just like NCD COPY with the /DELETE switch, which is acceptable on some network systems where GRAFT is not.

Suppose you want to delete the entire subtree named D:\NUBACK. You could use this command:

```
NCD RMTREE D:\NUBACK
```

When used like this, NCD will display a confirmation box to warn you what is about to happen. Sometimes a batch file creates a subtree for its own purposes and deletes it later in the same job. In that case, you might not want the confirmation dialog box to appear on the screen. The /BATCH parameter suppresses it.

> **Warning:** The /BATCH switch can be very dangerous. If you have the wrong directory name on the NCD RMTREE command, you could destroy a lot of files and you might not be able to recover them. Check the batch job and make sure it works perfectly before adding the /BATCH switch to it.

Displaying and Printing Trees

Use the /L switch to display or print a drive's tree or save it in a file. To display the tree for drive C: using nongraphics characters, enter this command:

```
NCD C: /L /NG
```

To save the tree for drive D: in a file named DTREE, use this command:

```
NCD D: /L:DTREE
```

FileFind

One of the most frustrating experiences is to forget what you named a file and/or what directory you put it in. FileFind can help you find files by name or by some key text. It will display found files, if requested, highlighting the key text.

FileFind has three additional capabilities. It will determine whether all the found files will fit on another drive; for example, you could ask it whether all the files named *.CDR will fit on the diskette in drive A:. It will let you view and change the attributes of found files. And it will generate a batch file

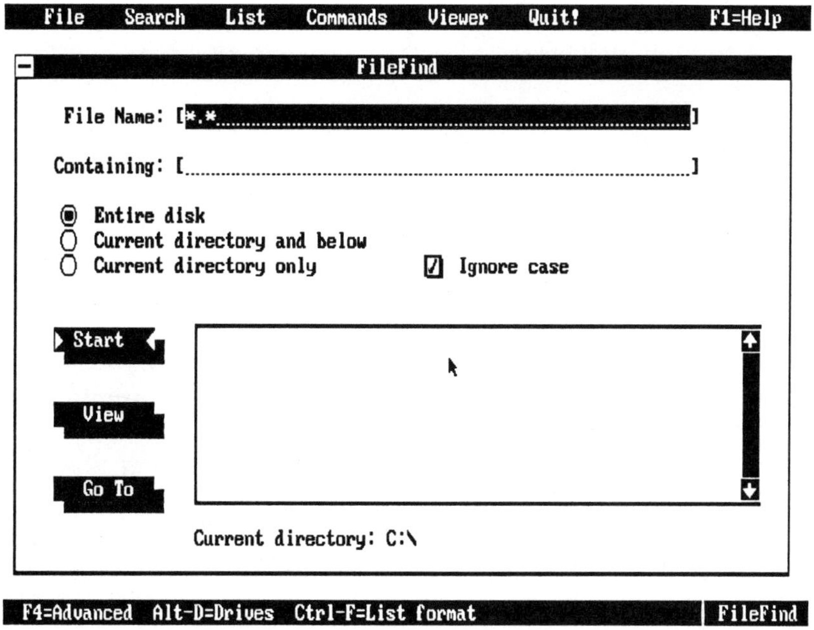

```
┌──────────────────────────────────────────────────────────────────┐
│  File    Search   List   Commands   Viewer   Quit!        F1=Help  │
├──────────────────────────────────────────────────────────────────┤
│ ─│                         FileFind                                 │
│                                                                    │
│   File Name: [*.*..................................................]│
│                                                                    │
│   Containing: [...................................................] │
│                                                                    │
│     ◉ Entire disk                                                  │
│     ○ Current directory and below                                 │
│     ○ Current directory only            ☑ Ignore case             │
│                                                                    │
│   ▶ Start ◀  ┌──────────────────────────────────────────┐ ▲       │
│              │                    ▶                        │        │
│              │                                            │        │
│     View     │                                            │        │
│              │                                            │        │
│              │                                            │        │
│     Go To    │                                            │ ▼      │
│              └──────────────────────────────────────────┘         │
│              Current directory: C:\                                │
│                                                                    │
└──────────────────────────────────────────────────────────────────┘
  F4=Advanced  Alt-D=Drives  Ctrl-F=List format            │ FileFind │
```

Figure 16-7   FileFind Initial Screen

that repeats a command for every found file. For example, you could create
a batch file that executes this command:

```
PRINT filename
```

for every file on drive D: containing the words "Norton Utilities." (Some of
the found files might not be printable, however.)

To start FileFind, select **File Find** from the Norton menu (**Tools** section)
or enter FILEFIND at the DOS prompt. Figure 16-7 shows the initial screen.

Searching for Files

Suppose you are looking for a file named BRESUME.DOC and can't remember what directory it's in. You would enter BRESUME.DOC in the **File Name**
text box and select **Entire Disk**. When you select the **Start** button, FileFind
searches every directory on the drive, listing all the files named
BRESUME.DOC in the list box (with full paths so you can tell the difference
between them).

Suppose you can't quite remember the name of the file, but you're pretty
sure it starts with B. You could enter B*.* in the text box. A much longer list

would result. To keep it short, you might want to limit it to the current directory or the current directory and below by checking the appropriate check box.

Suppose you can't remember what you named the file at all, but you know it contains the name "Barbara." You would leave the default value in the **File Name** text box and put Barbara in the **Containing** box. (You might also uncheck the **Ignore case** box so that you don't match "barbara" and "BAR-BARA.") This search will take much longer, since FileFind has to read through every file on the disk.

If you see the desired filename appear in the list box, you can interrupt the search. As soon as the search starts, the **Start** button becomes a **Stop** button. Select it to interrupt the search. You can continue the search from the point of interruption by selecting **Start** again.

When searching for text, you probably want to limit the search as much as possible. For example, if you know you're looking for a Word document, you could put *.DOC in the **File Name** box so that only DOC files are searched. You should also limit the number of directories to be searched if you can.

If the file you want isn't found in the current drive and/or directory, you can switch to other drives and directories. The **File** menu contains two options that let you change to a different **Drive** and a different **diRectory**. They work just like comparable options in other utilities.

When the search is done and you have finished with FileFind, you can go directly to the directory of a found file by highlighting that file and selecting the **Go To** button, which terminates FileFind and returns you to the command prompt with the highlighted directory active.

More Advanced Searches

The above search techniques should handle most of the searches you have to do. But sometimes you have to go even further to find the missing file.

The **Search** menu offers two options that let you refine your search. **Search drives** opens a dialog box that lets you select multiple drives to search. Suppose you have three hard drives and you don't know which one the missing file is on. Open the **Search Drives** dialog box and select all three drives. Then return to the main screen and continue the search as usual.

Advanced search opens the dialog box shown in Figure 16-8. You can use this dialog box to limit an extensive search—especially a search for text rather than filenames—so that it doesn't take so much time. For example, suppose you know that the desired file was last modified around April of 1991. You might specify **Date is after** 3-15-91 and **Date is before** 5-15-91. If you wish, a time can be included with a date, as in 6-13-92 5:10 PM.

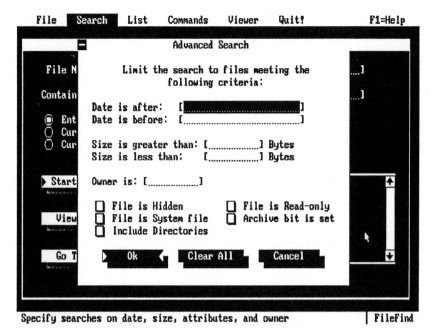

Figure 16-8   Advanced Search Dialog Box

If you know that the desired file runs to about three pages, you could specify **Size is greater than** 2000 **Bytes** and **Size is less than** 8000 **Bytes.** (A full double-spaced page runs 1000 to 2000 bytes.) This will be a great timesaver, as FileFind won't have to search long files. And of course, if you know any of the file's attributes, you should check them.

If a network drive is included in the search, you can also specify a network owner to limit the number of files searched.

Notice that you can choose to include directories as found files, if desired. For example, if you want to list every file that starts with TRI, you might also want to include directories in the list.

The options that you select on this dialog box stay in effect until you change them or terminate FileFind. You can reset them to their default values by selecting the **Clear All** button. The message "Advanced search is on" appears on the main FileFind screen to remind you that some advanced search options are in effect.

Viewing Found Files

You might find it necessary to look through the found files to decide which ones you want. You don't have to wait until the search finishes. As soon as the first file shows up in the list box in Figure 16-7, you can start viewing it.

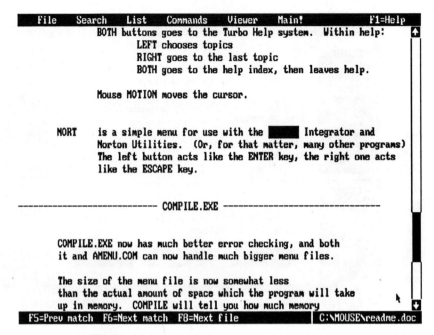

Figure 16-9   View File Screen

Highlight a filename and select **View**. Figure 16-9 shows the screen that appears, which is always a text view (there is no hex option).

Scroll through the file using normal means. If pointers appear at the ends of rows, you can scroll left and right using the mouse or Left and Right arrow and Ctrl-Left arrow and Ctrl-Right arrow.

Use the F7 key to see the previous file in the list or F8 to see the next one when these options appear on the status line.

If you searched for a key word, it will be highlighted on the screen. F6 scrolls to the next occurrence in the same file, if there is one, while F5 scrolls to the previous one. The status line lets you know which keys are valid.

After the search itself has finished, you can add one more feature to your file viewing. You can add or change text in the **Containing** field. Whatever text appears in that field will be highlighted in the files you view, even if that text wasn't used during the search itself. The F6 and F5 functions will be available to scroll between highlighted occurrences.

Manipulating the List

Once the file list has been built, you might find that you want to rearrange it and/or print it. The **List** menu, shown in Figure 16-10, offers several options to manipulate the list.

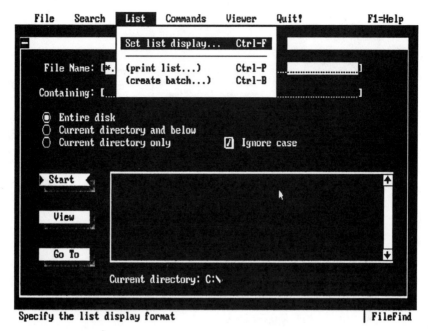

Figure 16-10   List Menu

The **Set list display** option opens the dialog box shown in Figure 16-11, which lets you select information to be displayed and the display order.

The **Print list** option opens the dialog box shown in Figure 16-12, which lets you print a copy of the list or save it in a disk file. The control box in the middle lets you select the format of the list to be printed or saved.

At the bottom are several check boxes. **Print text search occurrences per file** adds to each file name a value showing the number of times that the search text was found in the file. For example, if you searched for "Barbara" and an entry in the list says "AMCDOC 7," then the word "Barbara" appears seven times in AMCDOC.

Print directory totals adds to the list the total number of files that were found in each directory, and the total number of bytes and matches in those files. **Print totals for entire list** adds a last line totaling the entire list.

Setting Attributes and Date/Time

The **Commands** menu contains two options that are very similar to Disk Editor features. **Set Attributes** lets you change the attributes of all the files on the list. A dialog box lets you select attributes to be turned on and off. Suppose you want to turn off the read-only attribute wherever it appears in

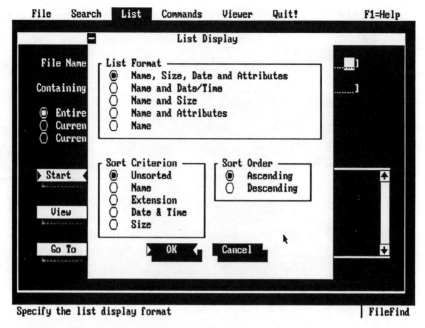

Figure 16-11   Set List Display Dialog Box

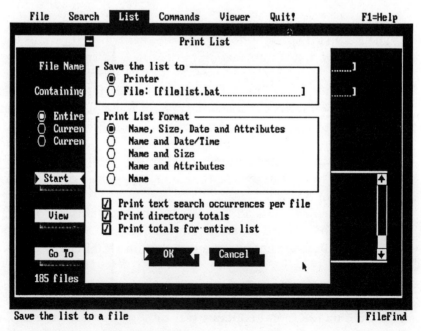

Figure 16-12   Print List Dialog Box

the current directory. Use the **Advanced search** function to select all files with the read-only attribute. Then use **set Attributes** to turn it off for the found files.

The **set Date/Time** function lets you set the date and time stamp for all the found files.

Determining Target Fit

Suppose you want to copy all the found files to drive A:. Will they fit? Select **Target fit** from the **Commands** menu to find out. Figure 16-13 shows the message box that appears. This message tells you how many bytes are actually in the files, then how many bytes they take up on the source drive (because of whole clusters being allocated). The third line tells you how many bytes the same files will take on the target drive (which may have a different cluster size). And the fourth line tells you how much space is actually available on the target drive. The final line tells you whether or not the files will fit.

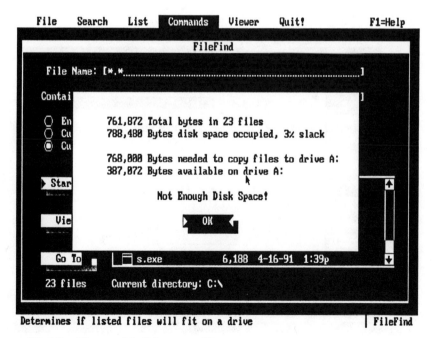

Figure 16-13   Target Fit Message Box

Creating a Batch File

This function can save you lots of time if you want to process a group of found files with the same command. For example, suppose you want to copy all the files containing "Norton Utilities" to the diskette in drive A:. The slow way is to print the list, then manually copy each file. Instead, you could instruct FileFind to generate a batch file containing the following line for every found file:

```
COPY filename A:
```

To generate a batch file, select the **Create batch** option from the **List** menu, which opens the dialog box shown in Figure 16-14.

Check the **Save full path** option if you want FileFind to include the path with each filename. If you have searched more than the current directory, you will need this option.

The **Directory title line** option causes FileFind to generate a line for each directory in which a file was found. The line states the full path of the directory and can be used for switching directories in the batch job.

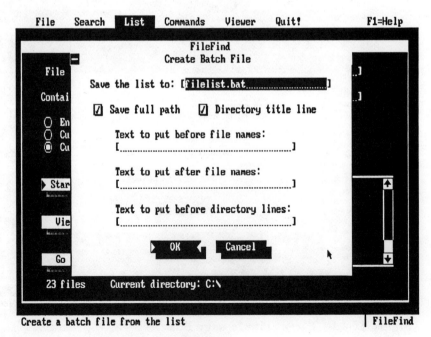

Figure 16-14   Create Batch Dialog Box

Each directory line immediately precedes the list of files that were found in that directory.

In the above example, you would put "COPY" in the box labeled **Text to put before file names**. You would put "A:" in the **Text to put after file names**. If some of the found files are actually directories or if you have generated directory lines with **Directory title line**, you might want different processing for the directories. For example, you might want to put "NCD" before each directory line to switch to that directory in preparation for the next set of files.

When you select **OK**, FileFind generates the batch file. Then you have to leave FileFind and get to the command prompt to actually execute the file. If you used the default filename of FILELIST.BAT, you would enter the command FILELIST at the DOS prompt to execute the generated file.

> **Warning:** You should view the batch file first to make sure it contains the commands and files you intended.

Going to a File's Directory

When no files have been found yet, the **Go To** button is not available. After there are files in the list box, you can use **Go To** to exit FileFind to the directory of the currently highlighted file. For example, suppose you searched for a file and have decided that the file named ACELINKS.WP1 in D:\WP\SCRIPTS is the one you want. You could move the highlight to ACELINKS.WP1 in the list box, then choose **Go To**. You will exit FileFind and D:\WP\SCRIPTS will be the current directory. You are now ready to copy, delete, edit, or whatever you wanted to do with this file.

The FILEFIND Command

Table 16-3 shows the format of the FILEFIND command, which you can use in place of the menus and dialog boxes for some of the FileFind functions.

If you're familiar with DOS's filenaming rules, you'll recognize a difference here—the drive name *: specifies that all drives be searched (including network drives and RAM drives).

Sorting Directories

The DS (directory sort) utility can be used to sort directories. It's faster and easier than Speed Disk when all you want to do is sort directory entries, not

---

Table 16-3   FILEFIND Command Reference

Format:

FILEFIND [*filename*] [*search-text*] [*switches*]

filename	File to search for; can include wildcard characters; the following symbol can be used for a drive name: *: Search all drives
search-text	Text to search for

Switches:

/S	Include subdirectories
/C	Search current directory
/CS	Case sensitive (pay attention to case of search-text)
/A	Search files with archive attribute
/A+ or /A-	Turn archive attribute on or off
/R	Search files with read-only attribute
/R+ or /R-	Turn read-only attribute on or off
/HID	Search files with hidden attribute
/HID+ or /HID-	Turn hidden attribute on or off
/SYS	Search files with system attribute
/SYS+ or /SYS-	Turn system attribute on or off
/CLEAR	Remove all file attributes
/D (*mm-dd-yy*)	Set the date to *mm-dd-yy*

---

optimize a hard disk. Figure 16-15 shows the dialog box that opens when you enter DS at the command prompt or select **Directory Sort** from the Norton menu.

The current directory appears in the list box. Select the **Change Dir** command button to work on a different drive or directory.

Note: Hidden and system files are not listed and will not be sorted.

Specifying the Directory Order

There are two ways to control the order of entries in the directory. You can choose one or more options from the **Sort Order** control group. And you can drag individual entries around in the list box.

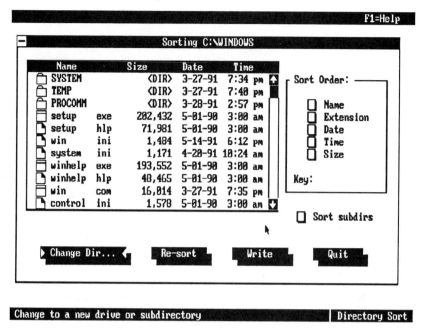

Figure 16-15 DS Dialog Box

When you check an item in the **Sort Order** box, several things happen at once. A number indicates the sequence in which it was selected; 1 appears next to the first item you check, 2 next to the second item, and so on. A plus sign appears to the right of the item. And the key letter of the item name appears next to **Key** at the bottom of the control group. Each of these items has significance.

The sequence number indicates the order of the keys. The entries are sorted first according to the first selected item. If two or more entries have the same value for that key, the second key determines their order. The third key is used only if two or more items have the same first and second keys.

The **Key** field also shows the order of the keys. A value of **SEN** means that Size is the first key, Extension is the second key, and Name is the third key.

The plus sign next to a key means that entries will be sorted in ascending order using that key. Alphabetic keys (name and extension) are sorted in ASCII sequence. The size key is sorted from small to large. And the date and time keys are sorted from early to late. You can toggle between a plus sign and a minus sign, which reverses the order, by clicking on the sign or by moving the cursor to that key and pressing the + or – key.

When you have set up the **Sort Order** you want, select the **Re-sort** command button to sort the directory entries. This button sorts the directory in memory only; it doesn't make any changes on disk. But you'll see the new order in the list box.

> **Note:** Subdirectories are automatically placed first in the directory, regardless of sort order.

Once you have the general order you want, you can reposition individual entries by moving them in the list. Drag an entry using the right mouse button. Or highlight it and press the Spacebar to tag it, use the arrow keys to position it, then press the Spacebar or Enter to untag it and fix it in its new position.

When all the entries are in the desired order, choose the **Write** button to actually rewrite the directory.

> **Note:** You can't write a sorted directory back to a network drive, an ASSIGNed drive, or a SUBSTed drive.

Sorting Subdirectories

By default, only the current directory is sorted. To sort its subdirectories at the same time, using the same sort keys, check **Sort subdirs**. When you do this, changes are automatically written to disk as soon as they're made. A dialog box warns you that this will happen.

Putting Changes into Effect

If you make a move that would cause DS to forget the most recent work that you've done, DS prompts you to save it. For example, if you change the sort keys but don't choose **Re-sort**, then choose **Change Dir**, DS asks if you want to "Apply sort order before changing directories."

If you move some entries around but don't choose **Write**, then choose **Quit**, DS asks if you want to "Write changes before quitting."

The DS Command

Table 16-4 shows the complete format of the DS command. If you specify one or more sort keys, the sort job is done from the command line and the DS dialog box does not appear. So if you want to be able to view the order and play with it, don't put a sort key in the command.

Table 16-4   DS Command Reference

To open the DS window:

```
DS [path]
```

To sort the directory without opening the window:

```
DS sort-keys [path] [/S]
```

path	Identifies the directory to be sorted
sort-keys	Specifies the order to sort the directory; prefix a minus sign (–) to reverse the order

N	Name
E	Extension
D	Date
T	Time
S	Size

/S	Includes subdirectories

Looking Ahead

You've now seen all of the Norton Utilities' graphic utilities. The next chapter introduces a set of utilities that work straight from the command line without opening up any windows or dialog boxes. They're quick and easy to use when you want to accomplish a specific function. For example, suppose you can't find the file named MYDAY.REV. Rather than starting up FileFind, you can enter the command FL MYDAY.REV. In just a few moments, FL will show you where all the files of that name are located on the current drive.

The command-line utilities can't do everything that their graphics counterparts can do. But for limited functions, you'll often find them handier.

17

COMMAND-LINE
UTILITIES

The command-line utilities have traditionally been one of the Norton Utilities most popular features. They tried removing them from Version 5 of the Norton Utilities, thinking that each one had been adequately replaced by graphic functions. But they have been brought back in Version 6 by popular demand. As you read about these utilities, you'll recognize that there are alternative ways of accomplishing most of the functions. The advantage of the command-line utilities is that they work very quickly without taking the time to open windows.

Changing File Attributes, Times, and Dates

Suppose you're preparing a diskette full of files to ship to customers. You want to make all the program files read-only, and several crucial data files should be system files. The other files should have no attributes. Furthermore, all the files should have the same date and time stamps—perhaps 12:00 noon on the day of shipment. If you simply copy the files from your hard disk, they will have the same attributes and date/time stamps as the source files, except the new copies will automatically be given the archive attribute. You could set the attributes, times, and dates using FileFind or Disk Editor, but you might find it quicker and easier to set them with the FA (file attributes) and FD (file date) commands. Also, it's easier to set up a batch file to do the job repeatedly because these are command-line commands requiring no dialog boxes or user interaction.

Table 17-1   FA Command Reference

Format:

FA [*filespec*] [*switches*]

Switches:

/A	Displays files with positive archive attribute
/A+	Turns on archive attribute for specified files
/A-	Turns off archive attribute for specified files
/DIR	Displays directories
/DIR+	Turns on hidden attribute for specified directories
/DIR-	Turns off hidden attribute for specified directories
/HID	Displays files with positive hidden attribute
/HID+	Turns on hidden attribute for specified files
/HID-	Turns off hidden attribute for specified files
/R	Displays files with positive read-only attribute
/R+	Turns on read-only attribute for specified files
/R-	Turns off read-only attribute for specified files
/SYS	Displays files with positive system attribute
/SYS+	Turns on system attribute for specified files
/SYS-	Turns off system attribute for specified files
/CLEAR	Turns off all attributes for the specified files
/P	Pages output messages
/S	Includes subdirectories
/T	Displays totals only
/U	Displays "unusual" files

The FA command can be used not only for changing file attributes but also for displaying them, whether or not you want to change them. Table 17-1 shows the complete format of this command.

Displaying File Attributes

If you enter the FA command with no parameters, it displays the file attributes of all the files in the default directory. For a short directory, the result looks something like this:

```
FA
File Attributes, Copyright 1991 by Symantec Corporation

 D:\
        treeinfo.ncd        Archive
        comlist.img         Archive
        image.idx           Archive Hidden Read-only System
        image.bak           Archive        Read-only
        image.dat           Archive        Read-only

        5 files shown
        0 files changed
```

You could include a parameter to specify a different drive and directory and to limit the filenames that are listed. For example, all of the following could be useful FA commands:

`FA C:`	(displays all the files in the default directory on drive C:)
`FA D:\NEWSET`	(displays all the files in the specified directory)
`FA *.SYS`	(displays only files that match *.SYS in the current directory)
`FA C:\*.SYS`	(displays only files that match *.SYS in the specified directory)

You can also limit the list to files having a particular attribute or set of attributes by specifying one or more of the attribute switches with no + or – sign. In this instance, you can consider DIR just as if it was an attribute. For example, suppose you want to see the names of all the subdirectories in the current directory. You could enter this command:

```
FA /DIR
```

Of course, you could include a drive, path, and/or filespec to access a different directory and/or limit the files that are selected. If you specify more than one attribute, only files that have *all* the specified attributes will be listed. Suppose you want to see all the files that have both the hidden and system attribute in the root directory of drive C:. The complete transaction might look something like this:

```
FA C:\ /HID /SYS
File Attributes, Copyright 1991 by Symantec Corporation

 C:\
     io.sys                        Hidden           System
     msdos.sys                     Hidden           System
     image.idx            Archive Hidden Read-only System

     3 files shown
     0 files changed
```

Don't combine /DIR with other attributes. FA doesn't recognize any attribute but DIR for subdirectories, so if you specify any other attributes, no subdirectories will be selected.

Another way to select files is by using the /U switch, which causes any "unusual" file to be listed; that is, files that have any positive attributes except DIR.

If the displayed list of files scrolls off the screen, use the /P switch to page it, much like /P pages the output from the DIR command. To see files from the entire subtree headed by the specified or implied directory, use the /S switch.

Changing File Attributes

To change file attributes, add a + or – sign after the attribute switch; + turns an attribute on, while – turns it off. For example, the following transaction turns on the read-only attribute for all EXE files in the C:\ directory.

```
FA C:\*.EXE /R+
File Attributes, Copyright 1991 by Symantec Corporation

 C:\
     egacolor.exe        Archive          Read-only
     egamode.exe         Archive          Read-only

     2 files shown
     2 files changed
```

Notice that FA lists the files that were selected and changed.

You can select files to be changed using the same techniques you use when listing files. If you include some attribute switches with no + or – sign, FA selects files that have those attributes and then changes whatever attributes you specify. For example, suppose you want to turn on the hidden attribute for all files that are currently read-only. You could use this command:

```
FA /R /HID+
File Attributes, Copyright 1991 by Symantec Corporation

E:\NUBOOK
      tab14-1.doc                  Hidden Read-only
      tab17-1.doc                  Hidden Read-only
      tab17-2.doc                  Hidden Read-only

   3 files shown
   3 files changed
```

You can use the /U switch to select unusual files, the /S switch to include the entire subtree when selecting files, and the /P switch to page the output listing.

To clear (turn off) all the attributes of the selected files, no matter which positive attributes each one has, use the /CLEAR switch. To hide directories, use /DIR+; to unhide them, use /DIR−. You can include a path on the command line with /DIR+ or /DIR−, but don't include any other switches.

To suppress the list of filenames and show just the total number of files changed, add the /T switch to the command line.

Changing the Time and Date

Table 17-2 shows the format of the FD command, which changes the time and date stamps of files. You must include a filespec with this command. If you use it without the /T and /D switches, it assigns the current time and date to the selected files. If you use /T or /D without any time or date values, it zeros the time or date entries.

Suppose you want to set the time and date on all the files in the \SHIPPER directory to the current time and date. You would use this command:

```
FD \SHIPPER\*.*
```

Suppose instead you want to set them to 12:00 noon on 5/10/92. You would use this command:

```
FD \SHIPPER\*.* /T:12:00 /D:5/10/92
```

Table 17-2   FD Command Reference

Format:

FD *filespec* [*switches*]

Switches:

/D:[*date*]	Sets the date for all specified files
/T:[*time*]	Sets the time for all specified files
/P	Pages output messages
/S	Includes subdirectories

If you find the punctuation in the /T and /D switches confusing, you can omit the colons (:) that come after /T and /D, and you can use dashes instead of slashes in the date. So the above command could look like this:

```
FD \SHIPPER\*.* /T12:00 /D5-10-92
```

Locating Files

Once your hard disk directory structure becomes somewhat complicated, it's easy to forget where you put a file. You've already seen how Norton's FileFind can be used to locate missing files. But the FL (file locate) and TS (text search) commands can solve many problems without starting up a graphic utility. FL locates files by name while TS searches for a text string.

File Locate

Suppose you have lost the TREE1.PRN file. You know it's somewhere on the current drive, but you don't know which directory it's in. You can find it easily with the FL command, which is shown in Table 17-3.

An FL transaction might go something like this:

```
FL TREE1.PRN
E:\NUBOOK
        tree1.prn        380 bytes  12:00 pm  Tue May 11 1993

E:\TREES
        tree1.prn        380 bytes  12:00 pm  Tue May 11 1993

2 files found
```

Table 17-3   FL Command Reference

Format:

FL [*filespec*] [*switches*]

Switches:

/A	Searches all drives
/F [*n*]	Finds *n* files; default is 1
/P	Pages output messages
/T	Searches path files only
/W	Lists output in wide format

FL searches all the directories on the current drive and lists every instance of TREE1.PRN that it finds. In the above example, it found two copies of the same file, one on E:\NUBOOK and one on E:\TREES.

You can add a drivename to the filespec to search a different drive, but you can't specify a path since FL always searches all directories on the specified drive(s). To search all drives, use the /A (all) switch. Even the diskette drives are searched when you use /A, so you'll have to provide diskettes or the command will abort. You can also search just the directories in your current search path using the /T switch.

Listing Multiple Files

When you use a generic filename with FL, it lists all files that match the filename in all searched directories. For example, suppose you want to list all your COM files on the current drive. You could enter this command:

FL *.COM

Other FL Switches

You could add the /T switch to list all the COM files in your search path or the /A switch to list all COM files on all drives. If the listing gets too long, use the /P (page) switch to pause after each page or the /W (wide) switch to list filenames only, five across. The /F*n* switch limits the list to the first *n* matching files; if you omit the *n*, only the first matching file is listed. You can also interrupt the listing by pressing any character key. When it's interrupted, you can resume it by pressing any character key or kill it by pressing Ctrl+C.

If you omit an extension on the filename, all extensions are found. That is, if you search for TREE1 with no extension, FL will list entries for TREE1.PRN, TREE1.RPT, TREE1.DOC, and TREE1.X. This creates a slight problem in searching for a file that has no extension, but all you have to do is put a period after the filename to indicate that you don't want to match all extensions, as in:

```
FL TREE1.
```

If you don't specify a filename, FL lists all the files on the current or specified drive(s).

Which is better, FL or FileFind? For straightforward file searches, FL is faster. And you can redirect the output to a printer or to a file. But FileFind has many capabilities that FL doesn't, such as creating batch files and viewing found files.

Text Search

Suppose you've lost a file and have no idea what its name is. But you know the file contains the word "Barbara." Table 17-4 shows the format of the TS command, which will search the disk for a text string.

Searching through Files

Suppose you know that the file you want has not been deleted. You could search through all the files on the current drive looking for the word "Barbara" with this command:

```
TS \*.* Barbara /S
```

The filespec *.* tells TS to search all the files in the root directory. The /S switch tells TS to include all its subdirectories. This search could take a long time. Anything you could do to limit the number of files to be searched will help. For example, if you know that the desired file was created by Microsoft Word and has the extension DOC, you could change the command to:

```
TS \*.DOC Barbara /S
```

This will shorten the search time considerably. Limiting the number of directories searched will also help. Suppose you're pretty sure the file is in the C:\STAFFRES directory. You could change the command to read:

```
TS C:\STAFFRES\*.DOC Barbara
```

Table 17-4   TS Command Reference

To search through files:

```
TS [filespec] [search text] [/A] [/CS] [/EBCDIC] [/LOG]
[/S] [/T] [/WS]
```

To search entire disk:

```
TS [search text] /D [/A] [/Cn] [/CS] [/EBCDIC] [/LOG] [/WS]
```

To search erased files:

```
TS [search text] /E [/A] [/Cn] [/CS] [/EBCDIC] [/LOG] [/WS]
```

Switches:

/A	Automates search (answers Y to all prompts)
/Cn	Starts the search at cluster n
/CS	Does a case-sensitive search
/D	Searches entire disk
/E	Searches erased files only
/EBCDIC	Searches data stored in EBCDIC format
/LOG	Formats output for logging to print or a file
/S	Includes subdirectories
/T	Displays totals only
/WS	Searches data stored in WordStar format

This search will take very little time because you're searching a limited set of files in only one directory.

If the files you're searching are in WordStar or EBCDIC format, be sure to add the /WS or /EBCDIC switch.

The Search Text

Select your search text carefully. Try to come up with a single word that is somewhat unique to the desired file. Phrases containing several words can be dangerous because most word processors insert formatting codes between words, and TS will not see the similarity between "operant conditioning" and "operant● conditioning" where ● represents a formatting code (such as the start of a new line). Search text containing more than one word must be enclosed in quotation marks.

By default, TS ignores case when searching for text. "Barbara" matches "barbara" and "BARBARA." Use the /CS switch to make the search case sensitive, in which case "Barbara" will match only "Barbara" and not "barbara" or "BARBARA."

Output from TS

You have a lot of control over the output of the TS command. By default, TS displays information about each match and asks if you want to search for another. In a file search, it looks like this:

```
Text Search, Copyright 1991 by Symantec Corporation

Searching C:\STAFFRES\tablerb.res

Found at line 3, file offset 265

American Society for Applied Behavioral Technologies

Ever since she has joined our staff, Dr. Barbara Tabler has
Education
Ms. Tabler received her PhD in Behavioral Psychology from th

Search for more (Y/N)?
```

You can see the filespec on the second line. The third line shows the exact location of the found string in the file. Next, several lines from the file surrounding the found string are shown so that you can see the context of the string. Each paragraph is one line, and they seem choppy because any paragraph longer than 80 characters extends off the right end of the screen. Sometimes the found string itself can't be seen because it is so far down in the paragraph that it is pushed off the right end of the screen. But you should be able to see enough to tell if this is the file you want. If not, press Y to continue searching. When you press N, the search ends immediately and the command prompt returns.

Automating the Output

If you don't want to respond to each matching string, use the /A switch to automate the search. This switch causes TS to assume a Y answer to every "Search for more" prompt. All you have to do is watch the screen carefully and press Esc when you see the file you want. You can also press Pause to pause the output temporarily, and press any character key to resume it.

Saving the Output

If you would like to save the output in a disk file or print it, use the /LOG switch to automate it and format it for print, in which case the paragraphs are formatted to fit inside normal margins so you can read all of them. For each match, about seven lines are printed, with the matching string on the fourth line. On the command line, use the > or >> symbol to redirect the output to a printer or file. In DOS, the > symbol redirects output to a port or a file; if the file already exists, its contents are replaced. The >> symbol does the same thing, except that it appends the output to the end of an existing file instead of replacing it. Suppose you want to print the output from the above search. You would adapt the command to look like this:

```
TS C:\STAFFRES\*.DOC Barbara /LOG > PRN:
```

If instead you want to create or replace the TEMPOUT file, you would use this command:

```
TS C:\STAFFRES\*.DOC Barbara /LOG > TEMPOUT
```

To append the output to the end of TEMPOUT instead of replacing it, use this command:

```
TS C:\STAFFRES\*.DOC Barbara /LOG >> TEMPOUT
```

If TEMPOUT doesn't exist, TS will create it whether you use > or >>.

Totals Mode

Suppose you don't want to see the text of the found files. The /T switch puts TS in totals mode, where it lists the names of every found file and a summary at the end, like this:

```
TS C:\STAFFRES\*.DOC Barbara /T
Text Search, Copyright 1991 by Symantec Corporation

Searching contents of files

    C:\STAFFRES
        tabler.doc
        laruso.doc
        newadds.doc
        leader.doc
```

```
colton.doc
backup.doc
```

```
6 files found containing the text "barbara"
```

Searching Clusters

You can use the /E switch to search the available clusters or the /D switch to search the entire disk. The output looks something like this:

```
TS Barbara /D
Text Search, Copyright 1991 by Symantec Corporation

Searching unused data space (erased file area) of disk

Current drive is C:
Press the letter of the drive to search...
```

After you press the appropriate drive letter, the messages continue:

```
To copy text into a file, enter the file specification
including the drive letter, or press enter to not copy
  File:
```

In most cases, you'll want to enter a filespec so that you can rescue the clusters you find. But if you plan to just locate clusters this way and use UnErase to create the file, just press Enter. If you do enter a filespec, it must represent a different drive from the one being searched. After entering a filespec, the messages continue:

```
Searching C: cluster number nnnn, sectors nnnnn - nnnnn
```

You'll see the cluster and sector numbers spin as the search take place. When a match is found, the numbers freeze to show the cluster and sector numbers, and this message is displayed:

```
Found at byte offset 517

This project will require approximately 15 staff-days to be
Either the Santa Barbara facility or the new facility at Los
7.12.2 Other Direct Costs
Other direct costs will include purchase of networking equip

Copy this cluster into output file (Y/N)?
```

If you type Y, the entire cluster is copied into the file that you designated before. If you type N, it isn't copied. In either case, the next question is:

```
Search for more (Y/N)?
```

If you type Y, the search continues as before. When you press N, the search is terminated and the command prompt returns.

Searching clusters takes time; you can save time with the /Cn switch if you know the desired text isn't in the early clusters. For example, suppose you have already searched up to cluster 5000. Now you want to continue. You could enter this command:

```
TS Barbara /D /C5000
```

Prompt Mode

If you don't enter enough parameters in the command for TS to figure out whether you want to search files, erased files, or the entire disk, TS will prompt you for the information it needs. You can enter a TS command with no parameters at all if you wish. Then all you have to do is respond to prompts. But you won't get the chance to specify such switches as /Cn, /A, or /WS.

Determining File Sizes

Suppose you want copy all the CHAP*.DOC files from your current directory to the diskette in drive A:. Will they fit? The FS command can tell you. Table 17-5 shows its format.

If you use FS without a *target drive:*, it shows you how many bytes the specified files occupy on their current drive. This includes slack space

---

Table 17-5   FS Command Reference

Format:

FS [*filespec*] [*target drive:*] [*switches*]

Switches:

/P	Pages output messages
/S	Includes subdirectories
/T	Displays totals only

---

allocated to the files. It also shows you how much total space is used and available on the specified drive. A sample transaction looks like this:

```
FS CHAP*.DOC
File Size, Copyright 1991 by Symantec Corporation

  E:\NUBOOK
    chap12.doc        19,968 bytes
    chap13.doc        23,040 bytes
    chap11.doc        25,600 bytes
    chap09.doc        32,768 bytes
    chap10.doc        14,336 bytes

     115,712 total bytes in 5 files
     118,784 bytes disk space occupied, 2% slack

  Drive usage
    21,291,008 bytes available on drive E:
     1,978,368 bytes unused on drive E:, 9% unused
```

You can see that the files themselves occupy 115,712 bytes but they're using up 118,784 bytes on the hard disk because of slack at the ends of clusters. You can also see how much space is used and available on drive E:.

But what if you copy those files to the diskette in drive B:? The diskette has a different cluster size, so how much space will they need on that drive? By adding a *target drive*: parameter to the command, you can find out, as in this example:

```
FS CHAP*.DOC B:
File Size, Copyright 1991 by Symantec Corporation

  E:\NUBOOK
    chap12.doc        19,968 bytes
    chap13.doc        23,040 bytes
    chap11.doc        25,600 bytes
    chap09.doc        32,768 bytes
    chap10.doc        14,336 bytes

     115,712 total bytes in 5 files
     118,784 bytes disk space occupied, 2% slack

     116,736 bytes disk space needed to copy to B:
     118,784 bytes available on B:, enough disk space
```

```
Drive usage
   21,291,008 bytes available on drive E:
    1,972,224 bytes unused on drive E:, 9% unused
```

Notice the lines added just above the "Drive usage" lines. They tell you that the selected files will occupy 116,736 bytes on drive B: and that, since there are 118,784 bytes available on drive B:, they will fit on that diskette.

The /T switch suppresses the file listing and displays the totals only. Suppose you want to find out exactly how much of your hard drive is currently wasted in slack. You could enter a command like this:

```
FS \*.* /S /T
```

The /T switch causes FS to list totals only. The *.* filespec causes every file to be counted, starting with the root directory. Actually, you could omit the *.*, which is the default when no other filename is specified. The /S switch causes every subdirectory to be included. FS lists the totals for every subdirectory. At the end, it shows a summary like this:

```
Total of all files found
   18,700,451 total bytes in 556 files
   19,283,968 bytes disk space occupied, 3% slack

Drive usage
   21,291,008 bytes available on drive E:
    1,970,176 bytes unused on drive E:, 9% unused
```

The answer is in the third line of the summary—3 percent of the hard drive is wasted in slack. Actually, that's not too bad.

Printing Files

If you've ever used DOS's PRINT program to print a text file, you know that it has some shortcomings. Norton's LP (line print) has several advantages over PRINT:

- It can print on PostScript printers.
- You can specify different printers for different files without having to reboot.
- It doesn't need to be initialized.
- It is not a TSR, so it doesn't take up memory space when it's not in use.

- It can handle files in WordStar and EBCDIC format.
- It gives you some control over page formatting, including headers, page numbers, and line numbers.
- You can send a setup string to the printer.

About the only disadvantage of LP when compared to PRINT is that it doesn't run in the background. That is, you have to wait for the file(s) to finish printing before you get the command prompt back and can continue with another task.

Table 17-6 shows the format of the LP command. As you can see, it can have a lot of parameters, but the basic command can be as simple as LP CONFIG.SYS.

Table 17-6   LP Command Reference

Format:

`LP [filespec] [device] [switches]`

Switches:

/Tn	Specifies top margin of n lines
/Bn	Specifies bottom margin of n lines
/Ln	Specifies left margin of n characters
/Rn	Specifies right margin of n characters
/Hn	Specifies page height of n lines
/Wn	Specifies page width of n characters
/TABn	Specifies tab stops every n characters
/Sn	Specifies n line spacing
/Pn	Specifies starting page number
/N	Turns line numbering on
/80	Specifies print size of 80 characters per line
/132	Specifies print size of 132 characters per line
/Hn	Specifies header format of 0, 1, or 2
/EBCDIC	Prints EBCDIC encoded files
/WS	Prints WordStar compatible files
/PS	Prints on PostScript printer
/SET:filespec	Sends specified file to printer as setup string

The Default Line Print

Figure 17-1 shows the printout format you get when you enter an LP command without any switches. It uses these default parameters:

- .5" margins on all sides
- 8.5" by 11" paper size
- Single spacing
- Page numbering is on; first page is number 1
- Line numbering is off
- Tabs are set at every eight columns
- Print width is 80 characters per line
- A one-line page header shows the filename and the current day, date, and time

Specifying the File to be Printed

You can use a specific or global filespec with the LP command. If a global filespec causes more than one file to be printed, each file is printed separately, starting on its own page one.

If a file was formatted by WordStar, it might not print correctly. Because of the way WordStar stores formatting information, the first character of every word might be printed as an extended character such as ß or ç. You can clear up the problem with the /WS switch, which strips out the formatting information and prints the correct character. (Some other applications also use WordStar-style formatting and will benefit from the /WS switch.)

Many mainframe computers use the EBCDIC (Extended Binary Coded Decimal Interchange Code) method of storing character data instead of ASCII. If you need to print out a file that uses EBCDIC code, simply use the /EBCDIC switch.

Specifying the Printer

DOS has a standard name for every output port: LPT1: through LPT*n*: for your parallel ports and COM1: through COM*n*: for your serial ports. It also uses the name PRN: to refer to the main printer, which is usually attached to LPT1:, but your system might redirect it to another port.

```
README.TXT              Thursday, June  6, 1991 3:51 pm              Page 1


DEVICE DRIVERS
--------------

Device drivers are programs that let the operating system recognize devices
that are not a part of the computer (for example, a modem, printer, or
mouse).  Some device drivers are already installed with MS-DOS.  Other
device drivers, called installable device drivers, can be installed as you
need them.


ANSI.SYS--Installable Device Driver
-----------------------------------

ANSI.SYS, an installable device driver, lets you use ANSI escape sequences
in real mode.  An ANSI escape sequence is a series of characters developed
by the American National Standards Institute.  You use these escape
sequences to define functions for MS-DOS.  Specifically, you can change
graphics functions and affect the movement of the cursor.

Following is a description of two options you can use with the ANSI.SYS
device driver.

/L

The function of this option is to retain the number of screen rows for
application programs that return the number of screen rows to the default,
25.  You change the default with the MODE command.

/K

The function of this option is to prevent ANSI.SYS from using extended
keyboard functions when an enhanced keyboard is installed.

For more information on the ANSI.SYS device driver, and the MODE command,
please see the Microsoft MS-DOS User's Reference.


HIMEM.SYS--Installable Device Driver for Extended Memory
--------------------------------------------------------

Capabilities
------------

HIMEM.SYS, an installable device driver, conforms to the XMS (eXtended
Memory Specification) version 2.0.  It allows MS-DOS programs on 80286 and
80386 systems with extended memory to access the extended memory
independent of machine configuration.  It also allows MS-DOS programs to
use an extra 64K region of memory for code and data.  This region is
located just above the 1 MB boundary.
```

Figure 17-1 Default LP Format

If you don't specify a printer port in your LP command, LP assumes PRN:. To use another printer, simply include its port name after the filespec, as in:

```
LP README.TXT COM1:
```

If it's a PostScript printer, be sure to add the /PS switch.

Formatting the Page

Use /T*n*, /B*n*, /L*n*, and /R*n* to set the top, bottom, left, and right margins, respectively. The top and bottom margins are specified in number of lines, with six lines to the inch. If you want a 1.0" top margin and a 1.5" bottom margin, specify /T6 /B9. The left and right margins are specified in number of characters, with 10 characters to the inch.

Use /H*n* to change the height of the page, specified in number of lines at six lines per inch. Use /W*n* to change the width of the page, specified in number of characters at 10 characters per inch.

Use /S*n* to change the spacing from 1 (single spacing) to 2 (double spacing), and so on. Use /132 to set the character spacing to 132 characters per line (compressed print) and /80 to return it to 80 characters per line (normal). Only IBM-compatible printers will respond to the /80 and /132 switches.

By default, tabs are set at every eight character positions. Use /TAB*n* to change the setting. For example, to set tabs at every inch, specify /TAB10.

Headers and Numbering

A header can be printed on every page of the file, in the top margin. LP offers three header formats:

/H0	No headers.
/H1	The filename and today's date and time are printed on line 1.
/H2	The filename and today's date and time are printed on line 1 and the file's date and time are printed on line 2.

The default is /H1. Use /H2 or /H0 to select one of the other formats.

By default, pages are numbered starting on page 1. Use the /P*n* to specify a different starting page number, as in /P125 to start with page 125. Use /N to number every line.

Sending a Setup String

Some printers will respond to a setup string that will do such things as select a font, a ribbon, or a paper tray. You need to consult your printer manual to find out what codes it responds to. Use the /SET parameter to send a setup string to your printer at the beginning of a print job.

> **Note:** You can't use setup strings with PostScript printers.

To use a setup string, create a separate ASCII file that contains the string. Then use /SET:*filespec* to send the file to the printer. In the setup file, specify codes in these formats:

nnn	A decimal number representing any of the 255 characters of the extended character set. You must use three digits, so include leading zeros, if necessary. See Disk Editor's ASCII Table for the characters and their decimal codes.
x	A letter representing Ctrl+*x*. For example, if your printer manual says that Ctrl+Y selects the red ribbon, you would enter \\Y in your setup file.

Normal ASCII characters are entered as is.

Looking Ahead

Have you noticed that your old familiar DOS commands such as COPY and DIR seem to be acting a little differently, and definitely better, since you installed the Norton Utilities? That's because the utilities include NDOS, a powerful substitute for DOS's command processor. The next chapter shows you how to get the most out of NDOS, which has a lot of new commands and features as well as many improvements to the traditional commands.

18

NDOS

If you have used your computer since installing the utilities, you have probably been using NDOS, perhaps without even realizing it. NDOS (which stands for Norton DOS) is a command interpreter, or *shell*, that replaces DOS's usual command interpreter—COMMAND.COM—to provide improved functions as well as additional functions.

A good example of an improved function is a *global* DEL (delete) command—that is, a DEL command that uses wildcards in the filespec to delete more than one file. Under DOS it looks something like this:

```
C:\JDOCS>DEL *.BAK
C:\JDOCS>
```

You get no feedback on what files were deleted and which ones couldn't be deleted because of hidden, read-only, or system attributes. NDOS's version shows which files are deleted and which ones aren't:

```
c:\jdocs\>DEL *.BAK
Deleting c:\jdocs\nu.bak
Deleting c:\jdocs\new17.bak
Access denied: "c:\jdocs\new17-1.bak"
Deleting c:\jdocs\new17-4.bak
Deleting c:\jdocs\new17-6.bak
```

```
Access denied: "c:\jdocs\new17-10.bak"
    4 file(s) deleted
c:\jdocs\>
```

There are similar improvements to many DOS commands. In addition, there are many familiar commands that have new parameters. The DIR command, for example, has a /2 switch to display the file list in two columns instead of the usual one. The DEL command lets you specify multiple files and includes a /P switch to prompt you for permission to delete each selected file. The CLS command lets you specify new colors for the cleared screen.

Also included are a host of new commands and features. New commands include such things as DESCRIBE, which associates descriptive text with a file's directory entry, and CDD, which changes both the drive and the directory at once. New features include the ability to recall and edit previous commands, combine two or more commands on the command line, and include lists of filespecs where you can use only one in DOS.

NDOS is so full of features that it would take a separate book to explain completely. This chapter describes all the features and shows how to use the ones that will be the most useful at first. For more information about the other NDOS features, the NDOS reference book that is included in the Norton Utilities package documents every feature.

There will be some overlap between NDOS and other Norton Utilities because NDOS was originally developed as a separate product and was merged into version 6.0 of the Norton Utilities. In this chapter, we'll stress those NDOS capabilities that can't be accomplished better with one of the other utilities.

Starting Up NDOS

When NDOS is installed with the utilities, it starts up automatically when it is booted and is the primary command interpreter. An immediate clue that NDOS is in control is a lowercase command prompt (DOS's normal command prompt is uppercase). To make sure which command interpreter is in charge, enter the VER command, which requests the version number of the active command processor as shown below:

```
C:\>
VER

DOS version 5.0
NDOS, Norton Utilities version 6.0
```

If only DOS is mentioned, NDOS isn't installed.

Starting NDOS from the Command Prompt

If the system isn't yet set up to start NDOS automatically, it can be started up from the command prompt using the NDOS command, which has this format:

```
NDOS [switches]
```

Table 18-1 shows some of the NDOS command switches. (Your NDOS reference manual lists the complete set.) Once you decide which switches you want to use regularly, you'll probably want to add the NDOS startup command to AUTOEXEC.BAT. Or you could start it up from CONFIG.SYS, as you'll see in "Installing NDOS from CONFIG.SYS."

> **Tip:** Fewer and simpler switches can be used by copying NDOS.COM and NDOS.OVL to the root directory of the boot drive. The following discussion assumes you did this and we won't talk about how to use parameters when these two files are somewhere else.

The /P switch makes NDOS your primary command interpreter, causing it to replace COMMAND.COM in memory. Both NDOS and COMMAND.COM are not needed at the same time, so some memory space can be saved by including the /P switch on the command that starts up NDOS.

Table 18-1   Common NDOS Command Switches

/A:n	Sets the alias list size, from 256 to 32000 bytes; default is 1024.
/E:n	Sets the environment size, from 256 to 32000 bytes; default is 512.
/H:n	Sets the history list size, from 512 to 8192 bytes; default is 1024.
/L:path	Identifies the location of the NDOS.OVL file and sets the COMSPEC variable.
/P	Makes NDOS the primary shell and runs AUTOEXEC.BAT.
/S:x	Sets the NDOS swapping mode: E Swaps to expanded memory N No swapping X Swaps to extended memory D Swaps to disk

Some things that should be considered when starting up NDOS from the command prompt:

- When the /P switch is used, AUTOEXEC.BAT is reexecuted as NDOS is installed.
- You must reboot to reinstall COMMAND.COM as the primary shell.
- NDOS will execute a file in the root directory of the boot drive named NSTART.BAT or NSTART.BTM as it starts up. You can place whatever startup commands you want in the file. What's the difference between NSTART and AUTOEXEC? NSTART is executed every time you start up NDOS, whether or not the /P switch is used. Also, it can contain NDOS commands that DOS doesn't recognize.
- When you start up NDOS from AUTOEXEC.BAT, any subsequent commands in AUTOEXEC.BAT won't be executed unless you terminate NDOS.

Installing NDOS from CONFIG.SYS

If you decide to use NDOS as the primary command interpreter, make the SHELL command in the CONFIG.SYS file similar to this:

```
SHELL=C:\NDOS.COM C:\ /P [switches]
```

> **Tip:** Setting up NDOS with the CONFIG.SYS SHELL command does not affect your ability to use the DOS 5 Shell, which is started up by entering a DOSSHELL command at the command prompt.

The switches are the same as those shown in Table 18-1, except /L is not needed because the second parameter (C:\) identifies the location of the NDOS.OVL file and tells NDOS how to set up the COMSPEC variable. COMSPEC is explained below, but for now just keep in mind that it's necessary to set COMSPEC properly if you want to use NDOS as the only command processor. You can't have more than 32 characters in a SHELL command after the name of the shell file (NDOS.COM in this case), so if you need to use more characters, put them in a separate file and use the @*filespec* switch on the SHELL command line. For example, you could enter an NDOS command like this:

```
SHELL=C:\NDOS.COM @C:\NSWITCH.TXT
```

In this case, C:\NSWITCH.TXT is an ASCII file containing the rest of the text for the SHELL command. NDOS will read and use the information as it starts up.

> **Tip:** If you make an error in the SHELL command, you'll end up in "boot limbo," where you can't boot from the hard disk so you can't fix the problem that is preventing you from booting. Make sure you have a good bootable diskette available *before* you change the SHELL command in CONFIG.SYS.

NDOS Swapping

NDOS saves memory space by bringing most of its program into conventional memory only when no application is running. The process of moving itself in and out of memory is called *swapping*. By default, NDOS stores the swapping portion—which is contained in the NDOS.OVL file and runs to about 80K—in whatever is the best possible place for your system: extended or expanded memory, a RAM drive, or a hard drive. A startup message tells where the swapping portion has been placed, and the /S switch can be used to control the swapping location if the automatic choice is not acceptable. The /S:N switch turns off swapping altogether, placing the entire NDOS program in conventional memory, which you should do only if NDOS is trying to use a diskette drive for swapping.

Environments

Every command interpreter needs an *environment*, which is simply a memory buffer where the interpreter stores information that is near and dear to its heart, such as the path and prompt settings.

Both DOS and NDOS let you use the SET command to define your own environmental variables, which can be used to pass variable information to batch files and programs. You'll see how to use some NDOS environmental variables later in this chapter.

By default, NDOS sets up a 512-byte environment. That's more than enough space for the standard environmental variables. You can use the /E switch to make it as small as 256 bytes or as large as 32000 bytes, which would give you lots of room for your own variables. Append a U to the switch (as in /E1024U) to place the environment in upper DOS memory instead of conventional memory if there's room up there and if the system is set up to access upper memory blocks.

Exiting from an Application to NDOS

Many applications let you exit temporarily to the shell, run a few commands, then use EXIT to return to the application. Chapter 4 shows how to do this from Disk Editor, for example. You can also do it from programs such as Microsoft Word, WordStar, and DOSSHELL. Some applications invoke the command interpreter without your knowing it to process file and directory management requests such as Copy and Delete.

When you call a command interpreter temporarily from an application, the program that is called is determined by the COMSPEC environmental variable, which is set by the second parameter on the SHELL command. No startup parameters are passed to a command interpreter started up this way. So if you need startup switches such as /S and /E with NDOS, you must create an environmental variable named NDSHELL using a command like this:

```
SET NDSHELL=/S:X /E512U
```

Include whatever switches you use when starting up NDOS at other times.

The NSTART file is executed every time you start up NDOS. Avoid including commands in NSTART that should not be executed more than once, such as commands to start up TSRs.

Getting Help with NDOS

The first NDOS feature you should learn to use is the online Help system, which you can start up by pressing F1 at the command prompt or by entering the command HELP. Either method opens the window shown in Figure 18-1. You can scroll through the index for a complete list of NDOS topics and select specific topics to read about. To bypass the index and open the Help window for a specific NDOS topic, type the topic at the NDOS command prompt and press F1 or enter HELP *topic*.

General NDOS Features

A host of NDOS features makes it easier to work effectively at the command prompt.

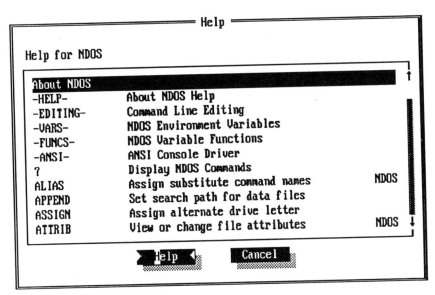

Figure 18-1   NDOS Help Window

History List

NDOS remembers all of the commands you enter. You can recall and scroll through the command "history" list with the Up and Down arrow keys. Table 18-2 shows the keys for editing the command line.

The HISTORY command (no parameters) displays the entire history list. Type part of a command and press Up or Down to recall a particular command from the history list. Keep pressing Up or Down until you find the command you want. Then press Enter to execute it again.

Inserting Filenames

Insert filenames from a directory into the current command line with F9 (or Tab), F8 (or Shift-Tab), and F10. F9 starts at the top of the current or specified directory and works down; each time you press it, the next filename replaces the current one. F8 returns to the previous filename. F10 appends the next filename to the previous one instead of replacing it. Type a path and/or a partial filename or global filename before pressing F9 to recall only files from the specified directory that match the global filename or that complete the incomplete one.

Table 18-2   NDOS Command Line Editing Keys

Key	Function
Left	Moves left one character
Right	Moves right one character
Ctrl-Left	Moves left one word
Ctrl-Right	Moves right one word
Home	Moves to beginning of line
End	Moves to end of line
Insert	Toggles between insert mode and overstrike mode
Del	Deletes character at cursor
Backspace	Deletes character to left of cursor
Ctrl-L	Deletes word to left of cursor
Ctrl-R	Deletes word to right of cursor
Ctrl-Backspace	Same as Ctrl-R
Ctrl-End	Deletes line to right of cursor
Ctrl-Home	Deletes line to left of cursor
Esc	Deletes entire line
Ctrl-D	Deletes the command from the history list and displays the previous command
Ctrl-E	Displays the last command in the list
Ctrl-K	Saves the current command in the history list but does not execute it; clears the line
Alt-255	Places the next character in the command instead of interpreting it as an editing key; use before Ctrl-D, Ctrl-E, etc., when you need to type them in a command
F3	Recalls the last command from DOS's command template
Up	Displays previous command in history list
Down	Displays next command in history list

Multiple Filespecs

ATTRIB, COPY, DEL, DIR, LIST, MOVE, REN, SELECT, and TYPE can have multiple filespecs. In these same commands, several filenames can be attached to one path with semicolons, as in:

```
DEL C:\*.BAK;*.OLD D:\*.BAK;*.OLD
```

Combining Commands

Combine several commands on one command line with a caret (^). The following command deletes all the files on A:, copies some files to it, then displays the new directory:

```
DEL A:*.* ^ COPY *.DOC A: ^ DIR A:
```

All NDOS commands set exit codes indicating whether the command was successful; some other programs also set exit codes. For commands that set exit codes, use && to connect two commands so that the second command is executed only if the first one succeeded. The following command copies CHAP1.DOC to A:, then deletes the source file *only if* the copy was successful:

```
COPY CHAP1.DOC A: && DEL CHAP1.DOC
```

Use || to connect two commands so that the second command is executed only if the first one failed. The following command removes the subdirectory named TEMPDIR, but if RD fails, the directory is displayed so you can see what the problem is:

```
RD TEMPDIR || DIR TEMPDIR
```

> **Warning:** The behavior of commands connected by && and || is unpredictable if the first command doesn't set an exit code. All NDOS commands set exit codes. For other commands, check the program's documentation to see if exit codes are set.

Batch Files

The BTM (batch-to-memory) extension creates batch files that execute much faster because NDOS reads them into memory all at once. Avoid starting TSRs from BTM files; they cause gaps in memory that waste memory space. Rename your current BAT files as BTM files for faster processing as long as they don't start up TSRs. Don't rename AUTOEXEC.BAT; DOS won't execute AUTOEXEC.BTM during booting. Use the command LOADBTM OFF in a batch file to switch out of BTM mode so you can load a TSR; use LOADBTM ON to return to BTM mode. For example, the following lines could be used in the middle of a BTM file to start up a TSR named GRAB:

```
LOADBTM OFF
GRAB
LOADBTM ON
```

NDOS permits 128 numbered variables (%0 to %127) in a batch file. You can also use the %& variable to insert all parameters from the command line into the batch job. For example, suppose a batch file named P.BTM contains this command:

```
FOR %%F IN (%&) DO PRINT F
```

Suppose you execute P.BTM with this command:

```
P A.TXT B.TXT C.TXT D.TXT E.TXT
```

NDOS will substitute all five parameters for the %& in the FOR command so that the command that is executed is:

```
FOR %%F IN (A.TXT B.TXT C.TXT D.TXT E.TXT) DO PRINT F
```

Inserting a number between the % and the &, as in %n&, changes the meaning of the variable slightly. Instead of substituting all the parameters from the command line, NDOS substitutes only those from the nth variable to the end of the command line. For example, suppose you revise the preceding FOR command to read:

```
FOR %%F IN (%3&) DO PRINT F
```

Now if you execute the batch file with the same command shown above, the FOR command will be interpreted like this:

```
FOR %%F IN (C.TXT D.TXT E.TXT) DO PRINT F
```

Another batch variable, %#, inserts the count of parameters into the batch job. Suppose P.BTM contains this command:

```
ECHO I have processed %# files.
```

If P.BTM is executed with the same command line shown previously, the ECHO command would be interpreted this way:

```
ECHO I have processed 5 files.
```

DOS and NDOS include a SHIFT command, which shifts all the command line parameters to the left, so that the second parameter becomes the first parameter, the third becomes the second, and so on. SHIFT was originally designed to get around DOS's ten-variable limit. Since NDOS lets you have up to 128 variables, you probably won't need SHIFT. But if you do use it for some reason, keep in mind that it affects the results of %&, %n&, and %# as well as %0 through %127.

Parameters are separated on the command line by spaces, tabs, or commas; the following expression constitutes four parameters:

```
SAN DIEGO, CA 92101
```

Use quotes to include commas, tabs, or spaces inside a parameter; the following constitutes one parameter:

```
"SAN DIEGO, CA 92101"
```

Single quotes are stripped from a parameter when it is passed to a program or batch command, but double quotes are passed.

When you interrupt a batch job, NDOS displays the message "Cancel batch job (Y/N/A)?" Press A to cancel the entire batch job, including any higher-level batch files that called the current file. Press Y to cancel the current batch job, returning to a calling batch job if there is one. Press N to cancel the current command only; continue with the next command in the current file.

Redirection

Both DOS and NDOS let you use > to redirect normal messages (but not error messages) from the monitor to a device or file. The >> redirection symbol appends redirected output to the end of a specified file. The < symbol redirects input from the keyboard to a device or file. With NDOS, you can also use >& to redirect both normal and error output from the monitor to a file or device. The following command deletes a group of files and prints both normal and error messages:

```
DEL *.DOC >& PRN
```

Use >&> to redirect only error messages to a file or device. The following command deletes a group of files and prints only the error messages; normal messages are displayed on the monitor:

```
DEL *.DOC >&> PRN
```

Other NDOS Features

You can enter up to 255 characters per command in NDOS, as opposed to 127 for DOS. Wildcard characters (* and ?) can appear anywhere in a global filename or extension. The following filespec, for example, selects files containing TR anywhere in the filename and 5 anywhere in the extension:

```
*TR*.*5*
```

When an NDOS command has more than one switch, you can group the switches together with one slash, as in:

```
DIR /C /4 /B   or   DIR /C4B
```

Differences in Familiar Commands

NDOS includes improvements for most of the DOS commands. The ones that are unchanged are BREAK, CHCP, CTTY, DATE, EXIT, GOTO, TIME, VER, and VERIFY. This section shows you how the other commands have been changed.

APPEND

APPEND sets up a search path for data files much as PATH does for programs. The DOS version includes a facility for modifying the path after it's set, but NDOS doesn't. You must use COMMAND.COM if you really need to change the APPEND path. You can start up COMMAND.COM as a secondary shell just long enough to run APPEND, then exit back to NDOS.

> **Warning:** APPEND can be a dangerous facility, causing programs to be confused about what directory—and even what file—is being accessed. If you must use APPEND, study it carefully to make sure you understand how it works and, especially, its pitfalls.

ATTRIB

The ATTRIB command displays and changes file attributes (but not as usefully as Norton's FA command). The NDOS version of ATTRIB includes a /D switch to view and change subdirectory attributes and an /S switch to include files from the entire subtree headed by the current or specified directory. Also, you can use +S and –S to change a file's system attribute.

CD or CHDIR

In DOS, one period means the current directory and two periods mean the parent directory. In NDOS, you can keep adding periods to go further up the tree. The following command moves up two levels in the directory tree:

```
CD ...
```

CLS

The NDOS format for CLS looks like this:

```
CLS [[BRIGHT] [BLINK] foreground-color ON background-color]
```

The foreground color sets the color of displayed text and graphics. BRIGHT and BLINK apply to the foreground color only. You can use these colors: BLACK, BLUE, GREEN, RED, MAGENTA, CYAN, YELLOW, WHITE. All the keywords can be abbreviated to three letters, so you could set the screen to use bright white text on a blue background with this command:

```
CLS BRI WHI ON BLU
```

COPY

You've already seen that NDOS's COPY command lets you use multiple filespecs. You can also add several switches: /M, /P, /Q, /R, and /U. /M selects only modified files to be copied but does not turn off the archive bit. /P (for Prompt) displays each selected filename and prompts you for permission to copy it. /Q (for Quiet) suppresses the list of copied filenames. /R (for Replace) warns you if a file already exists in the target directory and asks for permission to replace it. /U (for Update) copies a file only if the source version is newer than the target version (according to the time/date stamps) or if there is no target version.

DEL or ERASE

DEL and ERASE are two names for the same command, which deletes files. NDOS permits multiple filespecs in this command. The /P switch prompts for permission to delete each selected file. The /Q switch suppresses the list of deleted files, which NDOS normally supplies. The /Y (for Yes) switch suppresses the "Are you sure?" message when you try to erase all the files in a directory. The /Z (for Zap) switch ignores hidden, system, and read-only attributes, deleting all files that match the filespecs.

DIR

NDOS's DIR command permits multiple filespecs and has many new switches. The default output from NDOS's DIR looks like this:

```
DIR *.SYS


Volume in drive C is FIXED DISK    Serial number is 16B2:8B0E
Directory of  c:\*.sys

config.sys       163   6-09-91  3:12p Sets up hardware environment
himem.sys      11304   5-01-90  3:00a Extended memory manager
myfig.sys        119   5-25-91  9:29a Save old config.sys
work.sys           0  11-18-90  3:36p
       11,586 bytes in 4 file(s)        16,384 bytes allocated
    6,252,544 bytes free
```

You can see a lot of differences from a DOS DIR—the files are listed in lowercase and in alphabetical order, the filename and extension are connected by a period, the file description is shown if there is one, and the summary lines include the number of bytes in the listed files as well as the number of bytes allocated to them.

The NDOS DIR command has a wide variety of switches to control the format and contents of the directory listing, as shown in Table 18-3. Most of these switches are self-explanatory, but let's take a closer look at /A, /O, /V, and /N.

The /A switch selects files with specified attributes. Without any suffixes, it displays all files that match the filespecs, including hidden and system files. If you specify one or more attribute suffix, only files that have those attributes are displayed. If you use a minus sign before an attribute, only files that don't have that attribute are selected. One handy use for the /A switch is to see only the subdirectories, which can be done with this command:

```
DIR /AD
```

To see all the subdirectories in the subtree, add an /S switch to the above. To list everything but directories, you would use this command:

```
DIR /A-D
```

Table 18-3   New DIR Switches

Format:

```
DIR [switches] [filespec...] ...
```

Switches:

/A[x...]	Selects files with specified attribute(s)

	A	Archive
	D	Directory
	H	Hidden
	R	Read-only
	S	System

Prefix an attribute with a minus sign (–) to select files that don't have that attribute

/O[x...]	Sorts file list in specified order

	D	By date/time stamp
	E	By extension
	G	Groups subdirectories at the beginning of the list
	I	By description
	N	By filename
	S	By size
	U	Unsorted

Prefix an order code with a minus sign (–) for descending order

/1	Displays a single column (default)
/2	Displays two columns
/4	Displays four columns
/B	Displays list of names only
/C	Uses uppercase
/J	Justifies names
/K	Omits header lines
/L	Uses lowercase (default)
/M	Omits summary lines
/N	Restores default format
/S	Includes subdirectories
/T	Displays attributes instead of description
/U	Displays summary lines only
/V	Sorts vertically

By the way, /A and /O are exceptions to the rule that you can group switches together. NDOS interprets any letters you put after an A or an O as suffixes for that switch. This can result in an error message or in the wrong information being displayed. Put other switches before the A and O, or use separate slashes to keep them apart.

/O sorts the displayed list according to the specified parameters. The list is automatically sorted by name unless you specify other sort keys. Use a minus sign to reverse the order of a particular key. For example, the following command sorts the displayed list in descending order by size and for files of the same size, in ascending order by name:

```
DIR /O-SN
```

You might find the /V switch handy when displaying multiple columns. By default, NDOS sorts horizontally. That is, the first file is shown in column 1, the second in column 2, the third in column 3, and so on. If you would prefer the files to be sorted so that the first column shows the first part of the list, the second column shows the next part, and so on, use the /V switch.

If more than one filespec is included, NDOS sorts them separately. All the files matching the first filespec are listed first, then all the files matching the second filespec, and so on. But if the filespecs are connected with a semicolon, they are sorted into one list.

The following example shows the two separate file lists that result when the filespecs are separated with a space:

```
c:>DIR *.COM *.EXE
  Volume in drive C is HARD DISK 1    Serial number is 1678:5CCA
  Directory of  c:\*.com


command.com    46246  12-13-90  4:09a
egatest.com     6563   7-24-87  7:16p
ndos.com       10603   4-29-91  6:00a
      63,412 bytes in 3 file(s)          67,584 bytes allocated
   7,491,584 bytes free


  Volume in drive C is HARD DISK 1    Serial number is 1678:5CCA
  Directory of  c:\*.exe


egacolor.exe   13350   7-24-87  7:15p
egamode.exe    15456   7-10-87  4:59p
      28,806 bytes in 2 file(s)          30,720 bytes allocated
   7,491,584 bytes free
```

Now watch what happens when the two filespecs are connected with a semicolon:

```
c:>DIR *.COM;*.EXE
  Volume in drive C is HARD DISK 1    Serial number is 1678:5CCA
  Directory of  c:\*.com;*.exe

command.com     46246   12-13-90  4:09a
egacolor.exe    13350    7-24-87  7:15p
egamode.exe     15456    7-10-87  4:59p
egatest.com      6563    7-24-87  7:16p
ndos.com        10603    4-29-91  6:00a
     92,218 bytes in 5 file(s)       98,304 bytes allocated
  7,491,584 bytes free
```

You can change formats in midstream when using more than one filespec. Any switches in the middle of the command apply only to subsequent filespecs. The /N switch comes in handy for restoring the default format in the middle of a command.

If you would prefer a different default format from the one NDOS provides, you can create your own by setting the DIRCMD variable in the NDOS environment using a command in this format:

```
SET DIRCMD=switches
```

Put this command in AUTOEXEC.BAT or NSTART.BTM to set up the default switches you want every time you boot.

FOR

The FOR command causes a command to be repeated for every item in a set of variables. For example, the following command prints three files:

```
FOR %F IN (CONTRACT.TXT ATTACH.TXT CAVEAT.TXT) DO PRINT %F
```

The %x symbol (%F in the example above) identifies the variable to be replaced by each item in the parentheses. With DOS, you must use the symbol %x in FOR commands at the DOS prompt but the symbol %%x in FOR commands in batch files. NDOS permits either symbol in either place. In addition, DOS permits only a single character as the name of the variable, as in %F in the above example, but NDOS permits names up to 80 characters long, as in %FILENAME or %TEXTFILE. The word DO is also optional in

NDOS. And you can use multiple levels of FOR statements (called "nesting") in NDOS, so the PRINT %F command in the above example could be replaced by another FOR command.

Even though NDOS makes FOR more flexible and useful, it's still not a very friendly command. You'll find the SELECT command, explained under "SELECT" later in this chapter, a much easier way to apply one command to multiple files when you can't use multiple filespecs (and sometimes when you can).

IF

The IF command executes another command if a condition is true. For example, the command shown below copies a file from A: to C: only if it doesn't already exist on C:

```
IF NOT EXIST C:NU.INI COPY A:NU.INI
```

Table 18-4 shows the conditions you can use with NDOS. Most of them are not available with DOS. You can reverse the effect of any condition by preceding it with NOT.

You'll learn more about using IF ERRORLEVEL in Chapter 19.

MD or MKDIR

The NDOS difference from regular DOS in MD is that multiple pathnames can be used to create more than one directory at once, as in:

```
MD C:\TEMPY D:\TEMPY E:\TEMPY
```

PATH

If DOS encounters an invalid pathname in the program search path, it displays an "Invalid path" message and continues searching. The "Invalid path" message can be a surprise, as you might not be aware that the search path is in use. NDOS simply ignores an invalid path and goes on to the next directory in the search path.

PAUSE

The PAUSE command pauses execution of a batch file and displays the message "Press any key when ready...". In the DOS version, you can include

Table 18-4   NDOS IF Conditions

String comparisons:

string1==*string2*	Condition is true if the two character strings are equal
string1 EQ *string2*	Condition is true if the two character strings are equal
string1 NE *string2*	Condition is true if the two character strings are not equal
string1 LT *string2*	Condition is true if the first character string is less than the second character string
string1 LE *string2*	Condition is true if the first character string is less than or equal to the second character string
string1 GT *string2*	Condition is true if the first character string is greater than the second character string
string1 GE *string2*	Condition is true if the first character string is greater than or equal to the second character string

Exit code comparisons:

ERRORLEVEL *n*	Condition is true if the preceding program's exit code is greater than or equal to *n*
ERRORLEVEL EQ *n*	Condition is true if the preceding program's exit code is equal to *n*
ERRORLEVEL==*n*	Condition is true if the preceding program's exit code is equal to *n*
ERRORLEVEL LT *n*	Condition is true if the preceding program's exit code is less than *n*
ERRORLEVEL LE *n*	Condition is true if the preceding program's exit code is less than or equal to *n*
ERRORLEVEL GT *n*	Condition is true if the preceding program's exit code is greater than *n*
ERRORLEVEL GE *n*	Condition is true if the preceding program's exit code is greater than or equal to *n*

Existence comparisons:

EXIST *filespec*	Condition is true if the specified file exists
ISDIR *path*	Condition is true if the specified directory exists
ISALIAS *aliasname*	Condition is true if the specified alias has been defined

a message in the command, but it will appear on the screen only if Echo is on. In the NDOS version, the message replaces the standard "Press any key" message and is displayed whether Echo is on or off.

PROMPT

The PROMPT command defines the command prompt. Table 18-5 shows a list of characters that insert special information into the prompt. The standard NDOS prompt is pg, which displays the current drive and directory in lowercase letters followed by a right angle bracket (>).

In DOS, you can use the PROMPT command to set up the screen with bells and whistles using the ANSI.SYS device driver. You can't do this in an NDOS batch file because NDOS doesn't repeat the command prompt while processing a batch file. But you can use the ECHO command to accomplish the same function. You need to send an escape character to the screen to start an ANSI.SYS command, and you can do this in an ECHO command by typing Ctrl+X,e. The Ctrl+X displays as an up arrow (↑).

Table 18-5 PROMPT Special Characters

$B	Vertical bar (|)
$C	Open parenthesis (
$D	System date
$E	ASCII escape character
$F	Close parenthesis)
$G	Right angle bracket (>)
$H	Backspace
$L	Left angle bracket (<)
$N	Default drive letter
$P	Current drive and directory (uppercase)
$p	Current drive and directory (lowercase)
$Q	Equal sign (=)
$S	Space
$T	System time (*hh:mm:ss*)
$V	Version number
$X*d*:	Current drive and directory (uppercase) where *d:* is the drive
$x*d*:	Current drive and directory (lowercase) where *d:* is the drive
$Z	Shell nesting level
$$	Dollar sign ($)
$_	Starts a new line

RD and RMDIR

The RD (or RMDIR) command deletes subdirectories. Unlike DOS, NDOS lets you specify more than one pathname and/or use wildcards in the pathname to delete more than one directory at once.

REM

REM is used to add comments to a batch file or CONFIG.SYS. With NDOS, you can have up to 255 characters in each comment.

REN and RENAME

The REN (or RENAME) command renames files. With NDOS, you can include multiple filespecs in the command. NDOS also offers two more switches: /P and /Q. /P displays each new filename and prompts for permission to rename it. /Q suppresses the list of renamed files.

DOS does not permit you to put a path with the new filespec, but NDOS does. If the path specifies a different directory (which must be on the same disk), the file is moved to that directory as it is renamed. For example, the following command moves all the DOC files starting with CHAP to the OLDCHAPS directory and changes their extension from DOC to OLD:

```
REN CHAP*.DOC \OLDCHAPS\CHAP*.OLD
```

Renaming is a zippy way to move a file since the only data that moves is the directory entry. The file data stays where it is.

SET

The SET command creates or modifies variables in the NDOS environment. With no parameters, it displays the entire contents of the environment. Since the NDOS environment can be very long, you can use /P to break the output into pages. /R:*filespec* loads the environment from a file, which is much faster than including all the necessary SET commands in a batch file. The environment file should not contain SET or ALIAS commands, just lines like those that are displayed when you use SET to view the environment, which look like this:

```
variable=value
```

> **Tip:** Use SET > *filespec* to create a file containing the current environment.

When you have created an environment file, you can edit it using any ASCII editor to add or remove lines. To document its contents, add comment lines starting with a colon (:).

NEW NDOS VARIABLES

NDOS includes several new variables and functions. Some of the common ones are shown in Table 18-6. These are internal variables so you won't see them in the environment, but you access them just like environmental variables. For example, to see the exit code set by the last program, enter:

```
ECHO %?%
```

The variable functions require parameters in square brackets. For example, to see the amount of free disk space on drive A:, listed in kilobytes, you would enter:

```
ECHO %@DISKFREE[A:,K]%
```

SHIFT

The SHIFT command is used in a batch file to change the position of the parameters on the invoking command line. Used without parameters, it shifts all the parameters one position to the left so that the second parameter becomes the first parameter and is substituted for %1 in the batch job.

The NDOS version of SHIFT lets you specify a numeric parameter to indicate how many times the parameters should be shifted to the left. A minus sign shifts them to the right. For example, the following command would shift all the parameters three positions to the right, so that the first parameter becomes the fourth parameter and is substituted for %4 in the batch file:

```
SHIFT -3
```

TYPE

The TYPE command displays the contents of a file. With NDOS, you can include multiple filespecs in the command to display several files one after

Table 18-6   Common NDOS Variables

Internal Variables:

?	Supplies the exit code of the preceding program
#	Supplies the number of command line parameters
CMDLINE	Supplies the current command
_CWD	Supplies the current drive and directory
_CWP	Supplies the current directory
_DATE	Supplies the system date
_DOW	Supplies the day of the week
_TIME	Supplies the current time

Variable Functions:

Note: Parameters are required and must be enclosed in square brackets, as in @DOSMEM[B].

@DISKFREE[d:,B|K|M]	Supplies the free space on the specified drive, in bytes, kilobytes, or megabytes
@DOSMEM[B|K|M]	Supplies the amount of free DOS memory in bytes, kilobytes, or megabytes
@EXTENDED[B|K|M]	Supplies the amount of free extended memory in bytes, kilobytes, or megabytes
@XMS[B|K|M]	Supplies the amount of available extended memory
@EMS[B|K|M]	Supplies the amount of available expanded memory

the other. Use /P to pause after each page. Use /L to add line numbers to the display.

> **Tip:** See "LIST" later in this chapter for a better way to display files.

VOL

The VOL command displays the volume label of a drive. The NDOS version lets you specify multiple drivenames, as in:

```
VOL C: D:

Volume in drive C is FIXED DISK    Serial number is 16B2:8B0E
Volume in drive D is SECOND HD     Serial number is 16B2:8B0E
```

New NDOS Commands

NDOS doesn't stop with improving the DOS commands. It also gives four dozen (!) new commands, to do everything from keeping a log of all the commands to creating an alias for a command.

SETDOS

The SETDOS command lets you set up the NDOS configuration using the switches shown in Table 18-7. You probably won't need to use any of these switches. In most cases, NDOS works fine with the default settings.

The /Hn switch can come in handy to keep short commands out of your history list. Use /H10 (or so) to avoid storing simple commands like CD \, DIR, and VOL.

If you redirect command output very often, you might prefer to set the /N1 switch. Table 18-8 compares the effects of /N0 and /N1. In effect, if you redirect output to an existing file with >, >&, or >&>, NDOS will clobber (replace) the existing file. But if /N1 is set, the existing file is not clobbered. This is called the "Noclobber" variable because it protects files from being clobbered accidentally. Also, if /N1 is set and you redirect output using >>, >>&, or >>&>, it is appended to an existing file, but it will not create a new file if there is no existing file.

You can override the "Noclobber" feature in a single command by appending an exclamation point (!) to the redirection symbol. For example, suppose

---

Table 18-7   Common SETDOS Switches

Format:

```
SETDOS [switches]
```

Switches:

/Hn	Identifies the shortest command to save in the command history list, from 0 to 256; default is 0
/Mn	Identifies default command line editing mode; /M0 uses overstrike mode (default); M1 uses insert mode
/Nn	Determines whether output redirected by > can clobber (replace) an existing file; /N0 lets it clobber the file, /N1 doesn't
/Un	Determines case of displayed filenames; /U0 uses lowercase (default), /U1 uses uppercase
/Vn	Determines command echoing in batch jobs; /V0 suppresses echoing unless Echo is on, /V1 echos commands regardless of Echo

Table 18-8   Effects of /N0 and /N1

Redirection symbol	Type of output	Effect of /N0	Effect of /N1
>	standard	create or clobber	create only
>>	standard	create or append	append only
>&	standard and error	create or clobber	create only
>>&	standard and error	create or append	append only
>&>	error only	create or clobber	create only
>>&>	error only	create or append	append only

the /N1 variable has been set and you want to redirect all output from a DEL command to a file named SHAVED, creating a new file or replacing the existing one. You would use this command:

```
DEL *.TNT >&! SHAVED
```

More Redirection Commands

As long as we're talking about redirection, let's look at a couple of new ways NDOS lets you redirect information: Y and TEE.

Y combines two or more sources of input into one output. (The name Y graphically depicts two inputs being combined into one output.) Its basic format looks like this:

```
Y filespec...
```

When you enter the command, Y first takes input from the standard input device. By default, the standard input device is the keyboard. But when you use piping, the piped data from the preceding command becomes the standard input. This is how most people use Y. Y then appends the specified file(s) to the output.

Y sends its output to the standard output device. By default, this is the monitor. But you could pipe the output to another command or redirect it to a device or file. Suppose you want to combine the output of a DIR command with the DIRLOG file and print the output without saving it. You could use this command:

```
DIR | Y DIRLOG > PRN
```

The TEE command does the opposite of Y—it redirects a single input to two or more outputs. Its format is:

```
TEE [/A] filespec...
```

By default, the input comes from the standard input device (the keyboard or a pipe) and the output goes to the standard output device (the monitor or a pipe) as well as to the specified file(s). Most people use TEE in the middle of a piping command to save intermediate output in a file. For example, the following command both saves on disk and displays in separate pages the directory of the current drive:

```
DIR /OEN /AADHRS /S \*.* | TEE C-5-15.DIR | MORE
```

The first portion of this command obtains a sorted listing of all the files (all attributes, all subdirectories) on the current drive. The listing is piped to the TEE command, which saves it in the file named C-5-15.DIR. TEE also pipes the listing to the MORE command, which displays it in pages.

By default, TEE will clobber (replace) an existing file with the new data. The /A switch causes the output to be appended to the specified file(s) rather than clobbering them.

Command History

The HISTORY command displays the entire command history list. Use /P to pause after each page. /F (for Free) deletes the current list. /R followed by a filespec loads the history list from the specified file. Suppose you want to set up a standardized history list. Either create the file with an ASCII text editor or use the following command to preserve the current history:

```
HISTORY > HISTLIST.SAV
```

You could then edit HISTLIST.SAV with an ASCII editor. To load the list you would enter this command:

```
HISTORY /R HISTLIST.SAV
```

To prevent new commands from being added to the list, which might overlay current commands, enter this SETDOS command:

```
SETDOS /H256
```

Logging Commands

Another way to save commands is to log them to a file with the LOG command, which has this format:

```
LOG [/W filespec | ON | OFF | text]
```

To turn logging on, use LOG /W *filespec* or simply LOG ON, which uses the default filespec of \NDOS.LOG on the boot drive. All subsequent commands are recorded in the log file until logging is turned off again with LOG OFF. LOG with no parameters displays the current LOG status, ON or OFF.

Logging helps record your activities for a particular project by recording a date/time stamp with each saved command, as in:

```
04/07/92 10:12:27 COPY A:*.* D:\TEMPSET
```

You can add narrative explanations to the file with the LOG *text* command. Because of the date/time stamps, log files do not make good sources to load the history list from.

Some New File Management Commands

Managing files seems to be a constant task for PC users. NDOS includes several new file management commands to make life a little easier. Their formats are shown in Table 18-9.

MOVE

MOVE moves a file from one drive/directory to another. To move all the files from drive A: to the current directory, enter this command:

```
MOVE A:*.*
```

You can specify a target filename if you move only one file. For multiple source files, the last parameter, which identifies the target, must be a path only.

MOVE attempts to move files by renaming them; that is, the directory entry is moved from the source to the target directory. This is much faster because the file itself is not copied. But if it isn't possible—for example, if the target directory already has an entry with that name—MOVE copies the source file to the target location and deletes the source. You'll see a warning message if the source can't be deleted because of its attributes.

Table 18-9   NDOS File Management Commands

MOVE [*switches*] *source... target*
    Moves files(s) from source to target
      /P   Prompts for each selected file
      /Q   Suppresses list of files
      /R   Prompts for replacements

DESCRIBE *filespec* "*description*"
    Attaches description to file's directory entry

LIST [*switches*] *filespec...*
    Displays file(s) in scrollable format
      /H   Removes high-order bit (for WordStar format)
      /S   Reads from standard input instead of file
      /W   Wraps text at right margin

SELECT [*switches*] [*command*] (*filespec...*)
    Displays file list so you can select files for processing with command
      /A[*x...*]   Selects files by their attributes (see DIR for details)
      /O[*x...*]   Sorts file list before processing (see DIR for details)

EXCEPT (*filespec...*) *command*
    Executes command for all files except the specified ones

DESCRIBE

When you have a thousand or more files, it's easy to forget what some of them are. The DESCRIBE command lets you attach descriptions that appear in a directory listing (you can see an example on page 374). The following command attaches a description to CHAP01.DOC:

DESCRIBE CHAP01.DOC "Strangers in our Midst"

A description can be up to 40 characters long. You can describe both files and subdirectories. The descriptions are stored in each directory in a hidden file named DESCRIPT.ION. If you copy, move, or delete a file using any NDOS internal command such as MOVE, the description is automatically fixed, too. But if you use a command that is external to NDOS, such as DOS's

XCOPY, NDOS doesn't know you've done something to the file and can't fix the description.

LIST

LIST displays a file somewhat as TYPE does, but you can scroll around in the file using the cursor movement keys. Table 18-10 shows the keys to use when examining a file with LIST. The one to remember is F1, which pops up the Help window for LIST, in which you can review the other keys.

Use /H if the file is in WordStar format and produces extended characters at the beginnings of words. Use /W to wrap the right margin if lines are too long to fit on the screen. The /S switch lets you use LIST with piping to examine output from another command. For example, you could examine the current directory with this command:

```
DIR | LIST /S
```

Now you can scroll up and down in the directory, search for specific names, and so on.

Table 18-10   LIST Maneuvering Keys

Home	Displays the first page of the file
End	Displays the last page of the file
Esc	Exits the current file
Ctrl+C	Terminates LIST
Up	Scrolls up one line
Down	Scrolls down one line
Left	Scrolls left 8 columns
Right	Scrolls right 8 columns
Ctrl+Left	Scrolls left 40 columns
Ctrl+Right	Scrolls right 40 columns
F1	Opens online help window for LIST
F	Searches for string (a dialog box asks for the string)
N	Finds the next matching string
P	Prints the file on LPT1

SELECT

Have you ever wished you could display a directory and select files from it to copy, delete, or otherwise process? The SELECT command lets you do just that. Suppose you enter this command:

```
SELECT COPY (*.*) A:
```

SELECT displays a screen similar to the one in Figure 18-2. Notice the instructions in the top line. To copy NEW18.DOC and TYPOS.DOC, you would do this:

1) Move the highlight to NEW18.DOC.
2) Press the + key to tag it.
3) Move the highlight to TYPOS.DOC.
4) Press the + key to tag it.
5) Press Enter to copy the tagged files.

You can include any command with SELECT. Multiple filespecs are permitted, and you can use the /A and /O switches to select and sort files as with DIR.

When the global filespec(s) are enclosed in parentheses, SELECT issues a separate command for each file selected. But if they are enclosed in square brackets, SELECT issues one command including all the selected filespecs. Execution is much faster when square brackets are used, but be careful that

```
  21 chars │ ↑ or ↓ Selects │ + Marks  - Unmarks │ ENTER to run │ Page  1 of  1
copy (*.doc) a:                                      Marked:    0 files      0K
appsumm.doc    19456   5-03-91  2:24p
chartest.doc    5120  10-04-90  3:09p
macrocnv.doc    7676  10-04-90  2:35p
new18.doc      60416   6-20-91  3:13p
os2_note.doc    2509  10-04-90  3:09p
printers.doc    3118  10-04-90  1:07p
typos.doc       2560  10-04-90  3:09p
word_dca.doc    3608  10-04-90  3:41p
word_rtf.doc    1578  10-04-90  3:41p
```

Figure 18-2   Sample SELECT Display

the command doesn't exceed DOS's 127-character limit for external commands or NDOS's 255-character limit for internal commands. Also, the command must permit multiple filespecs.

EXCEPT

Sometimes it's easier to specify the files you don't want to process rather than the ones that you do. The EXCEPT command lets you do that. For example, to delete all files except the program files in the current directory, you could enter this command:

```
EXCEPT (*.COM *.EXE) DEL *.*
```

EXCEPT works by setting the hidden attribute temporarily for the specified files. It has no effect on commands that ignore the hidden attribute. If you abort EXCEPT before it gets the chance to clear the attributes, use FA to clear them.

Additional Directory Management Commands

NDOS includes some directory management commands that you've probably wished for. Table 18-11 shows the formats of the new directory management commands.

CDD

If you want to change to a different drive and directory, you need two commands with DOS. NDOS lets you do it with one CDD command. To change to \NEWDOCS on drive D:, you would enter this command:

```
CDD D:\NEWDOCS
```

Like NDOS's CD, CDD lets you use more than two periods when moving up the directory tree.

Table 18-11   NDOS Directory Management Commands

CDD *path*
> Changes drive and directory

GLOBAL *[switches] command*
> Executes command in the current directory and its subdirectories
>
> /I   Ignores exit code
>
> /Q   Suppresses display of directory names

PUSHD *path*
> Pushes current drive and directory onto directory stack and switches to specified drive and directory

POPD [*]
> Removes top directory from directory stack and switches to it
>
> *   Clears directory stack

DIRS
> Displays directory stack

GLOBAL

The GLOBAL command lets you apply another command to an entire subtree, as in the following, which copies all DOC files from the current subtree to A:

```
GLOBAL COPY *.DOC A:
```

All selected files are copied to the same target directory even though they come from different source directories.

GLOBAL is meant to be used with commands that don't have their own /S switches, such as COPY and MOVE. It has a /Q switch to suppress the display of directory names. GLOBAL will terminate prematurely if the included command returns a nonzero exit code for any file unless you specify the /I (for "Ignore exit code") switch.

Stacking Directories

Are you annoyed when a batch job changes the default drive and directory? You can avoid this problem in your batch files with PUSHD and POPD.

PUSHD places the current drive and directory on top of a stack of directory names in a memory buffer and switches to another drive and directory. POPD removes the top directory from the stack and switches to it.

You could use PUSHD and POPD in a batch file like this:

```
PUSHD C:\GRABBER
GRAB
POPD
```

The PUSHD command preserves the current drive and directory and switches to C:\GRABBER. The next line starts up a program named GRAB. The POPD command restores the original drive and directory that was preserved by PUSHD.

Aliases

If the same command is used repeatedly, the keystrokes can be shortened by setting it up as an alias. For example, suppose this command is often used to list the current subtree in scrollable form:

```
DIR /S | LIST /S
```

You could use the ALIAS command to assign this command the name DD like this:

```
ALIAS DD 'DIR /S | LIST /S'
```

Now whenever you want to execute the command, simply enter DD.

Using Aliases

Using an alias has two major advantages over recalling a command from the history list. First, you don't have to search for the right command. Second, an alias won't be overwritten by later commands. The main advantage of an alias over a batch file is that it's stored in memory so it's accessed much faster. Of course, batch files can be more complex because they can have more than one command line, but you can do a lot with an alias using IF, piping, and commands combined with ^, &&, and ||. You can also reference other aliases.

If command combinations are used when defining an alias, you must enclose the entire alias value in backquotes ('). If the preceding example didn't have backquotes, NDOS would try to process the command line as an ALIAS command piped to a LIST command.

Variables can be used in an alias definition. For example, the preceding alias could be adapted to allow for one or more parameters to be entered with the DD command:

```
ALIAS DD 'DIR %& /S | LIST /S'
```

To display a scrollable list of all the hidden program files in the current subtree, you would enter this command:

```
DD /AH *.COM *.EXE
```

NDOS would expand this command to:

```
DIR /AH *.COM *.EXE /S | LIST /S
```

Other Alias Uses

Enter ALIAS without parameters to view the entire alias list. The /P switch pauses the list after each page. Redirect the output to a file to preserve the current set of aliases on disk. Use the following command format to load aliases from one or more files:

```
ALIAS /R filespec...
```

(Don't use backquotes in a file of alias definitions.)

UNALIAS

Remove aliases from the environment with the UNALIAS command. To remove individual aliases, specify their names, as in:

```
UNALIAS DD CO SHOW
```

To remove all aliases, use an asterisk (*), as in:

```
UNALIAS *
```

Editing the Environment

The ESET command lets you edit an environmental variable or an alias. Enter the name of the item you want to edit. ESET displays the entire item so you can edit it using NDOS's command line editing facilities (see Table 18-2). For example, you would enter the following command to edit the DD alias definition:

```
ESET DD
```

UNSET

UNSET works just like UNALIAS but on environmental variables instead of aliases. To remove several variables from the environment, enter a command like this:

```
UNSET MYDIR MYCHAP
```

To remove all environmental variables, enter this command:

```
UNSET *
```

Warning: Using an asterisk with UNSET removes variables needed by DOS, NDOS, and the Norton Utilities, such as PATH, PROMPT, COMSPEC, NDSHELL, and NU. You might have other applications that need environmental variables, too.

Dressing Up the Screen

Color and graphics help make command output more effective. Simple graphics can be added to the screen with the commands shown in Table 18-12. Most of these commands overlap functions provided by Batch Enhancer, which is explained in the next chapter.

Receiving Batch Input

When messages and menus are displayed in a batch job, you often need to receive input from the keyboard before continuing. Table 18-13 shows a few commands that allow for that.

You can input either a single keystroke or a line terminated by the Enter key. Either way, the entered value is assigned to the specified environmental variable, which can then be tested with IF commands. For example, suppose you have displayed a menu offering Quick format, Safe format, or DOS

Table 18-12   Color and Graphic Commands

COLOR [BRIGHT | BLINK] *foreground-color* ON *background-color*
  Sets the screen color

DRAWBOX *upper-row left-column lower-row right-column style*
[BRIGHT | BLINK] *foreground-color* ON *background-color* [FILL
fill-color]
  Draws a box

	style	The type of border
	0	No border
	1	single line
	2	double line
	3	single top and bottom, double sides
	4	double top and bottom, single sides

DRAWHLINE *row column length style* [BRIGHT | BLINK]
foreground-color ON *background-color*
  Draws a horizontal line

	style	The type of line
	1	Single
	2	Double

DRAWVLINE *row column length style* [BRIGHT | BLINK]
foreground-color ON *background-color*
  Draws a vertical line

	style	The type of line
	1	Single
	2	Double

Table 18-13   Batch Input Commands

INKEY [/W*n*] [*text*] %%*variable-name*
  Reads a single keystroke from the standard input and assigns it to the specified
  environmental variable

	/W*n*	Times out after waiting *n* seconds
	text	Displays text as a prompt

INPUT [/W*n*] [*text*] %%*variable-name*
  Reads a line from the standard input and assigns it to the specified
  environmental variable (parameters are the same as for INKEY)

---

format. You could input and process the user's response with these commands:

```
INKEY %%FTYPE
IF %FTYPE% EQ Q FORMAT /A /Q A:
IF %FTYPE% EQ S FORMAT /A A:
IF %FTYPE% EQ D FORMAT /A /D A:
```

Branching in Batch Files

DOS and NDOS both offer a GOTO command to branch to another location in a batch file. NDOS has several additional commands to control the order of execution in a batch file, as shown in Table 18-14.

CALL and GOSUB both cause another block of statements to be executed, after which NDOS returns to the command following the CALL or GOSUB command. Both commands come in handy in IF commands when you want to execute a block of code instead of a single command. For example, suppose a menu in AUTOEXEC.BAT offers the user a choice of startup configurations labeled memory (M), quick (Q), or protection (P). Each choice results in five to ten commands being executed. You could store the commands for each choice in separate batch files named (for example) MEM-START.BAT, QUSTART.BAT, and PROSTART.BAT. The following lines in AUTOEXEC.BAT would execute the desire batch file:

```
INKEY %%STARTX
IF %STARTX% EQ M CALL C:\MEMSTART.BAT
IF %STARTX% EQ Q CALL C:\QUSTART.BAT
IF %STARTX% EQ P CALL C:\PROSTART.BAT
```

Table 18-14 Batch Control Commands

CALL *filespec*	Executes a secondary batch file
GOSUB *label*	Executes the subroutine starting at *label*
RETURN	Returns from a subroutine
DELAY [*seconds*]	Pauses for a specified number of seconds
QUIT	Terminates the current batch file
CANCEL	Terminates all levels of batch file processing

Another way to handle the same problem is to have MEMSTART, QUSTART, and PROSTART labels in the AUTOEXEC.BAT file and use GOSUB to execute them. That part of the batch file would look something like this:

```
INKEY %%STARTX
IF %STARTX% EQ M GOSUB MEMSTART
IF %STARTX% EQ Q GOSUB QUSTART
IF %STARTX% EQ P GOSUB PROSTART
QUIT

:MEMSTART
...
...    (commands for MEMSTART)
...
RETURN

:QUSTART
...
...    (commands for QUSTART)
...
RETURN

:PROSTART
...
...    (commands for PROSTART)
...
RETURN
```

In this routine, the INKEY command reads the user's input from the keyboard. The three IF commands determine which subroutine is executed. The QUIT command is important because it keeps NDOS from falling down into MEMSTART after the third IF command. QUIT doesn't have to immediately follow the third IF, but it must come somewhere before the MEMSTART label.

Tip: In some batch file situations, usually where a major error has been identified, CANCEL is a better choice than QUIT because it terminates not only the current batch file but also all levels of calling batch jobs.

Each subroutine starts with a label and ends with RETURN, which is crucial to return to the command that called the subroutine.

Table 18-15   IFF Command

IFF [NOT] *condition* THEN ^*command1* ^ELSE *command2* ^ENDIFF
Executes *command1* if *condition* is true or *command2* if it's false

Notes: Use the same conditions as for the IF command (see Table 18-4).
Command1 and command2 can be combined commands.
Command1 and command2 can be IF commands. Up to 15 levels of
nesting are permitted.

IFF

The IF command often gets you into awkward situations, where you can't
quite control all eventualities. The IFF command, shown in Table 18-15, is
often easier to work with, especially when you want to do one thing if the
condition is true and another if the condition is false. For example, suppose
a batch file contains this command:

```
INKEY %%YN Would you like to reformat the disk (Y/N)?
```

If the user enters Y, you want to call the FORMDISK.BAT file. If the user
enters any other character, you want to call the NOFORM.BAT file. There's
no easy way to do this with the IF command, but it's easy with IFF:

```
IFF %YN% EQ Y THEN ^ CALL C:\FORMDISK.BAT ^ ELSE CALL
C:\NOFORM.BAT ^ ENDIFF
```

The first part of this command (IFF %YN% EQ Y THEN ^ CALL
C:\FORMDISK.BAT) calls the FORMDISK batch file if a Y is entered. The
second part of the command (^ ELSE CALL C:\NOFORM.BAT) calls
NOFORM if anything else is entered. The final part (^ ENDIFF) is required
to mark the end of the command. Sad to say, the carets (^) are also required.

Other NDOS Commands

A few of the new NDOS commands defy categorization, so we've grouped
them into a miscellaneous "other" category. Table 18-16 shows these other
NDOS commands.

Table 18-16   Other NDOS Commands

FREE [d:...]	Displays total disk space, total bytes used, and total bytes free on current or specified drive(s)
MEMORY	Displays total RAM and free RAM, total and free EMS (expanded memory), total and free XMS (extended memory), total and free environment space, total and free alias space, and total history space
SWAPPING [ON | OFF]	Enables or disables NDOS swapping
TIMER [/S]	Starts or stops stopwatch; /S displays elapsed time without stopping watch
KEYSTACK [keys]	Stores keys in keyboard buffer

FREE and MEMORY

Use FREE to find out quickly how much space is left on a disk; it takes less time than DIR or CHKDSK. Use MEMORY to see your memory sizes. It's not as thorough as the information provided by Sysinfo, but it's fast.

SWAPPING

The SWAPPING command disables and enables NDOS swapping. You might find it desirable to disable swapping if you're swapping to disk and are trying to run a long batch job, because NDOS will swap after every command, slowing the batch job down considerably. Use this command to turn swapping off:

```
SWAPPING OFF
```

While swapping is off, the swapping portion of NDOS will take up about 80K of conventional memory. To resume swapping after the batch job, enter this command:

```
SWAPPING ON
```

You can find out whether swapping is on or off by entering SWAPPING with no parameters.

TIMER

The TIMER command makes a single stopwatch available. The first TIMER command turns it on. The next TIMER command turns it off and displays the elapsed time. If you enter TIMER with an /S switch, the elapsed time is displayed but the watch is not stopped.

KEYSTACK

The KEYSTACK command lets you automate commands in batch files that normally require keyboard input. To use KEYSTACK you must first load the KEYSTACK driver during booting by placing this command in CON-FIG.SYS:

```
DEVICE=C:\NU\KEYSTACK.SYS
```

Then place a KEYSTACK command in a batch file to load up the keyboard buffer with the keystrokes you want the next program to receive when it reads from the keyboard. Your NDOS reference manual includes tables of codes to represent keys such as Enter (13) and F1 (@59). Use 0 as a separator between values where you want the program to stop reading. That is, to store three different Enters in the keystack, you would use this command:

```
KEYSTACK 13 0 13 0 13 0
```

Keep breaks in mind when trying to figure out what keystrokes you need to fully automate a program. DOS checks the keyboard buffer often to see if you have pressed Ctrl+C or Ctrl+Break, and you must store enough key-strokes in the buffer to account for those break checks as well as the keystrokes the program needs. (If you use DOS's BREAK ON command to force DOS to check for breaks more often, you'll have to put even more keystrokes in the buffer.) Figuring out the correct sequence of keys is often a trial-and-error process.

Looking Ahead

As you've seen in this chapter, NDOS includes a lot of features to build better batch programs. But why stop there? Norton's Batch Enhancer pulls out all the stops in batch programs. You can add sound (even music), graphics, time delays, and more. The next chapter shows you how.

19

BATCH ENHANCER

A DOS batch file is somewhat like a program except that it's made up of commands to be executed at the command prompt. They might be DOS commands such as DEL and DIR, Norton Utilities commands such as SFORMAT and IMAGE, NDOS commands, and commands for any other software you have.

Batch files let you set up permanent copies of procedures that you repeat often. Suppose that, whenever you run your desktop publisher, you have to unload Disk Monitor and Norton Cache first, then switch to the drive and directory containing the desktop publisher. Then you enter the command DP to start up the application. When you terminate the desktop publisher, you always reload Disk Monitor and Norton Cache. You could make up a batch file containing these commands:

```
DISKMON /UNINSTALL
NCACHE /UNINSTALL
CDD C:\DESKTOP
DP
NCACHE /EXT
DISKMON /PROTECT+ /LIGHT+
```

If the file containing the above commands is called DESK.BTM, you would enter the single command DESK to execute all the commands in the order listed. (The last two commands would not be executed until the desktop publisher terminates.)

Batch Basics

A batch file must be an ASCII file with extension BAT, as in DESK.BAT. If you're using NDOS, batch files can have the more efficient extension BTM. You can create it with DOS 5.0's Edit or your word processor, but be sure to save it in ASCII format so that it has no special headers or formatting. Each line should contain one command and should be terminated by a carriage return. To execute a batch file, enter the filename without the extension at the DOS prompt.

If you place a batch file in a directory that's included in your system's search path, it will be executable no matter what drive or directory is current. In that case, make sure that all the commands it contains will work from any drive and directory. Include complete paths with specific filenames; you might also need to include a complete path with the command name if the referenced program isn't in your system's search path. For example, this command might work only when C:\PRESTO is active (where RECORD is a program command and TODAYS.LOG is a filename):

```
RECORD TODAYS.LOG
```

To make it work from any drive and directory, you could enter it like this:

```
C:\PRESTO\RECORD C:\PRESTO\TODAYS.LOG
```

Or you could include a command in the batch file to switch to C:\PRESTO, like this:

```
CDD .C:\PRESTO
RECORD TODAYS.LOG
```

The first solution leaves the original drive and directory active when the batch job terminates, while the second leaves C:\PRESTO active.

DOS Batch Commands

DOS and NDOS provide a number of commands that can be used to make batch files more effective, some of which are shown in Table 19-1. The REM command lets you document the batch file with comments which are ignored

---

Table 19-1   Common Batch Commands

```
ECHO [ON|OFF|message]
```
Turns command echoing on or off or displays *message*
```
GOTO label
```
Transfers execution control to line starting with :*label*
```
IF ERRORLEVEL n command
```
Executes *command* if exit code equals or exceeds *n*
```
REM comment
```
Ignored by DOS (used to insert comments in batch files)
```
@ command
```
When prefixed to a command, suppresses command echoing for that command only

---

by DOS when executing the file. For example, you might create this file to delete all files, including read-only files, from the current directory:

```
REM This batch job empties a directory.
REM The following command removes the read-only
REM attribute from all files so they can be deleted.
ATTRIB *.* -R
REM The following command deletes all the files
DEL *.*
```

The ECHO command controls what messages the user sees while the batch job is running. By default, the user sees all commands (including REM) and their output messages. ECHO OFF suppresses all subsequent command lines, so that only the output messages appear on the screen. Since ECHO OFF doesn't suppress itself, people usually prefix it with @ to suppress the ECHO OFF command, too.

ECHO followed by any text other than OFF and ON causes that text to be displayed, even when ECHO is off. Use ECHO message to display messages during a batch job, as in this file:

```
@ECHO OFF
REM This batch job clears a directory.
FA /R-
DEL *.*
ECHO All files should now be deleted. Run DIR to be sure.
ECHO ***** End of batch job *****
```

When you run this job, you will see only the output from the FA, DEL, and ECHO commands.

Decision-Making in Batch Jobs

The IF and GOTO commands let you make some elementary decisions about what to do next in your batch job. In particular, the IF ERRORLEVEL command comes in handy to see if the previous command was successful before executing the next one.

See Table 18-4 for a list of all the conditions that can be used with IF when NDOS is in the command interpreter. The sample IF commands shown here will work with either DOS or NDOS.

Many programs set an exit code when they terminate, indicating whether or not a problem was encountered. An exit code of 0 usually indicates no problems while higher numbers indicate some type of problem. For example, the Image program sets an exit code of 0 if the image file was successfully captured. If the disk was full, it sets an exit code of 3. Any other kind of error (such as a write-protected diskette) produces an exit code of 1.

Suppose you want to run Image from a batch file and check the exit code. If it's not 0, you want to display this message: "Image unsuccessful. Fix the problem and try again." You could use these commands in your batch file:

```
IMAGE
IF ERRORLEVEL 1 ECHO Image unsuccessful. Fix the problem and try again.
```

The IF command executes the ECHO command for any exit code of 1 or higher. But if the exit code is 0, the ECHO command is bypassed.

Frequently you need to execute several commands when the IF command is true, and perhaps several others if it's false. The GOTO command lets you do that. GOTO *label* transfers DOS to a line that starts with :*label*, as in this example:

```
GOTO ENDING
REM The next two commands are skipped...
DEL B:
COPY A: B:
:ENDING
DIR B:
```

When DOS executes GOTO ENDING, it skips down to the line starting with :ENDING and continues from there, so the next command executed is DIR B:.

You can combine IF ERRORLEVEL and GOTO to create alternate branches in your batch job. For example, suppose you want to display the message "Done!" if Image succeeds. If it fails, you want to display "Try again!" Here's the routine you could use:

```
IF ERRORLEVEL 1 GOTO FAILED
ECHO Done!
GOTO ENDING        ← very important!
:FAILED
ECHO Try again!
:ENDING
REM This is the end of the routine
```

If the exit code is 0, the GOTO FAILED command is bypassed, so the next command executed is ECHO Done! The GOTO ENDING command is important to bypass the other branch, starting at :FAILED, which should be executed only when the exit code is 1 or greater.

The general structure of a two-part branch using IF ERRORLEVEL and GOTO looks like this:

```
IF ERRORLEVEL code GOTO label
     [commands for false branch]
GOTO ENDING
:label
     [commands for true branch]
:ENDING
     [continue with other commands]
```

Note: We use the label ENDING in the above structure and in all our examples, but it is not required. Any label will do.

You can create even more complex branches, testing for many different values. Because the IF command is considered to be true if the exit code equals *or exceeds* the specified code, you have to start with the highest value and work down. The general structure for a four-way branch would look like this:

```
IF ERRORLEVEL code4 GOTO label4
IF ERRORLEVEL code3 GOTO label3
IF ERRORLEVEL code2 GOTO label2
     [commands for codes less than code2]
```

```
:label4
     [commands to handle code4 and above]
GOTO ENDING
:label3
     [commands to handle code3 and above]
GOTO ENDING
:label2
     [commands to handle code2 and above]
:ENDING
     [continue with other commands]
```

The first IF statement handles all exit codes at *code4* and above. Since it contains a GOTO command, only error codes less than *code4* will reach the second IF statement, which handles those equal to or greater than *code3* (but less than *code4*). Likewise, the third IF statement handles exit codes equal to or greater than *code2* (but less than *code3*). As long as each IF command includes a GOTO command, only exit codes below *code2* reach the fourth line.

Let's look at how you could display a separate message for each possible error code generated by Image:

```
IMAGE
IF ERRORLEVEL 3 GOTO DISKFULL
IF ERRORLEVEL 1 GOTO GENERROR
ECHO The image was successful
GOTO ENDING
:DISKFULL
ECHO The disk was full and the image was not made
ECHO Delete some unnecessary files from the disk
ECHO And try again
GOTO ENDING
:GENERROR
ECHO Something prevented the image file from being made
ECHO Make sure the disk is formatted and write enabled
:ENDING
ECHO **** End of job ****
```

NDOS provides options to make branching logic simpler. For example, you can test for exit codes equal to, greater than, and less than a specific value. And the IFF command lets you control true and false branches in one command. Chapter 18 explains these features.

You might never want to create a batch file this complex, but you will see later how to take advantage of multiple branches to create menus with the Batch Enhancer commands.

DOS offers more batch commands than the ones we've discussed here. We've shown you the ones that will be useful in combination with the Batch Enhancer commands.

Enhancements

The Norton Utilities includes a set of commands that will work both at the NDOS command prompt and in batch files to add color, sound, flexibility, and a few miscellaneous functions that DOS doesn't provide.

Table 19-2 shows the commands that Batch Enhancer provides. Although they're designed for use in batch jobs, all but BE EXIT, BE JUMP, and BE GOTO work directly at the command prompt, so you can try them out while reading about them. They work even faster in NDOS than in DOS because in NDOS they're internal commands. (But BE EXIT, BE JUMP, and BE *filespec* are not internal NDOS commands.)

> **Note:** Typing BE ? at the command prompt displays the complete list of Batch Enhancer options on the screen. Typing BE *command* /? or just *command* /? at the NDOS command prompt displays a list of options for the specified command. You can also look up the NDOS versions of these commands using NDOS's on-screen help system.

BEEP

The BEEP command sounds the computer's alarm. In its simplest form, with no parameters, it plays a single beep. You can control the frequency (pitch) with the /F switch, as in:

```
BE BEEP /F1000
```

Most humans can hear tones in the range of 20 to 20,000 cycles per second (Hz), but older humans sometimes can't hear the extremes of that range.

The BE BEEP command uses /D*n*, /R*n*, and /W*n* to control the duration, repetitions, and pause (wait) between repetitions. For example, to play a 440Hz tone for a full second (18/18ths of a second), repeated five times with a 1/6-second (3/18s of a second) pause between tones, you would use this command:

```
BE BEEP /F440 /D18 /R5 /W3
```

Table 19-2   Batch Enhancer Commands

BE ASK *prompt*[,*keylist*] [DEFAULT=*key*] [TIMEOUT=*seconds*]
[ADJUST=*n*] [*color*] [/DEBUG]

keylist	List of valid keys
DEFAULT=*key*	Default key if user presses Enter or times out
TIMEOUT=*seconds*	Number of seconds to wait for user input before using default key
ADJUST=*n*	Adds *n* to exit code
color	Color of prompt
/DEBUG	Displays the exit code

BE BEEP [*switches*]
BE BEEP [*filespec*] [/E]

/D*n*	Duration of $n/18$ths of a second
/F*n*	Frequency of n cycles per second (Hz)
/R*n*	Repeat n times
/W*n*	Wait $n/18$ths of a second
filespec	Executes a tone file
/E	Displays quoted comments from tone file

BE BOX *top left bottom right* [SINGLE|DOUBLE] [*color*]

top	Top row of box
left	Left column of box
bottom	Bottom row of box
right	Right column of box
SINGLE|DOUBLE	Single or double lines
color	Color of box

BE CLS [*color*]

color	Screen color specification (see "Colors" below)

BE DELAY *n*

n	Delay of $n/18$ths of a second

BE EXIT
   Exits a script file

(continued)

Table 19-2   *(continued)*

BE *filespec* [[GOTO] *label*]

filespec	The script file to be executed
label	The line to start at in the script file

BE JUMP *label1*[,*label2*[,...]] [/DEFAULT:*label*]

label	A label in the same script file

BE MONTHDAY [/DEBUG]

/DEBUG	Displays the exit code

BE PRINTCHAR *character repetitions* [*color*]

character	The character to be printed
repetitions	The number of times to print it
color	The color to print it in

BE ROWCOL *row column* ["*text*"] [*color*]

row	Row to position cursor in
column	Column to position cursor in
"*text*"	Text to display at new position; must be in quotes
color	Color to print text in

BE SHIFTSTATE [/DEBUG]

/DEBUG	Displays the exit code

BE TRIGGER *hh*:*mm* [AM|PM]

hh	Hour to continue the batch job; use 24-hour time unless AM|PM is included
mm	Minutes to continue the batch job
AM	Hours before noon
PM	Hours after noon; 12:00 PM is noon, 12:00 AM or 0:00 is midnight

BE WEEKDAY [/DEBUG]

/DEBUG	Displays the exit code

BE WINDOW *top left bottom right* [*color*] [SHADOW]
[ZOOM|EXPLODE]

top	Top row of window
left	Left column of window

(continued)

Table 19-2 *(continued)*

bottom	Bottom row of window
right	Right column of window
color	Colors of window foreground and background
SHADOW	Displays a see-through shadow under window
ZOOM	Zooms window onto screen
EXPLODE	Same as ZOOM

BE SA *main-setting* [*switches*]
BE SA *color* [*switches*]

main-setting	Can be NORMAL, REVERSE, or UNDERLINE
/N	Do not set border color
/CLS	Clear screen
color	Foreground and/or background colors

Colors

[[*intensity*] *foreground*] [ON *background*]

intensity	Can be BOLD or BRIGHT (which are the same) and/or BLINKING
foreground *background*	Can be WHITE, BLACK, RED, MAGENTA, BLUE, GREEN, CYAN, or YELLOW

For more complex tunes, you can create and reference a tone file. Each line in the tone file consists of a set of BEEP parameters to describe one tone. In a tone file, the slash that precedes each switch is optional. You can also include comment lines that start with a semicolon. To play the opening phrase of Beethoven's Fifth Symphony, you could create a tone file like this:

```
; "Beethoven's Fifth (sort of)"
; (notes are approximate since fractional
; frequencies are not allowed)
/F400 /D3 /R3 /W1
/F320 /D9
```

The tone file must be in ASCII format, just like a batch file. If its name is C:\BEET5, you would play it like this:

```
BE BEEP C:\BEET5
```

The /E switch causes any comments inside quotes to be displayed while the tone file is being played. If you add an /E to the above command, it would cause "Beethoven's Fifth (sort of)" to be displayed.

DELAY

The DELAY command pauses the execution of the batch file for the specified number of clock ticks (each tick is about 1/18 of a second). To pause the batch file for a full second, you would enter this command:

```
BE DELAY 18
```

DELAY comes in handy primarily when the output from various commands scrolls by too quickly, and you want to give someone a little more time to take it in. It also can be used to create an audible pause between two beep commands.

Graphic Displays

In addition to playing tunes, you can dress up the normally dull DOS screen with color and graphics, using several Batch Enhancer commands.

In order for these commands to work properly, you have to load a driver called ANSI.SYS during booting. Add this statement to your CONFIG.SYS file if it isn't already there:

```
DEVICE=path\ANSI.SYS
```

Use the *path* of the directory containing your DOS files (probably C:\DOS).

Because monitors vary so widely, the effect of the graphics commands are not the same on all of them. Be sure to check them out to see what they do on your monitor(s).

Screen Attributes

You can change the screen colors and attributes with the SA command. One form of the command selects foreground and background colors. The background is the field on which graphics and text are displayed while the foreground is the text and graphics. For the DOS prompt screen on a color monitor, the background is normally black and the foreground is normally white. To display black text on a magenta background, you would enter this command:

```
BE SA BLACK ON MAGENTA
```

The entire screen, including existing foreground material, immediately changes to black on magenta. All SA parameters can be abbreviated to three letters, so this command could be entered as:

```
BE SA BLA ON MAG
```

Use /CLS to clear the screen when the colors change. It has the same effect as a separate CLS command.

When you change the background color, you can specify the /N switch to leave the border unchanged, creating a frame around the text area. To use white on black with a magenta border, you would use these two commands (in the order shown):

```
BE SA ON MAG
BE SA ON BLA /N
```

You can specify an intensity attribute before the foreground color, as in BRIGHT RED or BLINKING BLUE. Blinking causes all the foreground data on the screen to blink on and off, which can be somewhat disconcerting, but attention-getting.

Note: If used, the intensity attribute must precede the foreground color.

The other format of the SA command controls the entire color scheme. NORMAL resets the screen to normal white on black. REVERSE swaps the current foreground and background colors. UNDERLINE works on monochrome monitors only. The following command creates blinking red text on a black background:

```
BE SA BLI RED ON BLA /CLS
```

Suppose you want to display the message "Don't forget to back up your new files" while you play a little tune; the message should blink in blue on black for five seconds, then return to white on black. Assuming that the message and the tune are in the tone filenamed C:\BACKTUNE, you would use this series of commands:

```
@ECHO OFF
BE SA BLI BLU ON BLA /CLS
BE BEEP C:\BACKTUNE /E
BE DELAY 90
BE SA NOR
```

Note: There is a bold (or bright) black, which comes out as a dull gray.

Drawing Boxes

Messages like the preceding one are frequently more effective if they appear in boxes, carefully positioned on an otherwise blank screen. Several Batch Enhancer commands let you create this type of effect.

The BOX command draws a box according to your specifications. Suppose you want to draw one that starts at row 3, column 10, and extends to row 7, column 70. You would use this command:

```
BE BOX 3 10 7 70
```

Figure 19-1 shows the result.

By default, the box is drawn with a single line in the default foreground color. Specify DOUBLE (or DOU) for a double line. You can also specify the foreground and background colors using the same parameters that you use with SA. For example, the following command draws a blue box on a white background:

```
BE BOX 3 10 7 20 BLU ON WHI
```

When you specify a color, the box is drawn with double lines by default, so you have to specify SINGLE for a single line. The specified colors affect only the box itself. The background is behind only the lines that make the box; it doesn't even fill the box. If you want to fill the box with a background color, you need to use the WINDOW command, which is discussed shortly. You can use BOLD or BRIGHT and BLINKING in front of the color parameter, as in BOLD GREEN ON BLACK. When BLINKING is used, the lines creating the box blink, but not the background or any other text on the screen.

D:\NUBOOK>be box 3 10 7 70

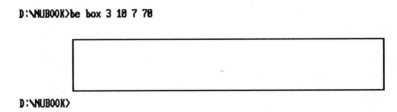

D:\NUBOOK>

Figure 19-1   Sample Box

Printing Repeated Characters

The PRINTCHAR command displays a repeated character. For example, to draw a line of asterisks across an 80-column screen, you would use this command:

```
BE PRINTCHAR * 80
```

The major advantage of PRINTCHAR over ECHOing 80 asterisks is that you can specify the color, as in the following command:

```
BE PRINTCHAR * 80 BRI RED
```

You can specify a background color, which appears only behind the displayed characters and does not affect the rest of the screen. You can also specify BOLD or BRIGHT and BLINKING with the foreground color.

Positioning the Cursor

You can position the cursor anywhere on the screen with the ROWCOL command. You can even include text in the command to be displayed at that position. You would usually use ROWCOL to display a message at a specific location, such as inside a box. The screen shown in Figure 19-2 was created with this series of commands:

```
@ECHO OFF
CLS
BE BOX 10 10 20 70 DOUBLE
BE ROWCOL 15 30 "Please contact Hillary Jordan, ext. 543"
BE ROWCOL 22 1
```

It's essential to turn off ECHO to create a display like this. If it's on, the DOS prompt and the next command are displayed after CLS, after BOX, and after

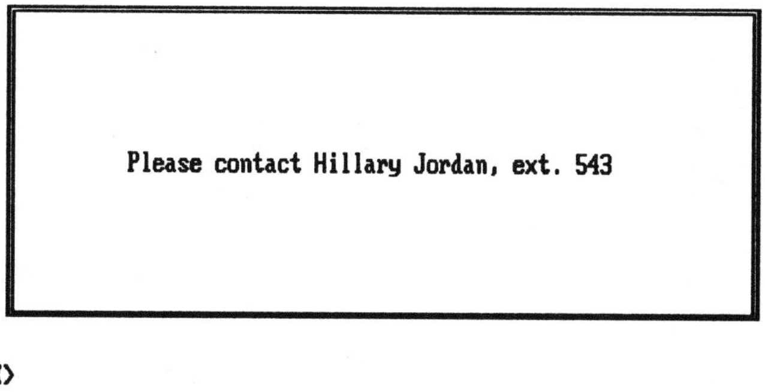

```
┌─────────────────────────────────────────────┐
│                                               │
│                                               │
│        Please contact Hillary Jordan, ext. 543│
│                                               │
│                                               │
│                                               │
└─────────────────────────────────────────────┘
```

D:\NUBOOK>

Figure 19-2   Example of ROWCOL

ROWCOL, ruining their effect. You should also position the cursor afterward so that the DOS prompt that appears after the job is finished doesn't
appear in the middle of the box.

Drawing Windows

The WINDOW command creates a more sophisticated box on the screen,
which always has a double border. The difference between a window and a
box is in what goes on inside the border. A box defines only the lines that
create the rectangle. Any foreground or background material that lie within
the rectangle are not affected. A window defines the entire area enclosed by
the rectangle. Any previous material is overlaid by the window.

If you specify a foreground color, it applies not only to the border but to
all text and graphics that fall within the border. A background color fills the
entire window area, not just the border.

The following set of commands beeps and displays a warning message in
flashing black print on a red window. The result is quite dramatic:

```
@ECHO OFF
CLS
BE WINDOW 10 10 20 70 BLI BLACK ON RED
BE BEEP
BE ROWCOL 13 38 "WARNING!"
BE ROWCOL 16 15 "You are about to delete all data from your hard disk!"
BE ROWCOL 22 1
```

The EXPLODE option causes the box to zoom onto the screen. The
SHADOW options displays a see-through black shadow under the window,

such as you have seen with many of the Norton Utilities dialog boxes. You can't see it on a black screen, but it shows up nicely on a colored one.

Interacting with a User

A good general-purpose batch job often needs to offer alterative actions for the user to select from. As a simple example, you could create a job called CACHE.BAT that starts up the Norton Cache in either extended or expanded memory, depending on what the user selects from a menu. You could use WINDOW combined with ROWCOL like this:

```
@ECHO OFF
CLS
BE WINDOW 10 10 20 70 BLACK ON BLUE
BE ROWCOL 12 15 "Where would you like the Cache?"
BE ROWCOL 14 15 "(P)   exPanded memory"
BE ROWCOL 15 15 "(T)   exTended memory"
BE ROWCOL 18 15
BE ASK "Press P or T" pt
```

The first two lines of this batch job turn off ECHO and clear the screen. Then a black-on-blue window is displayed with the menu text arranged neatly inside it. The ASK command waits for the user to type a key, then sets an exit code according to which key was typed. The keylist following the prompt determines which keys are valid and what exit codes will be assigned. ASK assigns exit code 1 to the first key (reading from left to right), 2 to the second key, and so on. The Esc key triggers exit code 0. So in the above example, if the user types P (in uppercase or lowercase), the exit code is 1; for T or t, it's 2; for Esc, it's 0. Any other key produces a beep and the user must try again.

You could follow the ASK command with a series of IF ERRORLEVEL commands to process the exit code. Don't forget to work from high to low. In the CACHE.BAT example, the entire branching routine might look like this:

```
BE ASK "Enter P or T" pt
IF ERRORLEVEL 2 GOTO EXTENDED
IF ERRORLEVEL 1 GOTO EXPANDED
REM The following command handles ERRORLEVEL 0
GOTO ENDING
:EXTENDED
NCACHE /EXT
GOTO ENDING
:EXPANDED
```

```
NCACHE /EXP
:ENDING
BE ROWCOL 22 1 "**** END OF JOB ****"
BE ROWCOL 23 1
```

Let's look at how this routine works. After the ASK command gets an answer from the keyboard and sets the exit code, the first IF ERRORLEVEL command is executed. It branches to :EXTENDED if the exit code is 2; that is, if the user typed a "t". Otherwise, the second IF ERRORLEVEL command is executed, which branches to :EXPANDED if the user typed a "p". If the user pressed Esc, the GOTO ENDING command is executed.

If you don't include a keylist, ASK accepts any input, sets a high exit code, and continues with the next command. You can use this feature to force the user to respond to a message by pressing any key. The following job runs Image on the diskette in drive A:, but gives the user a chance to change the diskette first:

```
@ECHO OFF
CLS
BE WINDOW 10 10 20 70 WHITE ON BLU
BE ROWCOL 14 15 "Insert target diskette in drive A:"
BE ROWCOL 16 15
BE ASK "Press any key when ready"
BE ROWCOL 22 1
IMAGE A:
```

In this job, the first three lines turn ECHO off and set up a white-on-blue window on a blank screen. The next three lines display a neatly arranged message and wait for the user to respond. When the user presses any key, the last two lines position the cursor for after the job and execute the Image program.

You can specify a default key for the keylist with the DEFAULT=*key* option. The default will be triggered if the user presses Enter without typing a key or if the ASK command times out. All other keys have the same effect as when there is no default.

The ASK command will wait forever for user input unless you establish a timeout factor with TIMEOUT=*seconds*. If you do specify a timeout, be sure to also specify a default key, because that's the key that's triggered if the user times out.

The ADJUST parameter causes the amount specified by *n* to be added to the exit code. It is intended to be used in complicated loops involving several layers of menus. Most people never use or need this parameter.

Batch Enhancer Script Files

> **Tip:** All Batch Enhancer commands that set the error level have a
> /DEBUG switch that helps you in testing and correcting the batch file
> by displaying the error level.

If you use the same set of Batch Enhancer commands in many different
batch files, you can create a file of Batch Enhancer commands, called a *script*
file, to be executed somewhat like a tone file. For example, you might create
a script file called WIN that contains these commands (the BE is optional in
a script file):

```
SA WHI ON BLU /CLS
WIN 20 10 50 70 BLA ON RED
ROWCOL 25 15
```

This sets up a window and positions the cursor for whatever message you
want to display in the window. To use this script file, you could use these
commands:

```
BE WIN
ECHO Press any key to start copying
```

When the BE command is followed by a filename such as WIN, it causes that
script file to be executed. In this particular case, the WIN file sets up the
window, then the ECHO command displays a message in it.

Script-File Branching

A script file can contains only BE commands. Well, technically, it can contain
anything at all, but only the BE commands are executed. You can't use NDOS
commands such as IF or GOTO in a script file because BE will ignore them.
When you need to branch in a script file, the BE JUMP command takes the
place of the NDOS branching commands. It's easier to use and understand,
but it works only from within a script file.

Follow the word JUMP with one or more label names. If the current exit
code is 1, JUMP goes to the first label; if it's 2, the second label, and so on.
If it's 0 or greater than the last label listed, it goes to the label specified in
/DEFAULT:*label* if there is one. Otherwise it simply falls through the JUMP
command to the next line in the script file.

Let's look at how you could use a script file to make the screen blue on Monday but green the rest of the week. In your AUTOEXEC.BAT file, you'd place a command something like this:

```
BE COLORMON.BES
```

The COLORMON.BES file, which must be a script file, would look something like this:

```
WEEKDAY
JUMP OTHER MONDAY
:OTHER
SA BLACK ON GREEN
EXIT
:MONDAY
SA BLACK ON BLUE
```

The BE WEEKDAY command sets the exit code to 1 on Sunday, 2 on Monday, 3 on Tuesday, and so on. On Sunday, JUMP goes to :OTHER. On Monday, it goes to :MONDAY. On any other day, it doesn't jump but simply falls into :OTHER.

You can add a GOTO parameter to the BE command to jump immediately to a particular label in a script file. For example, suppose you want to execute a different part of the script file named MONTH.BES depending on the day of the month.

```
BE MONTHDAY
IF ERRORLEVEL 25 GOTO LATE
BE MONTH.BES
EXIT
:LATE
BE MONTH.BES GOTO MONTHEND
```

The MONTHDAY command sets the exit code to a value from 1 to 31 representing the day of the month. It it's 25 or over, IF ERRORLEVEL 25 jumps to :LATE, which executes MONTH.BES starting at the line labeled :MONTHEND. Otherwise MONTH.BES is executed starting at the beginning.

BE includes an EXIT command to terminate a script file before the last line. Don't try to use EXIT to terminate a regular batch file, because the DOS EXIT command terminates the secondary command processor, if there is one. Use EXIT only in script files.

Time/Date Functions

The BE TRIGGER, BE MONTHDAY, and BE WEEKDAY functions can be used to set up jobs to be performed at specific times. You've already seen how MONTHDAY and WEEKDAY work. TRIGGER delays the batch job until a specific time, as determined by your system clock. To send some faxes after 8:00 pm when the long-distance rates are cheaper, you could create this batch job:

```
BE TRIGGER 8:01 PM
FAX command...
```

You would start up this job when you're done using the computer for the day, because it ties up the computer until 8:01 pm. Then the FAX command is executed.

Miscellaneous BE Commands

The BE SHIFTSTATE command sets an exit code that tells you which shift keys are pressed, as shown in Table 19-3. If more than one key is pressed, BE SHIFTSTATE adds them together, so an exit code of 3 means that both Shift keys are pressed and an exit code of 9 means that Alt-Shiftright is pressed. You can use BE SHIFTSTATE after any command requiring keyboard input, such as BE ASK, INPUT, INKEY, and PAUSE.

The BE REBOOT command reboots the computer, which you might want to do in a batch job after processes such as making changes to CONFIG.SYS or AUTOEXEC.BAT.

Table 19-3   BE SHIFTSTATE Exit Codes

code	meaning
1	Shiftright key
2	Shiftleft key
4	Either Ctrl key
8	Either Alt key

Looking Ahead

Well, there is no more ahead as far as this book is concerned; we've reached the end of the road. But we hope there is much more ahead for you as you continue to use the Norton Utilities on a daily basis to protect your data, occasionally rescue a file or two, and make your life a little easier with the utilities' simplified functions.

EMERGENCY RESCUE PROCEDURES

This appendix can help you rescue data from a disk in straightforward situations, such as unerasing a file that you just erased or unformatting a disk that you just formatted. For more complex situations, such as unerasing a file that you erased two weeks ago, you will be referred to the appropriate chapter.

You should never add any new data to a disk when you know you need to rescue something from it, because DOS might write the new data on top of the very data you want to rescue, completely obliterating it. This means that, when you know you need to rescue data from a disk, you should never do any of the following operations to the disk:

- Copy any files to the disk, not even to update an existing file.
- Install or update any software on the disk.
- Start up any programs from the disk (the program might create a temporary work file as it starts up).
- Modify existing files in any way.
- Add a volume label.
- Create any new directories.
- Reformat the disk.

- Run any of the following Norton Utilities (or comparable utilities from other vendors), all of which create, modify, or move files:

  Disk Tools (Make a disk bootable; Recover from DOS's Recover)

  Diskreet

  Erase Protect

  File Fix

  Image

  Norton Change Directory (NCD)

  Norton Disk Doctor II

  Safe Format

  Speed Disk

  WipeInfo (Don't wipe unused clusters)

- The following utilities are safe to use as long as you don't save any reports to disk:

  System Information

  FileFind (Don't create a batch file)

  Calibrate

- Don't use any of the following DOS commands, all of which create temporary files or otherwise modify the data on the disk:

  BACKUP

  COPY

  FORMAT

  LABEL

  MKDIR (MD)

  MORE

  PRINT

  RECOVER

  REPLACE

  RESTORE

  XCOPY

  Also, don't redirect output to the disk or use piping.

If the problem disk is your boot drive, don't boot or reboot from it, as the boot procedure might run some of the above programs. If you must boot, do it from drive A: with a diskette that does not contain an AUTOEXEC.BAT file.

The remainder of this appendix contains step-by-step procedures for rescuing data in these categories:

Recovering files (page 433)

Unformatting disks (page 434)

Recovering a Disk from the DOS RECOVER Program (page 438)

Recovering Files

You can recover data files such as word processor documents, databases, spreadsheets, and graphics. Avoid recovering a program file or any files that support a program, because you won't be able to examine the file to see if it was recovered correctly. Instead, reinstall the program to recover the file.

You can recover your file easily if one of the following conditions is true:

- Erase Protect is in effect for the drive and file type AND the file was deleted recently (like today).

- You have not done *anything* to the drive since deleting the file.

If neither of these conditions is true (or you're not sure), you may be able to recover the file anyway. Try the following procedure with your fingers crossed. If it doesn't work, you still might be able to rescue some of your data, but you'll have to read Chapters 1 and 9 first.

Note: If you need to recover a group of files, it's safest to recover them one at a time, starting with the smallest one.

Step 1:   If you need to boot, do it from a diskette in drive A: that contains no AUTOEXEC.BAT.

Step 2:   If the Norton Utilities are not installed on your hard drive, place Norton Utilities Emergency Disk (#2 for 5.25" diskettes) in drive A: and switch to that drive, if necessary, by entering the following command:

```
A:
```

Step 3:   Enter the following command at the DOS prompt, where *path* identifies the directory the file was erased from (you can leave it out if the file was erased from the directory that is now current) and *filename* is the name of the erased file:

```
UNERASE [path\] filename
```

For example, if you erased the file named STRATA.DAT from the directory named GEOL, which is a child of the root directory on drive D:, you would try to recover it by entering the command UNERASE D:\GEOL\STRATA.DAT.

If all goes well, you will see a message like this, which means that the file was successfully recovered and you are finished:

```
strata.dat    15,777 bytes  10:06 am Sun Dec 9 1990   RECOVERED
```

If you get the message "Bad command or filename," the UnErase program was not found. Go back to step 2, make sure you insert the correct disk in drive A:, and try again.

If you see any of the following messages, make sure you used the correct path and the correct filename. If you did, you probably will have to use a manual recovery technique to rescue as much data as possible; read Chapters 1 and 9 to learn how to do this.

```
No erased files matching [path\] filename
Not recovered. The file's data space is being used by another file.
```

Step 4: If the file was recovered, read it using whatever application created it. If it looks okay, you have finished recovering it. If it contains some incorrect data, which might be nonsense data or text from another erased file, or if it is missing any data, then you need to remove or adjust the clusters manually; read Chapters 1 and 9 to find out how. (If the file was a worksheet or database, you might also need to read Chapter 13 on File Fix.)

UnFormatting a Disk

Use this procedure if you accidentally reformat a disk and want to recover the former data from it. Unformatting will be most successful if all of the following conditions are true:

- Nothing has been added to the disk since it was reformatted.
- It was not made bootable during (or after) formatting.
- A disk label was not added during (or after) formatting.
- Image data was stored on the disk during formatting. (Chapter 3 explains Image.)
- DOS's format (or a DOS-style format) was not used on a diskette.

If any but the last condition is false, try the following procedure anyway. You still might be able to recover a good portion of the disk. But if you used a DOS-style format on a floppy diskette, the former data was wiped out and cannot be recovered.

Important! If at any step you don't get the message described, do not continue with the procedure. Press Esc repeatedly until you get back to the DOS prompt, then read Chapters 1 and 10.

Step 1:   If you need to boot, do it from a diskette in drive A: that contains no AUTOEXEC.BAT.

Step 2:   If the Norton Utilities are not installed on your hard drive, place Norton Utilities Emergency Disk (#1 for 5.25" diskettes) in drive A: and switch to that drive by entering the following command:

    A:

Step 3:   Enter this command at the DOS prompt, where *d:* is the name of the drive to be recovered:

    UNFORMAT *d:*

(If you need to recover a diskette in drive A: and the Norton Utilities diskette is currently in drive A:, go ahead and enter the command UNFORMAT A:. UnFormat will tell you when to insert the diskette to be recovered.)

The UnFormat screen should appear with this message: "Analyzing drive *x:*." Then the following question appears: "Did you previously use **IMAGE.EXE** or **MIRROW.COM** to save recovery info for drive *x:*?" (If you're not sure, answer YES.)

Step 4:   Select **Yes** (just press Enter).

If no files have been added to the disk since it was reformatted, you will see the question "Are you sure you want to unformat drive *x:*?" Go on to step 5.

If the disk currently contains files that have been added since it was reformatted, UnFormat displays the list of filenames with the question: "Are you sure you want to unformat it?" If more than a couple of files are listed, you should not continue with this procedure. Press Esc until you get back to the DOS prompt, and read Chapters 1 and 10.

If only a couple of filenames are shown, you can go on to step 5.

Step 5: Select **Yes** (just press Enter).

UnFormat searches the disk for image files, from the end to the beginning. You will see a map of the drive, animated to show UnFormat's search.

If no image files are found, the search might take a long time because UnFormat has to search the entire disk. Eventually, this message appears: "Unable to find any recovery info on drive x:." (There's a lot more to the message.) Skip to step 13.

If image info was found, you will see this message: "IMAGE Info Found!" (The message contains additional information.) Go on to step 6.

Step 6: (The following steps should be followed only if image information was found.) Examine the time and date information in the message carefully. Have you made any changes to the disk since then? If so, it would be better to unformat the diskette without an image file. Select **Cancel**, select **Quit** on the next dialog box, and start this procedure over; but at step 4, select **No** and skip to step 13.

If at least one image file is up-to-date, go on to step 7.

Step 7: If only one image file was found, select **OK** (just press Enter). If two image files were found, use the most recent one unless it was made *after* the disk was reformatted. In that case, use the previous one. Select **Recent** (press R) or **Previous** (press P).

When you've made your selection, the next box asks (for the last time) if you're *absolutely* sure you want to unformat the disk.

Step 8: Select **Yes** if you're absolutely sure (just press Enter).

The next box asks if you want to do a **Full** or **Partial** recovery.

Step 9: Select **Full** (just press Enter).

Message boxes keep you informed while UnFormat restores the disk. The final message should tell you that the drive was successfully restored and suggests that you run Norton Disk Doctor (and perhaps reboot). (If you don't get this message, quit this procedure and read Chapters 1 and 10.)

Step 10: Select **OK** (just press Enter).

The next box briefly explains UnFormat and gives you a chance to **Continue** or **Quit**.

Step 11: Select **Quit** (just press Esc).

The DOS prompt returns.

Step 12: You should now run Norton Disk Doctor on the disk to fix up any problems in the restored information. Enter the command NDD /QUICK and follow the directions on the screen.

When that's done, if any files are missing, you might be able to manually recover them; read Chapters 1 and 9 to find out how. (This ends the procedure for unformatting when image info was found.)

Step 13: (Use the following steps when image info was not found.) Select **Yes** (just press Enter).

UnFormat searches the disk for old directories. You will see an animated map and progress information. The search will take a long time on a high-capacity disk.

Eventually, you will see the message "Drive *x:* has been unformatted."

Step 14: Select **OK** (just press Enter).

You will see the message "Exit unformat and examine the disk to ensure that proper recovery was performed." This is followed by information about the filenames in the root directory.

Step 15: Select **OK** (just press Enter).

The next box briefly explains UnFormat and gives you a chance to **Continue** or **Quit**.

Step 16: Select **Quit** (just press Esc).

The DOS prompt returns.

Step 17: Examine the root directory of the recovered disk by entering the following command:

```
DIR x:
```

If the root directory contains subdirectories named DIR0, DIR1, etc., go on to step 18. If not, you have done as much unformatting as you can do. If files are still missing, you might be able to recover them with UnErase; read Chapters 1 and 9 to find out how.

Step 18: Examine each subdirectory by entering the following command:

```
DIR DIRn
```

DOS will list the contents of each subdirectory. You should be able to identify the subdirectory's former name by examining its contents. Write a list of the correct name for each subdirectory.

If the Norton Utilities are installed on your hard disk, you can use the following steps to rename your directories. If not, save the list of directory names until you have installed the utilities.

Step 19: If the utilities are installed, start Norton Change Directory by entering the following command, where *x:* is the name of the recovered drive:

```
NCD x:
```

The Norton Change Directory screen should appear showing an outline of the directories on the recovered drive.

Step 20: Highlight DIR0.

You can click on it if you have a mouse or use the arrow keys to move the highlight to it.

Step 21: Press F6.

A box opens on the screen which says "Type the new name for directory *x:*\DIR0."

Step 22: Type the correct name for DIR0 and press Enter.

The new name should replace DIR0 on the screen.

Step 23: Repeat steps 20-22 for DIR1 through DIR*n*.

Step 24: When all directories are renamed, press Esc.

This terminates Norton Change Directory, and the DOS prompt should reappear. You have completed the unformatting process. If any files are missing, you might be able to manually recover them using UnErase. Read Chapters 1 and 9 to find out how.

Recovering a Disk from DOS's RECOVER Program

Use this procedure if you ran DOS RECOVER on a disk and it renamed all your files FILE0000.REC, FILE0001.REC, etc. Use it also to recover files from a disk with a faulty root directory.

The Norton Utilities must be installed to use this procedure. If the drive in need of recovery was the one that contained the Norton Utilities, but you can't access them now, reinstall the utilities on another hard drive. If you don't have another hard drive, reinstall them on the drive you need to recover.

Step 1: Enter this command:

```
DISKTOOL
```

A screen should appear that briefly explains Disk Tools.

If instead you get the message "Bad command or filename," make sure you spelled the command correctly. If you did, then the utilities are not installed. You will have to install them before proceeding.

Step 2: Select **Continue** (all you have to do is press Enter).

The Disk Tools main menu appears, showing six functions in the left-hand column; one of the six functions is **Recover from DOS's RECOVER.**

Step 3:   Press the Down arrow key to move the highlight to **Recover from DOS's RECOVER**. Then press Enter. (If you have a mouse, you can just double-click on **Recover from DOS's RECOVER**.)

A dialog box explains the recover function.

Step 4:   Select **OK** (just press Enter).

A dialog box gives you a list of drives to recover.

Step 5:   Type the letter of the drive you want to recover.

If you chose a diskette drive, a dialog box asks you to "Insert the diskette to Recover into Drive *x:*." Do so and press Enter.

Then a warning message appears to tell you that you should use this procedure only in certain situations. It ends with "Do you wish to Recover Drive *x:*?"

Step 6:   If you really want to recover the indicated drive, select **Yes** (just press Enter).

The next message issues another warning and asks "Are you absolutely sure you want to Recover Drive *x:*?"

Step 7:   If you're absolutely sure you want to recover the indicated drive, select **Yes** (press the letter Y).

The recovery process begins. An animated map and progress boxes keep you informed. When it's finished, a message tells you that "Recover from DOS's Recover is complete," followed by some information about the names in the root directory.

Note: Like RECOVER, **Recover from DOS's RECOVER** assigns generic names to the files (FILE0000, etc.) and subdirectories (DIR0, etc.) in your root directory. The difference is that the Norton Utility identifies and restores all your subdirectories and their files so that you have to rename only the files and subdirectories in your root directory. In addition, it identifies many types of files and assigns the correct extension so that you know whether they are programs, word processor documents, spreadsheets, etc.

For hints on how to straighten out directory and filenames, see Chapter 12.

Step 8:   Select **OK** (just press Enter).

The first **Recover from DOS's RECOVER** dialog box reappears.

Step 9:   Select **Quit** (press the letter Q).

B

A DAB OF DOS

If you don't know anything about DOS, this appendix will get you started with the concepts and commands that you need on a regular basis. You will need to know many of these commands while learning to use the Norton Utilities. This is not meant to be an exhaustive discussion of DOS, which would take a book of its own. This is more like a basic survival course.

Drives

Your system will have at least one diskette drive and at least one hard drive. Your first diskette drive is named A:. If you have a second diskette drive, it is named B:. Otherwise, your only diskette drive is named both A: and B:, and you can use both names in commands that require two drives. (DOS will tell you when to insert the diskette for drive A: and when to insert the one for drive B:.)

Your first hard drive is named drive C:. This is probably the drive that you start your computer, or *boot*, from. If you have more than one hard drive, the others are named D:, E:, and so on. The other types of drives that you might use—such as a network drive or a RAM drive—are named with higher letters.

Starting-Up Your Computer—"Booting"

To boot from your hard drive, make sure drive A: is empty (for 5 1/4" drives, you can just make sure the drive door latch is open). Then simply turn on your computer. You will see various messages as your system performs a memory check, then reads drive C: and boots DOS. After DOS takes over, it looks on drive C: for a file named CONFIG.SYS, which contains commands to set up (*configure*) your hardware. You might see a variety of messages as programs that control your hardware (called *device drivers*) are loaded into memory. After it finishes with CONFIG.SYS, DOS looks for a file called AUTOEXEC.BAT, which contains commands to perform tasks that should be executed during booting. You will also see messages generated by these tasks—if any—as they are executed. Finally, DOS displays its command prompt on the screen. It probably looks like this:

```
C:\>
```

This prompt tells you that the root directory of drive C: is active and that DOS is ready to receive a command. Whatever you type on the keyboard will be displayed at the command prompt.

> **Note:** Someone may have altered your system so that a menu or some other program's screen (such as the Norton menu) appears instead of the command prompt. In that case, you will have to find out how to enter commands and run programs for your system.

Sometimes you need to reboot your system to get out of a program that is stuck, to clear memory, to reset your system to its just-booted state, or for some other reason. You can usually reboot by pressing three keys simultaneously: Ctrl-Alt-Del. This is called a "warm" start because it doesn't go all the way back to the beginning of the boot process, just back to the beginning of DOS. (The memory check is not rerun.) If rebooting doesn't work, then you can push the Reset button on the front of your computer, if you have one, to do a "cold" start, which goes back to the beginning of the boot process. If your computer doesn't have a Reset button, then you have to turn the power off, wait a few seconds, and turn it back on again to reboot.

Warning: Keep an eye on your drive lights and avoid rebooting or powering down when a light indicates that DOS is accessing any drive. By interrupting DOS before it finishes what it is doing, you could make some data inaccessible.

If your hard disk is in trouble, you might need to boot from a diskette in drive A:. You must have a bootable diskette to do this; that is, it must contain the DOS system files and the boot program. (To find out if a diskette is bootable, try it. You will see an error message if it's not.) Insert the diskette in drive A:, close the drive's latch if it has one, and turn on the computer (or reboot). Whenever drive A: contains a diskette, DOS boots from that diskette instead of drive C:.

Changing Drives

Whatever drive name appears in the DOS command prompt is the *active* drive (also called the *default* or *current* drive). DOS will read and write on this drive whenever you don't specify another drive in your commands. Immediately after booting, the boot drive is usually the active drive. You can make another drive active by entering that drive's name (with no other text) at the command prompt. For example, to switch from drive C: to drive D:, you would do this (the text you type is shown in bold):

```
C:\>D:      [press the Enter key]
D:\>
```

The new DOS prompt on the second line shows that drive D: is now active.

Directories

A directory is a list of the files on a disk, which DOS uses to find the files that you want. Every disk has at least one directory, located at the beginning of the disk and called the *root directory*. It's official name is \ (backslash). You can create subdirectories under the root directory to keep your directories fairly short and to group related files together. (Chapter 16 shows you how to create and manage subdirectories using Norton Change Directory.) It's very common for hard drives to have subdirectories, but diskettes often have only a root directory.

Active Directories

At any given point in time, every drive has an active directory where DOS reads and writes if you don't specify another directory in a command. Immediately after booting, the root directory on each drive will be active. The DOS prompt usually includes the name of the active directory for the active drive. This, in a sense, is the most active directory, since this is where DOS will look if you don't specify either a drive or a directory in your command. You can activate a different directory with DOS's CD command, which looks like this:

```
C:\>CD NORTON
C:\NORTON>
```

The new command prompt on the second line shows that the NORTON directory is now active on drive C:.

You can change active directories more easily with the Norton Change Directory command, which is explained in Chapter 16.

Viewing Directories

You can list the contents of a directory with the DIR command. A sample is shown below:

```
C:\HSG>DIR

 Volume in drive C is HARD DISK 1
 Volume Serial Number is 1553-0EFB
 Directory of  C:\HSG

 .                <DIR>       12-06-90    8:50a
 ..               <DIR>       12-06-90    8:50a
 ALIEN    HSG      16128 03-18-88    9:31a
 BUGS     HSG      27893 03-18-88    9:31a
 GRAB     EXE      20649 03-18-88    9:31a
 HS       CFG        512 12-06-90   10:29a
 HS       DAT     144464 03-18-88    9:31a
 HS       GDT      15660 03-18-88    9:31a
 HS       PSD        399 03-18-88    9:31a
 HSG      EXE     281678 03-18-88    9:31a
 TEMP     ASC          0 12-13-90    8:26a
        11 File(s)     11132928 bytes free
```

In this example, DOS listed the active directory because no other drive or directory was specified. You can specify a different drive and/or directory, as in these commands:

```
DIR A:              [lists the active directory on drive A:]
DIR \               [lists the root directory on the active drive]
DIR D:\BASIC        [lists the directory named \BASIC on drive D:]
```

The DIR command does not list all the information in a directory, only what DOS thinks you need to know. The Norton Utilities has features that let you see more.

Files

DOS stores all information on disk in files. A file might be a program, a letter, a database, a drawing, or what have you. You might have dozens of files on a diskette and hundreds (or even thousands) of files on a hard drive.

Filenames

Every file must have a name at least one character long. It can have up to eight characters in the main part of the name. It can also have an extension, which is a period followed by from one to three characters. All of the following are valid filenames:

```
JOHNBOY      C5      5TH       CARSON.NEV       FORMS.D
```

Filenames can contain letters, numbers, and some symbols, such as # % $ and !. They cannot contain spaces, periods (except to identify the extension), backslashes, or colons.

Some commands let you use a *global filename*. This is a nonspecific filename that might cause several files to be selected for processing. You use a question mark (?) to indicate an ambiguous character, as in CHAP?.DOC, which would select CHAP1.DOC, CHAP2.DOC, and CHAP3.DOC, but not CHAP10.DOC, since only one ambiguous character is called for. A space matches an ambiguous character, so CHAP.DOC would be considered a match. You can use an asterisk (*) to indicate that the rest of the name, no matter how many characters, is ambiguous. CHAP*.DOC would match CHAP.DOC, CHAP1.DOC, CHAP10.DOC, and CHAPTER7.DOC. (CHAP*.DOC is equivalent to CHAP????.DOC.)

Ambiguous characters can also appear in the extension, as in CHAP1.* (which is the same as CHAP1.???) or CHAP*.DO? (which is the same as

CHAP????.DO?). The most global filename of all is *.* (or ????????.???), which matches every possible filename.

Listing Files with DIR

You can limit the DIR listing to a specific file by including the desired filename in the command, as in DIR JOHNBOY. If the file is contained in the directory, it will be listed; otherwise the message "File not found" will be displayed.

If you specify a global filename, all files matching that name will be listed. The following example shows what happens when you use the global filename HS*.* with the DIR command.

```
C:\HSG>DIR HS*.*

 Volume in drive C is HARD DISK 1
 Volume Serial Number is 1553-0EFB
 Directory of  C:\HSG

HS         CFG        512 12-06-90   10:29a
HS         DAT     144464 03-18-88    9:31a
HS         GDT      15660 03-18-88    9:31a
HS         PSD        399 03-18-88    9:31a
HSG        EXE     281678 03-18-88    9:31a
         5 File(s)    11132928 bytes free
```

Paths

If you want to access or create a file in a directory that is not current, you must tell DOS how to find the desired directory. You do this by specifying a *path* along with the filename, as in this example:

```
\DATABASE\ADMIN\EMP.DB
```

This file specification tells DOS that the file named EMP.DB is in the ADMIN directory, which is a child of the DATABASE directory, which is a child of the root directory on the current drive.

Absolute Paths

The above file specification is an example of an *absolute path*; that is, it shows the complete sequence of directories from the root on down. An absolute path starts with a backslash (\) representing the root directory. The other backslashes are connectors between directories and between the final directory and the filename itself.

Relative Paths

You don't always have to specify an absolute path. Sometimes you can just tell DOS how to get to the desired directory from the current directory using a *relative* path, as in this example:

```
ADMIN\EMP.DB
```

This example says that EMP.DB is in the ADMIN directory, which is a child of the *current directory*. Because it does not start with a backslash representing the root directory, DOS assumes that you are starting with the current directory.

You can use the symbol .. to represent the parent directory in a relative path. The following example says that the CUST.DB file is in the SALES directory, which is a child of the *current directory's parent*:

```
..\SALES\CUST.DB
```

Other than the .. symbol, there is no way to go up or sideways in the directory tree with a relative path. If the desired directory is not descended from the current directory or its parent, you must use an absolute path to reach it.

Drive Names in Paths

If the desired directory is not on the current drive, you can prefix a drive name to the path, as in this example:

```
D:\INVOICES\D91.INV
```

This example says that the D91.INV file is in the INVOICES directory, which is a child of the root directory on drive D:.

You can prefix a drive name to a relative path if you're sure you know what the current directory on the targeted drive is. For example, the following file specification accesses the D91.INV file in the INVOICES directory, which is a child of the current directory on drive D:

```
D:INVOICES\D91.INV
```

Copying Files

DOS's COPY command lets you copy files. Its basic format is:

```
COPY source target
```

The *source* is the file(s) to be copied and the *target* is the location to receive the copies. The source might be a drive name, in which case all the files in the current directory of that drive are copied. It might be a specific filename if you want to copy just one file. It might be a global filename if you want to copy several files. Or it might be a directory name, in which case all the files in that directory are copied.

The target might be a drive name, causing the file(s) to be copied to the current directory on the designated drive. It might be a directory name, causing the file(s) to be copied to that directory. If the source is a specific filename, the target can be a specific filename, causing the source file to be copied as a new file with the specified target name.

Here are some sample COPY commands:

`COPY A: B:`	[copies all the files in the active directory on drive A: to the active directory on drive B:]
`COPY A:*.DOC  C:\`	[copies all the files that match the global filename *.DOC in the default directory of drive A: to the root directory of drive C:]
`COPY C:\NORTON A:`	[Copies all the files from the NORTON directory on drive C: to the default directory on drive A:]
`COPY CONFIG.SYS CONFIG.SAV`	[Makes a copy of CONFIG.SYS in the same directory, calling the copy CONFIG.SAV]

Summary

This is only a brief introduction to some of the most essential DOS commands and concepts. You'll probably want to know more about DOS and how you can control it as you get more comfortable with your system. The *Disk Companion* that came with your Norton Utilities documentation explains a lot more about how DOS works—especially how it manages your disks. For more information on DOS commands, see your DOS documentation (or any number of good books on the subject).

C

PROBLEM-SOLVING GUIDE TO THE UTILITIES

If you need to solve an immediate problem that isn't covered by Appendix A, you'll have to read the appropriate chapters in this book to find out what to do. You probably don't want to read the whole book until after you have fixed the problem. First read Chapter 1, which introduces the utilities and shows you how to interact with them. This appendix will help you decide which other chapters to read and which Norton Utilities to use right away. Then you can finish the book when your system is working again.

This appendix is organized in three major sections: Disks, Files and the FATs, and Directories. Turn to the section that you seem to be having problems with and find the closest description to your problem. It probably shows several utilities (and chapters) to try out. Try the first utility in the list first. It's the easiest to use and will probably fix the problem. But if it doesn't work, try the next one in the list. If you reach the bottom of the list and still can't solve the problem, call the Technical Support people at Symantec (the number is in your Norton Utilities documentation). They usually can walk you through a solution.

The utilities suggested in this appendix require some knowledge to apply; that's why we don't walk you through their use in Appendix A. Please don't try to use these utilities without reading the referenced chapters (and Chapter 1).

Disks

Floppy diskette—can't access

> **Note:** Try to access another diskette to make sure you don't have a hardware problem before using the following techniques. If you find a hardware problem, have the drive repaired.

- Use *Norton Disk Doctor* (Chapter 11) to diagnose and fix problems with the diskette's structure.
- Use *Revive a Defective Diskette* (Chapter 12) to refresh the physical formatting.
- Use *Safe Format* (Chapter 2) in safe mode to redo the logical formatting, followed by *UnFormat* (Chapter 10) to recover the directories and files.
- Use *Disk Editor* (Chapters 2 and 14) to access the physical sectors and copy whatever data you can find to another diskette.

Hard disk—can't access

> **Note:** This could be a hardware problem or the result of a weak CMOS battery. You might need to replace the battery or get the hardware repaired.

> **Note:** If your installed copy of the Norton Utilities is on the hard disk you can't access, and you don't have another hard disk to install it on, you won't be able to use System Information, which must be installed. You can use the other programs mentioned below from the un-installed Norton Utilities diskettes, though.

- Use *System Information* (Chapter 16) to see if it reports any hardware or CMOS problems.
- Use *Norton Disk Doctor* (Chapter 11) to diagnose and fix problems in the disk's structure.
- Use *Calibrate* (Chapter 5) to refresh the physical formatting.
- Use *Restore Rescue Disk* (Chapter 12) to restore the Partition Tables, Boot Records, and CMOS values.

Hard disk won't boot

> **Note:** This could be a hardware problem or the result of a weak CMOS battery. You might need to replace the battery or get the hardware repaired.

> **Note:** Boot from a floppy diskette to try the following solutions. If you find that you can't access your hard disk after booting, see "Hard disk—can't access."

- Use *System Information* (Chapter 16) to see if it reports any hardware or CMOS problems.
- Use *Restore Rescue Disk* (Chapter 12) to replace the Partition Table, Boot Record, and CMOS values from a rescue disk, if you have one.
- Use *Norton Disk Doctor* (Chapter 11) to locate and fix any problems in the disk's structure.

Physically damaged disk (need to recover as much data as possible)

> **Note:** It might not be possible to recover any data from a severely damaged disk. A repair technician might be able to rescue data in cases where you can't.

- Use *Norton Disk Doctor* (Chapter 11) to diagnose and fix problems with the disk's structure and extract data from bad clusters.
- Use *Calibrate* (Chapter 5) for hard disks or *Revive a Defective Diskette* (Chapter 12) for diskettes to redo the physical formatting.
- Use *Restore Rescue Disk* (Chapter 12) to restore the crucial system areas of a hard disk from a rescue disk (if you have one).
- Use *Safe Format* (Chapter 2) in safe mode to redo the disk's logical formatting followed by *UnFormat* (Chapter 10) to recover the directories and files.
- If all else fails, use *Disk Editor* (Chapters 2 and 14) to access the physical sectors and copy whatever data you can find to files on other disks.

Reformatted disk (need to rescue former files)

> **Note:** If you did a DOS-style format on a diskette, the former data cannot be recovered.

- Use *UnFormat* (Chapter 10) to recover the former directories and files.

Files and the FATs

Copy overlaid a file (need to recover former version)

- Use *UnErase* (Chapter 9) to search for clusters belonging to the copied-over version and make them into a new file.

Cross-linked files (reported by CHKDSK or some other program)

- Use *Norton Disk Doctor* (Chapter 11) to diagnose and fix problems in the FAT.
- You might also need to use *UnErase* (Chapter 9) to locate abandoned data in the unused clusters and append it to the appropriate files.

Corrupted database or spreadsheet files

- Use *File Fix* (Chapter 13) to rescue as much data as possible in the files.

Corrupted files (not database or spreadsheet)

- You might be able to use *Disk Editor* (Chapters 2 and 14) to examine the file, compare its structure to uncorrupted files, and fix up the damaged file's structure.

Erased file

- Use *UnErase* (Appendix A and Chapter 9) to recover the file.

Extraneous data in files

- Use *Norton Disk Doctor* (Chapter 11) to diagnose and fix problems in the FAT.

FAT errors (reported by DOS or any other program)

- Look up any DOS and CHKDSK messages in the Norton menu (Chapter 1).
- Use *Norton Disk Doctor* (Chapter 11) to diagnose and fix problems in the FAT.
- Use *UnFormat* (Chapter 10) to rebuild the FAT.
- Use *Disk Editor* (Chapters 2 and 14) to examine the FATs and fix up errors.

Missing data from a file

- Use *Norton Disk Doctor* (Chapter 11) to diagnose and fix problems in the FAT.
- Use *UnErase* (Chapter 9) to locate abandoned data in the unused clusters and append it to the file.

Missing file

- Use *FileFind* (Chapter 17) to locate a file when you've forgotten its name and/or directory.
- Use *Norton Disk Doctor* (Chapter 11) to diagnose and fix problems in the disk's structure and turn lost cluster chains into files.
- Use *UnErase* (Chapter 9) to find data in unused clusters and recover it in a file.
- Use *Disk Editor* (Chapters 2 and 14) to examine directories for abandoned or damaged entries and repair the directories.

Read/write errors in files (reported by DOS or any other program)

- Use *Norton Disk Doctor* (Chapter 11) to diagnose and fix problems with the disk's structure.
- Look up DOS messages in the Norton menu (Chapter 1).
- Use *Calibrate* (Chapter 5) for hard disks or *Revive a Defective Diskette* (Chapter 12) for diskettes to redo the physical formatting.

Zapped dBASE file

- Use *File Fix* (Chapter 13) to unzap the file.

Directories

Corrupted directory (except root directory)

- Use *Norton Disk Doctor* (Chapter 11) to diagnose and fix directory problems.
- Use *Disk Editor* (Chapters 2 and 14) to examine and fix up directory entries.

Corrupted root directory

- Use *Recover from DOS's RECOVER* (Chapter 12) to fix the root directory (even if you didn't use DOS's RECOVER).
- Use *Disk Editor* (Chapters 2 and 14) to examine and fix up directory entries.

Directory structure trashed by DOS's RECOVER program

- Use *Recover from DOS's RECOVER* (Chapter 12) to restore subdirectories and fix as much of the root directory as possible.

Erased directory

- Use *UnErase* (Chapter 9) to recover erased directories.

INDEX